THE STRUGGLE FOR LIBERATION

War and Militarism in African History

SERIES EDITORS: ALICIA C. DECKER AND GIACOMO MACOLA

Sarah J. Zimmerman
Militarizing Marriage: West African Soldiers' Conjugal Traditions in Modern French Empire

Lennart Bolliger
Apartheid's Black Soldiers: Un-national Wars and Militaries in Southern Africa

Alfred Tembo
War and Society in Colonial Zambia, 1939–1953

Myles Osborne, ed.
Making Martial Races: Gender, Society, and Warfare in Africa

Charles G. Thomas
Ujamaa's Army: The Creation and Evolution of the Tanzania People's Defence Force, 1964–1979

John Burton Kegel
The Struggle for Liberation: A History of the Rwandan Civil War, 1990–1994

The Struggle for Liberation

A History of the Rwandan Civil War, 1990–1994

John Burton Kegel

OHIO UNIVERSITY PRESS
ATHENS, OHIO

Ohio University Press, Athens, Ohio 45701
ohioswallow.com

Printed in the United States of America
Ohio University Press books are printed on acid-free paper ∞ ™

Hardcover ISBN 978-0-8214-2626-5
Paperback ISBN 978-0-8214-2627-2
Electronic ISBN 978-0-8214-2628-9

Library of Congress Cataloging-in-Publication Data available upon request

To my parents and de allerliefste

publication supported by a grant from

The Community Foundation for Greater New Haven

as part of the Urban Haven Project

Contents

Illustrations

MAPS

FIGURES

TABLE

Acknowledgments

Without the help of the Rwanda Defense Force I would not have been able to write the present history of the Struggle for Liberation. Thus, I would like to thank Minister of Defense James Kabarebe for allowing me to carry out my research. Major General Ferdinand Safari believed in the project and facilitated it from the start: obtaining the relevant permissions would have been impossible without his help. For his confidence, I am deeply grateful. Lieutenant General Caesar Kayizari discussed his experiences of the Struggle with me for hours on end and introduced me to many of his friends. General Kayizari: thank you for your insights and help. I also owe a special thanks to Senator Tito Rutaremara and Christine Umutoni, who explained to me in detail the nuances of the relationship between the RPF and RPA like only insiders can. Member of Parliament Logan Ndahiro shared an early version of the English translation of his book. The excellent series of articles he wrote for the *New Times* is a key point of departure for anyone interested in this history. Brigadier General Ronald Rwivanga also went out of his way to help make this book possible; thank you. At the Institute of National Museums of Rwanda, I was helped by Jerome Karangwa. Mugabo guided me around all of Mulindi and is a superbly informed guide. The manager of the Campaign Against Genocide Museum, Medard Bashana, was also kind enough to help me every time I visited. To all the others I interviewed or spoke to in Rwanda, thank you for your time. Last but not least, Lieutenant Colonel Ndore Rurinda, a superb historian at heart, helped me when I got my timelines confused, took the time to answer many questions, and advised me on whom to contact when I got stuck.

I would also like to thank all those whom I interviewed, spoke to, or corresponded with in Europe over the course of the past few years. Special thanks go to Lieutenant Colonel George Molyneux-Carter, who read several chapters and kindly put up with my incessant questioning. Tony Jackson:

without your insights into Rwanda and Burundi, this thesis would not have been the same. I must also mention Charles Cullimore, Mark Eyskens, and Paul Whiteway, who all responded in good form to my questions about their past. Marco Jowell, Harry Verhoeven, André Koppers, and Wiet van Banning helped me navigate the Rwandan scene and opened doors for me along the way; thank you. There are many who prefer not to be named, but you know who you are and my gratitude is great.

Anna Haward, Heather Faulkner, and the rest of the team at the UNHCR Archive run one of the most welcoming archives I have ever visited. I also owe a special thanks to Lore van de Broeck at the Africa Museum in Tervuren and Alison Seiler at the US Committee for Refugees, who both helped me find rare and enlightening documents. The Historical Freedom of Information team of the UK Foreign and Commonwealth Office deserve singular praise for their stellar work and patience with my repeated requests. Alicia Decker, thank you for your enthusiasm and support throughout this project. Philippa Burton provided invaluable help with textual editing, linguistics, and translations. Kellyann Falkenberg Wolfe made the excellent index. The team at Ohio University Press did a wonderful job polishing the text and getting the book to print.

Giacomo Macola is a superb mentor and even better friend. His grand historiographical command, eye for detail, and enthusiasm kept my research rigorous and on track.

Abbreviations

ADL	Association rwandaise pour la défense des droits de la personne et des libertés publiques
APROSOMA	L'Association pour la promotion sociale de la masse
BBTG	broad-based transitional government
BEM	*brevet d'état-major*
CADA	Commission d'accès aux documents administratifs
CLADHO	Comité de liaison des associations rwandaises de défense des droits de l'Homme / Collectif des ligues et associations de défense des droits de l'homme au Rwanda
CMF	combined mobile force
CND	Conseil national de développement
CRAP	Commandos de recherche et d'action en profondeur
DAMI	Détachement d'assistance militaire
FAR	Forces armées rwandaises
FAZ	Forces armées zaïroises
FCO	British Foreign and Commonwealth Office
FGT	France Génocide Tutsi
ICTR	International Criminal Tribunal for Rwanda
JMO	*journaux des marches et opérations*
MAM	Mission d'assistance militaire
MDR	Mouvement démocratique républicain
MRND	Mouvement révolutionnaire national pour le développement

NRA	National Resistance Army
NRM	National Resistance Movement
OAU	Organisation of African Unity
PARMEHUTU	Parti du Mouvement de l'émancipation Hutus
PL	Parti libéral
PSD	Parti social-démocrate
RADER	Rassemblement démocratique rwandais
RDF	Rwanda Defense Force
RPA	Rwandan Patriotic Army
RPF	Rwandan Patriotic Front
RPIMa	régiment de parachutistes d'infanterie de marine
SAP	structural adjustment plan
SHD	Service historique de la Défense
UNAMIR	United Nations Assistance Mission for Rwanda
UNAR	Union nationale rwandaise
UNHCR	United Nations High Commissioner for Refugees

Introduction

A Neglected Topic

SINCE THE MID-TWENTIETH CENTURY RWANDA HAS EXPERIENCED two civil wars. The first, known as the "Social Revolution," lasted from 1959 to 1964. It coincided with independence and led to a campaign of ethnic cleansing. As a result, many, mostly Tutsi, Rwandans fled abroad. The second is the "Struggle for Liberation," which started on 1 October 1990 and ran until 19 July 1994. During this war, the refugees who had been forced out of the country during the Social Revolution and in subsequent decades returned to Rwanda by military force under the aegis of the Rwandan Patriotic Front (RPF) and its military wing, the Rwandan Patriotic Army (RPA). The RPF was opposed by the government of President Juvénal Habyarimana and its armed forces, the Forces armées rwandaises (FAR).

The Rwandan Genocide started on 7 April 1994, following the death of President Habyarimana; over the course of a mere one hundred days, approximately 800,000 Tutsi and moderate Hutu were killed by Hutu Power gangs and militias supported by the FAR. Advancing from their zone in the north of the country, the RPA put an end to the Genocide by defeating the FAR, which had been shielding the ethnic militias. The defeat inflicted by the RPA on the FAR forced the latter to flee into Zaire, initially taking the moniker "ex-FAR." With it went between one to two million Rwandan refugees, who settled in North and South Kivu. This exodus paved the way for "Africa's Great War" in Zaire/Democratic Republic of the Congo from 1996.

During colonial times, Rwanda was the subject of an extraordinary amount of historical research, especially in view of its size and landlocked location. The main focuses of interest for many of these early scholars were the ethnic stratification of Rwandan society (Hutu, Tutsi, Twa) and the importance of the royal court.[1] After independence, the study of Rwandan history became the domain of a handful of dedicated scholars interested in the societies living on the shores of the African Great Lakes.[2] Though some of these would only publish their most significant work on Rwanda much later, their nuanced views of ethnicity would go on to supplant and problematize the ethno-racist ideas held by their colonial counterparts.[3]

The world of Rwandan studies was profoundly changed by the Genocide, as researchers, journalists, and human rights activists reported on one of the gravest human rights abuses of the twentieth century.[4] They documented the killings at the micro level, analyzed the international dimensions, and identified the culprits. In this last respect, the work of Alison Des Forges and her testimony before the International Criminal Tribunal for Rwanda (ICTR) are particularly noteworthy. Other scholars interested in exploring the origins of the mass murders also started writing about the role of the Church in the Genocide and the nitty gritty of Rwandan internal politics.[5]

Recently, the writing on Rwanda has turned away from the Genocide and its complex causes to postwar rule.[6] Most of the literature written directly after the Genocide was informed by a positive view of the RPF, the organization that stopped the Genocide as the international community stood by and watched. However, the RPF's inexperience in ruling a country and instances of revenge killings, combined with the almost insurmountable problems involved in rebuilding an utterly shattered nation still crawling with *génocidaires,* caused friction with otherwise friendly researchers. As the best among them explained: "There was not a precise turning point, it was an evolution. I went back to Rwanda in February 1995 and soon started to hear stories about the killing going on. I tried to access some of the mass graves that were being filled and found rapidly that taxi drivers were scared shitless of taking me there. . . . Later I found eyewitnesses to some of the massacres. By the time I left, I was under RPF security surveillance."[7]

Whatever goodwill researchers had left for the RPF dissipated during the First and Second Congo Wars (1996–1997; 1998–2003). In recent years, Filip Reyntjens, Susan Thomson, and Timothy Longman have all written highly critical books on post-Genocide governance.[8] Aside from one obvious answer to their criticisms—that there are no poor, post-conflict/genocide nations in unstable geopolitical areas that are doing significantly better than Rwanda, and many that are faring far worse—the existence of important gaps in the country's recent historiography means that these works are all based on an incomplete understanding of the post-Genocide political scene.

The origins of the RPF and RPA, in particular, have been sketched but not closely studied. Considering it was the RPF/A which started the war that ended in Genocide and that it was the same organization which stopped the cataclysm, its trajectory deserves fuller attention than it has received so far. What was the background of RPF/A members? Why did the RPF/A decide that military return was the only viable option? How was the RPF/A able to prepare for the Struggle for Liberation? How did the RPA recover from its initial setbacks? Why were RPF cadres and RPA soldiers so motivated? How did the RPA manage to beat a French-backed FAR? These questions warrant full discussion and unprejudiced consideration, since the history of this "rebel" movement also informs how it governs Rwanda today. If we ignore its background, how can we understand the choices it has made, and continues to make, in the post-Genocide period? Going a step further, we need to look at the history of the RPA and the FAR if we are to gain insight into the workings and mentality of today's Rwanda Defense Force (RDF), in both its military and nation-building roles. As Richard Reid has written with reference to the precolonial past, "war in itself . . . [is] a major force for social and political and economic change; war and soldiery . . . worked their way into African cultural, social and political narratives. Songs were composed for them, traditions developed around them, and identities forged through them."[9] These remarks are relevant for present-day Rwanda, where we can literally see this process taking place before our eyes.[10]

Another neglected aspect of Rwandan history is the Struggle for Liberation itself.[11] Though research has been conducted into the preparation of the Genocide and the international community's role in it, no scholar has placed the Struggle for Liberation at the heart of their narrative.[12] However, the preparation of the Genocide, the rise and fall of the moderate opposition, the degradation of the FAR from a respected fighting force to a genocidal militia, the role of the international community, the Arusha negotiations, and the end of the Genocide all took place in the context of the war. My contention, in sum, is that the Struggle for Liberation should form the bedrock of any genuine understanding of Rwanda between 1990 and 1994, and indeed beyond.

The aim of this book is to begin to address these two related gaps in Rwandan historiography: the origins and nature of the RPF/RPA, on the one hand, and the history and implications of the Struggle for Liberation, on the other. I will attempt not to fall into the well-known pitfall of military history, where research is reduced to "a chronology of generals and battles."[13] As such, particular attention will be paid to the roots of the war—going back to the Social Revolution of 1959–1964—and its effects on Rwandan society and politics, showing how the conflict formed, molded, and informed every decision taken by Rwandan politicians and generals at the time. At a grassroots level, the conflict also created an explosive atmosphere that was manipulated and exploited by the génocidaires.

Two works speak directly to this study's subject matter. The best single volume on the Struggle and the Genocide is Gérard Prunier's *The Rwanda Crisis: History of a Genocide.*[14] That this extraordinary book, written less than a year after the end of the Genocide, still holds pride of place in the current scholarship is a testament to the skill of the author, who also enjoyed exceptional access to key players in the events. Another book that looks specifically at the immediate antecedents of the Genocide is André Guichaoua's *From War to Genocide: Criminal Politics in Rwanda, 1990–1994,* originally published in French in 2010.[15] Guichaoua's mastery of Rwandan internal politics is second to none and builds on the often forgotten, but high-quality, *Les crises politiques au Burundi et au Rwanda (1993–1994),* which he edited in 1995.[16] Though these two books come closest to dealing with the questions that the present study seeks to answer, each was written with other primary objectives. Prunier, moreover, lacked access to many documents on the war that are now available. In fact, as late as 2008, Claudine Vidal could still point out that

> not much is known about the military actions of the armies that fought the 1990–1994 Rwandan Civil War. The sources of all orders, documents, reports, testimonials are mostly inaccessible, be they Rwandan, French or Belgian. Even when they are in the public domain, they generally relate to the Rwandan Armed Forces [FAR]. The lack of documentation is even bigger in the case of the RPF.[17]

An important caveat should be introduced at this stage. Rwandans are, quite rightly, picky about the names of the wars they have experienced. During a conversation with an RPA veteran, I asked him about the "Ugandan Bush War." His retort was that calling it a "'bush war' is a denigrated description of a legitimate struggle that changed things."[18] Following this exchange, I resolved to refer to it as the Ugandan Resistance War. In naming the two Rwandan wars explored in this book, I have followed the conventions of the victors. The Social Revolution was won by the pro-Hutu political parties that had been formed in the lead-up to independence in 1962. By overthrowing the Tutsi monarchy and installing a one-party dictatorship of the Hutu majority, they ensured they would remain in power until 1991. Equally, I call the second civil war the Struggle for Liberation, the name given to it by the RPF/A. The RPF sees the war it inaugurated on 1 October 1990 as a struggle waged by and for all Rwandans, inside and outside the country, to liberate themselves from the neocolonial government led by President Juvénal Habyarimana.[19] This is particularly important in the context of post-Genocide Rwanda, where the RPF wishes to stress the unity of the people rather than their divisions. Those who fought in the Struggle insist that their enemy was not the people of Rwanda or the Hutu, or even the FAR as a whole, but President Habyarimana's regime and, in its wake, the génocidaires and genocide ideology itself. Calling the war the Struggle for Liberation rather than the Rwandan Civil War also does more justice to the domestic opposition to the Habyarimana presidency—which was significant—as well as to the noncombatant projects of the RPF that made victory possible: the mobilization of Rwandans living outside Rwanda, fundraising activities, and the like. In addition, the name goes some way toward honoring the memory of all who fought for change in Rwanda and all too often gave their lives to stop the Genocide: not only the RPA, RPF, and domestic opposition, but also many ordinary Rwandans who helped save compatriots at great personal risk.

MILITARY HISTORY IN AFRICA

More broadly, this book aims to make a contribution to African military history, a field that remains altogether underdeveloped for two main reasons. First, it is mostly political scientists, journalists, and anthropologists who have engaged with Africa's conflicts. And these works, as Stathis Kalyvas has noted, pay scant attention to the actual experience of fighting.[20] It is unclear why this is the case. Squeamishness about bloodshed or slaughter can be ruled out, since books and reports on massacres and genocides abound.[21] Difficulty in accessing sources might be part of the problem, as veterans are seldom accessible, while documentary evidence, when it exists, is often under lock and key in military archives. However, as Richard Reid writes, the most important reason is probably that war is "simply not fashionable: African studies is as susceptible to the fad as any, and the kind of history produced in the last quarter of a century has had no place for men like Shaka, Mirambo or Mutesa. Their armies were redolent of the kind of high political history which a generation of scholars now eschewed."[22] While Reid refers to precolonial history his comment is just as valid for the postcolonial period. The point is neatly made by Timothy Stapleton: "African military history . . . largely emerged as a defined field after operational history had become undesirable leading to accounts of African conflicts devoid of details of fighting and described as . . . 'warless wars' making no impact on our broader understanding of the history of warfare."[23]

Second, the discipline of military history itself has until very recently been dismissive of African warfare. Military historians have long been aware of the ultimate Eurocentricity of their field, focused as it is on "the West"—Europe and the United States—and the way its societies wage and interpret conflict.[24] The "emphasis," as Jeremy Black put it, is "on the military history of . . . the west . . . ensuring that other states and societies appear primarily in order to be defeated—so that the 'non-west' is misunderstood when it is not ignored."[25] Self-awareness, however, has not helped remedy the problem.[26] In the introduction to the revised edition of *The Cambridge History of Warfare,* Geoffrey Parker notes that, like its "precursor, *The Cambridge Illustrated History of Warfare: The Triumph of the West* (2008), the approach adopted in [the] volume lays its authors open to the charge of Eurocentrism."[27] Parker raised three defenses against this accusation. First, that it would have been impossible to compress the history of warfare of all cultures into a single volume. Second, that to "merely pay lip service to the military and naval traditions of Africa, Asia and the Americas . . . would be an unpardonable distortion."[28] Third, and most important, he pointed to the fact that "over the past two centuries the western way of war has become dominant all over the world. In the nineteenth and twentieth centuries remarkably few states and cultures managed to resist western arms for long—and the few that did so usually succeeded by imitation or adaptation. The rise and development of this dominant tradition, together with the secret of its success, therefore seems worthy of examination and analysis."[29]

There are several problems with this statement. Hidden in Parker's reasoning is the implicit assumption that the study of defeated military cultures or structures is a less worthy pursuit. This is both slightly hypocritical (military historians, it needs scarcely be observed, have extensively studied Western armies that suffered defeat, the German army of the Second World War being a good example) and intellectually problematic, since in most cases close analysis of failure is at least as instructive as analysis of success. Even the ostensible dominance of Western armed forces and their "way of war" in the twentieth century can be called into question. The French failed to defeat the Front de libération nationale (FLN) in Algeria in the 1950s, while in Vietnam they and, later, the Americans tried in vain to impose their political order. In the post-WWII period, the British sought to hang on to Palestine but failed, just as they did in Cyprus and Aden. For its part, the Soviet Union proved incapable of defeating the mujahideen in Afghanistan in the 1980s. Even in counterinsurgency campaigns that have traditionally been considered a military success—Mau Mau in Kenya and the Malaysian Emergency—victory was only obtained at the price of abdicating political hegemony over the colonies in which they were fought. The Dutch, Portuguese, and South Africans also tried to hang onto their colonies and territories but failed as abysmally as the rest. Nor have the most modern armed forces proved more successful in recent times. The American-led invasions of Afghanistan and Iraq in the early 2000s have been unmitigated disasters. Western states have tried as hard as they did in the 1950s, 1960s, and 1970s, yet their coalitions have failed to impose their will by force on the two countries.

While Parker is clearly aware of the issue, the lack of attention that has been given to African warfare in general remains. The result, as the editors of the newly launched *Journal of African Military History* write, is that

> the very tropes of a primitive and barbaric Africa which have been dispelled within the political, social, and economic realms by expansive historiographies remain within the popular and sometimes even academic understanding of the military realm. While there are now nuanced portraits of complex and cosmopolitan civilizations present throughout African history explored within the body of academic work on the continent, the topic of military history is much more circumscribed.[30]

A good example is provided by celebrated military historian Martin van Creveld, according to whom "the entities" by which African modern wars "are waged resemble tribes—indeed they *are* tribes, or whatever is left of them under the corrosive influence of modern civilisation."[31] The problem with this characterization is that it denies African military institutions the prowess and adaptability that many of them possess. Fighting under conditions of material scarcity unknown to Western armed forces since the Second World War, African military groups have developed unique coping mechanisms. The same goes for military doctrine. In the case of the RPA, its commanders, led by Paul Kagame, drew inspiration from British, NATO, Soviet, and Chinese military doctrines and built upon them to suit their own needs. This raises questions on both rebel militaries and (foreign-trained) government armies. Might foreign tutelage of African armies have been less important than previously thought? After all, even in conflicts where foreign military support was undoubtedly essential, such as the Angolan Civil War, it is Africans who did most of the fighting. This also raises the question of unique African military traditions running from the (pre)colonial period to the present—in which interactions with noncombatants, for better or for worse, seem to be particularly important.[32] The image of the African soldier as a thinking, constantly adapting, efficient, and disciplined professional has been sorely lacking in the literature.

The inappropriateness of Eurocentric approaches becomes clear when we consider that the vast majority of people touched by conflict since the end of the Second World War were not situated in Europe or the United States, but in Africa and Asia. If military history wants to survive in the twenty-first century, it will have to engage with warfare in a more holistic way. It is only by moving away from an exclusive focus on Western armies and the Western way of fighting that military history can break out of its narrow confines and become a force that helps humanity understand its most destructive tendencies.[33]

To be sure, the present research will not contribute to reverse that "foreshortening" of African history that Reid rightly deplores;[34] there is simply not enough room in a monograph to tease out continuities and ruptures between the Social Revolution and the Struggle for Liberation, on the one hand, and earlier traditions of precolonial warfare in Rwanda, on the other. However, what this book aspires to demonstrate is that there is no reason why Africa's modern wars should not be approached from the perspective of military historical analysis—one which takes into account the wider political, economic, and social contexts of a given conflict.

MAIN THEMES AND ARGUMENTS

This book is organized according to a loose chronological structure, and each chapter contributes to its overall argument: that it is impossible to understand what happened in Rwanda between 1990 and 1994 without a thorough analysis of the military aspects of the conflict. The first chapter looks at Rwanda's pre- and early colonial history and presents a compressed explanation of the origins of two divisions that would prove important during 1990–1994: ethnicity (Hutu-Tutsi) and regionalism (North-South). Chapter 2 lays out the causes and effects of the Social Revolution with a view to showing the clear links, based on ideology, memory, and method, between the violence of 1959–1964 to that of 1990–1994.

Chapter 3 provides a new interpretation of Juvénal Habyarimana's rise to power in 1973. Until now it has been argued that Habyarimana's coup was carried out, in part, to protect the Tutsi minority in Rwanda.[35] However, previously underutilized diplomatic sources make it seem more likely that Habyarimana acted to protect his country against a Burundian-Ugandan military coalition and to safeguard Hutu hegemony.[36] This chapter, too, seeks to position the Struggle for Liberation within the context of Rwanda's troubled history. It closes with a brief discussion on the political economy of Rwanda under both Kayibanda and Habyarimana, and the important role of regionalism.

Chapter 4 looks at the Banyarwanda, that is, Rwandans living outside of the country, many of whom had fled the ethnic cleansing of the Social Revolution. It details how these refugees became, by force of circumstance, a force to be reckoned with in Uganda. The same chapter also shines light on the protracted negotiations between Presidents Yoweri Museveni and Habyarimana over the possible repatriation of Banyarwanda refugees. It breaks with the current narrative by describing the refusal of the Rwandan government to accept any return of refugees from 1960 right up to 1990. These negotiations have never received the attention they deserve, although they represented the last chance to avoid an outbreak of war. The RPF's decision to return to Rwanda by armed force is set in the context of these negotiations.

Following this extensive investigation into the background of the conflict, chapter 5 outlines the start of the Struggle for Liberation and the initial setback experienced by the RPA in October 1990. Chapter 6 explains how the RPA, its early defeat notwithstanding, was forged into one of the most disciplined rebel groups Africa has ever seen. The defeat of the French-supported FAR, the utter incompetence and vicious infighting within its officer corps, and the groundwork necessary to bring the warring parties to the Arusha negotiating table are discussed in chapter 7. Taken together, chapters 5, 6, and 7—the detailed chapters on the Struggle for Liberation—serve two main purposes. First, their blow-by-blow description of military operations hopes to provide a bedrock for further research on this period. Second, they reveal the effect of the ongoing conflict on the Rwandan domestic scene. War does not take place in a vacuum, but rather interacts with every other sphere, be it political, economic, or social.

Chapter 8 continues the analysis of the war but also looks closely at Rwandan internal politics. It describes how Rwanda's first true multiparty government included three ministers who would become the driving force for peace among the opposition parties: Prime Minister Dismas Nsengiyaremye, Minister of Foreign Affairs Boniface Ngulinzira, and Minister of Defense James Gasana. Chapter 9 shows how this triumvirate fought for peace at Arusha and the tactics used by hard-line Hutu Power elements within the government and the FAR to undermine them. It also provides new and detailed analysis of the RPF's February 1993 Offensive. The historian Christopher Clapham once argued that if the RPF had refused to negotiate altogether, things might have turned out differently during the Genocide in 1994: "Had the RPF advanced [in 1993], the territory under the control of the central government, and hence the scale of the killings would have been greatly reduced."[37] The relevant section in chapter 9 engages with this possibility by examining both the role of the international community and RPF ideology.

One of the fundamental arguments of chapter 10 is that the Arusha Accords *were* viable. A key element is that they were negotiated with a moderate government—which I believe negotiated in good faith and with the intention of seeing them through. However, only days after the accords were signed, the Nsengiyaremye-Ngulinzira-Gasana triumvirate was thrown out of government. It is their defeat, the rise of the ethnic militias—intimately connected with the slow but steady collapse of the FAR—as well as the institutional weakness of Rwanda's judicial and law enforcement bodies, that made the accords untenable. The problem was not the Arusha Accords per se, but the aforementioned elements, combined with the disengagement of the international community after they were signed.

Besides focusing on the role of the international community, scholars have focused on the willingness of Rwandans to obey orders to kill during the Genocide. One of the answers that became prevalent was that Rwandans were a particularly obedient people, as history had predisposed them to trust and act on orders from above.[38] While this theory was developed to explain the Genocide, it can easily be refuted by studying pre-Genocide Rwanda. As will be made clear in chapters 8, 9, and 10, Rwandans were anything but obedient and passive. In this regard, my findings fully support Peter Uvin's, who wrote that

> Rwandans surely, like all other people, know how to resist orders from above, pretend to execute them while really opposing them, passively sabotage or undo obligatory programmes, and the like. They do so on a daily basis when it comes to evading taxes, smuggling, avoiding mandatory meetings, escaping from community labor, engaging in petty crime, or illegally migrating. If they chose to follow orders to kill—deeply dramatic orders—and not others, it needs more explanation than their supposedly obedient nature.[39]

Finally, chapter 11 provides the first military history of the Rwandan Genocide. It shows how, between April and July 1994 the RPA, by now a capable and experienced fighting force, conducted the Campaign Against Genocide, defeated the FAR, and put an end to the ethnic massacres unleashed by the génocidaires.

SOURCES, METHODOLOGY, AND BIAS

One of the main problems with the existing primary source material on the Struggle for Liberation is its lopsided nature. Though many documents—most of which were collected by the International Criminal Tribunal for Rwanda—provide insight into the actions of the Rwandan government led by President Habyarimana, as well as the international players, there is almost nothing on the RPF/A. It was thus clear from the start of the project that new evidence would have to be found.

Interviews

Pride of place is taken by interviews conducted in Rwanda in 2017–2018 and in 2021. During three separate stints of fieldwork, I interviewed roughly twenty RPF political cadres and RPA veterans. These ranged from individuals who had held high positions during the Struggle (most notably, James Kabarebe, Caesar Kayizari, Tito Rutaremara, and Christine Umutoni) to midlevel commanders, foot soldiers, and grassroots mobilizers. In addition to the interviews in Rwanda, others were conducted in Europe with British, French, Dutch, and Belgian diplomats and soldiers. Though some of them had been interviewed before,[40] they had not spoken at length about their experiences during the Struggle.

Once I received my official permission (following a lengthy and exhausting process that needs not concern us here), the RPF cadres and RPA veterans I met were extraordinarily generous with their time. Some, like Lieutenant General Caesar Kayizari, Lieutenant Colonel Rurinda, and Christine Umutoni, spoke to me for a great many hours spread over several sessions. Toward the end of my stay in Rwanda, I also collaborated with the Institute of National Museums of Rwanda. Deputy Director Jerome Karangwa ensured that I was warmly welcomed at the Liberation Museum in Mulindi. I was expertly guided not only around the Mulindi Tea Factory hill, the RPF/A headquarters for a large part of the war, but also around the whole sector, being shown the valleys in which the combined mobile forces (CMF) had been formed, the routes used to smuggle supplies from Uganda, the old location of Radio Muhabura, and some of the northern battlefields. Despite the access I was given in Rwanda, I did not manage to interview everyone I would have liked to. Perhaps the most important gap in this respect is that I only interviewed one female RPF cadre and no female RPA veterans. Thankfully, I was able to contact Christine Umutoni at the start of 2019, and she has been extraordinarily generous with her time. Hopefully, her testimony will go some way toward redressing the balance, as women were an integral part of the RPF/A throughout the preparatory and military phases of the Struggle for Liberation.

Interviews, of course, pose challenging methodological problems, but oral testimony has been crucial to Africanists for a long time.[41] While there are obvious differences between "oral tradition" and life stories, there are similarities as well. Oral traditions come into existence when the people who experienced history pass it on to later generations. In a sense, this is what is happening in Rwanda today. Although no academic book has been written on the Struggle for Liberation, it is common enough for veterans to tell their stories to children and teenagers in schools and at public events. After having heard about my research, one RDF officer who was waiting alongside me at the Ministry of Defense volunteered that written work on the Struggle would be useful because "in Africa, we don't write things down, but we tell them to each other."[42]

Jan Vansina noted that "there exists quite a range of situations of performance depending on what is performed."[43] I would argue that an interview is one such performance. As Philip Roessler and Harry Verhoeven, who interviewed many of the same people I did, explain:

> From the onset, we never perceived of the set of elite interviews we hoped to conduct as merely neutral exchanges in which we as interviewers would somehow manage to extract information, recovering an "elusive truth" from a handful of gatekeepers. Rather, we see them as encounters in which knowledge was constructed and story-lines were spun, mediated through a range of human emotions, motivations, and foibles, including political calculus, personal biases, fickle memory, confusion, a tendency to rationalize one's actions retrospectively, and so on. Given the subject at hand, subjectivity was inevitable.[44]

In my experience, careful listening quickly builds trust and, while taking the above into consideration, I found my interviewees remarkably candid and open. The best way of ensuring the accuracy of the information learned from interviews is to crosscheck it with other interviews and archival material. As the reader will notice, this basic scholarly principle has been deployed throughout the present work. One case of subjectivity that I did notice regarded Uganda. The once strong relationship between Rwanda and Uganda deteriorated markedly in the lead-up to, and during, my visits. As such, quite a few of those I interviewed were, I suspect, more dismissive of the Ugandan role during the Struggle for Liberation than they would otherwise have been.

I was also able to interview Belgian, British, and French soldiers and diplomats in Europe. Usually, potential interviewees came on my radar as the original authors of archival documents. Most reacted graciously to my requests and spoke, or emailed, with me at length. The French—I am sad to say—were the only exception. As with the archival records in their possession (more on which below), I repeatedly ran into metaphorical defense lines made up of belts of barbed wire and trenches covered by machine guns and heavy artillery. The French Ministry of Defense and Ministry of Foreign Affairs refused to relay my requests to people who had been active in Rwanda. Those I found through other channels were usually deeply reticent to speak about their connection to Rwanda for fear of opening themselves up to character assassination by the media. Their fears were somewhat justified: while a wide body of literature criticizes the actions of French soldiers in Rwanda, no coherent defense had been mounted before the *Rapport Duclert,* commissioned by President Macron in 2019.[45]

I have tried to make up for the dearth of interviews with French personnel by paying special attention to the documents released in the context of the 1998 French Parliamentary Inquiry, also known as the Quilès report, and others that have been leaked or released over time.[46] However, due to the advanced state of the manuscript when the *Rapport Duclert* was released, I could not fully integrate many of its findings into the text. The declassified Foreign and Commonwealth Office reports and US diplomatic cables have also been useful in this respect, as they often dwell on the opinion of their French counterparts.

Online Documents

Catherine and David Newbury have argued that "recent accounts need . . . to be reversed. Instead of seeing history exclusively through the Genocide [as much of the current scholarship does] . . . one can only understand the Genocide through an understanding of Rwanda's history."[47] My approach to the formation of the RPF/A and the Struggle for Liberation takes up their call, and my goal is to examine the history of the 1990–1994 war in its own right, without working backward from the Genocide. Although this is not an easy task (historians cannot simply detach themselves from their ex post facto knowledge), I tried to put it into practice by drawing mainly on documentary evidence dating to the period before the outbreak of the Genocide.

A large amount of useful documentation is available online, if one knows where to look. There are two indispensable websites in this regard. The first is France Génocide Tutsi, which is run and maintained by Jacques Morel,[48] an independent researcher who has written extensively on France's role in the Rwandan Genocide.[49] Though his work has received little attention, perhaps due to the way he takes France to task, it is an excellent account of the French role in Rwanda. Morel's website lists many documents that are now publicly available (sourced from the ICTR, the French Parliamentary Inquiry, the Belgian Parliamentary Inquiry, and many more). The second is George Washington University's National Security Archive, which has methodically worked at obtaining documents, especially from the US government, through Freedom of Information Act requests.[50] It is invaluable for the US view on what was happening in Rwanda and at the Arusha Peace negotiations. As the US diplomatic corps in the Great Lakes at the time ranked among the best informed, these documents also shed light on many otherwise rather obscure events.

Equally important is the online archive of the ICTR.[51] Although the Tribunal has come under attack from various directions, its archive is one of its crown jewels. It is enormous and contains most of the transcripts and evidence—in English and French—of the major trials. While parts of the evidence of the ICTR have been consulted before, especially by Linda Melvern and André Guichaoua, the sheer size of the archive means that most of it has not yet been used for academic research. I, too, was forced to limit my scope to the transcripts and evidence produced during three of the most important cases: Military I, Military II, and Government II.[52]

Other valuable online archives are those of the United Nations, which contain most of the United Nations Assistance Mission for Rwanda (UNAMIR) archive, and that of the World Bank.[53] Unfortunately, the UNAMIR archives mostly contain material relating to the period after the Genocide. The website of the World Bank has a considerable number of reports on Rwanda from 1974 onward, including those of the 1991 Structural Adjustment Plan (SAP).[54] The latter could form the basis for a desperately needed study. While many authors have presented the SAP as one of the key destabilizing forces in Rwanda in the early years of the war, it has not yet received its own dedicated study. Another website that I used extensively is the Access to Archival Databases of the United States National Archives.[55] This database gives researchers access to large amounts of diplomatic cables sent by US diplomatic missions all over the world before 1980.

Archival Records and Other Written Primary Sources

This book also draws on previously untapped archival material originating from third-party organizations, such as the Office of the United Nations High Commissioner for Refugees (UNHCR), the British Foreign and Commonwealth Office (FCO), and the Belgian Ministry of Foreign Affairs (Federal Public Service Foreign Affairs, or FPSFA). The archives of the UNHCR in Geneva have not yet been used in relation to research on Rwanda or, as far as I know, the Congo wars. This is a shame, as they house large amounts of material in the form of minutes and reports on high-level private discussions, as well as on the details of peace negotiations and the organization's activity on the ground. UNHCR material proved especially valuable to explore the background of the RPF and the negotiations surrounding the return of the refugees to Rwanda (see chapter 5).

Though the British National Archives do not hold much material relating to Rwanda in the early 1990s, the FCO does. Because they are not held in a public archive, these records, which consist exclusively of diplomatic cables, can only be accessed by Freedom of Information requests. Throughout my research, I filled in four such requests and received much documentation, some of which has now also been made available to the wider public online.[56] In total, I was granted access to between three and four hundred pages of hitherto unexploited material.

The archive of the Belgian FPSFA, which houses the correspondence to and from the embassy in Kigali, forms another vital source. Most of this material has never been used by historians, although some of it was quoted in Ambassador Johan Swinnen's book *Rwanda: Mijn verhaal*.[57] The scope of the archive is tremendous and includes well over seven thousand pages of material. They have played an important part throughout this book, even though I was not allowed to access the documents dating to 1993–1994.

Given the ultimately insurmountable difficulties it posed, the Service historique de la Défense (SHD) in Paris warrants a fuller discussion. It was to be expected that the French military archives would not roll out the red carpet for a Dutch researcher working on the Rwandan Struggle for Liberation, but the effort required to access even a couple of boxes genuinely beggars belief. The first obstacle is that the archive's finding aid on Rwanda was itself classified. This forced me to travel to Paris, on 26 April 2016, just to see what material was available. I had naively thought I would be given a copy of the finding aid to peruse at my leisure. The director of the SHD soon dispelled my illusion, forcing me to go through the finding aid at the archives and immediately fill in a request form to indicate which documents I would like to see ("Don't even try more than ten boxes at once; it will be immediately denied"). Having requested the nine boxes that seemed most likely to yield results, I went back to the UK ("There is no point in trying to ask for boxes marked *Secret Défense;* in all my years here I have never seen one declassified").

On 30 May 2016, I received my first reply, which allowed me to view two boxes at the SHD.[58] The same letter clarified that access to two other boxes had been denied and that access to the remaining five boxes depended on declassification procedures. In early September 2016, I traveled to the SHD to view the documents contained in the two boxes to which I had been granted access. While some of these records had clearly been consulted by Bernard Lugan in preparation for his *François Mitterrand,* seeing the material in its entirety proved very useful indeed.[59] Having completed my work, I put in another request for five boxes, carefully selecting material similar to that which I had been able to access on my trip.

On 18 October 2016, I received another reply stating that access to the five boxes still in limbo was denied. Then, on 6 February 2017, my second declassification request was denied in its entirety.[60] Not willing to let things rest, I launched an appeal with the Commission d'accès aux documents administratifs (CADA). Several months later, CADA replied, upholding the earlier decision by the SHD that no documents would be released.[61] The absurd reason cited by CADA for turning down my appeal was that the requested documents had "no relevance" to the research I was conducting. On the contrary, the records in question could hardly have been more relevant to my purposes, as they consisted of several *journaux des marches et opérations* (JMO), that is, the military diaries of the French units that served in Rwanda in the early 1990s. After a year and a half of mind-numbing official requests for declassification, letters, and appeals, I gave up trying to extract any more information from the SHD.

In the light of these tragicomic experiences, one can imagine my frustration when the *Rapport Duclert* was published on 26 March 2021. Among the documents used by the Duclert's team were those which I had asked for starting in 2016—proving their relevance. They have now been declassified and should be open to the public in the Pierefitte-sur-Seine reading room of the French National Archives.[62] Although the *Rapport Duclert* was sorely needed and is a significant step forward compared to the French Parliamentary Inquiry, it came too late to be of much use to this work.

Besides archival material, this book also relies on personal memoirs and parliamentary inquiries.[63] Because of the methodological problems posed by personal testimonies written after the events—problems that are similar to those raised by oral interviews—I have always used these memoirs in conjunction with reports, cables, or documents written by, or about, the author during the war.[64] A similar approach has been adopted in the case of parliamentary inquiries. In general, the value of such inquiries lies not so much in the final reports they produced but rather in the sources, interviews, and documents that accompany them.[65]

Bias

In the course of their research, historians construct what they believe to be the truth and present it to their readers. Their version of the truth is hopefully informed by their sources rather than their emotions. However, the way researchers view their sources is moderated—consciously or unconsciously—by their ethics, life experience, politics, and a host of other factors. I am no different from my colleagues in this regard.

While both (former) RPF/A and FAR and government functionaries who served under the Habyarimana regime were given the chance to be interviewed for this project, it was only members of the first group who seized this opportunity. The result is that when I went to Rwanda, I spoke to many RPF and RPA members at length. Naturally they gave me their point of view. In this context it is impossible not to develop personal bonds and friendships (or quite the opposite) with those who take the time to speak with you. Awareness of these relationships, and reliance on other sources, is the best way to moderate the effect they have on one's research.

Even though I was unable to interview everyone I was hoping to and to gain access to every potentially relevant archive, I believe the material uncovered by my research is more than sufficient to tell the story of the Struggle for Liberation and its antecedents in a much more comprehensive and empirically sound way than has previously been attempted. It will be up to the reader, equally informed by their life experience and beliefs, to decide whether they agree.

1

The Origins of Rwanda

Ca. 1550–1959

ON 22 NOVEMBER 1992 LÉON MUGESERA STEPPED ONTO THE football pitch of the small Rwandan town of Kabaya. Sitting in the shade of the trees, or standing to make sure they picked up his every word, were about one thousand people. Most were MRND (Mouvement révolutionnaire national pour le développement) supporters, including some important figures like Colonel Laurent Serubuga. Others, especially Tutsi who lived in the surrounding area, had come because they feared they would be punished if they stayed away. Also in the crowd was a team from the Rwandan state broadcasting office, ORINFOR (Office rwandais de l'information). As Mugesera began his speech—"Long live our movement. May President Habyarimana have a long life. May we, the militants of the movement gathered here, have a long life"—the ORINFOR crew started an audio recording of what would become one of the most infamous speeches in Rwandan history.

Mugesera was a linguist—an academic who had studied abroad and taught at the National University of Rwanda. However, he had given up his academic post to become a propagandist for the MRND, the ruling party at the time. That day he presented two main themes to his audience. The first was regional. Kabaya was on the border of the provinces of Gisenyi (where the MRND had its main powerbase) and Gitarama (where the Mouvement démocratique républicain opposition party was strong). Recently the MDR had been doing well, which upset Mugesera. "Don't let yourself be invaded!" he commanded before explaining to the crowd that they should no longer turn the other cheek, but always strike back twice as hard instead. He continued, "Nothing more of what is called their flag, nothing more of what is called their cap, not even what they call their militants, must be allowed on our soil to speak!" In Rwanda everyone who belonged to a political party was labeled a "militant," even ordinary citizens. Building on this first call to violence, Mugesera turned to the Tutsi population of Rwanda, his second theme.

> Recently, I told someone [a Tutsi] who came to brag to me that he belonged to the PL [Parti libéral, a political party well known for including many Tutsi]—I told him "The mistake we made in 1959, when I was still a child, is to let you leave." I asked him if he had not heard the story of the Falashas, who returned home to Israel from Ethiopia? He replied he knew nothing about it! I told him "So don't you know how to listen or read? I am telling you that your home is Ethiopia, that we will send you by the Nyabarongo so you can get there quickly!" . . . Do not be afraid, know that anyone whose neck you do not cut is the one who will cut your neck. Let me tell you, these people should begin leaving while there is still time.[1]

Mugesera's speech is widely seen as a defining moment in the lead-up to the Rwandan Genocide. It was the first time a high MRND official called for the annihilation of the Tutsi.

A closer inspection of the speech shows that Mugesera reaches back into the past. He apparently expects his audience to be familiar with this history. But what do the Tutsi have to do with Ethiopia? And why is the regional conflict between the center-southerners (known as Nduga) and the northwesterners (known as the Kiga) so important? These are the main questions this chapter will deal with. To provide a satisfactory answer, we must, drawing primarily on the seminal work of Jan Vansina,[2] look back to the birth of Rwanda in the seventeenth century. Any attempt to start the story later—for example, at colonization in 1899, or independence in 1962—invariably ends up explaining Rwanda's history through the racist lens of colonial social-Darwinist theories. Such approaches conceal the intricacies of Rwanda's past social structures and ultimately fail to address one of the most important questions underlying the Genocide: What does it mean to be a Hutu or a Tutsi, and how did these categories come into being?

THE SOCIAL LANDSCAPE IN RWANDA CA. 1600

The Great Lakes region of Africa sits in the middle of the continent at the border between the great rainforest of the Congo River basin to the west and the vast savannas of Tanzania to the east. Splitting the two are the mountains of the African rift, which include the Rwenzori range, the Virunga volcanoes, and the Itombwe plateau. These mountains were created by the ever-widening split between the African tectonic plate, on the one hand, and the Arabian and the Somali plates, on the other. Lakes Edward, Kivu, and Tanganyika were created by the same process.

Rwanda sits at the center of the Great Lakes region and has rightly earned the nickname of "Land of a Thousand Hills." Its western border is formed of the jungle-clad Virunga volcanoes, Lake Kivu, and the Ruzizi River. Moving east, the jungle peters out and thousands of lightly wooded, steep-sided hills become the dominant geographical feature. Slowly but steadily these hills become less steep until they flatten out into the savanna-like plains and wetlands that flank the Akagera River. This river, which ends up in Lake Victoria and is therefore one of the sources of the Nile, forms the whole of Rwanda's eastern border with Tanzania.

One of the interesting aspects of the Great Lakes region is that it is home to its own historical cultural area. Southern Uganda, Rwanda, Burundi, and parts of northwestern Tanzania were all part of this interlacustrine culture. As Jean-Pierre Chrétien writes, the region

> seems to stand out for its high degree of cohesion. The region has centralised polities, common religious references, intense human density, and similar languages, all of which underline a contrast with neighbouring areas. These traits suggested a distinct cultural personality, at least in the state in which they were directly observed during the nineteenth century. Indeed, even if the region today is torn apart, its homogeneity is striking. The Great Lakes region is fundamentally different from the Congolese basin mosaic and the East African plateaus.[3]

Of course, there is a matter of scale, and the fact that the region was culturally similar does not mean that it was totally homogenous, in the same way that someone from Kent and someone from Leicester are both English, but not exactly the same. For example, in what was to become Rwanda, the people who lived to the south of Lake Kivu in a region called Kinyaga were quite different from those who lived in the region of Bugoyi, around the Virunga Mountains, who were in turn quite different from those who lived in Nduga, in the center of the country.[4] However, on the whole, the culture of the people in the Great Lakes region was distinct from that of those who inhabited surrounding territories.

If we zoom in on Rwanda around 1600 we find that the lineage was the most important social unit. It "included three generations: grandparents, their married sons, and their grandchildren."[5] Agriculture and cattle herding were the ways to make ends meet. By this time there had been cows in the region for hundreds of years, and most farmers had a couple of cows on their land.[6] Farmers generally lived in a lineage compound toward the top of a hill surrounded by their fields. There were few real villages but rather several lineages grouped on the same hill, their compounds sited some distance from one another. This can still be seen in Rwanda today. Besides the land on the sides of the hills, the farmers also used the valleys in between to grow crops or to forage. These, as can again still be seen in Rwanda today, are home to small streams and wetlands formed by rainwater quickly running down the steep sides of the surrounding hills. The water in these valleys is of great importance to the farmers, especially during the dry season.

Just like the farmers, herders also lived on Rwanda's hills, intermingled but some distance away from their agricultural fellows. Herders depended on cattle rather than on land for their survival. Normally the herds would graze in the vicinity of lineage compounds, but when the weather dried the grass and streams several lineages would group together and escort their herds to lands where good pastures and water could still be found. After staying there for as long as necessary they would return to their hills. Rwanda's herders, while much more mobile than the agriculturalists, were not nomads.[7] Both the farmers and the herders shared the same language and religion and lived intermingled.

A step up from the lineages were the many small kingdoms that ruled Rwanda. A Mwami, as a Rwandan king is called, usually controlled one or several of the hills that formed the center of daily life for ordinary people. According to the historian and anthropologist Jan Vansina, Rwanda's many small kingdoms were roughly subdivided into two types: the lineage territory and the principality. In lineage territories, land determined political power. The Mwami came from a lineage that supposedly "had come first and cleared the land."[8] Families that came to the territory later, or who were simply less powerful than the royal lineage, were allowed to settle a piece of land if they recognized the Mwami as their king and provided him with a regular "tribute in the form of labour, food and hoes."[9] Among scholars of the Great Lakes region this power structure is known as a patron-client relationship. In this case the patron was the Mwami, who provided land and royal protection, while the client was the family or lineage, which received land in exchange for recognizing the Mwami's overlordship. This system of "land servitude"[10] was also known as *ubukonde.* Lineage territories did not possess their own permanent armies, but in times of war all able-bodied men were called upon to fight for their Mwami.

In principalities, political power was in the hands of a ruling class of herder lineages. Among these, the patriarch of the most powerful lineage was recognized as the Mwami. In this kind of polity, the Mwami's court was important and included a permanent fighting regiment, to which the subchiefs of the kingdom, known as *abatware,* sent their sons to receive an education and to be trained in the art of war (and naturally also to serve as hostages, thereby guaranteeing their father's loyalty). The abatware also sent tribute to the Mwami's court in the form of labor and goods (hides, milk, meat, etc.).

Patron-client relationships within principalities were slightly different from those in lineage territories. In all of Rwanda, but especially in the principality, a cow had a value that went well "beyond its material products (milk, meat)." In fact, "the cow occupied an eminent place in these cultures and in the symbolism that governed their human relations (from dowries and gifts to dependency ties and fines)."[11] Because cattle, rather than land, were considered the most important form of wealth, that was what the patron-client relationship was based on. As in any other society, there were poor and richer lineages. If a young man of a poor lineage wanted to start a herd, or else increase the size of his existing herd, he would have to enter into an *ubugabire* patron-client relationship. The young man would go to the head of a lineage with a large herd and ask for a cow. In return for the cow the young man would promise to give the herder the first calf of said cow. In addition, he also promised "to aid his patron and to come to work for him when the need arose."[12] In this way the young man asking for the cow became the client of the herder, who in turn became his patron. After the death of the original cow, the contract would end.[13]

NDORI AND THE NYIGINYA KINGDOM

The size and importance of the small kingdoms and lineages of Rwanda waxed and waned. Occasionally some disappeared and new ones were established. The most important of the kingdoms, the Nyiginya Kingdom, was probably founded around 1650 in the center-south of Rwanda.[14] How this kingdom suddenly came about is difficult to explain, and there are some suggestions that its founder, Ndori, was a powerful warlord who migrated south with his herds and warriors from what is today Uganda.[15] Whatever the truth of the matter, the Nyiginya Kingdom would, over the next couple of centuries, grow to form the predecessor of modern Rwanda. However, this does not mean that the history of the Nyiginya Kingdom is the entire history of the country. Rwanda has dozens of regional histories, each with their own nuances, which cannot be covered here.[16]

One of the reasons for the success of the Nyiginya Kingdom was its high level of centralization. While Rwanda was familiar with patron-client relationships, such as the aforementioned ubugabire and ubukonde, they seem to have taken on a more structured and consequential role in the Nyiginya Kingdom. Mwami Ndori is said to have introduced a new form of ubugabire in his kingdom called *ubuhake*. The latter was "far more permanent and compelling to the client. . . . The relation therefore essentially traded political submission for military protection."[17] Initially, however, this relationship only existed between Mwami Ndori and his most important supporters.

Ndori also expanded the size of his military organization by recruiting additional companies of warriors besides the one commonly maintained by a Rwandan Mwami.[18] He regularly asked his clients to provide their sons when they reached maturity, so that a new company could be formed. The company was then trained in the ways of war by veteran warriors. Several years later the process would repeat itself and a new group of young men would form a new company. Ndori would then group several companies together, put them under a general, and give this newly formed army its own herds of cattle and land on which to graze them.[19] The resulting professional, semiconscripted standing army was unknown in Rwanda at the time and gave Mwami Ndori, and his successors, a major advantage over the rival kingdoms in the area.

Over the following centuries the Nyiginya Kingdom slowly expanded. One of the important internal struggles the kingdom had to face was the friction between the power of the Mwamis and that of the most powerful lineages. This "structural" tension, which sometimes took the form of open warfare and, at other times, that of court maneuvers and intrigue, can be divided into roughly two phases.

The first started around 1700. By this time, the kingdom founded by Ndori had been consolidated and the Mwamis focused on centralizing the state. On the strength of ubuhake, the kings claimed, and managed to have accepted, that all the cows within the kingdom belonged to them. After expropriating a couple of herders to make the point, herders were left with two options: either flee the kingdom or engage in an ubuhake relationship with a powerful lord or with the Mwami himself. The standing army that Ndori had pioneered was also refined. From now on, several permanent armies would guard the kingdom's borders. These armies were given cattle herds and land to sustain themselves and to provide for the needs of the royal court. In addition, membership of the armies became hereditary: each son would join the army of which his father had been a member.[20] Vansina sums it up as follows: Between 1720 and 1796, "a genuine centralization had occurred, resulting from the institutions of the royal *ubuhake* and the armies, which had become multiple and permanent. This centralization benefited the whole court, the elites as much as the king. The descendants of those great lords of yore were co-opted in a system that promised them more wealth and more influence than they could ever have acquired by themselves."[21]

The second phase began with the succession war that broke out in 1796. When Mwami Ndabarasa died, his sons went to war over the right to succeed their father. However, the deeper cause of the conflict was that there were not enough elite positions to satisfy the growing number of royal lineages at the court. Over the next seventy years, the kings would prove unable to reassert their power vis-à-vis their nobles. This meant that the noble families took much power for themselves, not least by increasing the number of ubuhake relationships, "to the point where . . . all the owners of sizeable herds and even some prosperous farmers were affiliated with a protector."[22] Indeed, while the ubuhake relationship was unequal, it did allow the client to rely on his patron for support in the event of another lineage having designs on his herds or lands. By the 1850s, a pyramid of patron-client relationships had come into being. At the top of the pyramid sat the king, who had as clients the most illustrious noble lineages, who in turn had less important families as clients, and so on, down to the smallest herders and, indeed, some farmers.[23]

Ironically, the civil wars and the increasing power of the elite noble lineages did not slow down the expansion of the kingdom, which encompassed most of modern Rwanda by 1867. This is because many of the conquests were conducted by powerful nobles themselves or on the initiative of individual army commanders. During this phase of expansion, however, the kingdom also ran into several regions that it could not conquer, or that it could conquer only with great difficulty. To the south was the Rundi Kingdom, which would go on to become the foundation for the modern state of Burundi. Then there were several regions within modern Rwanda, such as the northwest, around the Virunga Mountains, and Gisaka, in the southeast. There, the influence of the Nyiginya court remained limited at best due to strong local resistance.

HUTU AND TUTSI

Originally the word *Tutsi* had been used among herders in parts of the Great Lakes region to describe a small, wealthy, elite group in their midst. The royal lineages of the Nyiginya Kingdom were one of the groups who self-identified as Tutsi. This meant that as the power of the kingdom expanded, so did the importance of the term *Tutsi,* which, eventually, spread to most of the herders of central Rwanda. They used it to distinguish themselves from the farmers among whom they lived, "even if their social condition was but modest."[24]

In contrast to *Tutsi,* which described a herding elite, the word *Hutu* "was a demeaning term that alluded to rural boorishness or loutish behaviour used by the elite. Even before [King] Mazimpaka's time [ca. 1710–1766], masters at the court called their servants, even those who belonged to the Tutsi ethnic group, 'Hutu.'"[25] The Nyiginya armies are likely to have played an important role in the process that caused the word *Hutu* to be more closely associated with farmers. Within these armies, those who did the fighting were the cattle herders, while those who organized the supplies and carried extra weapons were farmers. These "'servants' were called Hutu in the Rwandan language."[26] Slowly, as time progressed, all farmers would be labeled Hutu, while the herders came to be labeled Tutsi. As the word *Hutu* could also mean "foreigners," the Nyiginya court also came to see any farmers living outside of their borders as Hutu.[27]

However, this does not mean that these categories were the main label by which people identified themselves. As Vansina explains, in the nineteenth century, Hutu "distinguished themselves as the 'people' of Bugoyi, Kinyaga, Nduga . . . not as 'Hutu.'"[28] This was particularly important in places where the court was unable to impose its will on account of distance. The Kiga of the volcanoes of northern Rwanda, for instance, "did not always accept the Hutu-Tutsi social parameters of the Court; instead there was a greater shared identity among people in these regions as . . . 'the people of the mountains.'"[29] People also often identified according to their clan, lineage, or chiefly allegiances. In addition Hutu and Tutsi were able to move from one category to the other through marriage or the acquisition/loss of wealth.[30]

Mwami Rwabugiri (reign: ca. 1867–1895) is a controversial figure in Rwandan history. In some circles, he is remembered as a warrior-king who managed to expand the kingdom to its maximum extent during his thirty-year reign. Jan Vansina, however, has provided a different reading of traditional material, arguing that Rwabugiri was a paranoid man who caused the unnecessary suffering of his people by waging too many wars—wars that proved costly and, ultimately, pointless. Following his death, practically none of the lands that he had conquered remained under the control of the kingdom. Instead, the people whom he had subjugated rebelled and reclaimed their independence.

However, for our purposes, the most important aspect of Rwabugiri's rule is that he introduced a new type of patron-client relationship that specifically targeted farmers. As there were no Tutsi farmers, this patron-client relationship and the new duties that it entailed de facto targeted the Hutu masses. By so doing, his policies polarized and sharpened what had hitherto been a relatively minor divide. "From this point on, 'Hutu' and 'Tutsi' would no longer designate a relative category with respect to class or dependency or occupation but became an absolute one."[31] One of these duties, *ubureetwa*, forced Hutu to spend about half their time working for a local Tutsi chief or notable.[32] The tasks assigned to Hutu included "collecting and drying firewood for the use of the hill chief's household, serving as his night watchman, fetching water, [or] cultivating the hill chief's fields."[33]

Rwabugiri's many military campaigns overextended the kingdom. Rebellions broke out even before his death; at some point in the early 1890s, the Hutu population around Giseke, in southern Rwanda, rose up in support of a pretender claiming to possess magical powers. Matters grew even worse when Rwabugiri passed away in 1895. Idjwi Island and Bushi (a region west of Lake Kivu) immediately broke away from the kingdom. Soon thereafter rebellions also broke out in other peripheral regions of the kingdom. Ndorwa and Bugoyi, in the north, and Gisaka, in the south, had only been recently conquered, and so local leaders led their people to battle against the Nyiginya Kingdom. These rebellions show how complicated Hutu-Tutsi relations were in Rwanda at the time, as well as the important role the kingdom played in shaping them. On the one hand, the people in these regions rose up as one, both herders and farmers. On the other hand, the rebellions seem to have had a certain anti-Tutsi character.[34] While the herders in the center of Rwanda, the heartland of the kingdom, self-identified as Tutsi, it seems that many herders on the periphery did not, or only marginally. So much so that, when faced with a fight for independence, their regional identity proved more important than whether they regarded themselves as Hutu or Tutsi, farmers or herders.

Rwabugiri's death was also followed by a succession war. Rutarindwa, the new Mwami who succeeded Rwabugiri, was at odds with the queen mother. Her position was exceptionally powerful in the Nyiginya Kingdom, second only to the Mwami himself. As Rutarindwa's mother had died, one of Rwabugiri's other wives, Kanjogera, had been designated queen mother. However, Kanjogera, herself from a powerful lineage, wanted her own son on the throne and schemed against Rutarindwa. Together with her brothers, they first eliminated the Mwami's most important supporters and then launched a coup d'état, during which Rutarindwa killed himself.[35] In February 1897 Kanjogera's son, Musinga, took the throne.

A German soldier, Captain Hans Gustav Ferdinand von Ramsay, arrived in Rwanda a month or two after Mwami Musinga (reign: 1896–12 November 1931) had been crowned. His mission was to extend German protection over the country. For the court his arrival was not wholly unexpected: Several German explorers had crossed through the territory over the preceding years, while Rutarindwa, during his brief period as Mwami, had even launched an attack on a station established by the Congo Free State at Shangi. Although the army sent to drive the Belgians out contained some of the kingdom's best warriors, it was decisively defeated, showing the court that firearm-wielding Europeans could not be trifled with.

Musinga, or at least his mother and her brothers (the Mwami was still in his early teens), was favorably disposed toward Captain Ramsay's offer of protection for several reasons. By allying the monarchy with an external force, young Musinga was able to consolidate his contested position as the new ruler of the kingdom. This was important as his claim to the throne was in fact illegitimate. Although several powerful nobles, including other sons of Rwabugiri, had supported him against Rutarindwa, they might well change their minds and make a play for the throne themselves. The Germans also offered him the opportunity of keeping the Belgians, who were advancing from the west, at bay. The horrors of the Congo Free State preceded them, and the court must have deemed it preferable to throw in its lot with the Germans.[36] In 1896, then, the Nyiginya Kingdom became a German protectorate.

HAMITIC HYPOTHESIS

When the first European explorers arrived in Rwanda in the late 1890s, they quickly realized that the country was run differently from many other African communities. It was a centralized kingdom. The country was ruled by one court, capable of raising thousands of warriors when needed, and a group of Tutsi herder aristocrats ruled over a mass of peasants called Hutu. At least that is what they saw through their colonial eyes. And what they saw demanded an explanation: Who and what were Tutsi and Hutu, and how had the difference between them come about? European colonists answered these questions with a racist fantasy that changed the way Rwanda worked and, ultimately, helped pave the way for Genocide. This fantasy is now known as the Hamitic Hypothesis.

At the time that the Europeans were trying to understand Rwanda, it was normal to speak of different human races, some of which were considered superior to others.[37] According to the leading scientists of the time there were at least two races in Africa. One was the Hamitic race, the descendants of the biblical Ham, the son of Noah. The Hamitic race included Ethiopians, because they were Christians, and Nubians, because they were the founders of the great Egyptian civilization. It was necessary to make this distinction because the scholars of the time could not—or did not want to—imagine that these two civilizations might be equated with the other African race which they considered inferior: the "Negroes."[38]

John Hanning Speke, an English explorer who had served in the British-Indian army, was aware of these theories when he set out on an expedition to find the source of the Nile in 1859. While he did not visit Rwanda, he did pass through Uganda, and he had on previous trips already visited Burundi. These regions were all part of the African Great Lakes and shared a similar, if not identical, culture. Both Burundi and Uganda had social categories similar to the Hutu-Tutsi in Rwanda. On his return, Speke wrote a book in which he argued that it was "impossible to believe, judging from the physical appearance of the Wahima [Tutsi], that they can be of any other race than the semi-Shem-Hamitic of Ethiopia. The traditions of the imperial government of Abyssinia go as far back as the scriptural age of King David, from whom the late reigning king of Abyssinia, Sahela Selassie, traced his descent."[39]

Despite many years of intermarriage Speke's Ethiopian Hamites had "maintained a high stamp of Asiatic feature, of which a marked characteristic is a bridged instead of a bridgeless nose."[40] Speke went on to explain that the cattle herders of the Great Lakes, who called themselves Hima or Tutsi, were actually the descendants of Ethiopian cattle herders who had conquered large parts of Africa and then settled there, "leaving the agricultural aborigines to till the ground."[41] Speke's ideas were readily recycled by all who followed. They became part of the official ideology by which both the Germans and, later, the Belgians ruled Rwanda and Burundi.[42]

The success and longevity of the Hamitic Hypothesis can in part be explained by the fact that it suited the needs and hopes of many European colonizers. On a theological-historical level, the theory was anchored in the Bible. The sons of Ham were part of the European cultural canon, and the notion that they had subjugated large parts of Africa and the peoples who inhabited it was a comfortable parallel to the colonial project. On a scientific level, the fantasy of a Hamitic Ethiopian race, which was actually "European under a black skin,"[43] fit right into the social-Darwinist ideas of the era. The alleged biological differences between the so-called Hutu and Tutsi "races" were therefore emphasized. Doctors and ethnologists set about measuring the size of noses, the height of foreheads, ears, and lips to prove that the Tutsi were not "Negroes." According to a Belgian doctor, "The Hamites [Tutsi] are 1.90 m tall. They have straight noses, high foreheads, thin lips. . . . Women, when they are young, are really beautiful; they also have a slightly lighter complexion than that of men."[44]

As late as 1957, R. Bourgeois, who had served as the deputy and, later, temporary resident (governor) of Rwanda, published the first of his three-volume work on the history and customs of Rwanda and Burundi. He took his work seriously and his opus ran to more than sixteen hundred pages. Yet even after the racially fueled insanity of the Second World War, he still ventured into racial speculations:

> If we go upwards towards the north [from Rwanda], first following the Ethiopian plateau, then gradually approaching the Nile and this up to 25° north latitude, we find the domain of the Ethiopians proper, intermediaries between the Whites and the Negroes. The Massai form the extreme vanguard of the Ethiopians towards the South. Geographically and somatically, outposts of the Ethiopian race are also constituted in the east by the Bahima [Tutsi] group in the middle of the Negroes between lakes Victoria, Edward and Kivu.[45]

The Hamitic Myth is not grounded in scientific evidence. In some oral traditions there is a hint that the founder of the Nyiginya Kingdom, Ndori, or his group of followers, might have come from Uganda.[46] There is also some archaeological evidence that he might have brought some pottery with him that was different from the dominant style in Rwanda at the time.[47] But as explained above, Uganda was in essence part of the same cultural region as Rwanda. Neither the Nyiginya Kingdom nor the polities that had preceded it were the products of the conquest of a "Negroe" race by a "Hamitic" Ethiopian race. What the region witnessed instead were "the internal movements at the center of a civilization, one that had been developing for two millennia."[48]

The Hamitic Myth turned a complex and at times adversarial Hutu-Tutsi relationship into a racial time bomb. Over the next sixty years, the idea that Tutsi and Hutu were two different races, and that the superior Tutsi originally came from Ethiopia and submitted the inferior Hutu, became accepted as fact by Rwandans themselves. This development can be attributed to several key factors. First, there were only limited opportunities for education during the colonial period. The best schools in the colony were the seminaries run by Catholic missionaries (the grand seminary at Kabgayi and the small seminary at Mugera) and the school for the sons of chiefs known as the Groupe scolaire d'Astrida.[49] These educational institutions, where the Hamitic Myth was part of the curriculum, served to form both the Tutsi and, much later, the Hutu elites.[50] On a broader level, most primary education in the country was delegated to missionaries, who, again, would have been firm believers in the Hamitic Myth. Second, as we shall see in the next chapter, the Tutsi monarchy and the elite aristocratic families of the kingdom used the Hamitic Myth to cement their own power. They simply had no reason to oppose a historical narrative that gave them more power and riches than they had ever had before. Finally, the European colonial officials who held the balance of power in Rwanda believed the myth and found it instrumental to their aims.

THE GERMAN AND BELGIAN PERIODS

German rule, which lasted from 1897 to 1918, did not entail the wholesale subjugation of Rwanda or the abolishment of the monarchy. Around 1900, colonial powers were still limited in their capacity to project power into the heart of Africa. The main objective of the Germans was to have their rule over Rwanda and Burundi accepted by other European powers and to maintain a small permanent presence in the territory. So the monarchy was left alone, and Mwami Musinga and the Nyiginya elites were allowed to rule nearly autonomously.[51] It was one of the best examples of colonial indirect rule.

As mentioned above, regionalism was an important factor in Rwanda. The people in the peripheral parts of the kingdom who had regained their independence on Rwabugiri's death identified strongly with their region. This identity was so entrenched that it often superseded the Hutu-Tutsi cleavage. The people from the heartland of the Nyiginya Kingdom, who were called the Nduga, were seen as unwelcome invaders. Gisaka, the region which covers southeastern Rwanda, is a good example. During the 1901 Rukura revolt in Gisaka, Tutsi warriors from the region sided with the rebels.[52] More generally, Tutsi who were displaced from power by the Nduga "resented the extension of royal control as much as did the Hutu."[53]

However, the most important regional cleavage was that between the center, Nduga, and the northwest, known as the Kiga. The people in Kiga had rebelled against the kingdom on the death of Rwabugiri. This region was ruled by several Hutu lineages that were proud of their warrior traditions. Musinga tried numerous times to break the resistance of the north and to install his clients to rule the region. However, he and his clients were never particularly successful, even with the assistance of European missionaries and the German authorities. The Kiga would not be fully absorbed into the kingdom—or, by that point, the Belgian protectorate of

Ruanda-Urundi—until around 1920.[54] By then, the animosity between the Nduga and the Kiga ran so deep that it would re-emerge after independence.

Belgium took over control of Rwanda from Germany as a League of Nations mandate territory at the end of the First World War. Like the Germans before them, the Belgians administered the country through a system of indirect rule. The start of Belgian rule had been accompanied by the high-sounding promises of the "civilising mission." In particular, the administration wanted to consolidate "the authority of indigenous leaders, while ensuring they operate within the limits of equity and legality."[55] In practice this meant that the Belgian colonial administration, who believed in the Hamitic Myth, worked toward creating a chiefly class that was exclusively Tutsi. The Groupe scolaire d'Astrida and its predecessor, the École de Nyanza, were an important part of this process. As a colonial report explains, "This school is exclusively meant for the children of the noble Tutsi race of Rwanda, and especially the sons of its chiefs, who form 259 of the 342 pupils in 1930."[56] Those Tutsi who were not destined to be chiefs but who were educated at the school could expect to be granted the very limited number of jobs in the civil service that were open to Africans. The alliance between the monarchy and the Belgians thus assured that the Tutsi increasingly consolidated an exclusive hold on power in Rwanda.

What did the Belgians receive in return? The administration needed the power of the monarchy, the chiefs, and the subchiefs to mobilize Hutu labor for the colonial economy. Although official policy tried to prevent those same chiefs and subchiefs from making excessive demands on the labor force for their own needs, the reality of the Great Depression quickly changed priorities. As Brussels made clear that Ruanda-Urundi would no longer be able to count on subsidies from Belgium, the importance of African labor and, therefore, of chiefly cooperation skyrocketed.[57] As it was Hutu who had to bear the brunt of this policy, which forced them into even more unpaid work, they sought ways to reduce the burdens placed on them by looking for protection from notables or missionaries or by other forms of resistance. However, as Des Forges writes, "for all their different pathways seeking redress, many Rwandans saw Belgian rule as the beginning of the 'time of the whip.' Hutu bore its sting most often, but Tutsi suffered from it occasionally as well."[58]

Chiefs and subchiefs often exploited their increased authority. For instance, they might call up more people than were demanded by the administration and set them to work on their own crops. On other occasions, they confiscated the small compensation set aside for people who worked on infrastructural projects.[59] Similar abuses included local authorities pocketing the wages paid to those who worked for European firms.[60] As the courts were controlled by these very chiefs and notables, exploited Hutu had few avenues for redress.[61] Even though the Belgians knew about these abuses,

> the abilities of Rwandan authorities to circumvent any controls were generally more effective than the controls themselves. In fact the system worked also to the benefit of the European community, including the administrators themselves. Consequently, the Administration was caught in the vice of assuring "adequate" administrative authority in the hands of the chiefs on the one hand, and professing the desire to control the abuses on the other. The administrative system was predicated on the basis of chiefly power; only individual administrators were concerned about abuses.[62]

However, the cooperation between the Mwami, the aristocracy, and the Belgians was not free from tensions. Musinga had never liked the Belgians and continued to profess traditional Rwandan beliefs rather than converting to Catholicism. This earned him the enmity of both the missionaries and the colonial administration, which deposed him in November 1931, replacing him with his son Rudahigwa. Nonetheless, the "cohesion of oppression" based on the alliance between the Mwami and the Tutsi aristocracy remained in place until after the Second World War. Between the 1930s and 1940s, most Hutu farmers were not only second-class citizens but were also forced to work for an increasingly demanding colonial administration, on the one hand, and for their traditional chiefs and patrons, on the other.

The Second World War brought about both the most extreme exploitation that Rwanda had ever experienced and—eventually—relief from it. As Belgium threw its colonies behind the Allied war machine, Rwandans were forced, from 1942 onward, to contribute sixty days per year to the war effort.[63] Colonial exactions, failing rains, and various crop-killing diseases caused one of the worst famines in the country's history. Known as Ruzagayura, it killed between 36,000 and 225,000 people in 1943–1944.[64] However, the aftermath of the war brought some solace. When the League of Nations was dissolved in 1946 and its duties taken over by the United Nations, Ruanda-Urundi, as the territory was then known, changed in status from a Class B Mandate under Belgian administration to a UN trust territory. While not much changed in practice, with Belgium remaining in control on the ground, the long-term purpose of UN trusteeship was to lead the country to independence on the terms "and the freely expressed wishes of the peoples concerned."[65]

* * *

By the eve of independence Hutu and Tutsi were firmly established in the minds of almost all Rwandans as unchangeable racial categories. Roughly 85 percent of the population was considered Hutu and 14 percent Tutsi (the remaining 1 percent were Twa, pygmies who were discriminated against by all). Identity cards reported a person's ethnicity and one's chances in life were largely determined by this racial label that was passed on from father to child. As we have seen, the process that created two ethnic groups was a long one. While the Hutu-Tutsi opposition existed in Rwanda before the arrival of the Europeans, it was based on connection to the royal family and the Nyiginya Kingdom, and on whether one was a farmer or a herder. It could also change. The two categories were not fixed in stone. In short, the Rwandans, regardless of whether they were Hutu or Tutsi, were one people, "not distinguished by language, culture, history or geographical space."[66]

It was the arrival of the Europeans and the introduction of the Hamitic Myth that created Hutu and Tutsi as races. Colonization then ingrained the ideas to such an extent that, almost one hundred years after the arrival of the first Europeans, Léon Mugesera was able to announce, in a hate-filled speech on a football field deep in rural Rwanda, that all Tutsis were Ethiopians and that if they were killed and thrown into the Nyabarongo, one of the sources of the Nile, they would float back to where they belonged. And not only could he say it, but he could also assume that his audience would understand.

Regionalism was another key issue. The gradual expansion of the Nyiginya Kingdom and the inability of the court uniformly to impose its ways meant that the independent-minded Kiga people of the northwest of Rwanda remembered the days when they had been free from interference from the Nduga from the center of the country. As we will see in the next chapters, the first forty years of independent Rwanda were dominated by a struggle between the Hutu political elites from these two regions.

2

The Social Revolution and Independence

1959–1964

ON 6 NOVEMBER 1959, IN THE SOUTHERN TOWN OF TAMBWE, the cousin of the Rwandan queen Asteria Basinda and her son Paul Kagame, just two years old, stood looking out to the other side of the valley. Plumes of smoke arose as an armed mob set fire to the houses of local Tutsi, killing all who tried to resist. Having finished their murderous work, the mob turned their attention to the next hill: "They started shouting and making a lot of noise, saying that we were escaping and that they had to hurry, to come and get us before we could leave."[1] Asteria and her son got lucky that day. Before the mob could reach them, a car sent by her cousin the queen picked them up and brought them to the safety of the Royal Palace at Nyanza. Soon after, it became clear that Rwanda was no longer safe for Tutsi and so the family fled north, to Uganda, where Paul would grow up in a refugee camp. Years later, during the opening days of the Struggle for Liberation, Kagame would take command of the Rwandan Patriotic Front (RPF) and lead it to victory against the genocidal forces of the Rwandan government.

On 10 November 1960, almost one year to the day after the attack at Tambwe, Juvénal Habyarimana, a Hutu from the northwest of the country, sat in front of the selection committee that would decide which recruits would be allowed to join the first officer course of the Rwandan Garde nationale. The twenty-three-year-old was exactly the kind of man the Belgian trainers would be looking for; he was tall and broad-shouldered, had studied for a year at the most important university in Belgian Congo, known as the

Lovanium, and was solidly Catholic. Just three years later, now a captain, Habyarimana found himself in command of the Garde nationale.[2] He would go on to become president of Rwanda and commander in chief of his country in the battle against the RPF.

Little is known of Habyarimana's role during the Social Revolution (1959–1964), as Rwanda's first civil war is known. What *is* known is that the persecution of the Tutsi, one of the core elements of the war, did not end in 1959. A roving correspondent for the *Sunday Times* reported the following in early 1964:

> Every figure from 8,000 to 15,000 has been given to me as the number of Batutsi [Tutsi] . . . slaughtered by the Bahutu [Hutu]. . . . The reprisals have been in two waves. The first was from late December to the first week of January—the more or less systematic slaughter at the behest of the government . . . of any visible male Batutsi and often mothers of male children. The second wave, till last week, was the rounding up of any Batutsi of conceivable influence for good or evil. They were loaded into trucks and machine-gunned by the nearest river, where after mutilation the bodies were dumped. . . . 142,000 refugees.[3]

It is impossible to understand Rwanda's second civil war, "The Struggle for Liberation" of 1990–1994, without a thorough knowledge of the Social Revolution. Nowhere is this more obvious than in the case of the two men discussed above.

BELGIAN COGNITIVE DISSONANCE

The colonial powers, mortally wounded by the Second World War, were forced one by one to relinquish their hold over the millions of people they had oppressed for so long. India and Pakistan won their independence from the United Kingdom in 1947. They were followed by Indonesia in 1949, after a long and bitter war against the Netherlands. But it was not just a decline in military might that heralded the end of empire. Powerful ideas about self-determination and the dignity of *all* human beings became increasingly widespread in the aftermath of the horrors of the war. The Atlantic Charter, issued by President Franklin Roosevelt and Prime Minister Winston Churchill in 1941, held that "all peoples" should be able to "choose the form of government under which they will live."[4] In 1945 the United Nations was founded, followed shortly by the Universal Declaration of Human Rights. Together these changes heralded a radical shift in the world's perception of colonial empires. Although it did not vanish overnight, colonialism increasingly appeared as the oppression of other peoples and countries, rather than a noble enterprise.

The Rwandan road to independence was strongly influenced by these international events. After the First World War and the defeat of Germany, the country, together with Burundi, had been taken over by Belgium as a League of Nations mandate territory—rather than a colony. After the Second World War, League of Nations mandates had become UN trust territories. This meant that the Belgian administration of Ruanda-Urundi was obliged to prepare Rwandans for "self-governance or independence" by way of their "freely expressed wishes,"[5] a fact that caught the Belgian administration unprepared.

New Belgian administrators and missionaries arriving in Rwanda after the Second World War were markedly different from their predecessors. Their social backgrounds were more varied, and many had liberal or socialist sympathies, unlike their solidly Catholic conservative forebears. Most had also experienced the horrors of the German occupation of Belgium and were much more skeptical of racial ideology.[6] These new arrivals, especially the missionaries, "began to create opportunities for Hutu, increasing enrolment in church schools and cultivating educated Hutu,"[7] something that would have been unthinkable only a decade earlier.

In some cases the effects were immediate, and a small Hutu elite (or, perhaps more appropriately, counter-elite) started to develop. This elite was led by men like Grégoire Kayibanda, Aloys Munyangaju, and Joseph Gitera. Kayibanda had been a seminary and school teacher, but became really influential in 1953, when he took up the post of coeditor of *L'Ami,* a magazine specifically geared toward the Catholic elites of Rwanda. Then, in 1955, Kayibanda gained the editorship of *Kinyamateka* (the Chronicler), a magazine with a circulation of more than 22,000.[8] Under the leadership of Bishop Laurent Déprimoz, the missionary Arthur Dejemeppe, and Kayibanda, *L'Ami* and *Kinyamateka* "shifted from a top down focus on the monarchy to a more grassroots emphasis on social justice, the Hutu peasantry and democracy."[9] Munyangaju, for his part, founded his own newspaper in 1956, but then took on the editorship of *Temps nouveaux d'Afrique* in 1958. Gitera, a businessman, had been educated at church schools in Kabgayi and Nyakibanda. Rather than work as an editor for an established newspaper, he founded his own: *Ijwi rya rubanda* (Voice of the little people).[10] According to the Belgian governor general, the views expressed by this small intelligentsia encountered the favor of a growing constituency, as they "reflected a tendency which in confused form was already part of the consciousness of a great many members of [the Hutu] social group."[11]

However, the importance and speed of these changes surprised the Belgian administration, which soon found itself out of step with reality. No Hutu was allowed to join the Groupe scolaire d'Astrida until 1945. By 1950, R. Bourgeois, a teacher at the school, noted that while he was happy to see both Hutu and Tutsi pupils, "all the candidate-chiefs were Tutsi, the administration would not tolerate a single Hutu amongst them."[12] When a mission of the UN Trusteeship Council visited Ruanda-Urundi in October 1948 to check on the progress of the Belgians, it was disappointed. The administration had promised to start democratizing the Rwandan political system, but the mission judged that "over-cautious and timid experiments are not enough; the machinery must resolutely be set in motion."[13] Other visiting missions in 1951 and 1954 re-emphasized that more Rwandans should join the territorial administration, that Rwandans should be included in the legislature, and that a process of democratization should be started as soon as possible.[14]

It seems that UN pressure did have a marked effect on the Belgian administration: the visiting mission of 1948 advised that the highest strata of Rwandans and Burundians should be allowed to travel abroad, and in 1949 the Mwami of Rwanda visited Belgium.[15] In 1948 and 1954, respectively, Mwami Rudahigwa abolished uburetwa and ubuhake, the two most hated forms of customary obligation that tied clients to their patrons. However, Belgian administrators had to use mental gymnastics to justify their actions; after all, they were helping dismantle a system that they or their forebears had helped create. The conclusion of a report sent by the Belgian administration to the UN in 1954 shows the narrative that was used to work around this:

> Thirty years ago, Ruanda-Urundi was an entrenched bastion of the feudal system. One could observe there the whole range of abuses that such

> a regime entails. These abuses were committed in broad daylight, no sanction repressed them.
>
> From the outset, the Belgian administration endeavoured to rectify the situation: success was not always proportionate to the scale of the efforts, as these were often met with both the hostility of the great [the Tutsi] and the apathy of the small [the Hutu]. However, today one can say that both sides have grasped the thinking that governed and still governs the action of the European administration of the Trust Territory, and that they have adjusted to it.[16]

The quote typifies the hypocrisy (or perhaps confusion) of the Belgian administration. Indeed, it was the Europeans—the Germans and then the Belgians—who had introduced the concept of a Hutu-Tutsi division based on race, who had helped the monarchy solidify its monopoly on power (thus enabling abuses throughout the system), who had relied on the monarchy's support for economic gain, and who had instituted an educational apartheid that specifically banned Hutu from positions of power. The effects of this string of policies would become clear during the 1956 elections.

THE 1956 ELECTIONS

The 1956 elections seem to have been a spur-of-the-moment decision by Governor Jean-Paul Harroy.[17] On 4 August he wrote a letter in which he decided on an immediate "popular consultation" in which every male Rwandan would be allowed to vote for the lowest administrative body, the electoral college of the sub-chieftaincy.[18] The elections were to be held at the end of September. The objective of this consultation is unclear. First, the structure of the administration of Rwanda meant there was no chance the election could have a significant effect on the higher levels of government. This set the stage for disappointment among the electorate. No matter what people voted for, they would hardly see any changes at the highest echelons of government. Second, the timeline for the election did not allow for any kind of proper preparation. The chiefs and subchiefs of Rwanda were informed at the beginning of September and the elections took place on 30 September. In some places the population was only informed of the upcoming elections seven days before election day![19]

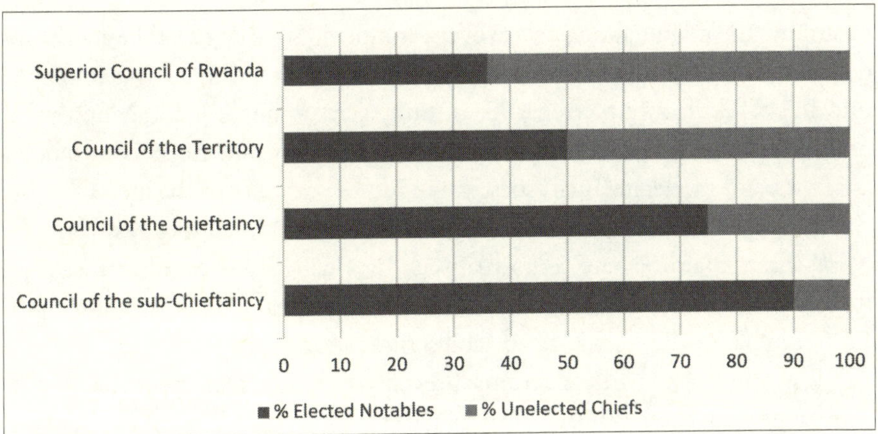

FIGURE 2.1. The Rwandan political system as of 1952. The political system that was introduced in 1952 and 1953 was supposed to be a step toward democracy, but it was heavily tilted toward unelected chiefs who were appointed by the Mwami. The country consisted of nine territories, 46 chieftainships, and 603 sub-chieftaincies in 1952.

In the first "election," held in 1953, the unelected subchiefs drew up lists of local notables who were eligible to vote. These notables then voted among themselves to see who would actually sit on the council of the sub-chieftaincy. The notables on the council of the sub-chieftaincy then voted on a limited number from their own ranks who would sit on the council of the chieftaincy and so on.

The 1956 elections were for the council of the sub-chieftaincy. On the day of the elections those eligible to vote were given a ballot at the entrance to the voting station. Each voter would write on their ballot four names of the local men they would like to see as a member of the electoral college of the sub-chieftaincy—there were no candidates to choose from. If they could not write, they would be assisted by scribes especially recruited for that purpose. They would then cast their vote by putting the ballot in a special urn. As the votes were counted, a list was made of the names of the people who had received the most votes. From that list of names, the sub-chief would then choose who he wanted as a member of his electoral college. While the entire male population of Rwanda voted for the sub-chieftaincy level, the effect of the vote on the councils of the territory and the Superior Council of Rwanda remained limited.
Source: Jacques J. Maquet and Marcel d'Hertefelt, *Elections en société féodale: Une étude sur l'introduction du vote populaire au Ruanda-Urundi* (Brussels: Académie royale des Sciences coloniales, 1959), 29–30, 99, 199, 132, 210–11, 216

When political parties define their election platform, they usually set the national agenda for years to come. However, Rwanda had no political parties—the result of a Belgian policy as restrictive as that which existed in Congo. Furthermore, the election timeframe did not allow the development of a debate to determine the main national issues of the moment. So what exactly were Rwandans voting for, or against? In Rwanda some organizations could have stepped into this void, if only there had been time. One example is the Mouvement politique progressiste (MPP), which included among its members both moderate Hutu and moderate Tutsi (such as the future president of Rwanda Grégoire Kayibanda before he became an extremist). As historian J. J. Carney explains, the MPP "charted a moderate course between nationalism and ethnicism, striving to improve relations between Rwandans and Europeans while avoiding 'anti-European nationalism' and . . . 'social discrimination based on race.'"[20]

Rushing ahead with elections prevented these covert political parties (one might call them "clubs") from playing a useful role. The choice between candidates became binary. The vote was for either a Tutsi or a Hutu candidate. Indeed, both Belgian administrators and scholars saw the vote through a distinctly ethnic lens. One of the most senior administrators, R. Bourgeois, the adjunct-resident of Ruanda-Urundi, wrote that

> the results of the year 1956 cement the impressive retreat of Tutsi authority in Rwanda: . . . the feudal class are in the process of collapse. . . . These elections are a historic event for Rwanda: the realisation of a wish included 26 years ago by the vice governor general in his program of 25 September 1930: "The dominated class must become aware of its rights." . . . I am happy to have participated, for a quarter of a century, in this awareness raising, and to have drawn up the instructions that organised the current elections.[21]

The administration had also commissioned a study into the elections. Conducted by two eminent scholars, Jean-Jacques Maquet and Marcel d'Hertefelt, it too was fully focused on the ethnic implications of the elections:

> In the feudal kingdoms of Ruanda and Urundi, political relations were based on a principle of fundamental inequality between men, which translated as paternalism among superiors and dependence among inferiors. Those in command were considered superior because they belonged to the minority Tutsi caste. These conquering herders, who probably came from the North-East several centuries ago, had succeeded in imposing their domination, to a different extent in Ruanda and Urundi, and even in the various regions of each of these countries, over the mass of Bantu-speaking cultivators, the Hutu, and on the minority of hunters and potters, the pygmoid Twa.[22]

These two quotes neatly demonstrate the cognitive dissonance that dominated Belgian thought. On the one hand, Maquet, d'Hertefelt, and Bourgeois all subscribed to the Hamitic Myth—that the Tutsi were a superior Hamitic race from Ethiopia which had subjugated the Hutu and the Twa. This myth was the foundation upon which the colonialists—the Germans and Belgians—had based their organization of Rwanda, changing the Hutu-Tutsi divide from a social into a racial matter. At the same time, the administrator Bourgeois, who had worked for decades to spread the Hamitic Myth and who educated Tutsi chiefs at the racially segregated Groupe scolaire d'Astrida, was well pleased for his role in helping the Hutu regain their rights—rights which they had been largely deprived of during colonialism.

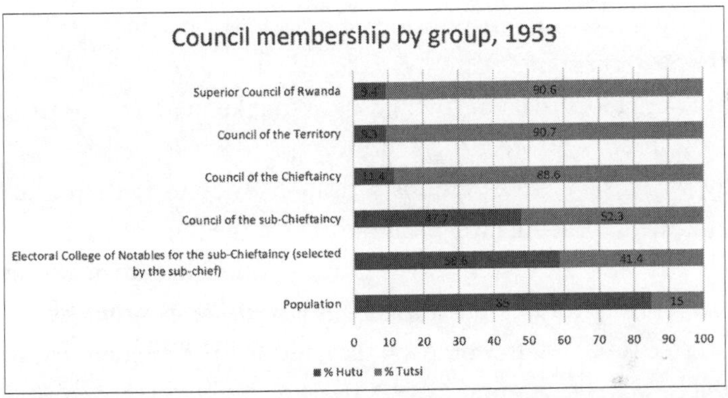

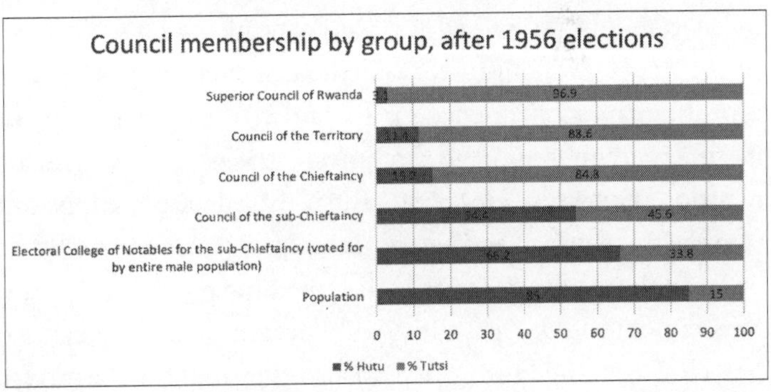

FIGURES 2.2 AND 2.3. The results of the 1956 "popular consultation." The 1956 elections were for the electoral college of notables for the sub-chieftaincy. As can be seen, the electoral system excluded Hutu from proper representation, even after the elections. *Source:* Jacques Maquet and Marcel d'Hertefelt, *Elections en société féodale: Une étude sur l'introduction du vote populaire au Ruanda-Urundi* (Brussels: Académie royale des Sciences coloniales, 1959), 29–30, 99, 199, 132, 210–11, 216

INDEPENDENCE

The effects of the 1956 "popular consultation" were twofold. On the one hand, it deeply disillusioned the growing Hutu counter-elite, which eventually found a spokesman in Kayibanda in 1957, when he joined the newly formed Mouvement social muhutu (MSM).[23] They had expected the democratic reforms to help remove the gulf in power that separated Tutsi from Hutu, but the political system at the time did not allow for this to happen. On the other hand, the UN-supported road to independence and the steadily growing political awareness of the Hutu posed a problem for the Tutsi monarchy. As a minority controlling the monarchy and the civil service in the country, the royal establishment felt that any free and fair elections would fundamentally undermine its position of power. The oscillating views of the Belgian administration must also have played a role in convincing the monarchy and its councillors that they would have to take matters into their own hands if they wanted to protect their future.

Consequently, when the United Nations Visiting Mission to Trust Territories in East Africa came to visit Ruanda-Urundi in 1957, the Superior Council of Rwanda, which was fully controlled by conservative Tutsi, had an appeal at the ready. This *Statement of Views* argued that "self-government is the normal culmination of trusteeship. . . . It would be difficult at the present stage to specify when it will be possible to grant us self-government, but we are anxious that we should be trained for self-government now."[24] A well-educated elite, so the *Statement* continued, was the only vehicle that would allow a smooth transition to independence for Rwanda. What is especially interesting is that, in an apparent attempt to circumvent the issue, the *Statement* does not once mention the words "Hutu" or "Tutsi." Faced with the UN-supported principle of universal suffrage and the Hutu majority, the monarchy and High Council believed that only accelerated self-government centered around a consolidated, Western-educated, Tutsi elite would permit the maintenance of the status quo.

However, the Hutu elite had also prepared for the arrival of the UN Mission. Their reply to the *Statement of Views* was the Bahutu Manifesto, written by Kayibanda and eight others, which clearly stated the grievances felt by the Hutu. The preamble immediately comes to the point:

> The indigenous racial situation is of course a domestic matter, but what can remain purely domestic or local nowadays? How can it remain hidden

from view now that the indigenous and European political positions appear to confront each other? Political, social and economic conditions are complicated by a racial conflict which seems to grow increasingly acute. The advantages of modern civilization are, it would appear, being made available through education, predominantly to one recipient—the Mututsi—thus making for more difficulties in the future than are presented by what is often called today "the difficulties which divide us." No solution of the Mututsi-Belgian relations can be durable until the fundamental difficulties between the Mututsi and the Muhutu are settled.[25]

While the *Statement of Views* pretended that no Hutu-Tutsi question existed, the manifesto took a diametrically opposed view. In fact, it argued that a solution to the ethnic problems was the sine qua non for self-governance and independence. Having outlined the issue, most of the rest of the manifesto lays out propositions to help end inequality. First, the manifesto recommends a change in the state of mind, "which is sarcastically called 'respect for the culture and customs of the country.'"[26] Second, in the economic realm, it calls for "the abolition of the corvées. . . . The legal recognition of individual land ownership in the Western sense of the word. . . . Freedom of expression."[27] Third, on the political plane, it recommends "that laws and customs should be codified . . . that Bahutu should in fact be promoted to public office."[28] And, finally, it asks that Hutu should no longer be excluded from secondary and tertiary education.

These statements of intent by both groups could have facilitated a dialogue and probably overcome many of the tensions. Indeed, various observers have pointed out that the Hutu and Tutsi had much in common and that their differences were not always as significant as they sometimes appeared. Prunier, for one, argues that the income gap between the two groups on the eve of independence was, on average, negligible,[29] while the UN Mission itself noted that

> traditional conceptions are giving way and the elite of the old regime are coming up against a new elite. It will not be long—and indeed there are already indications of this—before the traditional political structure and the respect for feudal institutions will be as irksome to the rising generation of young educated Batutsi as to the new Bahutu elite. In time, and perhaps in the fairly near future, the new generation of

> Batutsi or Bahutu will have more in common than will the young generation of Batutsi with the old. In the same way the Bahutu elite will become increasingly interested in ensuring that all enlightened elements of the population as a whole participate in the direction of the country's affairs, whether Batutsi or Bahutu.[30]

By April 1958, even the Mwami could not continue turning a blind eye to the Hutu-Tutsi problem, and a special commission on social relations was established to investigate the issue. If there was a time for reconciliation, it was now, and had the moderates on both sides triumphed, Rwandan history would have taken a different course. But extremists quickly moved to prevent constructive dialogue. A group of old Tutsi close to the monarch drafted a note to the special commission, stating that "the relations between the Tutsi and the Hutu have always hitherto been based on servitude, so that there is no foundation for brotherhood between us. . . . As our kings conquered the country of the Hutu and killed their petty kings, how can they now claim to be our brothers?"[31] Then, when the special commission made its recommendations in June of the same year, both the High Council and the Mwami sidelined the advice being proffered and insisted, as in the *Statement of Views,* that institutional reform have top priority. On the opposite side, the aforementioned Joseph Gitera, owner of the *Ijwi rya rubanda* newspaper, launched a diatribe against various elements most dear to the monarchy, further inflaming the situation. The main target for his attack was Kalinga, the royal drum, which Gitera thought should be abolished.[32] Legends about the dynastic drums, one of the key attributes of royalty, went all the way back to the founder of the Nyiginya Kingdom, Ruganzu Ndori, who was believed to have found his dynastic drum after many tribulations, "a feat that in this region announces the birth of a new Kingdom."[33] As Jan Vansina explains, "In the ideology of the Great Lakes region a kingdom only exists when it has a dynastic drum." If the drum is lost, the kingdom itself is also lost.[34] While there is no doubt that the drum decorated with the testicles of vanquished Hutu princes was an affront to the Hutu, it was also one of the key dynastic symbols of power that held enormous emotional, traditional, and ceremonial value—something no Mwami could afford to give up.

In what had become a clearly tense situation, and while political tracts were being vigorously exchanged between the opposing parties, the High

Council asked for a working group to be dispatched from Belgium to study the political problems of Rwanda. This group arrived on 22 April 1959. As a similar group had ended up recommending the granting of internal autonomy to the Belgian Congo in early 1959, its arrival was met with expectation in Rwanda.[35] The Belgian working group was strongly lobbied by the traditional Tutsi powers and, on 28 April, it concluded that full internal autonomy should be reached by 1960 "based on a healthy democracy."[36] This posed a problem to both groups. While the demand for rapid independence emanating from Tutsi elites had been satisfied, the Belgian experts envisaged an institutional dispensation based on mass participation, as opposed to elite privilege. For its part, the Hutu elite had achieved its goal of democratic participation, but independence would be coming much sooner than they had hoped for. With both groups now readying for the final showdown, tension in Rwanda became electric.

On 25 July 1959, after having watched the movie *The Lords of the Forest* in Bujumbura, Mwami Mutara III visited his Belgian doctor. Shortly afterward he died, probably due to an antibiotic allergy. The state of the country is summed up by Vansina, who was in Rwanda at the time: "The death of the Mwami was declared over the radio on Saturday evening. The public for the most part learned of it on . . . 26 July through announcements made during Sunday morning mass. . . . Everyone was immediately aware of the extent of the crisis. All stayed at home."[37]

The UN Mission added that "there were numerous highway incidents. . . . The bulk of the population was afraid and stayed at home or went out armed."[38] While there was some discussion about the possible abolition of the monarchy or the introduction of a constitutional monarchy, a new Mwami, Kigeli V, was named during the burial ceremony of Mutara III.

It was at this point that openly political organizations started being formed. On the Hutu side, two political parties were founded. The first, the Parti du mouvement de l'émancipation Hutu (PARMEHUTU), the successor of the Mouvement social muhutu (MSM), was founded by Kayibanda on 9 October 1959. The second, the brainchild of Aloys Munyangaju and Joseph Gitera, was called l'Association pour la promotion sociale de la masse (APROSOMA). There is disagreement about which of these political parties was more extreme. Both included radical elements. While PARMEHUTU was an exclusively Hutu party that framed the issues of the time in stark

Hutu-Tutsi terms, this also applied to some elements within APROSOMA. APROSOMA generally tried to present itself as the party of the poor, including the *petits* Tutsi. Yet one of its most important members, Joseph Gitera, was described by contemporaries as "a veritable fanatic"[39] and by later historians as "a populist, demagogue, a mythical Christian and somewhat unbalanced personality" and as "devoutly Catholic and passionately anti-Tutsi."[40]

On the Tutsi side, there were two main parties as well. The more important Union nationale rwandaise (UNAR), founded on 3 September 1959, stood firmly for the traditional system and supported the monarchy and Tutsi privilege come what may. This party was also the main force calling for quick independence, which attracted support from unexpected corners. Communist China funded the party because it considered it anticolonial and, thus, anti-Belgian. The party also made cross-border alliances with Patrice Lumumba's MNC.[41] The moment UNAR accepted aid from the People's Republic of China, the Belgian government definitively switched its support from the Tutsi monarchy over to the Hutu parties. In the Cold War world, communist-supported monarchists were more of a threat to the established order than a mass peasant movement. A more moderate voice was the Rassemblement démocratique rwandais (RADER), founded on 14 September 1959. Led by the moderate and progressive Chief Bwanakweli, the party was happy, on occasion, to work with both PARMEHUTU and APROSOMA. However, it was never as popular as the other three big parties and was often left on the sidelines. RADER was considered pro-Belgian by many of its supporters, as it was not in favor of immediate independence.

With the political parties out in the open, a concerted campaign of intimidation got underway. People received death threats, while the coffee and banana plantations of select individuals were destroyed at nighttime. Both camps seem to have been guilty of this, and the moderates on each side quickly lost ground, being treated as "traitors" to the cause and allies of the opposition.[42]

THE SOCIAL REVOLUTION: THE FIRST RWANDAN CIVIL WAR

While incidental violence must have begun in September 1959, it was on 1 November 1959 that the first proverbial shots were fired of what is known in Kinyarwanda as the Muyaga or, in English, the "Social Revolution." The

Muyaga is "a strong but variable wind, with unpredictable and destructive gusts."[43] While both "Muyaga" and "revolution" capture some of the severity of the events that swept through the country, I would argue that this period is best understood as a first Rwandan civil war.[44] This civil war lasted from November 1959 to early 1964 and culminated in a series of massacres.

On 1 November, a prominent Hutu, Sub-Chief Dominique Mbonyumutwa, was beaten up by several young Tutsi. The following day, large crowds of Hutu protested in Gitarama and the day after that several Tutsi notables were killed while visiting the house of Chief Gashagaza.[45] That night, groups of Hutu went to Tutsi houses in Ndiza, setting them on fire and driving away the inhabitants. Between 4 and 13 November, arson attacks spread from Gitarama to the Kigali, Gisenyi, Ruhengeri, and Kibuye districts, roughly the northwestern corner of the country.[46] According to the UN:

> Incendiaries set off in bands of ten. Armed with machetes and paraffin . . . they pillaged the Tutsi houses they passed on the way and set fire to them. On their way they would enlist other incendiaries to follow the procession while the first recruits, too exhausted to continue, would give up and return home. . . . Generally speaking the incendiaries, who were often unarmed, did not attack the inhabitants of the huts and were content with pillaging and setting fire to them. The most serious incidents involving tragic wounding and death occurred when the Tutsi were determined to fight back, or when there were clashes with the forces of order.[47]

In *The Deadly Ethnic Riot,* Donald Horowitz describes a "deadly ethnic riot" as "an intense, sudden, though not necessarily wholly unplanned, lethal attack by civilian members of one ethnic group on civilian members of another ethnic group, the victims chosen because of their group membership."[48] The UN report referenced above concurred that the attacks were partly planned. "It seems that the incendiaries were in most cases people of simple mentality who committed the worst excesses without realizing what they were doing. They burned and pillaged because they had been told to do so and because the operation did not seem to involve great risk and enabled them to seize loot in the victims' huts."[49] It, however, shied away from naming possible culprits in the planning of the unrest.

Even though the UN report and others argued that the intent of the arsonists was to chase away Tutsi rather than to kill them, it is difficult to imagine that no widespread violence accompanied these bands intent on burning down houses. It would be naive to think that a fairly well-organized and armed group like the Tutsi would allow their houses to be burned down without resisting at all.[50] Indeed, British missionaries who found themselves at the heart of the *jacquerie* insisted that many of the arsonists went out to kill and burn.[51] In some districts, almost all Tutsi houses were burned down. Yet, one should also keep in mind that, in the context of this general breakdown of law and order, many personal scores were settled and that the divide did not always follow the Hutu-Tutsi distinction. For example, on 6 November 1959, in a precursor to the regional struggles that would follow, a group of Rwandans from the northwest of the country came down to participate in the arson. When they reached Rubengera, in the west, they found all the locals, Hutu and Tutsi alike, ready and waiting under the command of a local chief, and were promptly put to flight after having fifty-eight of their group killed.[52]

By 6 November, the Mwami and UNAR had recovered from their surprise and were ready to strike back at those they held responsible: the PARMEHUTU and APROSOMA leadership. Having initially gathered several thousand armed men around Nyanza to protect the Mwami's compound by reactivating "the almost forgotten system of army regiments,"[53] they now switched to offensive action. Groups were formed with the objective of killing or arresting specific Hutu leaders. As Lemarchand points out, these groups were far more organized than the arsonists plundering the countryside and were formed around a core of traditional military organization.[54] Again, nuance is important, since the UN report pointed out that "each commando party amounted to some hundreds of persons or more, including a majority of Hutu, but the leaders were generally Tutsi or Twa."[55] It seems that, in many cases, Hutu still supported the Mwami and other traditional authorities, something which must be kept in mind to form a clear idea of the composition of the refugee population (see below). These commandos roamed almost freely around the country, killing APROSOMA sympathizers. On 8 November, one of these groups entered Astrida (Butare) and assassinated Polepole Mukwiye and his brother, two important Hutu leaders, and abducted the former's family.[56] Another group even crossed the Burundian border and surrounded the house to which Joseph Kanyaruka, a key APROSOMA man, had fled. There, they killed Kanyaruka and a relative, spearing them fifty-three and fifty-one times, respectively.[57]

From the outset, this widespread fighting, which the minister of Belgian Congo and Ruanda-Urundi, August De Schryver, would later call "a small-scale civil war," proved impossible to control for Belgian authorities.[58] With only about three hundred police officers for the whole country, there was not much the Belgians could do to protect the victims of the violence. While an emergency plan was put in place and extra police called in from Usumbura (Bujumbura), the Belgians—whose military operations were run by Colonel Guy Logiest—were only able to act after reinforcements from Congo started arriving on 6 November. However, the UNAR offensive in the south meant that these troops were moved to deal with that threat, leaving the arsonists in the north largely unchecked. This, combined with pro-Belgian sentiments among the Hutu, meant that it was the Tutsi and their allies who felt the brunt of the Belgian crackdown.[59] Between 8 and 9 November, four extra companies were called in from Congo, including Belgian para-commandos.[60] On 10 November, a slaughter was prevented on Save Hill, which was home to Joseph Gitera and the headquarters of APROSOMA. Several UNAR commandos comprising thousands of armed men surrounded the hill "in the hope of destroying the nest of APROSOMA."[61] Only the timely intervention of the district administrator with several soldiers, hand grenades, and a megaphone managed to convince the attackers to stand down and withdraw.[62] On the same day "sources close to the Belgian authorities in Usumbura . . . said . . . that there were hundreds of dead in the fighting [throughout Rwanda], but no precise figures could be obtained."[63]

By 14 November 1959, a semblance of order had been restored. This first phase of the civil war had been won by the PARMEHUTU and APROSOMA. Belgian authorities were faced with the immediate problem of what to do with the chiefdoms that had now become vacant. Many of the former Tutsi chiefs had been killed or forced away during the violence and needed to be replaced. Others had been implicated in the counter-violence and had to be removed. Following "public opinion," Colonel Logiest and the Belgian resident-general filled up the vacant posts with mostly Hutu candidates.[64]

TABLE 2.1. CHIEFDOMS IN RWANDA

	1 November 1959	1 March 1960
Chiefdoms	*45*	*45*
Vacant chiefdoms	2	1
Tutsi chiefs	43	22
Hutu chiefs	-	22
Sub-chiefdoms	*559*	*531*
Vacant sub-chiefdoms	-	17
Tutsi subchiefs	549	217
Hutu subchiefs	10	297

Source: Trusteeship Council, *Visiting Mission to Trust Territories in East Africa, 1960: Report on Ruanda-Urundi* (New York: United Nations, 1960), 86.

While the Belgians had declared the country pacified, instances of violence and arson continued. As the country prepared for the communal elections that the Belgian authorities had planned for June 1960, the situation got worse. When the visiting UN Mission approached Nyundo parish in March 1960, it noted that most of the people lining the road were PARMEHUTU supporters, but that at the parish itself there were schoolchildren, nuns, and others who were pro-UNAR.[65] After the UN Mission left, violence gripped the region and the huts of many Tutsi—and, presumably, UNAR supporters—were burned. Over one thousand people took shelter at the parish until the arrival of soldiers eventually put an end to the ethnic riot.[66] At the end of March, when the UN Mission arrived in Cyangugu, it was informed by the district commissioner that some huts had been burned there as well.[67] Other torchings took place around the same time in Byumba and Gisenyi, while between ten and sixteen arson attacks were carried out in Butare district in April.[68]

Besides filling the vacant chiefdoms, the Belgians were faced with several other challenges in the aftermath of the November violence. The main issue came from the thousands of refugees whose homes had been burned and who had fled to other parts of the country, or were seeking to move abroad, for security. By April 1960, their number had reached twenty-two thousand.[69] Some were put in refugee camps in Nyamata, while others sought refuge in churches and parishes throughout the country. As large-scale resettlement was out of the question—the Belgians were reticent to use force to resettle the refugees—and the refugees did not want to return home while the perpetrators of the violence against them remained unpunished, many refugees started moving abroad to Uganda, Congo, Burundi, and Tanzania. It is crucial to note that the refugee population was not solely made up of Tutsi. As Lemarchand writes: "Among the refugees were many Hutu, some of whom are now living in exile with their former lords. It is symptomatic of the persistence of traditional ties within the Hutu community that so many of them would rather go into exile than shift their allegiance to the new regime."[70]

What Lemarchand forgets is that many Hutu had come to the aid of their Tutsi compatriots during the fighting in November 1959 and had taken up arms against the incendiaries. It therefore seems likely that they would have been perceived as collaborators and would have been denied a place in the new regime. While it would take these refugees some time to get organized, for many, it was clear from the start that their objective should be a return to their home country, if necessary, by force of arms.[71]

As interethnic relations continued to deteriorate, one of the most contentious political issues was the role of the Rwandan Mwami in the post-independence state. On this score, RADER, APROSOMA, and PARMEHUTU formed a common front and demanded that the Mwami relinquish much of his power and that some of the traditional symbols, like the Kalinga war drum, be replaced by more inclusive regalia. When Mwami Kigeli V refused outright, he was forced into exile under Belgian pressure. UNAR, incensed, boycotted the June 1960 communal elections, a strategic error that handed an enormous victory to the Hutu political formation, now known as the MDR-PARMEHUTU.[72] The MDR-PARMEHUTU victory was so significant that it alienated APROSOMA, which formed a new common front with UNAR and RADER. This, combined with UNAR success in swinging international public opinion in its favor, led to a UN vote supporting its goals, which in turn convinced Belgium that a reconciliation conference was necessary. The colloquy of Oostende, held on 7–12 January 1961, pushed back national elections to 1961 and resolved that a separate vote would be held on the issue of the Rwandan monarchy.[73]

To prevent any possible reversal of its victory in the local elections, on 28 January 1961, PARMEHUTU staged a gathering in Gitarama for Rwanda's elected officials, the majority of whom were MDR-PARMEHUTU. The assembly, contrary to the spirit of the referendum announced during the colloquy of Oostende, voted that Rwanda would become a democratic republic. This assembly and its resolutions were supported by Belgium and its most important man on the ground, Logiest. The result was that Kayibanda, who had been provisional prime minister, was declared prime minister. Before the evening was out, he had formed a cabinet and was the de facto political power in Rwanda.[74]

The period between June 1960 and June 1961 coincided with one of the lulls of this first civil war. Refugees outside Rwanda, though clearly wanting to return, had not yet had the chance to organize themselves into a real threat. The main possible flashpoint, the Gitarama meeting, had been patrolled by Belgian troops and had not provoked large-scale protests by either UNAR or RADER. The absence of a UNAR challenge might be explained by internal divisions: while UNAR supporters inside Rwanda were interested in working within the newly established political framework, the members who had taken refuge abroad had no interest in working with MDR-PARMEHUTU.

As Belgium released political prisoners in June 1961—many of whom had presumably been held since November 1959—and with the elections looming, violence again broke out in Rwanda. "Clashes between Parmehutu, Aprosoma and UNAR partisans in southern Rwanda killed hundreds [and] destroyed over 3,000 homes. . . . Parmehutu and UNAR factions clashed . . . in July 1961 culminating in a major battle east of Kigali that left 130 dead."[75] When the general elections finally took place in September, they consolidated power in PARMEHUTU hands. In the separate referendum, the monarchy was definitively rejected. The fighting in late 1961 produced a significant number of refugees, and people were still fleeing Rwanda in January 1962.[76]

ETHNIC CLEANSING

It was also at this point that Rwandan refugees in surrounding countries began launching attacks into Rwanda—primarily from Congo and Burundi. These attackers were called Inyenzi, "cockroaches," a moniker which the Inyenzi appropriated as a badge of honor due to the toughness and stealth of the creature.[77] A Rwandan Ministry of Foreign Affairs circular puts the number of incursions into Rwanda between March 1961 and May 1962 at no less than thirty-six.[78] Whether all these attacks can be laid at the feet of the Inyenzi is questionable, as many included cattle rustling, while others occurred deep into Rwanda, rather than on the border. Still, this report, though clearly biased, shows that the Inyenzi posed a significant threat to the new Rwandan government and that their attacks were in all likelihood much more frequent and significant than has hitherto been assumed. It also sheds some light on the smaller Inyenzi raids, which targeted local MDR-PARMEHUTU party members or police and army posts. The report also indicates that the Inyenzi would burn Hutu huts on their forays into Rwanda. In July 1962, a French officer in Burundi confidently wrote the following:

> Colonel Logiest explained to me his confidence in the National Guard [Garde nationale, as the Rwandan army was called until 1972] and the stability of the regime. . . . The unit just annihilated two Tutsi gangs without incurring any losses. On 5 July a hundred men, of which only twenty had modern weapons, penetrated the area of Kisenyi: 50 of them were killed in the field. Moreover, during an attack on the Nyantare police station, the *Garde* took ten prisoners and killed two Tutsi. Out of about sixty men only a dozen had modern weapons. In both cases the support of the population favourable to the regime was crucial in reporting the rebel movements.[79]

After such raids, the local population often took revenge on the Tutsi living in, or close to, the area of the Inyenzi attack. They were routinely blamed for helping the Inyenzi, showing them the way, or being the cause of the attacks.[80] A particularly ferocious case of revenge killing was recorded around Byumba toward the end of March 1962, when between 1,000 and 3,000 Tutsi were killed.[81] In June and July of the same year, Inyenzi groups crossed the border once more and attacked villages and Garde nationale patrols.[82] On 11 July a group of sixty attacked the Garde nationale post at Niakatale. However, the Belgian commander, who had served in Congo and Katanga, had been forewarned of the attack by British authorities. As the Inyenzi attacked, twenty-one were instantly killed by automatic weapons. Others surrendered after they had been injured and their leader killed. However, "most were so brave that even after capture they refused to give any intelligence."[83] By mid-1962, it was estimated that there were 150,000 refugees from Rwanda in neighboring countries.[84]

The latter half of 1963 saw the most serious and concerted effort by the Inyenzi to retake power in Rwanda. On 30 November, a force of 3,000 armed Tutsi, on its way to Rwanda, was intercepted and disarmed by the Burundian armed forces.[85] However, this defeat did not break the Inyenzi spirit, and they attacked again on 21 December 1963. Operating in smaller groups, they crossed the Burundian-Rwandan border undetected and carried out a surprise attack on the Rwandan army camp at Kibungo. "Early in the morning of the 21st, when the main attack was launched by 25 to 30 spear-bearing Tutsi, the Rwandan platoon at Kibungo consisting of 36 soldiers under the command of a sergeant turned and fled at the sight of the Tutsi invaders."[86] After this successful attack, the Inyenzi, having captured a jeep, truck, and some firearms, moved toward the large refugee camp around Nyamata to gather more support. From there, they moved on Kigali, but were confronted at the Kazenze bridge, situated only twenty kilometers from Kigali, by a Belgian-led platoon of the Garde nationale. A firefight ensued, and at least two Rwandan soldiers were killed before the Inyenzi were scattered. Around one hundred prisoners were taken by the Garde nationale after the battle.[87]

The response to this attack was particularly severe. Several Tutsi residents of Kigali were arrested, taken to Ruhengeri, and executed by firing squad.[88] Other local Tutsi were immediately killed: "12 were machine-gunned by Bahutu National Guardsmen in the fortnight immediately following the foray from across the border with Burundi to the south on December 20."[89] As other Inyenzi attacks took place between December 1963 and February 1964, the reprisals grew increasingly worse until the media worldwide started talking of genocide.[90] Impressions of the situation are best gleaned from newspaper reports from the area. The correspondent of *Le Monde* in Butare wrote in mid-January:

> It is in the Gikongoro prefecture . . . that this repression seems to have reached its peak. Encouraged by certain authorities, the Hutu attacked Tutsi huts: armed with spears and clubs, they massacred all the Tutsi they could find and threw their corpses in the river. Four thousand Tutsi managed to take refuge at Kadwa Mission and two thousand five hundred at Cyanika Mission. The others, seven or eight thousand, are probably dead. The Nyabarongo is carrying corpses. . . . People speak of thousands of dead in the prefecture of Shangugu [Cyangugu] and of other massacres in the North.[91]

A correspondent for *The Times* reported that

> massacres are being carried out by groups of Hutu organised on a local basis and armed mostly with pangas. . . . Since the Government's first reprisals on the refugee camps, the massacres have spread throughout the country and, as far as observers can tell, seem to be completely indiscriminate. Parties of panga armed Hutu arrive at a Tutsi hut and call for the head of the house. He gives himself up, hoping he will be taken to the local police station, but is seldom seen again, unless his savagely mutilated body is found. . . . With killings going on at the rate of 1,000 a day for the past month it is feared that President Kayibanda's target is the whole 250,000 [Tutsi in Rwanda].[92]

A group of Dutch missionaries described what they saw upon arriving at a mission station: "A very young missionary, unshaved, covered in mud and totally exhausted opened the heavily barricaded door. He smoked incessantly. 'That's how I stay awake,' he said, 'I have not slept in a week. We have 2,600 refugees here. They are the survivors of the 15,000 refugees in our district. All the others have been murdered. 1,900 refugees sleep in the church in shifts.'"[93]

These slaughters encouraged more Inyenzi attacks, none of which were successful. On 6 February 1964, *Le Monde* reported that several thousand Inyenzi had launched an attack on Rwanda from Kivu Province, in Congo, on the previous day. A Swedish missionary who witnessed the events said that "they launched a suicide attack. . . . They were massacred by Rwandan troops as soon as they crossed the border."[94] The First Rwandan Civil War came to a close in 1964, as Inyenzi attacks petered out following their failure to seize power.[95]

* * *

For a number of reasons, we must understand this entire period as a single historical episode: the First Rwandan Civil War. The most important consideration is that the struggle over who would be in power in post-independence Rwanda was not decided until 1964. Prior to this, the Inyenzi still believed they could win. In other words, the almost continual violence in Rwanda between November 1959 and 1964 had the same motive on both sides: the seizure of political power. Political scientist Mahmood Mamdani has argued that "the revolution was not a bloodbath." Rather, it was "the attempted restoration that followed that opened the gateway to a blood-soaked political future for

Rwanda."[96] However, it was not the counterattack of the Mwami and the Inyenzi after the start of the Social Revolution that inaugurated the bloodbath. The killing had started immediately and lasted continuously until 1964. The massacres of Tutsi were unnecessary from a military point of view. Indeed, they had another motive. They spoke to a crucial ambition of the Revolution: the total destruction of all Tutsi political force within the country. The Social Revolution was the bloodbath that opened the gateway to a horrific future.

Estimating the death toll of the First Rwandan Civil War is difficult because of conflicting evidence. It is also difficult to know when double counting occurred or when reporting, as honest as it might have attempted to be, simply could not encompass the whole truth. Rwandan geography is extraordinarily rugged and large parts of the country would simply have been outside the gaze of European journalists or Belgian authorities, on whose evidence most of the casualty numbers are based. It follows that the number of people killed during this period could have been much higher, if many deaths were unobserved, or much lower, if massacres were over-reported. It is, however, safe to conclude that several tens of thousands died during the fighting and massacres between 1959 and 1964.

When we look at the entire period of the Social Revolution, from 1959 to 1964, the similarities with the later Struggle for Liberation and the ensuing Genocide are striking. First, this was when the idea was born of a possible regime change initiated by refugees from outside Rwanda. Second, the Tutsi within Rwanda were targeted as punishment for attacks originating from outside the country. The rhetoric that accompanied these killings would be echoed in the early 1990s. Third, the climax of the conflict was, in both cases, an orgy of violence that dwarfed what had preceded it. These similarities can only be explained by evoking the widespread, strong, and enduring memory of the Social Revolution. The actors on the Rwandan scene in 1990–1994 were not operating in a vacuum, but in the context of the memories of the past. Juvénal Habyarimana was twenty-three years old when the Social Revolution started. This was a formative time for him and some of his colleagues who would go on to hold important positions in the Rwandan army during the Struggle for Liberation. By ejecting thousands of Tutsi and Hutu from Rwanda, the Social Revolution laid the foundations for the Struggle. Stranded outside the country, these refugees would become increasingly intent on returning home. Come 1990, they decided to do so by force.

3

From Kayibanda to Habyarimana

1959–1990

ETIENNE UGEUX, A JOURNALIST WORKING FOR THE WELL-known Belgian newspaper *Le Soir,* entered Rwanda from Tanzania on 5 July 1973. Around noon, as he was returning from a visit to a model farm, he heard that the army had overthrown the current government and arrested the president. Indeed, only hours earlier the Belgian ambassador had sent the following message to Brussels:

> general habyarimana and the garde nationale have seized power in a bloodless coup d'etat STOP i went to see the general who told me that the officers of the garde nationale could not continue in a climate of political tension that was leading towards genocide STOP in these conditions he has decided to suspend political life for one or two years STOP president kayibanda is under the protection of the garde nationale STOP[1]

Unfazed, the reporter continued toward Kigali. All seemed surprisingly calm. As on any other day, women "transported pots of banana wine on their head to the next market," while "men and boys brought sacs of green coffee." The only oddity were the military checkpoints that had been set up along the road, but the soldiers were friendly and well-mannered and "we left each other with great gestures of friendship."[2] As Ugeux approached Kigali, where armored cars sat guarding strategic points, the soldiers became stricter, and at one checkpoint he was told to get home quickly as a curfew was about to start. A week later, as it became clear that the coup had been a success—no serious bloodshed or unrest had taken place—Ugeux was the first foreign journalist who was allowed to interview Major General Juvénal Habyarimana.[3]

Between independence (1962) and the start of the Genocide (1994), Rwanda was ruled by two presidents. The first, Grégoire Kayibanda, ruled the new republic until 1973, when he was deposed in the manner described above. During Kayibanda's presidency regionalism became particularly important, and it has been rightly identified as one of the causes of the coup. After the coup Habyarimana became president, and he would remain in power until his assassination in 1994.

Although regionalism, one of the main themes of this chapter, has already been identified by historians as an important contributor to the 1973 coup, many of the details surrounding it remain murky. Using new source material, this chapter will bring nuance to some of the existing historiography and offer a wider perspective on Major General Habyarimana's role and Rwanda's precarious international position. It will also add clarity to Kayibanda's death in 1976. Some historians have suggested the former president was starved to death or that he had his skull crushed in with a hammer on the orders of Habyarimana. This line of reasoning, based on rumors, becomes especially attractive when looking back at Rwandan history through the lens of the Genocide, as it neatly sets the scene for the portrayal of Habyarimana as a ruthless despot who would lead his country to mass slaughter. However, the truth seems more mundane.

THE KAYIBANDA YEARS

Following the 1959–1964 Social Revolution, Rwanda could best be described as a dictatorship of the majority. A Dutch diplomat wrote that Kayibanda was an "absolutist ruler,"[4] while a Brit noted that the president's party, PARMEHUTU, was the "only organised political force in Rwanda. There are in the country no unions. There is no intelligentsia or bourgeoisie class. There is no press. . . . Rwanda must be considered a one party state."[5] After the long period of Tutsi and Belgian rule, so PARMEHUTU's thinking went, it was now the turn of the Hutu to rule the country. In *The Rwanda Crisis: History of a Genocide,* Gérard Prunier explains the official ideology as follows: "Hutu were the silent demographic majority [85 percent of the population], which meant that a Hutu controlled government was not only automatically legitimate but also ontologically democratic."[6] In the elections of 1965 Kayibanda won 95 percent of the vote and PARMEHUTU a corresponding share of the National Assembly. This effectively marginalized the remaining opposition party, APROSOMA, and gave Kayibanda a free hand in appointing his cabinet. While the elections were conducted in a de facto one-party state in which PARMEHUTU and the national administration were wholly intertwined at every level, it should be kept in mind that Kayibanda had been one of the key figures in Rwanda's road to independence and the abolition of the monarchy.[7] Indeed, the same British diplomat was forced to admit that "there [was] no doubt that Mr. Kayibanda [had] a strong popular following throughout Rwanda."[8]

However, it would be incorrect to assume that ethnicity alone could ensure unity. While the Hutu of Rwanda, under the leadership of President Kayibanda and his PARMEHUTU party, had been generally united during the Social Revolution, cracks soon appeared within this ethnic-based coalition. One of the most important fissures was between the North and the South-Center of Rwanda (the regions that Rwandans call Kiga and Nduga, respectively). The people of the North, ensconced in their mountains, were the last to be conquered by the Nyiginya Kingdom. They thought of themselves as distinct from the rest of Rwanda, something that was emphasized by slight linguistic differences between the two regions. Although the Northerners were also Hutu, they felt that the Social Revolution had not brought them what they wanted: a return to the days before the monarchy, when the region enjoyed semi-independence. As Lemarchand writes, "The thrust of their 'revolutionary' efforts in the 1950s aimed at turning the clock back to the golden age of pre-Tutsi days."[9] However, President Kayibanda and PARMEHUTU saw the North as part of Rwanda and were unwilling to accept any special dispensations for the region. A particularly thorny problem revolved around land rights. Before the imposition of the Nyiginya Kingdom, the local Kiga/Hutu aristocracy had maintained power through various patron-client relationships (ubukonde). During the monarchic period these relationships had been taken over by Tutsi close to the Mwami. Now that the Social Revolution had expelled most of the Tutsi from the region, the old Hutu aristocrats expected to regain their former positions. This was unacceptable to President Kayibanda, a moderate socialist who had fought for the removal of Tutsi-Hutu patron-client relationships throughout the country.[10]

Besides dealing with regional tensions, Kayibanda also had to juggle tensions within his own party. One of the ways he seems to have done this was by letting certain ministers get away with embezzlement and graft, a behavior he himself did not indulge in. As a Dutch diplomat noted: "The first impression the President made on me at this event was an exceptionally friendly one. The ease and simplicity of the man do not obscure a deliberate personality, capable of discussing various subjects in surprising depth."[11] He was, moreover, also seen as a "man of high character, incorruptible and frugal,"[12] who "at night and on weekends would return to his small farm."[13] However, both the Dutch and the British diplomatic missions in Kigali noted that several of his ministers were of a lower caliber. For instance, one report described "the [new] Minister of Public Works, Mr. Charles Kanyamahanga, until recently Director General of the Department of Mines, [as] unsavoury and it is widely rumoured that he finds difficulty in keeping his fingers out of the till."[14] Another noted ironically that while the government had "followed [Kayibanda's] example" at the start of his presidency, most ministers had now "been converted to supporters of the welfare state, even though it is for the moment only symbolised by a couple of dozen Mercedes Benz 250 cars, and a remarkable rise in the consumption of champagne per head of the government."[15] As most of the members of Kayibanda's government were from the south-center of the country the feeling spread quickly that the North was being deprived of the benefits of government.

Northerners were key in the Rwandan Armed Forces, with Major Habyarimana, the head of the army (the Garde nationale), being the most prominent. There were several others as well, including Habyarimana's brother-in-law, Commander Pierre-Célestin Rwagafilita, and Major Alexis Kanyarengwe, who would become the head of the *sûreté*. Keeping these "violence specialists" on his side would be crucial if Kayibanda was to remain in power.[16] This is why Kayibanda made Major Habyarimana the new minister of the National Guard and Police (i.e., minister of defense), replacing the southerner Calliope Mulindahabi, "a fat useless oaf," according to an unkind British assessment.[17] The Belgian advisers who remained in the country after independence proved to be another key factor in the relationship with the military. These advisers enjoyed an exceptionally good working relationship with their Rwandan colleagues and remained within the chain of command until 1973, which meant they actually commanded a significant part of the Garde nationale.

The loyalty of this group from the north was demonstrated when, in 1967, Lieutenant Joachim Maramutsa, a Hutu from the north, attempted a coup d'état.[18] He was by all accounts an intelligent and aggressive man who had been educated at the Grand Seminary of Nyondo, in Gisenyi. He was known to Belgian military assistants as "the First Consul," a reference to Napoleon Bonaparte. The plan was for the police from Ruhengeri to advance on Kigali while the Kigali police took key points in the city. Maramutsa would then lead his company from Camp Kanombe and take the house of President Kayibanda. However, at the last moment, the Kigali police withdrew from the coup and exposed the conspiracy.[19] This failed coup shows that Kayibanda had mollified northerners by making Habyarimana minister of defense in 1965; the rest of the Garde nationale did not join Maramutsa.

As long as the relationship between the president and the minister of defense remained cordial, and the country stayed on course without too much disturbance, Kayibanda's rule was secure. However, on 29 April 1972, violence erupted in neighboring Burundi when Hutu rebels attacked the Tutsi government and army. While the complex causes of that violence fall outside the scope of this study, it should be noted that the Hutu-Tutsi dichotomy was the lens through which events in Burundi were seen in Rwanda. The initial outbreak of violence in April was followed by brutal suppression by the Burundian Tutsi army. In fact, as Lemarchand wrote, it "was not so much a repression as a hideous slaughter of Hutu populations. The carnage continued unabated until August. By then, almost every educated Hutu was either dead or in exile."[20]

In total, between one hundred thousand and two hundred thousand mostly Hutu people were killed in Burundi in 1972. Many of the Burundian Hutu fled to Rwanda, where they settled in refugee camps and among families, and told of their harrowing experiences. The events in Burundi came at a difficult time for Rwanda. After ten years of independence, the initial euphoria of the Social Revolution had abated and a certain stagnation set in. Increased corruption, the north-south rivalry, and the slow pace of economic development all weighed on the regime. Another issue was the failure to bring about the promised advancement of the Hutu in the education system, and this is the cause Kayibanda used to try to reinvigorate his flagging rule.

As one might expect from a president who had overseen the massive violence against the Tutsi in 1959–1964, he exploited the ethnic card.

Between 40 and 45 percent of students at Rwanda's two elite institutions, the National University and at the Groupe scolaire in Butare, were Tutsi. Historian Filip Reyntjens explains that Tutsi pupils were "admitted solely on the basis of their previous results and not—like certain Hutu students—thanks to the political status of a parent. They worked harder knowing very well that the opportunity for secondary or higher education was incredible for them and would not present itself again."[21] Another reason must have been that the pre-1959 education system had favored the Tutsi and ten years of change would not have been enough for the effects of the Social Revolution to be felt. In November 1972 Hutu students at schools in Save and Byimana threatened and attacked their teachers: "For the first time there were racist motives. According to students there are too many European and Tutsi staff."[22] To the chagrin of the Belgian Embassy in Rwanda, the culprits were immediately released from custody. President Kayibanda's party poured fuel on the fire when one of its publications, *Le Mois,* announced in its December issue that it was the forces of "reaction and neo-colonialism" that were behind the success of Tutsi pupils. In other words, *Le Mois* argued that the European and Tutsi teachers in the schools were purposely setting back Hutu students.[23] Soon Tutsi students and their teachers were being harassed at schools all over the country.

In January 1973 the work and residency permits of most private, so non-governmental, foreigners in Rwanda were revoked. On 12 February students at the College de Kigali started rioting, demanding the return of the students who had been expelled for threatening teachers and Tutsi students in the preceding months.[24] In addition, they did not want the Tutsi who had stopped going to school to return to their classes.[25] Later in the week several European teachers at the College de Kigali were threatened and forced to flee from their homes. The Swiss director of the school was also forced to resign and was replaced by a Rwandan. At the university in Butare similar incidents led to the deaths of several students and forced Tutsi students to abandon their medical studies.[26]

Rather than quelling the unrest, on 22 February, the government of Rwanda made the situation worse by imposing a quota of 15 percent on Tutsi working in the private sector.[27] The Belgian diplomatic service noted that the situation in Rwanda four days later was as follows:

> The purge in which Tutsi are removed from schools and companies is practically universal. There is some resistance, for instance from the Governor of the National Bank and from Deutsche Welle. The European population is anxious, especially because the government is not acting openly and everything is happening in the shadows. Lists of unwanted Europeans, including Belgians, have been drawn up in Kicukiro (Brothers Salesians) in Kigali (Hôtel Kiyovu, Hôtel des Diplomates) and Butare (I.N.R.S.).[28]

By the end of the month deadly riots were taking place throughout Rwanda. Tutsi were the main targets, especially if they were students, members of the clergy, or private-sector employees. As the government refused to act, the rampage spread to the countryside, where the huts of Tutsi families were burned down by armed gangs. "These sporadic riots, which at first bore a clear ethnic character are currently degenerating into banditry which victimises the Hutu as much as the Tutsi."[29] The violence also quickly took on a regional and political character. In the north, Hutu from the south and center of the country were faced with violence and forced to flee, while the properties of certain politicians also came under attack.[30]

In order to stop what was quickly escalating into civil war, the police and army were finally deployed on 1 March 1973. However, it took them about two weeks to restore order. Belgian Ambassador Frans Baekelandt reported on 6 March that although "the intervention of numerous police and military units" *was* restoring order, there

> were still casualties, especially at Kabgayi, where a number of injured at the Josephites monastery have since passed away. On Saturday there still was relatively much banditry, and yesterday Tutsi women and children [about thirty] were thrown in the river [and drowned] in Kigali. . . . We are receiving numerous messages of plundered and torched Tutsi homesteads and exterminated Tutsi families.[31]

When the dust finally cleared it was possible for the diplomatic corps in Kigali to try to piece events together. According to the Belgians—by far the most knowledgeable of the foreign powers in Rwanda—there was a rift at the highest level of the Rwandan government. On the one hand, there was a group of hardliners who had actively encouraged the persecution of the Tutsi in order to revitalize the spirit of the Social Revolution among the people. The most important member of this group was Foreign Minister Munyaneza. They were opposed by a group of moderates, including Colonel Habyarimana; the governor of the National Bank of Rwanda, Jean Birara; and Secretary of State for Planning Dr. Emmanuel Hitayezu.[32] While it is unclear where President Kayibanda stood within these constellations, it seems that he agreed with the hardliners.[33] We must remember that this was the president who had overseen the massacres of the Tutsi between 1962 and 1964 and had no qualms about the death of his fellow countrypeople. Had he been opposed to the violence, he could have acted sooner to stop the massacres, especially as he would have been able to count on the support of Habyarimana. His flagging government also stood to gain from this popular reinvigoration of the Social Revolution.[34] According to Ambassador Baekelandt:

> The current balance of the riots is as follows: between one hundred and fifty and two hundred dead [later unofficially revised to one thousand], between five and six thousand refugees of which the majority will return home, in a quarter of Rwandan municipalities Tutsi homesteads were systematically torched, a thousand students and a hundred teachers have disappeared from secondary and higher education and a thousand educated Tutsi are unemployed. . . . The disappearance of Tutsi from schools and enterprises *was something the government wanted and covertly organised. Ambitious politicians at times showed great zeal in this.* They are co-responsible for the violence against the rural Tutsi population which eventually degenerated into gangsterism.[35]

While other diplomatic missions in Rwanda were probably largely reliant on their Belgian colleagues for information, both the Dutch and the Americans agreed with Baekelandt.[36] In November 1973, after Habyarimana's coup, the Dutch consulate in Kigali looked back on the events of the year as follows:

> In mid-January the work and residency permits of all foreign private citizens were suddenly revoked. . . . At the same time pressure was exerted on all foreign entities to reduce their Tutsi staff to 10% of the total and appoint a Rwandan—read Hutu—as the second man in management. That this "Tutsi witch-hunt" was indeed planned was shown

> by the fact that posters with the names of Tutsi employees who had to disappear were pasted onto foreign companies and education institutes at night. . . . Deutsche Welle . . . had to fire its staff of Tutsi technicians. . . . The Sabena office was suddenly entirely empty, with the exception of its Belgian manager. . . . Outside of the cities, Tutsi farmers who often lived in isolation were attacked, driven out or murdered by their Hutu neighbours. . . . *It is certain that former president Kayibanda and, amongst others, his radical Minister of Foreign Affairs, well known in the Netherlands as the former Rwandan ambassador Munyaneza, were behind the removal of the Tutsi.*[37]

It took the government of Rwanda until March 1973 to restore order throughout the country.[38] Only then, on 23 March, did Kayibanda deliver a speech to the nation, in which he announced that the goals of the 1959 Revolution had to be pursued peacefully. He went on to say that discipline was crucial, that regionalism should be abandoned, and that disloyalty would be punished.[39]

While this speech was ostensibly aimed at those who had caused the troubles, it seems it also had another audience: northerners who might be thinking of taking advantage of the disturbances to launch a coup attempt. Otherwise, the reference to regionalism made no sense, as Hutu and Tutsi lived intermingled throughout Rwanda. Removing Tutsi from jobs and schools was not a regional affair. This is all the more plausible since, on 6 April 1973, the Archbishop of Kabgayi, Monsignor Perraudin, told the US ambassador that "he believed there had been 'small' coup attempt thwarted by loyalty of National Guard and 'most' ministers."[40] Soon afterward, Colonel Habyarimana was promoted to major general and Major Kanyarengwe to lieutenant colonel. So President Kayibanda managed to weather the initial storm. The country was shaken and his rule challenged, but the bulk of the Garde nationale remained loyal, and the president managed to show that he was not "soft" on the Tutsi. However, there does seem to have been a perceptible shift in power from the office of the president to that of the minister of defense.[41]

Just as matters were calming down, the Rwandan government started expelling the European and Asian business community. As they left the country the latter received the word "fraudster" stamped in their passport.[42]

Perhaps this was Kayibanda's attempt—inspired by Idi Amin's expulsion of Asians from Uganda just months before—to use xenophobia to bolster his popularity at home.

Only a fortnight later, the president was faced with another problem linked to Burundi. On 12 May, Burundian Hutu refugees in Kigali and in Refugee Camp Lilima "received a message telling them to prepare for an attack on Burundi" to overthrow President Micombero's government.[43] Major General Habyarimana was interrupted while at mass to deal with the situation. However, at such short notice, the Garde nationale was unable to prevent up to one thousand Burundians from heading to the border. As heavy fighting erupted in northern Burundi, close to the Rwandan frontier, the Burundian government led by President Michel Micombero warned Rwanda to move the Burundian refugee camps in Rwanda away from the border areas or face consequences.[44] It is hard to determine whether the Kayibanda government did truly try to stop the refugees' incursion into Burundi, or if some elements within the government continued to support them. The situation took an ominous turn on 14 May, when President Amin of Uganda asked the Burundian Embassy in Kampala "to send a telegram to President Micombero informing him that Uganda is ready to assist him to crush the invasion by rebels who attacked his country from Rwanda and Tanzania over the weekend."[45] That night the Rwandan Minister of International Cooperation, Munyaneza, attended a dinner at the Belgian Embassy and told the ambassador that the government of Rwanda was "worried over possibility of Burundi retaliation against Rwanda for refugee attack."[46]

Rwanda found itself in a difficult strategic situation. If Micombero attacked in retaliation for the raids emanating from Rwanda, and Uganda moved in at the same time, the small Garde nationale would not be able to defend the country. It would face a war on two fronts, with Belgian-trained Burundian troops in the south and the numerically superior Ugandan army in the north. Kayibanda was caught in a bind. If he addressed the nation, distancing himself and his government from the predominantly Hutu incursions into Burundi, he risked the ire of the people. On the other hand, if he said nothing, the Burundi-Uganda threat would increase by the day. So, on 15 May, Minister of International Cooperation Munyaneza boarded a small plane to Goma with the intention of transferring from there onto a commercial flight to Kinshasa. The US Embassy in Kigali speculated that the purpose of his mission was to persuade Mobutu Sese Seko, the president of Zaire, of Rwanda's innocence regarding the "Burundi situation" and maybe even to obtain his "intercession with Amin on account [of the] latter's reported promise [to] assist Burundi against outside attack."[47]

To make matters worse, the Belgian government now threatened to end the military assistance mission to the Garde nationale unless Rwanda agreed to specific terms. Belgians who were part of the military assistance team would be taken out of the chain of command, exempted from guard duty, and required to wear insignia that distinguished them as Belgians.[48] These measures seem specifically designed to ensure that Belgian military in Rwanda would not be on the front line in any conflict. Until then, Belgian officers had retained several command positions in the Garde nationale and carried out much of the operational planning. The Belgians might have been mindful of the fact that there were also Belgian officers training the Burundian army and that a possible conflict might see Belgians fighting Belgians. Thus, continued Belgian support was partly dependent on Rwanda's ability to reconcile with Burundi. All these factors gave Habyarimana important reasons to overthrow the Kayibanda government. Not only had Kayibanda put the country in mortal danger by allowing the tension with Burundi to escalate, but he had also been shown to lose control during the anti-Tutsi pogroms of 1972. On top of that, the withdrawal of Belgian military support to Rwanda would lead to the ruin of Habyarimana's Garde nationale. It was not, however, Habyarimana who made the first move.

At 23:00 on 4 July 1973, the governor of the National Bank of Rwanda, Jean Birara, was summoned to the president's office. Upon entering, he found President Kayibanda and about ten of his close supports from the south and center of the country waiting for him. Kayibanda presented Birara with a document. Upon examination, Birara realized it was a petition from northerners to Major General Habyarimana complaining about being regularly bullied and sidelined by those from the center and south of the country. The signature under the petition was illegible and Birara, suddenly realizing his precarious position, denied any knowledge of the document. Kayibanda spat in his face as Birara quickly fled. At 00:30 it was Habyarimana's turn. What passed between the president and his general is unknown, but it seems that Kayibanda might have presented Habyarimana with a list of northerners who were to be purged from the administration and the army. What we do know is that, at the end of the conversation, Habyarimana—only thirty-six years old at the time and a powerfully built and well-trained soldier—would not be bullied into acceptance by the assembled party and ended up engaging in a fistfight with Secretary-General of the Presidency Ntalikure. Shots might also have been fired at Habyarimana as he made his escape.[49]

Habyarimana fled to Camp Kanombe, where several officers from the Belgian military assistance mission were quartered. Habyarimana knew he could trust them to take his side in the affair. On arrival at the barracks, he put in motion a pre-existing plan that had been designed by a Belgian officer in case of major insurrection throughout the country.[50] Garde nationale troops moved to capture key locations throughout Kigali while Habyarimana personally returned to the presidency with a military escort. At 04:30 he arrested President Kayibanda and six others who had been present earlier that evening.[51] Immediately after dealing with the president, Habyarimana had a conversation with Belgian Ambassador Baekelandt, during which he explained that President Kayibanda had been brought to his house in Gitarama where he remained under guard.[52] He must also have requested that Belgian military advisers in Rwanda continue in their role. Though the Belgian ambassador was initially instructed by Brussels to confine Belgian military personnel to their houses, Baekelandt "did not comply, permitting them to carry on usual technical functions like repairing equipment, and urgently requested approval of his position. He was relieved to receive approval. Ambassador Baekelandt believes it important not to drag feet on supporting Habyalimana [*sic*] in order to gain goodwill, or at least escape alienation, having in mind the long haul."[53]

Two days later, on 7 July 1973, Habyarimana had another meeting with Ambassador Baekelandt. Afterward, Baekelandt asked permission to travel back to Belgium where he intended to "argue for early and favorable response to Habyalimana's [*sic*] requests . . . to regularize Belgian military assistance along lines desired by Belgium."[54]

Internationally, the coup was well received. Besides Belgium, both France and the Federal Republic of Germany reported that diplomatic relations would remain unchanged.[55] Presidents Mobutu of Zaire and Micombero of Burundi sent telegrams of support to Habyarimana, and the radio in Burundi and Zaire broadcast in support of the coup.[56] Relations with Burundi quickly improved. A Rwandan delegation visited the country on 9 July to "spare no effort to improve fraternal and long-standing relations between Rwanda and Burundi,"[57] and Burundi president Micombero even visited Rwanda in October 1974.[58] Relations with Amin's Uganda were also restored when Habyarimana met him in Kabale, Uganda, on 30 July 1973.[59] Thus, within the space of one month, General, now President, Habyarimana had managed to reset relations with Burundi and Uganda, removing external threats to Rwanda, and to secure the support of Belgium—with its military aid—as well as that of France, the Federal Republic of Germany, and Zaire.

Internally the coup was justified by explaining that the Garde nationale thought Rwanda was "going down the drain" and that this "would lead to 'genocide,'" not of the type seen in Burundi (Hutu-Tutsi) "but rather between North and South Rwanda."[60] For ordinary Rwandans, there was cause for optimism. Indeed, the rapprochement with Burundi and its Tutsi-dominated regime was a signal to Rwandan Tutsi that they would be safer now than they had been under Kayibanda. The unspoken modus vivendi was that as long as they stayed out of politics, they would not be targeted for success in other fields such as business.[61] In addition, Habyarimana's accession to power gave new hope that progress in other fields was also around the corner.

THE DEATH OF KAYIBANDA

Many rumors have surrounded the death of President Kayibanda over the past few decades. In 1995 Prunier wrote that the former president had "most likely been starved to death by his [jailers]" on orders of Habyarimana.[62] This claim was repeated by the French Parliamentary Inquiry in 1998.[63] More recently Andrew Wallis argued in his book *Stepp'd in Blood* that Kayibanda was slowly being poisoned, again on Habyarimana's orders, before being "put . . . out of his misery with a hammer blow to the skull."[64]

Newly declassified archival documents from the Belgian Embassy in Rwanda tell a more mundane story. On 14 December 1976 around 09:30 Kayibanda felt chest pains and his son Pio asked for a doctor to be called. As Kayibanda lived under strict house arrest in Gitarama, the soldiers who guarded him went in search of a doctor. Around 16:00 in the afternoon they approached a Belgian doctor, Vandenbulcke, to ask if there was a Rwandan doctor to attend to Kayibanda. Vandenbulcke told them that Dr. Bendendale (despite his Belgian name, a local Rwandan) was on duty.[65] Bendendale made his way to Kayibanda's house, where around 18:00 he diagnosed his patient with an abdominal affliction and gave him a shot of penicillin.

As the evening progressed, Kayibanda's situation deteriorated. He died at 04:00 on 15 December. On the morning of 16 December, Abbot Massion and Dr. Bendendale arrived, and the latter pronounced the former president dead. The abbot then assembled all five of the country's bishops, including Vicar Apostolic Perraudin. They arrived around 15:30 and found already assembled: six of Kayibanda's eight children, Habyarimana's private secretary, Commander Elie Sagatwa, and a detachment of troops who were to assist with the funeral. Kayibanda was then buried in the garden of his house. According to the Belgian ambassador, "The whole ceremony was marked with great dignity; the authorities present showed humanity throughout."[66]

This is the version of events transmitted by the Belgian ambassador in Rwanda to the Foreign Ministry in Brussels on 20 December. The communication is marked "Secret" and "Très confidentiel," and there is no doubt that this is what the Belgians believed had happened. Considering the position of the Belgians in Rwanda, their close relations with the Catholic Church, Bishop Perraudin, the fact that a Belgian doctor was a witness to part of the events, and the presence of their military assistants who were close to their Rwandan colleagues, it seems likely that the embassy would have picked up any rumors of foul play. Therefore, it seems highly unlikely that Kayibanda was assassinated.

The theory that Kayibanda was starved also seems untenable. Perraudin and Massion had visited the president on 19 November to celebrate mass and did not report anything awry. In fact, they told the ambassador that the ceremony had been conducted "in a brotherly atmosphere with the active participation of the representative authorities; the deputy, the local commander, the head of the guard."[67] Perraudin's testimony carries much weight. He had known Kayibanda for a long time, and the former president had served as his private secretary in the late 1950s.[68] This does not exclude the possibility that Kayibanda may have been poisoned, although this too seems unlikely. The poisoning claim comes from either Jean Shyirambere Barahinyura's book on Habyarimana or from a confidential informant of Andrew Wallis. Barahinyura's account can be readily dismissed: his book was written with the obvious intention of slandering Habyarimana. He later went on to become one of the co-founders of the extremist CDR party (Coalition pour la défense de la République), which played a major role in provoking and executing the Genocide.[69] As for the anonymous informer, it is the choice of poisoning that is interesting. Poisoning is a cultural trope in Rwanda, and many deaths, even today, are attributed to it.

Finally, and in absence of a motive on the part of Habyarimana—why would he want to kill someone who had no power and posed no threat?—we must conclude, as the Belgian ambassador did, that "it seems like the death was due to a poorly treated heart attack following a diagnostic error."[70] Clearly the guards were slow to find a doctor; Kayibanda was under a strict regime and few people were allowed to visit him. However, the evidence does not suggest premeditated murder.

POLITICAL ECONOMY UNDER KAYIBANDA AND HABYARIMANA, 1961–1993

Presidents Kayibanda and Habyarimana sat at the top of a network of supporters. Besides a small group that might have been personally loyal to them, most of their supporters expected to be rewarded for their loyalty. During Kayibanda's reign it was those from the center and the south of the country (the Nduga) who profited. When Habyarimana took over, the roles were reversed and those from the northwest (the Kiga) had their chance to eat from the public trough. "Elite accommodation" had a very material dimension, and there were several instances in which Habyarimana fell out with senior army officers because they felt they were not being given enough of the pie.[71] These rewards often flowed through semiprivate, semigovernmental companies called parastatals. The main problem the two presidents faced was that Rwanda was a poor nation, and opportunities to reward their supporters were limited—even more so than in most other African countries.

Kayibanda had inherited one of the world's poorest economies, still largely based on thousands of semi-sufficient rural households scattered among the hills. Agriculture remained Rwanda's most important economic sector for two reasons.[72] First, it provided food for most of the Rwandan population and, second, it produced export crops (especially coffee) that could have financed the country's development. However, the agricultural sector faced serious problems. While Habyarimana was a strong supporter of food self-sufficiency, the country could not feed itself and "local and seasonal shortages ke[pt] the threat of famine ever present."[73] This was caused by explosive population growth, which farmers could only keep up with by "an expansion of cropland area and a reduction in fallow periods"[74] because the government failed to structurally invest, or help investment in, technical inputs such as mechanization and fertilizers.[75] The result of this failure in management was that the issues of overpopulation and land degradation reached a crisis point between the early 1980s and the 1990s. This had both direct negative results on national agriculture—the total output increased by 10 percent but per capita output decreased by 20 percent—and severe secondary effects.[76] Catherine André and Jean-Philippe Platteau carried out research into agriculture, off-farm income, land rights, and inheritance in the northwestern Kanama commune between 1988 and 1993. Their research is particularly interesting because Kanama had only one Tutsi resident, thus eliminating ethnicity as a significant analytical variable. The two investigators concluded that the "extreme scarcity of land and . . . the harsh realities of bare survival" were causing such severe tensions in the commune "that the social fabric was at a risk of falling asunder."[77]

Export agriculture also faced severe difficulties. A fledgling coffee crop represented Rwanda's biggest export. Coffee (and tea) were introduced into Rwanda by German and Belgian colonists in the period 1905–1920, and their cultivation was aggressively encouraged thereafter. They were supposed, on the one hand, to make the country more solvent and profitable and, on the other hand, to counter the dominance of Brazil on the international coffee market.[78] Between 1962 and 1989 the price of coffee was artificially inflated by the International Coffee Agreement (ICA). Both coffee-importing and coffee-exporting nations were party to this agreement, which regulated the amount of coffee that was sold on the international market each year. Normally such a cartel-based solution would have been unpopular with coffee-importing countries, as it would artificially increase the price of the commodity. However, policymakers in the United States, the world's largest coffee importer, quickly understood that by supporting the ICA, they could ensure the US had a big say in the International Coffee Organization, the governing body of the ICA, thus preventing coffee-producing nations from dominating it. In addition, with the Cold War raging in the background, it was in the interest of the US to prevent economic instability that might open the doors of South America and Africa to the Soviet Union and Communism.[79]

The new stability on the coffee markets was an enormous boost for President Kayibanda. A state-run marketing system was introduced when the original Trafipro cooperative was enormously expanded. This situation was hardly unique to Rwanda. As economic historian Philip Verwimp explains: "Governments throughout Africa promoted the cultivation of export crops for taxation purposes: a government-run agency buys the coffee (or another cash crop) from the smallholders for a fixed price. The state agency then processes the coffee and sells it on the international market. The justification for this institution is to guarantee the farmer's income. The farmer is protected from shocks in the world market by a fixed price."[80]

However, in practice, the profit made by Trafipro, and later Rwandex, was not held in reserve to ensure continued payment to farmers in the event of a drop in the world coffee price. Instead, it was used to fund government expenditure, which was heavily biased in favor of its core ethnic clientele: southern and central Rwandan Hutu. The result was that, besides enriching certain politicians, Trafipro was also used to control and oust northern Hutu businessmen and politicians from their positions.[81]

Coffee remained a political tool when Kayibanda was ousted from power in 1973, even though the benefits now flowed to Habyarimana's northern patronage network. While Trafipro was largely abolished, only surviving as a chain of state-controlled shops that sold basic consumables, the state continued to control the price at which coffee was bought in Rwanda through a marketing board called Rwandex. A boom in the price of coffee between 1976 and 1979 allowed the Habyarimana regime to increase the price paid to farmers from 45 Rwandan francs (RWF) in 1974 to 120 RWF in 1977. By setting the coffee price relatively high, the regime bound the rural coffee-producing population to itself.[82] In fact, the price that the government paid for coffee in Rwanda was so high that coffee was smuggled into the country from both Uganda and Zaire, where the state marketing boards bought coffee from farmers at a far lower price.[83] Effectively, this system took the labor of Rwandan coffee farmers and transferred it to an elite patronage network—run by Rwandans from the south of the country before 1973 and by northerners afterward—through biased government spending.

When Habyarimana came to power in 1973, he was successful in attracting large amounts of donor aid to Rwanda. This aid eventually reached such a staggering scale that its impact on the Rwandan economy must be briefly discussed. By 1989, 11.4 percent of Rwanda's gross national product came from development aid. Moreover, between 1982 and 1987, 70 percent of public investment was financed by foreign assistance.[84] The main problem of development aid was that uncaring donors did not follow the most obvious of guidelines when setting up their projects. The result was that instead of improving the country, aid sometimes compounded the negative trends already described in this chapter, especially the growth of socioeconomic inequality. Indeed, it was nigh impossible for Rwandans to get a job with an aid agency or to benefit from its resources or facilities in the absence of a patron. A farmer from the southern town of Muku explained in 1991 or 1992: "'We have only one project, that of the EEC [European Economic Community], which employs tens of people. No one gets a job without giving a bribe. We have been going there now for an entire week.'"[85]

In 1989 the ICA was not renewed and within a couple of years the price of coffee reduced by 50 percent.[86] The only way the Rwandan government could continue to pay farmers the set price (145 RWF) was by borrowing money. As mentioned above, the government had neglected to build up its profits from the sale of coffee into an emergency fund, using them instead for government expenditure that had benefited a select group of the population. Instead of profiting from the export of coffee, the purchasing scheme started costing the government, as it tried to cling on to one of its tools for earning the loyalty of Rwanda's farmers. But this policy was not sustainable and the price farmers were paid for coffee decreased from 0.90 USD per pound in 1989 to 0.40–0.50 USD per pound in 1993.

In a bid to consolidate his position, and under significant pressure not only from elite actors but also from the Rwandan people, President Habyarimana was finally convinced to accept a World Bank structural adjustment program (SAP) in 1990–1991, which would provide a large influx of aid to reduce the country's debt.[87] However, the conditions of the SAP struck a major blow at every level of Rwanda's social fabric. Rwandan farmers were hit hard. The first and most immediate measure was the devaluation of the Rwandan franc by 40 percent in November 1990, which, in turn, caused a 50 percent rise in the price of essential goods in Kigali. This was followed by another 15 percent devaluation of the RWF in 1992. Taken together, these developments meant that coffee cultivators took an enormous hit to their income, much of which was used to purchase food. By 1993, 31 percent of the population had to survive on less than a thousand calories per day.[88] Other SAP-induced measures included cutting the government budget deficit, which resulted in the laying off of many civil servants, the introduction of school and health care fees, and a restructuring or liquidation of government enterprises. However, these measures also undercut the strength of Habyarimana's position, among both his grassroots and his elite supporters, by reducing the ability of the president and his immediate circle to reward loyalty.

* * *

Kayibanda's fall from power was largely of his own making. While the common enemy of the Tutsi monarchy had united Rwanda's Hutu population, consolidating power proved much more divisive. In the decade after he seized power, he was unable to make good on the expectations of Rwandans. The economy did not grow as fast as they would have liked, education remained unattainable for many, and the proceeds of government flowed to the president's home region. Using the pretext of events in Burundi, Kayibanda tried to reinvigorate his flagging rule by turning to ethnic discrimination once again. However, this undermined Rwanda's international position by uniting Burundi and Uganda in a possible military alliance. In the confusion that followed, in which regionalism played an important part, Kayibanda was ousted by Habyarimana. The new president deftly realigned Rwanda's foreign policy and placed the former president under house arrest where he died from natural causes on 15 December 1976. However, Habyarimana was as unsuccessful as Kayibanda in creating a stable one-party regime. By the late 1980s massive corruption and the collapse of the ICA caused widespread unrest in Rwanda. In October 1989, *Africa Confidential* wrote of "an atmosphere of *fin de règne* in Rwanda. . . . It is being widely speculated that the president may either be overthrown or obliged to submit to a palace coup which leaves him as the head of state while the real power lies elsewhere."[89] The deteriorating situation in Rwanda was being observed with great interest by the Rwandan refugees who had been forced to leave the country between 1959 and 1964 and 1972 and 1973. It is to this group that we turn our attention in the next chapter.

4

The Story of the RPF

Exile, Organization, and Armed Return, 1964–1990

THE PREVIOUS CHAPTERS DISCUSSED POLITICAL AND ECONOMIC developments in Rwanda between the Social Revolution and the eve of the outbreak of the Struggle for Liberation. This chapter will look at roughly the same time span, 1959–1990, but focus on those who were forced to leave Rwanda as refugees, and on their desire to return home. These refugees settled throughout the Great Lakes region and played an extraordinarily significant role in Ugandan politics. Following a time of repression at the hands of the Obote II regime in the first half of the 1980s, they emerged victorious alongside Museveni's National Resistance Movement (NRM). This successful alliance provided them with the time and space to found the Rwandan Patriotic Front (RPF) and begin preparations for an armed return to Rwanda. In its concluding sections, the chapter discusses the attempts to negotiate the return of Rwandan refugees to their country of origin, and their failure. A quick and successful conclusion to these negotiations, combined with political reform in Rwanda, would have presented a chance for lasting peace in the region. However, as the unpromising negotiations dragged on, the RPF saw a unique opportunity to invade Rwanda and enforce the return of the refugees on its own terms.

THE ARRIVAL OF THE 1959–1964 REFUGEES IN UGANDA, CONGO, AND TANZANIA

Rwandans who fled the violence in their country in the 1959–1964 period, and crossed the borders into Uganda, Zaire, Tanzania, and Burundi, arrived in places with long ties to their country.[1] Although many of the refugees were Tutsi pastoralists, circumstantial evidence suggests that there were also many Hutu agriculturalists among them.[2] The historical context in each country of resettlement was different, but Rwandans living outside of Rwanda—known as Banyarwanda—generally consisted of three groups.

First, there was the group of Rwandans who had lived in Uganda since before independence. While they had a close cultural affinity with Rwanda and spoke Kinyarwanda—the defining symbol of the Banyarwanda community—the members of this group found themselves included in Uganda after the colonial powers delineated the border in 1910.[3] Technically, these Banyarwanda were Ugandan citizens; as will be seen below, however, they were often heaped together with the other two groups. The second group of Rwandans in Uganda consisted of economic migrants who had left their country of birth during the colonial era.[4] Reasons for these migrations were varied, but one important motivating factor was that Ugandans did not face the same excessive labor demands as the peoples of Ruanda-Urundi. In the Democratic Republic of the Congo, then still known as Zaire, similar dynamics were at play. Some of the Rwandans there, mostly Tutsi, had relocated to South Kivu in the precolonial period and were known as Banyamulenge. In addition, there were also, as in Uganda, economic migrants who had worked in the Congolese provinces of Kivu and Katanga during the colonial period (for companies like the Union minière du Haut-Katanga). The new 1959–1964 refugees were a third group. As they trudged across the border to escape the violence of the Social Revolution, they were initially settled in UNHCR-supported refugee camps, such as the Nakivale Refugee Settlement in Uganda, which would go on to become an RPF stronghold in the late 1980s. Combined, the Banyarwanda population was about one million.

The refugees generally received a cordial welcome in Uganda and Tanzania. Tanzania was newly independent and led by President Julius Nyerere. As a committed Pan-Africanist, it would have been unthinkable for Nyerere to turn his back on Rwandan refugees entering his country in 1959–1964. Vianney Shumbusho, who would go on to become an RPF political cadre, remembers arriving in Tanzania when he was nine years old. In October 1961, the family house was burned down by a mob and his schoolteacher father arrested. To escape, the family first fled to a local mission before deciding to leave Rwanda altogether. According to Shumbusho, the reception afforded

MAP 4.1. Uganda refugee settlements. Map by Brian Balsley.

to the refugees was friendly and they were first housed in UNHCR refugee camps. He also recalls that, soon after they were settled, "Nyerere even came to visit the refugee camps."[5] As the family had only covered about eighty kilometers during its flight, its members spoke the same language as the locals, and in 1964 the Tanzanian government gave the refugees some land to settle on permanently. Eventually, the refugees were also offered Tanzanian nationality, as "Nyerere could not understand how an African can be a refugee in an African country, it is not possible." Although Nyerere offered to naturalize the Rwandan refugees, Shumbusho asserts that he also "knew it could never be a replacement [for home]."[6]

The family of the brothers Ndore Rurinda and Logan Ndahiro had a similar experience. As they lived on the Rwanda-Uganda frontier, they had the opportunity to move into Uganda with their cattle and to return afterward, whenever politics heated up in Rwanda. However, by 1963, the situation had become untenable, and the family moved to Uganda permanently. They first went to Nakivale Refugee Camp but were then sent on to Kahunge and Kyaka I & II Refugee Camps, since there was more space for their cattle there. Generally speaking, the Ugandans around the refugee camps, though poor, are said to have been friendly toward the new arrivals from Rwanda. Thus it was that, over the years, the family was able to establish itself socially and gain a degree of economic security.[7]

Although the refugees were in the first instance keen to return to Rwanda as quickly as possible, the defeat of the Inyenzi (see chapter 2) meant their exile became permanent. From the start, Banyarwanda refugees "expressed on many occasions their keen interest in their children being able to continue their education."[8] This was mainly because Rwandan parents realized that if their children were ever to return to their country of origin, they would need an education. The refugees themselves quickly established primary schools in the camps. With UN support, these schools ensured that rudimentary primary education would not be lacking for the young of this—or the next—generation.[9] Shumbusho vividly remembers his Rwandan primary teacher telling them: "Young men, come and start studying because you are the only hope for us to return home."[10] Although Shumbusho got lucky and received a UNHCR scholarship for his secondary education, this was not the case for all Rwandan refugees, and the circumstances in Uganda, which is especially relevant to our story, merit special attention.

As the UN noted in 1964, there were "not sufficient places in secondary schools in the Kampala area [for the children from Rwanda] . . . furthermore the financing of their education [could not] be met by the authorities nor by the students themselves."[11] Nonetheless, the Ugandan government indicated that it would endeavor to find places for Rwandan secondary school students if international funds were made available.[12] While the experience of poverty was obviously widespread, it is by no means true that all Banyarwanda refugees were destitute upon arrival. Many brought large herds of cattle with them, a clear indicator of prosperity. The refugees also included many aristocrats and successful businessmen. Besides the UN, the Rwandan refugees, especially in Uganda, could also count on a number of allies in their search for an education.[13] In the first half of the century, several of their compatriots had moved to Uganda and had been educated in missionary or colonial high schools. Some had become politically active, while others had become acquainted with Ugandan elites. At King's College Budo, for instance, some Banyarwanda had been classmates of Mutesa II, the king of Buganda and the first president of independent Uganda.[14] Help also came from the churches. The shared piety between the Banyarwanda and Ugandans gave them a common point of reference and enabled "access [to] church resources, particularly training in skills and scholarships for higher education."[15]

These circumstances and connections explain how some Banyarwanda refugees managed to secure access to the best secondary institutions in Uganda. For example, Paul Kagame, who would later become chairman of the RPF and president of Rwanda, went to Ntare Secondary School, the same school as Yoweri Museveni, the current president of Uganda. Later, many key RPF members, such as James Kabarebe, Rose Kabuye, Aloisea Inyumba, Christine N. Umutoni, and Kayumba Nyamwasa, attended Makerere University.[16] University education abroad was made possible both by UNHCR scholarships and informal aid.[17] There were, for instance, unofficial philanthropic networks that helped the refugees, sometimes run by expats. Rather than supporting the UN or other NGOs, wealthy donors would help individual refugees by paying for their university education in Europe. While these students would often be registered as "Ugandans," "Tanzanians," "Burundians" or "Congolese," they were actually Banyarwanda refugees.[18]

The Banyarwanda's emphasis on education is illustrated by the trajectories of two refugee families interviewed by Catherine Watson in the early 1990s. They had fled Rwanda in 1962 and 1963, respectively. The first family had fourteen children, four of whom went on to obtain university degrees. Two of the others "have accounting diplomas, and one a diploma from a technical college. Two are teaching in Kenya. Three are officers, formerly in Uganda's National Resistance Army, and now in the RPA."[19] The second family had five children, three of whom obtained university degrees; the other two worked as a nurse and a computer operator. Three of the children live in Canada, Switzerland, and Tanzania.[20]

Despite their educational achievements, the Banyarwanda in Uganda and elsewhere did face significant problems on account of their origins and identity. Anti-immigrant stereotypes were rife, as attested by some of the interviews conducted by Ugandan academic Elijah Mushemeza in the early 2000s. For instance, one of Mushemeza's informants—an autochthonous Ugandan—accused the Banyarwanda refugees of "ha[ving] a language barrier. The old refugees had problems to learn the local language compared to the young. . . . Especially the Tutsi felt more comfortable in isolation." Another felt that "some were lazy. They did not want to join us in cultivation."[21] Distrust also took more malignant forms: "There was a belief that 'Banyarwanda are not trustworthy. A Munyarwanda (singular [of Banyarwanda]) can entertain you and kill you. Therefore, when you are dealing with him/her be conscious and careful.'"[22] Because of these feelings, passing as a Ugandan, Burundian, Congolese, or Tanzanian improved the Banyarwanda's chances in their country of residence. This was especially true in the education sector. Uganda was also still a developing country, and many Ugandans felt that the few places in their schools should go to Ugandans rather than to refugees. Again, Watson's research highlights the issue:

> "You change your name, you become meek, you lose yourself as a person, you hide away from your culture" said one refugee, who took on a Kinyankole name in order to get a place at a secondary school and then lived in fear that someone would expose her by addressing her in Runyankole, a language she did not know.[23]

This strategy, on the other hand, excluded them from UN aid. As a refugee explained:

> I was a small girl when our family ran to Tanzania as refugees. I had my primary education in the refugee settlement. At primary seven, I was given forms to fill for secondary admission. I recorded myself as a refugee. The headmaster advised me to change my identity to a Tanzanian because being a non-citizen would limit my chances of admission. The day I joined the secondary school, the headmistress, who was a Tanzanian of Malawi origin, called me to her office. She asked me, are you

> Rwandese? I said yes. She then asked, "Why did you claim to be a Tanzanian?" I told her my past experience. She changed my forms because she wanted me to benefit from UNHCR scholarship. The experience of identity crisis made me cry and I have never forgotten. Even when Tanzania naturalised us in 1978, I was always feeling that I am Rwandese, that is why I joined [the] RPF to fight for my return.[24]

THE BANYARWANDA IN UGANDA, 1971–1980

As the 1960s went on, the Banyarwanda refugees became involved in Ugandan politics. Their natural sympathy for the pro-monarchist Bahima, with whom they shared a close cultural connection, caused the second president of Uganda, Milton Obote—a fanatical antimonarchist—to consider the Banyarwanda refugees as political enemies. In 1969, he planned a census to count and identify all the refugees with a view to expelling them at a later date. As one Ugandan People's Congress government employee put it: "The Banyarwanda people are not trustworthy. You give them land, food, water and education and yet they support your opponents. Obote was right to find out how many they were in order to find an appropriate solution to them and rid the country of the problem once and for all."[25] Another reason for the particular timing of the census might have been that the UNHCR indicated in 1967–1968 that support for the refugee camps would soon be ending and that the Ugandan government would now be expected to take responsibility for their upkeep.[26]

However, before Obote had the chance to expel the refugees from Uganda, he was overthrown by his army commander Idi Amin in early 1971. In an effort to bolster his regime, Amin sought the support of some African minorities.[27] In the case of the Banyarwanda, for instance, he allowed the exiled Mwami, Kigeli V, to come to Uganda and provided him with a house and a car. Amin's pro-Banyarwanda policies, in turn, prompted many of their number to join his army and brutal secret service. It was at this time that many refugees moved out of the camps and into the surrounding areas, where they settled down as both pastoralists and agriculturalists.[28] Banyarwanda support for Idi Amin's presidency is a somewhat contested topic, and it seems that the community was split over how to deal with Amin. Though his presidency coincided with a time of prosperity for the Banyarwanda and some, like Stephen Ndugute, joined his army, others, such as Emmanuel Gisa, opposed his regime.

Gisa is now better known as Fred Rwigyema, a Banyarwanda refugee whose parents had fled to Uganda around 1959. He was educated in Oruchinga Valley Refugee Camp and Mbarara High School, but in 1976 he left school to join a group of FRONASA (Front for National Salvation) recruits on their way to Tanzania. FRONASA had been formed in 1972 by Yoweri Museveni as an opposition group in exile with the goal of overthrowing the Idi Amin regime. Rwigyema's motivations for joining FRONASA are uncertain. It is possible that he was intent on escaping the anti-Banyarwanda sentiments harbored by some Ugandans. He might also have been looking for adventure. In addition, he was a great friend of Museveni's brother, Caleb Akandwanaho (nom de guerre Salem Saleh).[29] Whether they had met at school or on their way to Tanzania to join FRONASA is unclear, though the former hypothesis seems more plausible. As Museveni had contacts with the Frente de Libertação de Moçambique (FRELIMO), the young men were taken for training to Mozambique after joining—though they probably also took part in military operations against RENAMO.[30]

In 1978, President Idi Amin invaded Tanzania in an attempt to deflect the attention of Ugandans away from the terrible domestic situation. This turned out to be a strategic miscalculation, as Nyerere's Tanzania was no pushover; not only was the Tanzania People's Defence Force (TPDF) more than willing to defend its country, but it was also joined in this by several groups of Ugandan dissidents. These groups included Tito Okello's Kikosi Maalum; Museveni's FRONASA, to which Rwigyema belonged; and the smaller Save Uganda Movement and Uganda Freedom Union. Though these movements had little in common other than a shared will to see Idi Amin deposed, they had agreed at the Moshi Conference of March 1979 that they would combine into the Uganda National Liberation Front (UNLF). In the event, not only did the UNLF and the TPDF expel the Ugandan invaders from Tanzanian soil, but following a brief war, they also drove on to Kampala and deposed Idi Amin in April 1979 (although it would take an additional month to mop up the rest of his army).

After its victory, the UNLF ruled Uganda until the 1980 national elections. However, in the period between the deposition of Idi Amin and the 1980 elections, a new Ugandan army was being formed from the disparate anti-Amin groups, and Museveni's FRONASA was largely dismantled. FRONASA cadres were instructed that they would have to be "re-trained."

In the process, over half of the troops were barred from continuing to serve in the Uganda National Liberation Army (UNLA). Significantly, all of the Banyarwanda in FRONASA, including Fred Rwigyema, were removed from their positions.[31] This process took place for two reasons. First, Obote and others within the UNLF wanted to sideline Museveni to clear their own path to power. Second, although Fred Rwigyema's charisma had garnered many Banyarwanda recruits for FRONASA during the advance from the Tanzanian border to Kampala, the Banyarwanda were still seen as Idi Amin's stooges and significant anti-Banyarwanda sentiment existed within Uganda. This is probably why none of them were allowed to join the UNLA. Two historical processes now unfolded simultaneously: the persecution of the Banyarwanda in Uganda, and the Ugandan Resistance War launched by Yoweri Museveni. Both will be discussed in the pages that follow.

THE PERSECUTION OF THE BANYARWANDA

Milton Obote returned to power following the contested 1980 elections, from which many Banyarwanda had been excluded.[32] For Obote, the Banyarwanda were a piece of unfinished business. Not only had he been antagonistic toward them before he was removed from power in 1971, but many Banyarwanda had also supported his enemy, Amin. Within Obote's party, the Ugandan People's Congress (UPC), anti-Banyarwanda sentiment was rife, and the Banyarwanda were considered responsible for many of the country's woes. In addition, Banyarwanda Catholicism also caused friction with the predominantly Protestant UPC.[33] The new president's first move against the Banyarwanda was to test the waters to see if it was possible to encourage them to leave Uganda and go back to Rwanda. The "govt is very keen on voluntary repatriation,"[34] reported T. M. Unwin, the UNHCR representative in Uganda, in May 1981. However, he went on, "discussions at all levels (also with Rwandan Ambdr) . . . indicated that the Rwandans were dead against it."[35] As Unwin explained one month later: "Before one of the recent 'summits' in which President Obote took part he (Obote) received an envoy from the President of Rwanda. The envoy told Obote plainly that Rwanda did not want the refugees back: and Obote is said to have answered equally plainly that Uganda would like them to go."[36]

One of the main reasons Obote wanted to get rid of the refugees was because "the Government was definitely concerned about the nefarious activities of some Rwandans and . . . said they had proof that many more Rwandans were concerned in such activities than their proportion of the population warranted."[37] The "nefarious activities" in question had to do with the ongoing Resistance War. Following his election loss to Obote, Yoweri Museveni had taken to the bush to wage a renewed guerrilla campaign against the newly installed Ugandan government. Two of his earliest and most important supporters were the aforementioned Fred Rwigyema and Paul Kagame, who were both from Banyarwanda refugee stock. Their presence attracted Banyarwanda volunteers to the National Resistance Army (NRA), the army of Museveni's National Resistance Movement.

However, the Banyarwanda also provided an easy scapegoat and target against which Obote could mobilize his supporters. Following a meeting with the Ugandan vice president in June 1981, Unwin again reported that

> the Rwandans knew they could not hope for much from the UPC Government. . . . He [the vice president of Uganda] did say that Govt. has a list of some (he thought) 10,000 people (souls, not heads of family) whom they wanted moved because they felt certain that these people constituted a security threat. . . . He warned that if nothing was done such was the ire of the people of Uganda against the Banyarwanda "who have been killing us for years" that . . . the people would take matters into their own hands with deplorable results.[38]

Rather bizarrely, in mid-July 1981, the Ugandan Army asked the UNHCR to make a list of Banyarwanda members of the Ugandan Army.[39] Clearly this list could only serve one purpose: to purge any remaining Banyarwanda from the army. Naturally the UNHCR could not, and would not, oblige with such a request. At the start of 1982, Unwin reported to Geneva that the Ugandan government planned "to sort out the 'legitimate' from the 'illegitimate'" Rwandan refugees. He thought it was likely that the Rwandans would be made

> into some kind of scapegoat for all the illegal action by the Ugandan Army which is taking place and continues to act in many places (though not most) in an undisciplined and vandal-like manner. . . . Mr. Otai, Minister of State in the Vice-President's Office, said words to the effect that something had to be done about the Rwandan refugees who were

> responsible for "all our troubles." . . . You will therefore see that the long-feared campaign against our charges seems to be getting under way.[40]

In September 1982, preparations were allegedly made by the Minister of State Security Affairs, Chris Rwakasisi, to evict the Banyarwanda from the south of Uganda. Local administrators were briefed to prepare the evictions, which would be carried out by the UPC Youth Wing, while a group of the Special Force would be on hand as backup.[41]

In this situation of enhanced tension, many Banyarwanda sought shelter in the refugee camps and settlements in southern Uganda. Others started crossing the border into Rwanda. A UNHCR official, Patrick de Sousa, who went down to southern Uganda to investigate the situation, found "several groups of recently displaced Rwandese carrying a few belongings on their heads. Other groups were in hired vehicles piled high with mats, pots and pans, and other hastily assembled personal belongings."[42] After interviewing the displaced, de Sousa realized that a local chief had ordered them to leave their homes, which were outside the designated refugee settlements. De Sousa spoke to the chief who told him that he "had received instructions to expel all refugees from his area. When questioned about the Bahutu who could not be presumed to be refugees—he said his instructions were to expel all Banyarwanda. I asked how many days' notice were given to families who had been settled for several years, and was told that they were just told to leave, and if they refused the armed force was used to hasten evacuation."[43]

On the way to the border or the refugee settlements, the Banyarwanda were often forced to pay bribes or leave their cattle at roadblocks manned by the Special Force.[44] It is particularly important to note that no distinction was made between Banyarwanda refugees, most of whom had by this time been in Uganda over seventeen years, and the migrants and nationals who had been settled in Uganda for much longer. This explains why support for the RPF would later come not only from the Banyarwanda refugees whose parents had left Rwanda in 1959–1963 but also from much-longer-settled Kinyarwanda speakers.

A lengthy justification for this coordinated persecution of the Banyarwanda was advanced by the chairman of the Mbarara District Council. In his statement, he explained that the spark had been the deaths of the head and a member of the local paramilitary youth who had been pursuing cattle rustlers. Exactly what happened is unclear, but it seems the deaths were an instance of friendly fire.[45] About the Banyarwanda in general the chairman explained that "it is difficult to keep a snake in the bed and you feel peaceful in your sleep."

> I would like to give a small account on little history of the matter. For the last twenty years, we have been generous enough to accommodate the Rwandese Refugees and normal aliens of Rwandese origin not knowing that we were nourishing a vesper [viper?] in our chest until recently we realized that they were dangerous criminals, killers, smugglers and sabotours [*sic*]. We had to choose one of the two things:
>
> 1. Harbour them for further period was selling out our National integrity of Independence.
> 2. Cleaning them from our society was receiving International repercussions so we chose the latter to safe-guard integrity through the Universal decision based on the following points.[46]

This campaign of ethnic cleansing, which continued more and less intensively until 1985, quickly caused the two large refugee settlements of Nakivale and Oruchinga to double in population and livestock as Banyarwanda were concentrated into them.[47] Though massive starvation was averted due to the quick UN response, the atmosphere in the camps was one of fear. The experience of fear was also shared by urbanized Banyarwanda. Many had moved to Kampala while Idi Amin was in power, and others, mostly youngsters, were in the capital for their schooling. For these Banyarwanda, everyday life became very precarious, as Ndore Rurinda attests: "When you are on a bus, approaching a checkpoint, you don't speak but you are tall and lanky and you can tell the people are watching you."[48]

While up to forty thousand Banyarwanda were reportedly willing or able to get to Rwanda, the Rwandan government was not keen on their return—and neither were the majority of the (mostly) Tutsi refugees.[49] After all, Rwanda was at this juncture still ruled by a Hutu-dominated one-party system. Rwandan refugees who did make it into Rwanda were confined to refugee camps.[50] One of the Banyarwanda to experience this was James Kabarebe, who would later go on to rise to the highest levels of the RPA. In 1982, when the Obote II government started pushing refugees back into the refugee camps and over the Rwandan border, he was among the latter. His parents had gone ahead, while he was part of a group of boys who were to follow with the refugees' cattle. As the group approached the Rwanda-Uganda border, which was demarcated by a shallow river, the Rwandan border guards would not let them cross. Rwanda, so they told the boys, was full. Kabarebe explains that this was the first time he was confronted with genocidal racism. "The guard told me: 'You guys, Uganda hates you, Rwanda hates you, which means even God hates you. This river flows to Ethiopia, so you can take the river back to where you came from. To Abyssinia.'"[51] Kabarebe and his age-mates were stuck: behind them stood the Ugandans, who were driving them out of the country; before them stood the Rwandan border guards. Eventually, after spending a full day in the river with their cattle, the boys took advantage of the cover of darkness and were able to cross into Rwanda and the Akagera National Park. They walked until morning, when they were caught. Their cattle were put into a corral for quarantine, but food and water within the enclosure were insufficient, and dead carcasses were littered throughout.

The group now scattered to look for their families. James and a few others wound up at Kibondo Refugee Camp. Before being allowed to enter the camp, the boys were forced to dig the graves for some of their fellow refugees who had died the night before. No members of Kabarebe's family were among the corpses, and he found his father, mother, and siblings in the camp. However, as he put it some thirty years later, "The situation was too hard, not good, it only was a place to die. And my siblings were getting sick with diarrhea."[52] Thus, after staying in the camp for two or three nights, he decided to go back to Uganda and join Museveni in the bush. Leaving at night, he walked back through the Akagera National Park alone. Near the border, he found people struggling to load cattle onto a truck. James offered to help in return for a ride to Kampala. In the capital, he found some of his old friends and headed for the bush. Later, in 1985, he would be sent back across the border to recruit youths from these camps for the NRA. After signing up about two hundred of them, he led them back across the border and to Museveni.[53] For the young Banyarwanda living in squalid conditions in Rwanda or Uganda and discriminated against by the government, joining Yoweri Museveni's rebels in the Luwero Triangle became an enticing option.

In September 1985 the Rwandan government decided it had had enough of the Banyarwanda refugees from Uganda. Without the agreement of the

UNHCR, but apparently with the tacit acceptance of the Ugandan government, it started an operation to push the refugees out of the existing refugee camps and back toward Uganda. While some refugees happily set out toward the border, most were uninterested in returning to a country from which they had been so violently ejected only a short time before. To get them to move, the Rwandan government started cutting off support to the refugee camp. A Belgian diplomat wrote that "the Rwandan authorities apparently gradually reduced the usual services granted to refugees, first those relating to socio-educational matters, and later food. . . . Considering the more frequent reluctant attitudes among the remaining refugees, the authorities were said to have hardened their methods, going so far as to embark classes of ignorant children, thereby forcing many parents to follow them."[54]

Between 6 and 15 September about ten thousand people were thus forced toward the border. However, the remainder of the refugees still refused to budge. Not only had the UNHCR made an official protest to the relevant Rwandan authorities on 18 September, but news had come from Uganda that there was heavy fighting going on around Mbarara. As Mbarara would have been the destination, or along the route, for many refugees, they were now "prepared to face the deteriorated living conditions in the camps rather than to venture out into an uncertain war zone."[55] Faced with a mass of uncooperative people, the Rwandan security services now showed themselves "inclined to resort to violence if necessary."[56] The Rwandan security services had received orders to "empty" the camps by the end of October. Their violent attitude and the continued boycott of support to the camps seemed to work as over the next month or so another six thousand to seven thousand people were forced into Uganda.[57] There is no doubt that this brutal pushback operation was one of the key factors responsible for the RPF's decision to return to Rwanda by force five years later.

THE RESISTANCE WAR

Before the 1980 elections, Museveni insisted he would challenge any electoral outcome that seemed unfair. When Obote won the election under suspicious circumstances, Museveni decided to challenge the result. While initially contemplated, a coup d'état was eventually deemed impractical. The FRONASA members who had survived the purge (see above) were mostly stationed either in the north of Uganda or far away from the capital. Being unable to draw on a significant force of loyal troops, Museveni could not be sure of success. Instead, he decided to take to the bush and launch a protracted insurgency campaign against the Obote II regime.[58] From Museveni's perspective, a protracted campaign had several advantages. First, FRONASA knew this kind of fighting from their experiences in Mozambique. Second, it would allow the FRONASA cadres scattered throughout the country to reassemble. And third, it would also prevent a possible collision with the Tanzanian troops that remained in Uganda.[59]

The attack that signaled the outbreak of the Resistance War was the raid on the Kabamba barracks—a training center—launched on 6 February 1981 by the "Kabamba 27." While the attack was launched by thirty-five men, only twenty-seven of them were armed, hence the name. Among them were Fred Rwigyema and Paul Kagame. As the duo had been purged from UNLF/UNLA, they were not stationed far away like other Museveni loyalists and could immediately join Museveni for the attack.[60] Rwigyema rapidly moved up the ranks: by May 1981, he was in command of one of the six units that made up the NRA. By 1985, he was put in control of a new NRA front around Fort Portal and, later that year, he even acted as overall commander while Museveni was out of the country—with Salim Saleh as his deputy.[61] Paul Kagame also played a leading role within the NRA. Having received intelligence training in Cuba during the conflict, he was promoted to major by the time of its conclusion in 1986.[62] With such charismatic Banyarwanda in the NRA, and the ongoing persecution they faced in the south of Uganda, it is not surprising that many Banyarwanda youth signed up for the NRA.

Throughout the first years of the destructive Resistance War, Obote was able to hang on to power. But as the NRA insurgency steadily gained ground, squabbling increased within the government army, the UNLA, undermining his position. In July 1985, infighting broke out in Kampala and, by the end of the month, Obote was deposed in a coup d'état by General Tito Okello. Okello had also been one of the members of the alliance that had deposed Idi Amin and could count on an especially strong backing from the northern Acholi ethnic group. However, he was unable to reverse the military gains of the NRA, which entered Kampala victoriously in January 1986.

The end of the war came as a huge relief to the Banyarwanda community, as the NRA's reputation preceded it. As Roger Winter explained, "When the NRA exited the bush and entered Kampala in early 1986, it was already a legend. Its reputation for discipline and the NRM's policy of no sectarianism were almost too good to believe. Its brain trust was highly educated, highly ideological, highly committed to Ugandan nationalism."[63] As *The Times* reporter William Pike also noted, "Morale, something which cannot be lied about, also appeared high. Soldiers, mostly young peasants from Buganda and Ankole, swiftly obeyed the orders of their officers, young university graduates and former government career soldiers."[64] In the wake of Museveni's victory over Okello, Rwandans within the NRA suddenly found themselves catapulted into powerful positions in the new government. Fred Rwigyema was made deputy minister of defense and held various high posts in the armed forces. Paul Kagame held key positions in the Directorate of Military Intelligence. Many Banyarwanda who had not yet joined the NRA now flocked to its banners. In many ways, the NRA guaranteed their safety. The nonsectarian policies within the organization and the key positions already held by Banyarwanda fighters meant they would be safe. In addition, an extra inducement came from the fact that they would now be the soldiers with the guns and could no longer be wantonly stopped at checkpoints.[65] Besides the quest for personal safety, there was a general feeling among the Banyarwanda community that military training would be useful in the future. While the idea of an armed return to Rwanda had not yet crystallized, the feeling that force might be required was certainly present.[66] A generational consensus had been reached because of the Obote II years: while older refugees had always wanted to return home, many of their children who grew up in Uganda had been quite content there. Obote II changed that, and when parents now told their children that "without your own country, you will always be persecuted,"[67] those words rang true.

THE FOUNDING OF THE RPF

The Banyarwanda refugee community had always maintained internal links through cultural and political clubs and organizations. One of these, the Rwanda Refugees Welfare Foundation (RRWF, founded ca. 1980), was mostly dedicated to alleviating the plight of fellow refugees. Those who were fortunate enough to benefit from advanced schooling at places like Makerere University would then go out to the refugee camps to help educate the children. They would take scarce basic supplies like chalk. Other comparable organizations included, for example, the Intore society for men and the

Nyampinga group for women in Kenya, which provided a forum for Rwandan culture. While these associations were not overt political movements, they were probably founded with a view to promoting political awareness among the Banyarwanda community.[68] Undoubtedly the most important and most political of these refugee associations was the Rwandan Alliance for National Unity (RANU), founded 1979. It had two main goals: (1) to discuss and address the problem of national unity in Rwanda, and (2) to search for a solution to the plight of the Banyarwanda. However, by 1985, it had become clear that RANU in its current form had failed to deliver on its promises. The organization lacked a clear vision and did not have the structure that could have turned such a vision into action.[69] In response to these problems, a "task force" led by Tito Rutaremara was formed to gather information from the refugee community around the Great Lakes. As William Cyrus Reed explains, "RANU sent Rwandan university students directly to the refugee camps in Central and Eastern Africa to initiate contact and gather information which was reported back . . . to the task force."[70] Tito Rutaremara adds:

> Now, in 1985 it is when there was a debate in RANU asking how we could make RANU a mass movement, and a dynamic mass movement. When they asked us to write a paper, I happened to write one, telling them that if we don't organise ourselves [we won't achieve much]. . . . Then I proposed in my paper, which was accepted, when Kampala was taken and I came back to Uganda. RANU asked me to form a task force where there were two military people and two [political cadres] and I was heading that task force in order to reorganise RANU, to make RANU a very dynamic and mass movement. . . . so we created the RPF.[71]

In December 1987, during a general congress, RANU morphed into the Rwandan Patriotic Front. The RPF's "8-point program" expressed a much clearer vision than RANU had embodied. This, in turn, meant that the vision could be transferred to the mass of Banyarwanda refugees living outside Rwanda. The key to achieving as wide a constituency as possible among Banyarwanda was to exclude no one. For that reason, it was decided that the new organization would be a "Front": as long as members agreed with the "8-point program," their personal political bent, be it socialist, liberal, or conservative, was irrelevant. In the same vein, the RPF argued that ethnicity belonged to the past and that all Rwandans, Hutu and Tutsi, were welcome to join. The program was as follows:

1. Restoration of unity among Rwandans;
2. Defending the sovereignty of the country and ensuring the security of people and property;
3. Establishment of democratic leadership;
4. Promoting the economy based on the country's natural resources;
5. Elimination of corruption, favoritism, and embezzlement of national resources;
6. Promoting social welfare;
7. Eliminating all causes for fleeing the country and returning Rwandan refugees back into the country;
8. Promoting international relations based on mutual respect, cooperation, and mutually beneficial economic exchange.[72]

An important part of this "big tent" ideology was opening up the RPF to women. RANU had been mostly dominated by older men, but the founding of the RPF changed that. Christine Umutoni, a Rwandan who grew up in Uganda from refugee parents, remembers that her struggle had not always been that of a return to Rwanda.[73] As a woman in a still very patriarchal society, her fight had consisted in getting an education and emancipating herself. She overcame the triple hurdle of being a refugee, a young person, and a woman, and started a law degree at Makerere University in 1982, just as the anti-Banyarwanda policies of the Obote II regime were intensifying. Many of the young Banyarwanda men at the university were inspired by the war being waged by Museveni and Rwigyema and would slip away to the bush. However, Umutoni explains that "though I was a rebel I was still apolitical."[74] Her sentiment changed when she lost touch with her parents as they were rounded up and forced back into a refugee camp by anti-Banyarwanda, pro-Obote forces. Though Umutoni was able to find them with the help of the UNHCR, it was now clear to her that she did not belong in Uganda.

At the end of her degree, and with the fighting around Kampala reaching a peak, Umutoni went to Kenya to live with her uncle, Dr. Joseph Mudaheranwa Karemera, who was a fervent RANU supporter. The local RANU cell would meet in the evening and discuss their plans to fundraise or otherwise support the NRA. Eventually, Umutoni's uncle and many of his friends also disappeared to go fight with the NRA. Despite her education, Umutoni had never been involved in any work related to RANU, although the stay at her uncle's had piqued her interest. Things changed when she returned to Uganda in 1987. One day, two young Banyarwanda NRA officers came to the dorm where she and her friends were staying, looking for recruits for a political school run by the NRM. After some back and forth in which Umutoni told the two that she was more interested in returning to Rwanda, they ended up giving her the details of an RPF political school instead.

When Umutoni arrived at the school there was some discussion about whether, as a woman, she should be allowed to join. One high-up commented that, because she had permed her hair, she "looked just like a Muzungu (white person)," ready to go back to Nairobi and would not be very useful.[75] Tito Rutaremara overheard the conversation and having just spent two decades in France, was less intimidated by the sight of an assertive, intellectual woman; he thought Umutoni would make a good recruit. After completing the course at the political school, Umutoni joined the secretariat full-time and helped prepare the December 1987 congress in which RANU officially became the RPF. Though some Banyarwanda women had joined RANU, the RRWF, or the NRA, they were only truly accepted after the founding of the RPF. As a consequence, many more started joining.[76]

The RPF leadership realized early on that if they were to turn potential political support into actual support, they would have to focus on mass mobilization and education. An important part of this process was a sensitization campaign, at the center of which stood the Cadre Development Schools. As an RPF member explains:

> To help in its mobilization strategy, the RPF set up permanent political schools in Uganda, Burundi, Tanzania, Kenya and Congo. The political schools were organized clandestinely in members' houses and houses rented by the RPF. Members who were to attend the political school would secretly assemble at the venue and clandestinely stay for about a month while participating in rigorous political discussions. Under the guidance of cadres, who had been through political schools themselves, political activity would go on day and night in all the regions. The

participants would prepare their own meals from supplies bought by the RPF. . . . Those cadres who wished were clandestinely put into the NRA military training schools to later become Ugandan soldiers waiting for the D-day.[77]

Nor were these schools limited to big cities like Kampala or Nairobi. They reached throughout the refugee community, all the way to the grassroots in the refugee camps, and the small villages where Banyarwanda had settled. Every RPA soldier or RPF political cadre I spoke to had attended one of these political schools. The themes discussed there were broad, the intention being to develop the critical thinking skills of RPF trainees. The liberation struggles of Africa, the Vietnam War, Cold War politics, and dialectical materialism were all on the menu. While the slant was slightly socialist, a main tenet of RPF philosophy was that all political doctrines, from socialist to conservative, were welcome, as long as they were consistent with the basics set out in the "8-point program." Often, cadres who had been through the Cadre Development School system would go on to teach themselves on subjects in which they specialized. One of the problems with RANU had been that only a few of its members worked full-time for the organization. Their political work had taken place alongside other career and family pursuits. This, as Tito Rutaremara explains, was a serious shortcoming: "If there are no people who are politically professional, who make sacrifice and start mobilizing, if you go and work on weekends then things won't be."[78] To tackle this issue, some graduates of the Cadre Development Schools were selected to become full-time political mobilizers, spreading the message and objectives of the RPF not just in the Great Lakes region, but also among the diaspora in Western Europe and North America.

Cultural associations were another key part of the drive toward mass mobilization. Many of these organizations already existed and served the cultural needs of exiled Rwandans throughout Africa and Europe. But as the RPF started mobilizing, these associations became overtly political. On the one hand, they made the RPF's political message known. They were a way to spread "the narrativization of the past glory of Rwanda . . . in order to create a sense of belonging . . . and history that transcended the experience of conflict."[79] As a political cadre explained: "Cultural activities were regularly carried out in all regions by officially registered Rwandan cultural organizations pulling huge Refugee populations. Youth and women groups' activities sprang up in all regions. The Front's structures at all levels gained strength within the Refugee communities in all the regions."[80]

On the other hand, they were used as fundraisers for the cause. During cultural events, especially in Europe and North America, successful Rwandans were asked to make donations to the RPF, so that one day they might return to their country. However, for all their importance, these donations were insufficient to finance the newly formed organization, with its political schools and full-time political cadres. Thus, besides donations, "all members of the RPF in the region were making contributions to the Front depending on their levels of income."[81] For prosperous businessmen, these contributions could be substantial; for salaried members, they might amount to pledging a percentage of their monthly income; for grassroots refugees, they might mean sacrificing a cow to the cause.[82] As one former RPF member explained:

> Each Cell, branch, region had an elected Finance member. The Cell Finance member would collect and remit to the branch and the branch finance members would all remit to the region's finance member who would in turn remit to the executive, the Commission of Finance. The Commission had staff who would move through all regions collecting the funds and mobilizing for more, identifying well-to-do members and friends of the Front and specifically soliciting funds other than ordinary contributions from them.[83]

The RPF also established several business ventures in Uganda. One of its businesses involved the importation of cement from Tanzania to Uganda. Cement was relatively cheap in Tanzania, but in Uganda, which was going through an intensive phase of reconstruction in the aftermath of the Resistance War, demand was high and cement could thus be sold for a handsome profit.[84] Companies controlled by the RPF and its sympathizers also supplied the NRA with its rations.

> It supplied all the NRA battalions with foodstuffs: maize and beans. This was done through its network because by design all supplies officers, intelligence officers and finance officers in all the NRA brigades were Rwandan. RPF cadres would be awarded tenders to supply these units by tender committees made up mostly of [these] officers and even

> if . . . some Ugandans comprised the committees, they would not know what was happening. Moreover, the brigade commanders, who were all Ugandan would be in the know because they had been briefed by Major General Rwigema [Rwigyema] who was their superior, comrade in arms and hero. The Finance and Audit department at the NRA headquarters was, again by design, controlled by Rwandan officers so payment to the RPF suppliers would be hastened so that more supplies to the units would be delivered. Since the RPF cadres delivered on time due to their prompt payment and the quality was always immediately found good, the few other competitors were thrown out. Even those [Ugandan companies] who managed to . . . [survive], their supplies were tested and found wanting in quality by the Rwandan supplies officers in the units. Since the NRA had to have supplies and there was an efficient supply system, for three years prior to the invasion, the RPF had a cash cow in supplies.[85]

Thus, grassroots collections, diaspora donations, percentages of members' salaries and some organization-wide business ventures seem to have made up the bulk of RPF income in the years leading up to 1990.

Though the stated intention of the RPF was to find a peaceful way for Rwandan refugees to return to Rwanda, it was clear from the start that a military option was on the table. This was signaled most clearly by the election of Fred Rwigyema as chairman of the RPF, and the immediate formation of its military wing, the RPA, in 1987. Thus, another important part of the sensitization campaign was to reach and specifically prepare Banyarwanda in the NRA for a return to Rwanda. The lead in this effort was taken by those Banyarwanda officers who were already sympathetic to the RPF cause. They would speak to Rwandans in their units, showing their own sympathy for the RPF and convincing them that their cause was worthwhile. RPF members within the NRA would use the cover of their formal duties to go around the country and talk to potential recruits.[86] They would also communicate orders and directives from the RPF to Banyarwanda officers. Besides indicating which soldiers might be open to approach by the RPF, another role played by these officers was to train young Banyarwanda refugees, as well as the RPF recruits who came from around the Great Lakes region, in preparation for a potential military attack on Rwanda. As 1990 approached, and the military preparations of the RPF accelerated, more refugees came to Uganda in preparation for the eventual showdown. Some joined the NRA directly, but others were trained in small training camps set up throughout Uganda and run by Banyarwanda officers in the NRA. The following experience can be assumed to have been fairly typical. X, whose family had fled to Congo from Rwanda in the early 1960s, came to Uganda from Zaire in mid-1990, when he was about sixteen years old. Having spent a month in a political school in Kivu, he was recruited by the RPF. When the agreed night came, he and others gathered near their village and were taken to the Zaire-Ugandan border, which they crossed at night. On the other side, Ugandan army trucks were waiting to pick them up and take them to a camp deep inside Uganda, where the recruits were trained for six months by Rwandan instructors. In December 1990, he joined the RPA at the front.[87]

THE HOLY SPIRIT MOVEMENT AND THE INSURGENCY IN THE NORTH

Soon after Museveni took power in Uganda, an insurgency developed in the north of the country. Led by Alice Lakwena, the Holy Spirit Movement (HSM) exploited feelings of discontent among the Acholi and soon threatened the survival of the new government. This new conflict proved a godsend for the burgeoning RPF. The NRA needed troops to fight the HSM, so its leaders were happy to turn a blind eye to the fact that many recruits were Banyarwanda from outside Uganda. "As the NRM government was busy recruiting cadres and soldiers to prosecute its new-found duty of running a State and fighting an insurgency in the north of Uganda, it was also, by default, aiding the political agenda of Rwandan refugees."[88] In return, Banyarwanda within the NRA fought hard against the rebels of Alice: "Most of the newly passed out soldiers of the NRA would be deployed to the North and all the young Rwandans would be so eager to go and serve under their Rwandan hero especially knowing they would acquire experience to use in Rwanda under the same commander. General Rwigema [*sic*] was very popular with the troops in the North. Indeed it was him who finally stopped the Alice Lakwena insurgency at a place called Corner Kilak."[89]

It is difficult to say to what degree the war in northern Uganda was a formative experience for the RPF. What is clear is that the core of the later RPA did fight in northern Uganda and that the war against the HSM was used as a training ground of sorts. Caesar Kayizari explicitly made the point in an interview:

> So, whenever we went to battle, we said "let us excel, it is a battle yes, but it is also a school." So cowards were identified then, in the beginning. "Come on, are you going to help us when you are a coward here?" All over in the North in the East. Jinja, Magamaga, Soroti, Corner Kilak. . . . Whenever an opportunity to go for other training came, we found a way of putting our guys to benefit from this further training: officer cadet, company commander, platoon commander, artillery. Support guns, support services, like communication.[90]

However, it should also be noted that while many top brass within the NRA must have known and condoned the actions of the RPF men within their organization, it seems unlikely they grasped their full extent. The Rwandans who found themselves in the Ugandan military intelligence made sure that any discontent about the RPF's activities within the NRA was never made public. Kayizari continues:

> So in 1989–90 the question on everybody's mind was when [will we cross into Rwanda]. We were getting fidgety because the intelligence information [was] that something was boiling under. The reason why it didn't go far was because we were in intelligence. So we knew how to drop it. It comes from the ground but doesn't reach the leadership because we put it in the freezer. I was the person in that department, so I know how many reports I diverted and of course on instructions from my boss.
>
> JBK: Kagame?
>
> Yes, or Fred, all of them. We knew it was a military code that anything [that put] our mission in jeopardy we must do all effort to make sure it does not succeed. And one of the ways we had to do it was to stop the information flow which would be used against us. But, and this is the peculiarity of us, we had to excel in our undertakings for Uganda, so that they keep at least—so that they need us. They say: "These are the best officers we have, these are the best soldiers we have, we need them." Because they had the war they were fighting.[91]

The relationship between the RPF and the NRA is full of nuance. Rwandans had been part of Museveni's inner circle since the first days of his fight against Obote. Fred Rwigyema was one of the best friends of Museveni's brother, Salim Saleh, and rose to top command positions both during the Resistance War and the war against the HSM. Major Paul Kagame, for his part, was close to Museveni himself and held key positions within the NRA military intelligence. Besides these two, other high-level RPF members within the NRA included Lieutenant Colonel Adam Wasswa and Major Chris Bunyenyezi; Major Dr. Peter Bayingana, who was the head of the NRA medical services; Sam "Kaka" Kanyemera, the head of the military police; and Stephen Ndugute. Besides these elite connections, a web of friendship forged in combat bound the Rwandans inside the NRA and their Ugandan counterparts. It seems it was these personal ties that allowed the RPF to use the NRA to an astonishingly effective degree. As explained above, the RPF used the NRA to train its own armed wing, the RPA, and to fund its political and military agenda. However, there does not appear to have been an official, formal "pact" between the NRA and the RPF that allowed this to happen. Rather, personal connections at every level of the NRA created sympathy among the Ugandans for the objectives of their Rwandan friends. The Ugandans also understood the worth of the Rwandans within their ranks in the fight against Alice Lakwena and the HSM. By 1990, the RPF had in effect created an army within an army, one that was ready to spring out of the NRA box as the RPA. However, while the RPF prepared for a possible military return to Rwanda, diplomatic negotiations were also being carried out between the Ugandan and Rwandan governments on the right of return of the Banyarwanda.

NEGOTIATING THE RETURN OF RWANDAN REFUGEES

Though the political situation had improved for the Banyarwanda in Uganda following the end of the Resistance War and the elevation of their patron, Museveni, to power, this did not mean that the anti-Banyarwanda sentiment on display during the Obote regime had simply disappeared. In fact, a deep suspicion of the Banyarwanda remained, as shown by the following letter, seemingly the brainchild of an ordinary Ugandan man from Mbarara in 1989.

> While it is accepted by the UNHCR that refugees should be given freedom by the host country, it is dangerous to give too much of it. An example is seen here in Uganda where refugees from our neighbouring Rwanda were given asylum but now have become a burden to the government. . . . The problem is that the Uganda nationals themselves are facing scarcity of land and employment because of these expatriates. All government and non-governmental departments are filled by these refugees. Worse still, these refugees are always assuming higher positions in the government and they have even filled the army. Now I would request the UNHCR to send these people to their camps and have all the control over them. Those who wish to go back to their country of origin should be allowed to do so freely. Again these refugees should not be allowed in the state army.[92]

This anti-Banyarwanda sentiment gave Museveni a strong reason to negotiate for the departure of the refugees. By solving the refugee problem, Museveni would cement his position of power in Uganda. More specifically, he might have aspired to engineer the departure of Banyarwanda officers within the NRA, for while they fought bravely, they were becoming an increasing political liability in the face of their unpopularity with the Ugandan masses. It is also possible that Museveni was under pressure from the RPF, whose chairman, Fred Rwigyema, was close to him, to feel out the possibilities for a peaceful return of most Banyarwanda to Rwanda. However, a high-level RPF political cadre said that the RPF was completely excluded from negotiations on the return of the Rwandan refugees.[93]

The Habyarimana presidency made its position clear to the new government in Uganda by broadcasting its "Position du comité central face au problème des réfugiés rwandais" on national radio on 26 July 1986. The main argument of the communiqué was that Rwanda was full and already lacked the resources to develop its existing population. In light of this, Rwanda could not possibly be expected to open its doors to the refugees. "Rwanda is absolutely unable to ensure even the food security of an increased population resulting from a massive return of Rwandan refugees. And the absence of food security generates, as we know, all other insecurities."[94] The communiqué further stated that the best solution to the issue of the Rwandan refugees was their naturalization in their country of residence. In its conclusion, the Rwandan note finally stated:

> Rwanda will continue to consider sympathetically requests for individual, free and voluntary repatriation in the light of the conventions to which Rwanda is a signatory and the regulations in force in Rwanda, which regulations provide, inter alia, that a refugee may be admitted to the country who;
>
> - Never carried arms against the Rwandan Republic;
> - Never participated in a subversive movement against Rwanda or any activities against the interests of the Rwandan Republic;
> - Demonstrates ability to provide for their subsistence and fulfillment needs once back in the country.
>
> That said, although cramped, overpopulated, and still on the list of the poorest countries in the world, Rwanda will always be a country of asylum within the framework of the Conventions it has signed. It now shelters thousands of refugees. However, whenever the conditions for their return to their countries of origin have improved, Rwanda will accede to their individual will to repatriate.[95]

The ostensibly generous tone of the note belies the truth. In particular, the note ruled out the possibility of a general return of Rwandan refugees and spelled out a number of criteria according to which virtually anyone could be excluded. What was considered a "subversive movement"? What was considered sufficient ability to "provide for subsistence and fulfillment"? The document also failed to set out any procedure for individual repatriations to Rwanda. In reality, this procedure, in which documents and evidence had to be presented to the Rwandan Embassy in Uganda, was utterly impractical. The limited capacity of the Rwandan Embassy to process such applications also ensured that only a minuscule trickle of Rwandan refugees would ever be repatriated by this route. Thus, what the communiqué actually did was to shut the door on any prospect of mass repatriation for Rwandan refugees.

UNHCR legal experts were also unconvinced by the communiqué. They set out their analysis in a legal report. To be sure, they conceded that "the demographic growth rate and living space being what they are in Rwanda, on the one hand, and, on the other, the economic potential of the country and its capacity for absorption being more than limited, the return of a population this size could, if we are not careful, degenerate into social unrest and create insecurity within the national frontiers."[96] In addition, the UNHCR agreed that it was easy to understand the worry by the Habyarimana presidency that foreign governments would support the armed return of Rwandan refugees. Yet, considering the extreme restrictions placed on refugees who wanted to return, it seemed to the lawyers that

> repentance or forgiveness are but empty words in the eyes of the Rwandan authorities! In addition, some vague and imprecise words, such as "subversive movement," "any activities," "interests of the Rwandan Republic," etc . . . seem to have been purposely used to give the Government of Kigali the broadest possible discretionary power which may be used without limitation or control.
>
> As for the last of these three conditions, namely "the ability to provide for their needs," it seems both difficult to demonstrate and to estimate, except perhaps for a refugee returning to Rwanda with millions of dollars, accumulated abroad, which they would plan on investing in their native country.
>
> Those are not the kind of refugees you see everywhere![97]

The UNHCR legal report adds in conclusion that the position taken by Habyarimana and the MRND (Mouvement révolutionnaire national pour le développement) was greeted with disquiet, if not outright hostility, by the countries that hosted large populations of Rwandan refugees. And this feeling was echoed by the refugees themselves.

That President Habyarimana and the MRND leadership would take such a hard stance on the issue and risk the ire of both neighboring countries and the refugees is peculiar, as they were well aware that, if their claims were left unresolved, the Rwandan refugees in Uganda might attempt an armed return. In fact, the aforementioned communiqué states explicitly that the Rwandan people would not accept the return of refugees with weapons in hand—a clear reference to the Rwandans within the NRA. Anton Verwey, the UNHCR delegate in Rwanda, explained that "during our various interviews with diplomats posted in Kigali, the link between the moment chosen for the publication of the position statement and in particular its paragraph referring to the return of armed refugees, and the existence of a large group of refugees within the ranks of Museveni's NRA, has been raised several times."[98] In fact, just a couple of months before the communiqué was issued, Rwandan Minister of Foreign Affairs François Ngarukiyintwali had written to the head of the Service central de renseignements about Rwandan refugees "operating in the NRA" who wanted to return to their country of origin by force.[99]

Habyarimana and his advisers must have come to the conclusion that the refugees were less of a threat in Uganda than if they returned to Rwanda. After all, the state Habyarimana controlled in the late 1980s was not much different from the one the refugees had fled during the Social Revolution. Ethnicity and support for the one-party MRND government were crucial for success. Schools still maintained ethnic quotas, identity cards included ethnicity, and Tutsi were excluded from the armed forces. It was thus more than likely that returning refugees would disturb the political status quo in Rwanda and demand equality before the law. Many of their number were Tutsi, and few of them were likely to support the MRND. Domestic opposition groups could also potentially rally to the refugees and form a common front against the MRND government. In sum, inviting the refugees back to Rwanda posed a direct threat to the Rwandan establishment. Moreover, besides the political threat they embodied, the refugees were not a group that would be easily suppressed. They were well organized and many of them were experienced soldiers who had deposed Obote through a successful insurgency.

In December 1987, a fifteen-head commission of the Organisation of African Unity made a tour of Uganda, and a local UNHCR representative reported that the

> matter [of the refugees] was discussed at length in meeting with African Ambassadors and with Minister of Local Government who proposed a regional meeting at highest level with all countries concerned to solve this issue (main problem lying with reluctance of Rwanda government to take back its nationals). . . . The ambassador of Rwanda approved the choice of a durable solution but warned that repatriation would have to be selectively applied.[100]

The subject was once more broached three months later, when President Habyarimana embarked on an official state visit to Uganda. He agreed with Museveni that the Rwandan refugees were, in principle, a Rwandan problem. However, as Rwanda would not be able to solve the issue alone, the two presidents agreed that a joint ministerial committee would be set up to find a solution.[101] The Uganda/Rwanda Joint Ministerial Committee on the Problem of Rwandese Refugees Living in Uganda met for the first time early in 1989.

While the Rwandan government had publicly agreed to find a durable solution, it proved unwilling to budge from the negotiating position set out in the 1986 communiqué. In early 1989, Habyarimana reaffirmed that

> the refugees . . . must fully understand that it is not because RWANDA does not fervently want all refugees to be able to return someday, but because it does not at all see how it would be possible, the constraints of the country having grown so much—the extreme land shortage, the precariousness of our resources, not to mention the extraordinary demographic growth which poses almost insurmountable challenges for us—that reasonably, humanly speaking, it is simply not possible to imagine the massive return of our refugees.[102]

Indeed, the preferred solution for the Habyarimana presidency remained the naturalization of Rwandan refugees in their countries of residence.[103]

Following their president's lead, the Rwandan delegation to the second meeting of the Uganda/Rwanda Joint Ministerial Committee, held in Kampala on 14–17 November 1989, maintained that despite the best intentions of the Rwandan government, any mass repatriation of refugees was simply impossible. The minutes of the meeting show the sparring that took place. First, the Rwandan delegation presented a paper setting out for the umpteenth time their view that the country was overcrowded and could not absorb any Rwandan refugees.[104] Because a return of the refugees was considered impossible, the head of the Rwandan delegation further insisted that the government of Uganda give serious consideration to the possibility of "naturalisation as provided by Article 34 of the 1951 Geneva Convention on Refugees [as] one of the possible solutions."[105]

However, the Ugandan delegation was clearly prepared for these well-known arguments and comprehensively rebutted them. The delegation of Uganda noted that

> these constraints were not unique to Rwanda and she should therefore not use them to abdicate from her obligations towards Uganda. Uganda

> also asserted that the concept of voluntary repatriation is based on the wish of the refugee to return to his country of origin once the circumstances that compelled him to flee have ceased to exist, regardless of the economic situation obtaining in his country of origin. Moreover, the grounds for refusing a refugee to return to his country of origin are clearly spelt out in the International Instruments on Refugees to which Rwanda and Uganda are parties. Those grounds do not include the constraints enumerated by Rwanda. If massive repatriation is problematic, a phased repatriation should be carried out over a given period of time once the magnitude of the problem is ascertained.[106]

Despite the difference of opinion, the two sides were able to agree that an Independent Committee of Experts would be set up by the UNHCR. This committee would establish how many refugees were currently residing in Uganda, and what they wanted. Three options were on the table: repatriation back to Rwanda, naturalization in Uganda, or resettlement in a third country. The committee would also try to establish the assets owned by each refugee.[107] Communications between the UNHCR representative in Kampala and members of the Ugandan government show that the latter considered this second meeting of the Joint Ministerial Committee to be a breakthrough. "There is a known militant faction within the Rwandese refugee community consisting mainly of the younger generation of refugees, which advocates return to the motherland, as a matter of right and principle. This group is reportedly involved in harassment of other refugees who hold different views. Nevertheless it is expected that those refugees especially in urban areas who have integrated, intermarried with Ugandans and hold civil service offices as well as the aged refugees will opt for naturalisation."[108] It seems the Ugandans expected enough refugees to opt for naturalization that the number wishing to return could be managed by the Rwandan government.

Between 27 and 30 July 1990, the Joint Ministerial Committee met for a third time. The main news at the meeting was that the UNHCR had not yet been able to complete the agreed-upon survey. This was partly due to differences between the Rwandan and Ugandan governments over the kind of questions that would be put to the respondents. After such differences were resolved, the deadline for the completion of the UNHCR report was set for 30 November 1990. As both governments would need time to digest the findings of the report, the fourth session of the Joint Ministerial Committee was scheduled for January 1991.[109]

Slowly but surely the Rwandan government had been giving ground, and 1990 saw them make the greatest concession to date. Roger Winter, the director of the US Committee for Refugees, wrote on 17 September 1990:

> The government of Rwanda has modified its heretofore persistent policy of limiting repatriation to very few individuals, admitted on a case-by-case basis. . . . Now, however, Rwanda has agreed with Uganda and UNHCR to embark on an exercise that would permit the 118,000 Rwandan refugees in Uganda to either repatriate or remain in Uganda and possibly pursue naturalization there. I believe Rwanda has agreed to this because:
>
> 1. It now (I think correctly) believes that, although the refugees universally say they want the right to repatriate, most will not themselves do so. Most of today's refugees were born in Uganda, the refugees will almost certainly not be in a position to reclaim their properties or obtain compensation, and Rwanda retains some undesirable practices regarding ethnic Tutsi.
> 2. It recognises there will likely never be a government in Uganda more hospitable to the refugee population than the current government.

Winter concluded by recommending that the Sub-Group on Africa consider the possibility of requesting Rwanda to "reconsider its current practises of"

> 1. Requiring residents to carry identification cards which indicate the holder's ethnicity (Hutu, Tutsi and Twa)
> 2. Maintaining ethnic limitations on participation in certain education and employment.[110]

The point made by Winter here is crucial. While many of the Banyarwanda, both refugees and earlier economic migrants, wanted to return to Rwanda, they did not want to find themselves in a society that would structurally discriminate against them. Thus, a mass repatriation would only take place against a backdrop of internal political reform. Furthermore, this concession by the Rwandan government certainly did not mean that the negotiations were over or that a unanimous solution had been found. Just a couple of days after Winter's message, the representative of the UNHCR in Kampala wrote to Ibrahim Mukiibi, the Ugandan minister of internal affairs, that the

> UNHCR is finalising arrangements to implement the various activities agreed upon culminating in the survey of the refugees during November/December 1990.
>
> However, as you are aware, UNHCR has faced a serious financial crisis since 1989. These financial problems remain unresolved as a result of which UNHCR has no monies available to fund planned activities relating to the survey. It is therefore necessary to make special requests to donors, in particular the European Economic Community (EEC) for contributions to facilitate implementation of the survey.[111]

Considering the importance of the report of the UNHCR Committee of Experts to the negotiations, and the doubtful prospect it would be ready by the agreed deadline of 30 November, it must have seemed unlikely that the next Inter Ministerial Committee meeting scheduled for January 1991 would make much progress.

This rather lengthy discussion of the negotiations conducted between the Rwandan and the Ugandan governments under the auspices of the UNHCR is of particular importance, since many historians and commentators are under the mistaken impression that the negotiations for the return of refugees had actually been concluded. This has obvious implications for judging the RPF's subsequent decision to invade Rwanda. André Guichaoua, for instance, writes that "the aggressive move by Rwandan refugees based in Uganda took place at a time when negotiations on the refugee issue had just been concluded, in August 1990, under the auspices of international organisations."[112] Prunier also argues that the RPF invasion took place to preempt the conclusion of the ongoing, but promising, negotiations.[113] Not only are these assertions incorrect, they also fail to locate the negotiations in their proper context. Ugandan authorities had on and off been contemplating the return of the Rwandan refugees since the Obote I presidency, and the refugees themselves had made their will to return to Rwanda abundantly clear for decades through organizations like RANU. Yet never had the Rwandan government, either under Kayibanda or Habyarimana, seriously entertained the possibility of a mass return. The insistence of the Rwandan government is shown by the pushback of Banyarwanda refugees from Rwanda after they had fled the persecution in Uganda. It is with this background in mind that the late 1980s negotiations must be measured. In the eyes of many Rwandan refugees, the long, drawn-out nature of the negotiations, and the fact that they still had not reached a settlement by the autumn of 1990, were a clear reaffirmation of their deeply held belief that the Habyarimana presidency had no genuine interest in their return.

CHOOSING A VIOLENT RETURN

The choice of a violent return by the RPF can be explained by the coming together of two historical factors. On the one hand, Rwandan refugees had been agitating for a return to their home country since their departure in 1959–1964. While the negotiations described above were seemingly making progress, they had been grinding on for almost four years with no end in sight. On the other hand, they now held a unique position within the Ugandan government and army, a position that—it was reasonable to expect—would not last indefinitely. As stated above, Museveni was not negotiating for the return of the refugees solely because they had helped him overthrow Obote. He was also mindful of the strong anti-Banyarwanda sentiments that existed among many Ugandans. The popular support for the pogroms committed against the Banyarwanda during the Obote II government had not suddenly dissipated.[114] In this context in which (as it were) every minute counted, the RPF leadership had to make a decision: wait for the conclusion of the negotiations between Rwanda and Uganda in the hope of an increasingly unexpected positive outcome—at best a return to Rwanda as second-class citizens—or seize the opportunity and start a military campaign to force a return on their own terms.

The background of the leading RPF members played a key role in influencing their choices. Most of the higher-ranking echelons had been part of the victorious insurgency against Obote and knew that armed struggle was a realistic option. In addition, the military preparations the RPF had been conducting since 1987 meant that, by 1990, they were as ready as they would ever be. A deep distrust of Habyarimana's motives was also common among RPF members. The Front's cadres remembered Habyarimana's argument about Rwanda being full—as they remembered the treatment they and their families had received when they had fled Obote's persecution in the early 1980s. Equally important for the RPF was that its members feared the Ugandan government would turn on them eventually. As one former cadre explains: "We were doing it against time, because as the Uganda government consolidated themselves the first jacket that they put off was the Rwandese. Because politically they had to shed us off. So we said let's do it quickly and take off the jacket first before they do it on us. Because that will give us a more and better way of doing it than when you are fired. When you are fired you are a vulnerable person."[115]

A good indication of the depth of concern of the RPF leadership were the precautions it took to keep unsympathetic elements within the Ugandan security services off its tail. Paul Whiteway, a British diplomat at the High Commission in Kampala, was told that

> security was a constant worry. If the RPA members had been discovered, they could have faced a court martial. However, the situation was made easier for them by the fact that Kagame was the Deputy Director of Military Intelligence. On at least one occasion, he received information that individual RPA members were under suspicion by the NRA. Forewarned, the suspects were able to escape before the net closed in on them. . . . Karemera said that one month before the 1990 invasion, the plans were known only to six individuals: Rwigema [Rwigyema], Kagame, Baingana [Bayingana], Karemera and two others.[116]

Fred Rwigyema and the other high-level commanders in the RPF must also have heard that the internal position of President Habyarimana was no longer as strong as it had been and that he might be toppled in a lightning strike. Weighing all these factors, the RPF decided the time was ripe and set the date for "option Z," a military return to Rwanda, for 1 October 1990.

* * *

Between the early 1960s and 1990s the Banyarwanda community, especially in Uganda, transformed itself from one of mostly disenfranchised refugees to a formidable political and military organization. Time and time again, forces beyond the control of the Banyarwanda influenced their actions: the repression of Obote II taught them how to fight, while the attitude of Ugandans—even after Museveni had come to power—convinced them that they would never be able to settle there permanently. Finally, the repeated refusal of Habyarimana to countenance the return of the Banyarwanda refugees left a small window in which military action could open the door to return. If there had been more time, or if negotiations for the return of the Banyarwanda had been concluded more rapidly, this violent option might not have proved necessary. But with the Ugandan intelligence services breathing down their neck, the RPF leadership understood that they would not be able to maintain their underground network much longer, forcing them to make a choice.

5

The Start of the Struggle for Liberation

October 1990

ON THE MORNING OF 1 OCTOBER 1990 TWO PLATOONS OF Rwandan Patriotic Army (RPA) soldiers, still wearing their Ugandan uniforms, took up positions at the Kagitumba border crossing. All that stood between them and Rwanda was the Muvumba River, which demarcated the frontier, and the bridge spanning it. Looking to the other side, they saw a small detachment of Forces armées rwandaises (FAR), the regulars assigned to border duty. However, there were no unusual heavy weapons emplacements or bustling activity. Clearly, the RPA had maintained the element of surprise it was counting on. Shortly after, at 10:00, they launched their attack and quickly overran the Rwandan border guards who put up minimal resistance and retreated after their commander was killed.[1] As the RPA troops crossed into Rwanda, they tore the insignia of Uganda's National Resistance Army (NRA) off their uniforms, signaling the operation was not an attack on Rwanda by Uganda but an armed return by Rwandan refugees. The two-platoon spearhead was followed by a company of soldiers led by Major Chris Bunyenyezi and then, in dribs and drabs, further RPA comrades. The soldiers, who had deserted from their NRA units, did not yet have a clear organizational structure. No RPA units had been formed prior to the attack and the chain of command was confused. The whole scene quickly degenerated into disorder. Fred Rwigyema, Sam Kaka, Steven Ndugute, and other RPA officers tried to organize their troops, whose morale remained high despite the overall sense of confusion. Luckily there was no more fighting for the rest of the day and a semblance of order had been imposed by nightfall. The chaos of the first day was a result of the way in which the RPA had mobilized. As explained in the preceding chapter, the RPA was a de facto organization within the NRA. Extricating itself from its "parent" organization without tipping off the hostile elements within the Ugandan security establishment had been no easy matter.[2]

It is likely that Fred Rwigyema made the decision to launch option Z, as the Rwandan Patriotic Front (RPF) called the armed return, at some point in September 1990. From 20 September onward, Rwigyema, based in his house in a Kampala neighborhood, started spreading the word that the RPA cadres should make themselves ready to move on very short notice. Major Sam Kaka, a close confidant of Fred and commander of the Military Police Battalion, was able to move through Uganda freely on account of his duties and authority. He spread the message to the many Banyarwanda with Theogene Bagire and 13 Battalion who were deployed at Bihanda; to the troops of Commander Cyzia of 129 Battalion; to 45 Battalion and the training wing at Mbarara, where Charles Musitu was the key RPA man. Others like John Bosco Mulisa (who was working as a brigade intelligence officer in Kasese) and John Bagabo came to Rwigyema's house in Kampala where they were told the news. On 29 September there was another series of meetings at his house and the decision was made from which there was no turning back.[3]

The first units to start moving were those of Major Chris Bunyenyezi. On 30 September 1990, the 306 Brigade of Uganda's NRA was ordered to travel from its bases in Soroti, in the south of the country, to Lira in the north. The movement was to be made in two parts. Most of the troops would go by rail, while the brigade's vehicles would be driven as there was no room for them on the train. After loading up the train and seeing their comrades off, the road-bound column left Soroti. However, instead of heading north it went south in the direction of Kampala. Major Bunyenyezi, the unit's commanding officer, had carefully selected those who would be accompanying him by road. Most were Banyarwandans, like him, and they had just deserted en masse from the NRA. Major Bunyenyezi stopped briefly in Kampala to receive last-minute instructions from Fred Rwigyema. Also in attendance was Major Sam Kaka. Both were told to take their troops, move to the Rwanda-Uganda frontier post at Kagitumba, and cross the next day.[4]

As Bunyenyezi's column moved off into the night, reinforced by other RPA cadres who were now slipping away quietly from their NRA barracks,

Major Kaka prepared his own troops. Even now that the operation was underway, and some within the NRA probably knew what was afoot, no one challenged the commander of the military police. The force he assembled was built around the core of his MP Battalion, which was almost exclusively made up of RPA sympathizers. They were joined by about a hundred Rwandan soldiers of President Museveni's Presidential Protection Unit who were brought over by two of their charismatic commanders, Charles Muhire and Charles Ngoga. Finally, there were about 300 troops from 31 Brigade, also barracked in the center of Kampala. Most of the troops took their personal weapons, and various miscellaneous items like radios, batteries, and rations. The whole group met up with Rwigyema, who had got his hands on various heavy weapons, and other Banyarwanda who were arriving from as far away as Fort Portal in western Uganda. Together they piled into a collection of army vehicles, private cars, minivans, and rented buses. With Kaka's MPs leading the column to dissuade any NRA troops from stopping them, they headed off toward Kagitumba around 02:30 on 1 October.[5]

All this movement did not go unobserved by the NRA. Many within the NRA, and especially the staff of its 1 Division, were suspicious of their Rwandan colleagues. Fred Rwigyema's communications specialists sat glued to their radio headsets: if the anti-RPF faction turned on them now, the entire operation would be a disaster. At some point during the night, a message came from the office of the Ugandan president: "Don't be afraid, if it is Fred who is going with his soldiers, they are not going to fight us. I think he must be returning home." It is unclear who sent the message as Museveni was not in the country. Was it a ruse by the Banyarwanda in the Presidential Protection Unit, or was it the work of sympathetic elements within the NRA?[6]

ABAHUNGU BAMBUTSE: THE BOYS HAVE CROSSED

As Fred Rwigyema prepared to give the order to cross the Ugandan-Rwandan frontier and attack the Kagitumba border post, he must have been feeling mixed emotions, including excitement that the RPF struggle was about to enter its military phase and marvel at how many RPA soldiers had turned up.

> Maj Chris Bunyenyezi actually took two full companies (about 180 men) with <u>all</u> weapons in his 307 Bde HQ armoury, plus their personal weapons when they went. They were in the Soroti area. . . . Some

MAP 5.1. The October 1990 Campaign. (1) On 1 October 1990 the Rwandan Patriotic Front/Army cross the Rwanda-Uganda border and advance toward Gabiro. (2) By 2 October the RPA and the FAR (Forces armées rwandaises) are engaged in heavy fighting around Gabiro. On 8 October the FAR, reinforced by Zairian troops, launches a strong counteroffensive around the town. (3) By 23 October the situation becomes untenable for the RPA and Kagame orders a fighting retreat. (4) The RPA starts moving to the Virunga Mountains to reorganize for the next phase of the war. On 3 November troops under the command of Ludoviko "Dodo" Twahirwa score a small but important victory at the Gatuna border post. (5) By hugging the Rwanda-Uganda border and fighting small actions with the FAR, the RPA manages to arrive in the Virunga Mountains by mid-November 1990. Map by Brian Balsley.

> anti-aircraft artillery, some "big guns" and at least one, probably two Katyusha (40 barrelled multi-barrel rocket launchers) went with Fred Rwigyema. He deployed them from the "reserve units" at Bombo. . . . At least 10% [of his force] are not Rwandan, but have gone in a spirit of adventure, or to be with their chums.[7]

But Rwigyema must also have felt trepidation: while many had answered the call, significant numbers of the RPA had not yet arrived due to the secrecy of the preparations. These included many commanders and soldiers who were stationed in the north of Uganda. For instance, the future commander of the Bravo Combined Mobile Force, Ludoviko "Dodo" Twahirwa, only heard that the RPA had crossed the border after 1 October and immediately made his way south to join his comrades.[8] Peter Kalimba, who would rise through the ranks to become an RPA liaison to the United Nations Assistance Mission for Rwanda, had a similar experience. He heard about the attack on BBC Radio, quickly packed his things, put his subordinate in charge of his NRA unit, and headed for the front. In Kampala, he met up with two other RPF stalwarts—Protais Musoni and Kamali Karegyesa—who were heading for the battlefield in a rented car. They all arrived on 4 October 1990.[9]

Many of the troops that came later had a rather adventurous journey. John Bagabo and his unit had been stopped and arrested at an NRA checkpoint close to Mbarara. When they arrived at the barracks where they were to be detained, they realized that several other RPA members had met the same fate. However, luck was on their side, as Ugandan major Reuben Ikondere showed up. He had been one of the original "Kabamba 27" and had spent a long time in the bush with Rwigyema, Kagame, and the other Banyarwanda in the NRA. Naturally sympathetic to the cause of his comrades in arms, Ikondere joked that rather than wasting their time in jail they ought to be traveling to the border. He waited until evening, by which time even more RPA troops en route to Kagitumba had been arrested at the various checkpoints in the area, and then gave them several trucks and additional weapons and sent them on their way south. It was the need for secrecy and the pell-mell arrival of RPA troops that led to the confusion on 1 October 1990.[10]

Two immediate decisions were made to restore order. First, four battalions were formed (1 Battalion under command of Chris Bunyenyezi, 4 Battalion under the command of Steven Ndugute, 6 Battalion under the command of Adam Wasswa, and 9 Battalion under the command of Sam Kaka).[11] While the creation of the battalions organized the force on paper, this did not mean that they immediately became highly effective fighting units. Although many RPA officers and troops were veterans, the new units did not have the benefit of the team spirit or combat power that comes from having trained and fought together. It would take time for these units, drawn from various NRA brigades and battalions, to get to know each other and coalesce into an effective battlefield force. Second, the troops, who were short on rations, were ordered to impound cows from local herders and prepare them for dinner. The herders were issued with IOUs that were to be repaid after the war.[12] Another effect of the secrecy and excitement that accompanied the mass desertion from the NRA was that supplies—especially food—were lacking. Despite the extensive preparations made before the outbreak of the war, it seems that in the rush to get to Kagitumba the RPA was not able to warn its civilian counterparts in the RPF. This meant that no proper supply lines had been set up before operations started.

Having done what they could, Rwigyema and his High Command prepared their moves for the following day. The RPA would advance on two axes. The first thrust was aimed directly south to Gabiro and its Camp Mutara barracks, which stood guard astride the road to Kigali. The second drive was headed for Nyagatare, an important town just west of the Kagitumba-Kigali road. By the end of the day on 1 October, news had reached the FAR that the RPA had crossed the border. Some reinforcements were immediately sent to Kagitumba to assess the situation, and a battalion was prepared to launch a counterattack the next day.[13]

While resistance had not been significant on the first day, on 2 October, the FAR attacked the RPA with the intention of driving it back into Uganda. Rwigyema positioned his troops on a number of strategic hills to repulse this assault and was observing the fighting when he was shot and killed by a stray bullet.[14] Officers in the RPA immediately realized the potential for demoralization if the news of Commander Fred's death spread throughout their force. Rwigyema was far more than an able battlefield commander. He was a talisman, enormously respected throughout the Banyarwanda community, and the architect of the military return. Therefore, it was decided that the news of Fred's death would be kept secret at first. The rest of the High Command held a meeting, and it was decided that Chris Bunyenyezi would be made chief of the High Command and that Peter Bayingana would take the post of chief of operations. Steven Ndugute, Sam Kaka, and Adam Wasswa would continue to lead their battalions and help hold everything together until Paul Kagame could arrive from the United States. Although they arguably lacked the fighting skill of Rwigyema, or the strategic grasp of Kagame, these were all capable officers in their own right. Bayingana, Bunyenyezi,

Kaka, and Wasswa had all fought with the NRA against Obote and, later, against the Holy Spirit Movement in northern Uganda. Many were surprised when Wasswa joined the RPA, as he was not generally known to be a Rwandan, despite bearing the facial markings commonly found in the Eastern Province. Ndugute had had a slightly different path. He had been a part of Idi Amin's army and had fought with the Uganda Freedom Movement against the Obote II regime. However, after the victory over Obote, he had joined the NRA in service of the Rwandan agenda.[15]

Although Rwigyema's death was a setback, it was decided that the RPA had no choice but to push onward. They still had the element of surprise, and if a decisive defeat were to be inflicted on the FAR, or if Kigali were to be captured, the war could still be won. So, after repulsing the FAR counterattack on 2 October, all units continued their advance. By the evening, Nyagatare had been captured, and fierce fighting was taking place around Camp Mutara and Gabiro. Gabiro Guest House was being used as a FAR headquarters, and the elite paratrooper battalion had been tasked with its defense.[16] The British Embassy in Kinshasa reported that "except for the Presidential Guard Company which remains in Kigali virtually all operational units are at the front. Rwandan troop strength is estimated at 3–4,000. Ground troops are supported by 3 Gazelle helicopters. . . . The consensus among European military observers is that the war has started badly for the GOR [Government of Rwanda]."[17]

In the confusion of the first days the FAR scrambled to make sense of what was going on. It reported to the Belgian military trainers in the country that attacks had also been launched from Tanzania and Burundi. There were also widespread fears of hundreds of infiltrators in civilian clothes, spread throughout the country. According to the French military attaché in Kigali: "It would seem that total disorganisation prevails in the Rwandan army at the moment. Its men also show no enthusiasm for combat. . . . Decisions are taken piecemeal, there is no strategy, no plan of action."[18] To get on top of the situation everyone who could be mobilized was. The students at the Gendarmerie training camp at Ruhengeri were dispatched to Kigali, the FAR's independent infantry companies that had already been in the process of being expanded were mobilized, and the instructors of the Centre d'entraînement commando at Bigogwe were formed into an ad hoc company.[19]

While the war had started badly for the FAR, things were not all going the way of the RPA either. The chaotic nature of the departure from Uganda and the death of their inspirational commander were beginning to catch up with the rank and file. While the news of Rwigyema's death was not yet officially out, the troops felt that something was off. One veteran explained: "You could feel there was chaos but we didn't know why."[20] Others heard rumors, but "we had no time to sit and think, it was all go, go, go."[21] Caesar Kayizari, one of the officers who heard of Fred Rwigyema's death only hours after it occurred, explains that many became demoralized, while others became reckless: "If he can die, who am I to remain alive?"[22]

A distinct disadvantage for the RPA was their lack of air power. While the FAR had taken some time to organize its air wing, from 4 October onward, air power started playing an increasingly important role in the fight. Two Britten-Norman Islander twin-engine utility aircraft flew reconnaissance missions, while French-built Gazelle helicopters armed with rockets and cannons attacked RPA targets on the ground. "Early on 4 October the Gazelles destroyed the invading force HQ at Kagitumba. It was thought unlikely that any occupants of the HQ would have survived."[23] On the same day a resupply column, which included a fuel tanker, was also hit by the same helicopters. While the RPA attack was still moving forward, it was threatening to run out of steam.[24]

However, on the night of 4 or 5 October the RPA received a welcome surprise. President Museveni's brother Salim Saleh, accompanied by David Tinyefuza, the minister of state for defense, and Henry Tumukunde, a senior major in the NRA, turned up to consider progress with Bunyenyezi and Bayingana. It is not known what was discussed, exactly, during the meeting. An educated guess would be that they communicated a message from Museveni—perhaps telling the RPF/A that they would have to negotiate if they were unable to quickly force a military solution—and arranged a liaison system so the RPA and the NRA would have a set method of communication for the rest of the conflict. The suggestion has also been made that the NRA agreed to provide the RPA with significant amounts of food, medicine, and munitions.[25]

PRESIDENTS MUSEVENI AND HABYARIMANA RESPOND

At this juncture, it is worth turning our gaze to the diplomatic front, which is key to understanding the remainder of the military campaign. Early on the morning of 1 October, at a New York hotel, President Yoweri Museveni of Uganda was awoken by aides and told there was an important phone call from home. The caller was the NRA's commander, Major General Mugisha Muntu. During the 1980s, Muntu had not agreed with the politics of his prominent pro-Obote family and had joined Museveni's rebels in the bush. He quickly rose through the ranks and became director of military intelligence—where one of his subordinates was Paul Kagame—a post he held until 1987, when he was sent to the Soviet Union for training. Following a two-year course, he returned to Uganda and was soon appointed army commander.[26] Known as an incorruptible, secretive, and serious soldier, Muntu now told his president that the Rwandans had deserted their units and crossed the border. Museveni, who was attending a meeting of the United Nations General Assembly, decided to call President Habyarimana, who was attending the same event and staying one floor below, to warn him about the impending attack and to reassure the Rwandan president that this was not an invasion of Rwanda by Uganda. While we do not know exactly what happened between the two presidents, Tito Rutaremara suggests that they came to an agreement. Museveni pledged to close the border to prevent RPF reinforcements from joining their comrades, and in return Habyarimana declared himself open to negotiations with the RPF/A who had crossed into Rwanda.[27] Despite the warning given by Museveni to Habyarimana, the question on everyone's mind was neatly formulated by *Africa Confidential:* "How much did President Museveni know, and when did he know it?"[28]

The Ugandan government made strenuous attempts to deny their involvement. The day after the invasion, the vice chairman of the National Resistance Council "and consequently the highest ranking Ugandan currently in the country," Alhaji Moses Kigongo, issued a radio statement condemning the RPF attack.[29] On 3 October, Major General Muntu himself briefed the defense attachés in Uganda. He explained that the Rwandans in the NRA had been interested in returning to Rwanda for a while, but that President Museveni had hoped a peaceful negotiated solution would be found. The British high commissioner in Kampala, Charles Cullimore, reported that

> the scale of the desertions which had taken place on Sunday had caught the NRA by surprise and the military intelligence staff were highly embarrassed. . . . Once Muntu had been warned about the incursion he had notified the GOU [government of Uganda] who informed

> Museveni. Muntu had personally briefed the Rwandan Chief of Staff by telephone. Road blocks had been set up . . . as of mid-day on 3 October, 80 NRA deserters had been captured.[30]

The Ugandan Army commander closed the briefing with his own assessment of the campaign that was now unfolding in Rwanda. In his opinion, Rwigyema would need to rise beyond ethnic lines to win; he would need "popular support, a destabilised government and a Rwandan Army with grievances against its own government if he was to be successful. None of these factors were in his favour."[31] High Commissioner Cullimore attended yet another briefing with a senior Ugandan government official on 4 October. During the briefing, the assembled diplomats were told that though the NRA had been aware of the activities and existence of non-nationals in its ranks, it had been reticent to expel them from the armed forces. This unwillingness to deal with the Banyarwanda within the NRA and the Ugandan government was partly a consequence of the fact that, as Prunier has suggested, there was "no way of stopping . . . [them] without a major politico-military showdown."[32] After the meeting, Cullimore reported to the FCO that

> on balance I am inclined to discount suggestions that the Ugandan Government as such connived in the incursion. . . . We have had a wide range of contacts since the invasion with ministers, officials and senior army officers and other channels, all of whom have appeared genuinely taken aback by what has occurred. I doubt if the Ugandans could so convincingly orchestrate this kind of response. However, I believe that some of the exiles colleagues, especially in the NRA and in parts of the South-West may have a good deal of sympathy with their cause.[33]

However, Ugandan protestations of innocence were somewhat ambiguous. While the NRA posted roadblocks on the routes leading to the south of the country and arrested Banyarwanda who were suspected of going to the front, they were cagey with third-party observers. British Defense Adviser Lieutenant Colonel George Molyneux-Carter toured the Uganda-Rwanda frontier several times. On 1 October, after hearing that some Ugandan troops had deserted and left to fight in Rwanda, he immediately traveled south to the border. He was stopped at a roadblock and given an escort of NRA who "in effect became my escort/guide group. . . . I did not see much, and the

NRA patrol kept me with them. I assume they took me where they could keep me away from danger, and keep me away from noticing things."[34]

On 18 October, he repeated the trip, this time with several NRA colleagues, and was given much more access. "I discovered that NRA operations to control general movement to/from the main border towns were efficient and regular, but because of the nature of the terrain, operations to deny border crossing in the 'bush' areas were ineffective and in fact almost impossible."[35] While the border closure could not seal the border, it made life difficult for the RPF. RPA members and recruits hurrying to the frontline were unable to travel in the open and were forced to waste precious time avoiding roadblocks. This often involved using poor-quality roads and trails, hampering the transport of supplies and munitions. Caesar Kayizari explains: "Museveni closed the door. We never mentioned it because tactically and strategically it was not proper, but he did not give . . . support."[36]

While Uganda was busy controlling the political fallout of the RPF attack on Rwanda, Habyarimana was mustering his own response. On 2 October, he had first called the son of the French president, Jean-Christophe Mitterrand—then adviser on African affairs in the presidency—to plea for French intervention. Gérard Prunier, who was in the office at the time, recounts the episode: "I was sitting in Jean-Christophe Mitterrand's office and he stopped talking to me to pick up the phone from Habyarimana. He did not try to disguise the contents of the conversation which was openly about sending troops to bolster the regime's defences."[37] After hanging up, Mitterrand turned to Prunier and, with a wink, said: "We are going to send him a few boys, old man Habyarimana. We are going to bail him out."[38] President François Mitterrand himself heard about the situation around that time and, after a brief deliberation with his ministers, gave the go-ahead for a French military intervention destined to protect French expatriates in Rwanda and to secure the airfield for a possible evacuation.[39] Direct military action against the RPA was not part of the mission.

Having secured French support, Habyarimana's next port of call was Belgium. He stopped there on the way back to Rwanda from the United States. On 3 October, he met King Baudouin and Prime Minister Wilfried Martens. He requested an immediate military intervention and received the support of the Belgian king, who wrote a letter to the government pleading for military assistance to Habyarimana. Belgian Foreign Minister Mark Eyskens supported the position of the king, but Prime Minister Martens did not want to be implicated in the internal affairs of a former colony and denied the request.[40] Yet, Habyarimana's trip to Belgium was not wholly ineffective, as the delivery of a shipment of arms from FN Herstal, which had already been paid for, was expedited.[41] In addition, the Belgian government did decide to send a military contingent to Rwanda to protect the expatriate community. When Habyarimana arrived back in Kigali on 4 October, he had reason to be pleased with his diplomatic efforts. French and Belgian troops were on their way and scheduled to land that evening and the following morning, respectively. On the other hand, the French government had refused to provide air support, and the RPF was still putting serious military pressure on the FAR around Gabiro.[42]

THE EVENTS OF 4 AND 5 OCTOBER 1990

As the events of the night of 4–5 October are contested, it is worth following the story of the French troops who departed for Kigali in some detail. The 4th company of the 2ᵉ régiment étranger de parachutistes (2 REP)—a crack Foreign Legion parachute unit that had formed the spearhead at Kolwezi in 1978—was selected to lead the French intervention. It was put on a twelve-hour alert at 17:00 on 3 October and departed for its staging post in Bangui, Central African Republic, in two airlifts at 03:00 and 05:45 the following morning. At this point 4th company was also joined by a radio-transmission-interception detachment from the 13ᵉ régiment de dragons parachutistes (13 RDP), a French special forces regiment that specializes in long-range reconnaissance and intelligence gathering.[43] At 15:00 this combined force set off for Kigali in two C-160 Transall aircraft. The French were unsure whether Kigali airport would be clear for landing, so the troops had all donned their parachutes in case an airborne assault proved necessary. By the time the aircraft approached Rwanda, the pilots had been able to establish communications with the control tower of Kigali airport and were assured by French military personnel who were already stationed in the country as advisers to the FAR, known as the Mission d'assistance militaire (MAM), that a parachute assault would not be necessary.[44]

After landing at 18:50, the officers of 4th company were briefed by the French military attaché and members of the MAM. They were told that the RPA was only sixty kilometers from the capital, within striking distance.

The French Embassy had also received "last-minute intelligence from the US Embassy that Kigali would be attacked that night."[45] Alerted to a possible confrontation, Captain Streichenberger, the commanding officer of 4th company, divided his troops to cover the airport, the French school, and the French Embassy. According to the military diary kept by the 4th company, fighting in Kigali started at 01:10 on the morning of 5 October.

> 01H10 Simultaneous attack by the rebels on the military installations in Kigali. The French embassy is in the line of fire between mobile rebel elements and Rwandan soldiers manning firing points in a military camp nearby.
>
> The same shots (small calibre and 14.5 mm) passed just over the French school. . . . The embassy was the target of the direct fire (most often coming from the Rwandans). A CRAP [Commandos de recherche et d'action en profondeur, i.e., an elite section for special missions] opened fire after being engaged. The French school was hit by stray bullets and was the occasional target of isolated snipers (Sk.S2.S4 did not open fire). Mortars were fired from around the industrial zone of Kigali (by Rwandans or rebels?). The situation at the airport was calm (S3). The shooting lasted all night.
>
> 03H00 New attack on the same targets and on the airport where 3rd section took fire from the rebels and especially from the Rwandan forces protecting the airport (particularly the control tower).
>
> . . .
>
> 08H00 Shooting stopped in Kigali. No [French] injured.[46]

The following morning the British Embassy in Kinshasa, which was also responsible for Rwanda, reported that

> since 2 am this morning there had been fighting all over town. Armed civilians of both tribal groups had emerged in support of the rebels. They appear to have been well prepared. Significant combat was continuing in the industrial zone and at Avenue Paul VI near the honorary consul's residence. Habyarimana was entrenched at the military school. The French Legionnaires held the airport. There had been numerous

casualties among the regular army. Mortars were distinctly heard during the night but not other heavy weapons.[47]

While these reports give the impression that a significant battle was fought, presumably between RPA elements and the FAR, this does not seem to have been the case. In fact, RPA veterans deny they ever got close to Kigali in October.[48] Exactly what happened that night remains unclear, and different hypotheses have been advanced. The first and most widely accepted is that President Habyarimana staged the attack on Kigali in an attempt to persuade the French troops on the ground to take an active anti-RPA position, rather than just protect French expats and property in Rwanda. Supporters of this theory also suggest that an additional reason for staging the attack was to justify the massive political repression and arrests that took place the following day. Another variant of this thesis suggests that the French actively participated in the masquerade.[49]

The second hypothesis, put forward by French historian Bernard Lugan, is that the fighting in Kigali was unintentionally triggered by nervous FAR troops, who started shooting, causing a cascade of other jumpy FAR troops to start shooting as well, in the mistaken belief that they were under attack.[50] A third hypothesis, proposed by Belgian ambassador Johan Swinnen in his memoirs, is that a coup against President Habyarimana may have been attempted by elements within the FAR.[51] In this scenario, the shooting might have consisted of exchanges between loyalists and putschists. While there is little solid evidence to back up this theory, it would certainly fit the FAR modus operandi. Coup attempts, or politicking within the officer corps, were not unusual, and the US Embassy had indeed been prewarned of the attack (see above). The question then arises of how the US Embassy obtained its intelligence. Did the government of Rwanda provide it as part of its masquerade to justify its political repression the following day, or did a group of FAR officers intent on a coup warn the US Embassy in a bid to win the superpower's support?[52] Other circumstantial evidence in support of the attempted coup theory comes from the timeline. President Habyarimana landed in Rwanda for the first time since the RPF invasion either late on 3 October or early on 4 October. This absence and his visit to Belgium before his return to Rwanda might have been interpreted as possible signs of weakness by rivals in the FAR.

The following day, 5 October, saw a spate of arrests throughout Kigali: "The Rwandan authorities had started an extensive round up of people suspected of complicity in, or sympathy with, the invaders including the heads of military intelligence and logistics, and numbers of prominent Tutsi civilians."[53] Thousands were arrested, and few groups were left unaffected: political opposition, business rivals of the ruling power, ethnic minorities, suspected RPF sympathizers, and elements within the FAR were all rounded up. While the government insisted that ethnicity did not play a role in the arrests, about 75 percent of those detained were Tutsi. The arrests quickly drew the attention of the international media and diplomatic community due to the horrific conditions in which the detainees were kept.[54] In Kigali central prison, 1,500 detainees only had one toilet. Food and water were distributed sporadically, with inmates sometimes going without for days. These political prisoners also endured beatings and torture from both the military guards and "ordinary" prisoners.[55] The human rights report drawn up by Belgian lawyers Eric Gillet and André Jadoul at the behest of the Comité pour le respect des droits de l'Homme et la démocratie au Rwanda (CRDDR) found similar occurrences in the southern town of Butare. Between 3 and 5 October, dozens of people were arrested, held in poor conditions, and sometimes tortured.[56] What these arrests clearly show is that Habyarimana feared internal opposition as much as the outside threat emanating from the RPF. This aspect would remain crucially important throughout the Struggle for Liberation. As Prunier points out, the "game was not two-sided as the later tragic events in Rwanda have tended to make onlookers believe, but in fact three-sided, between the Habyarimana regime . . . the internal opposition . . . and the Tutsi exiles."[57]

Later on 5 October, when the roundup was well underway, Habyarimana addressed the Rwandan people on the radio for the first time since the start of the invasion. After explaining the modalities of the attack, the president turned to the events of the previous evening:

> But we soon realised that even before this concerted attack, guerrillas of this same group [the RPF] had already infiltrated our country, and especially Kigali. These guerrillas are not numerous. Nevertheless, they can create disorder if we are not vigilant. This is how the few clashes occurred, the characteristic sound of which was heard by the inhabitants of Kigali last night. . . . These clashes allowed us, and still allow us, to annihilate these assailants.

Then the president turned to the arrests that were being carried out throughout Kigali:

> It hurts me deeply to see that these rebels hoped to find accomplices within our country. Whatever the reason that pushes certain Rwandans to provoke blood and disorder in their own country . . . this treason exceeds our comprehension.
>
> Naturally, this is only a tiny fraction of individuals, obviously misled, we do not know how. But we must follow all leads to check the situation.
>
> This is why possible arrests and interrogations in no way signify proven responsibility.
>
> Nothing would be more unjust, nothing would be more harmful for our country, than if some among us were tempted to confuse things. There can be absolutely no question of considering our brothers and sisters, whatever their ethnicity or region of origin, as responsible for what happened, absolutely not. The political maturity, the fundamental humanity of the Rwandan people are the best guarantors of our continued attachment to national unity, so we may continue to experience every day the peace and understanding that we have known for so long already, and that no one, or nothing, can nor will want to endanger.[58]

Habyarimana's speech is a masterpiece of ambiguity. On the one hand, he warns the Rwandan people that there are infiltrators on the loose who are beyond redemption. On the other, he insists that ethnicity should not be brought into the equation. For any listener with a knowledge of Rwandan history, the specter of ethnic violence is clear. However, for those not fully aware of the events surrounding the 1959–1964 Social Revolution, nor of Habyarimana's coup d'état, the speech must have sounded reassuring. In short, it pandered to the needs of ethnic Hutu extremists and the international community, while at the same time warning the domestic Tutsi population: "Support the government and you will be left alone. Step out of line and you will be punished."

Also on 5 October, a second French company from the 3ᵉ régiment de parachutistes d'infanterie de marine (3ᵉ RPIMa) arrived at the airport, followed by troops from Belgium and Zaire. While the mission of Belgian troops was similar to that of the French, the Zairians had been ordered to directly support the FAR in combat.[59]

PRESIDENT MOBUTU INTERVENES

The troops sent by President Mobutu were commanded by General Donatien Mahele, widely regarded as one of the few generals in Zaire to have achieved his rank on the basis of merit rather than nepotism. But his force was made up of a hodgepodge of units. There were elements from the Division spéciale présidentielle (DSP), the 31st Parachute Brigade, and the Service d'actions et de renseignements militaires (SARM). Technically these units were the best Zaire had to offer, and the parachute brigade was especially highly rated as "one of Zaire's most effective Army units."[60] The DSP was Mobutu's praetorian guard, and its troops were the best paid soldiers in the country. However, according to a CIA assessment, "growing discipline and more problems suggest that even the DSP [had] begun to feel the effects of the country's general economic deterioration."[61]

While the build-up took some time, there would eventually be about 1,400 Zairian troops in Rwanda. On 8 and 9 October, the Zairians and the FAR made their first concerted effort to push the RPA out of Gabiro.[62] Heavy fighting ensued at Gabiro and around Nyagatare, and both changed hands several times. While the arrival of the Zairians and their counterattacks were not enough to break the RPA, they did take pressure off the FAR. However, relations between the FAR and the Zairians quickly soured. The British Embassy in Kinshasa noted that "Zairian troops stationed in Kigali controlled the checkpoint at the entrance to the city and both expatriates and Rwandans complained of harassment, intimidation and theft."[63] By 13 October, the French defense attaché in Kigali reported that "the retreat of the Zairians from urban zones seems most probable," because "the behaviour of Zairian troops is a matter of concern for the Rwandan population as well as for expat communities. Indeed, traders, motorists, or simple passers-by, are fleeced daily at Zairian checkpoints."[64]

Relations on the frontline were hardly better. Looting was widespread, and most of the contents of the Gabiro Guest House were trucked back to Zaire. Consequently, when Zairian forces ran out of ammunition, the FAR refused to replenish their stocks.[65] However, most detrimental to the relationship between the FAR and the Zairians was a fratricide incident in which 46 Zairians were killed by friendly fire from the FAR. According to the French, the Zairians had failed to establish proper radio communications before going into combat and had been misidentified by a Gazelle helicopter that had consequently rocketed them.[66] There were also rumors of infighting within the Zairian contingent. Apparently General Mahele was shot by one of the members of the DSP, and Zairian members of parliament later speculated that Mahele had been sent to Rwanda to die.[67] By 17 October, Habyarimana could no longer tolerate the embarrassing behavior of his allies and asked Mobutu to withdraw Zairian troops from Rwanda. Again, we can count on some insightful commentary from the British Embassy in Kinshasa: "This whole episode has been an embarrassing debacle for Mobutu. His supposedly elite troops appear to have been guilty of widespread looting and worse and their military performance is said to have been abysmal too. They used up their ammunition too rapidly, and carried out little reconnaissance before engaging the rebels, thus suffering serious casualties."[68]

For all their shortcomings and unpreparedness, the Zairians did buy some breathing room for the FAR and stabilized the front.[69] Without the Zairian intervention, the RPF would probably have broken through the front line and captured Kigali. Indeed, throughout the first days of fighting, the performance of the FAR troops had also been very poor. The head of FAR military intelligence, Anatole Nsengiyumva—who interestingly had also been arrested on 5 October but was quickly released—had the following to say shortly after the invasion:

> In terms of the preparation of our soldiers, it is showing its inadequacies. Indeed, our men no longer respect fire discipline, many panic when they hear the first shot fired by the enemy, others lose their head and shoot right and left, and, more serious still, others simply desert their UNITS, change sides and go away. These are some of the phenomena that show that our men are not at all prepared for the task at hand.[70]

The report continued:

> The causes for this lack of preparation are multiple. First there was the economic context. Due to the meagre budget, the country was NOT able to earmark sufficient funds to ensure a decent training of our men. Often practise cartridges were lacking, as were real cartridges. Grenades can hardly be found anymore in the AR [Armées rwandaises], explosives are generally lacking, as is military engineering equipment, etc. So our men have not had time to train.[71]

The report ended on a depressing note:

> Add to this the lack of motivation of certain cadres. Officers and NCOs, as well as Cpx [Corporals] and Sdts [soldiers]. Indeed, many people currently enter military life simply to earn money, or to lead an easy life in which everything is paid for by the State. Therefore, the result cannot be more satisfying [than it is], and the suffered setbacks should not surprise anyone.[72]

By the time the Zairians left, the RPA had been significantly worn down. The High Command had been unable to fully recover from the death of Fred Rwigyema. His plan had been a blitzkrieg straight to Kigali, but now the RPA found themselves stranded, unable to advance further than Gabiro.[73] As Museveni had closed the border, supplies were slow in arriving, while FAR helicopters, which had regular supplies of ammunition from France, remained a nuisance. The FAR were also increasingly able to deploy their light armor effectively—mostly French-built Panhard AML armored cars armed with 12.7 mm machine guns, MILAN wire-guided anti-tank missiles, and 90 mm guns. The flat, savanna-like terrain of northeastern Rwanda was perfectly suited for these vehicles. While the RPA had some heavy weapons, it proved difficult to deal with these armored cars. According to James Kabarebe, "The situation was pathetic, we were totally in disarray."[74]

THE ARRIVAL OF PAUL KAGAME

Around the second or third week of October 1990, Major Paul Kagame arrived to take command of the RPA. Kagame had been following a course at the United States Army Command and General Staff College at Fort Leavenworth, Kansas, when the RPA attacked Rwanda. After the start of the attack, Kagame had tried to make contact with Rwigyema but had received no reply. A few days later, he heard that Fred had been killed, and he immediately prepared to return to Rwanda. He asked a friend, the Ugandan ambassador at the UN (another example of the RPF-Uganda link), to arrange visas for himself and his pregnant wife. On 8 October, the two flew from New York to London. There, Jeanette Kagame boarded a plane to Brussels, where a sister of Paul lived. Kagame himself, after picking up $80,000 from a London sympathizer, boarded a plane to Addis Ababa.

After spending a few days in Addis, Kagame made his way by plane to Entebbe on 14 October. At the airport, he was picked up by friends in the Ugandan intelligence services. "The person who picked me up took me to his house and another friend from intelligence came to see me."[75] After spending the night at his friend's house, Kagame was driven to the border. The guards there were also helpful and allowed him and his Ugandan intelligence escort to pass. When Kagame arrived at the front, he was shocked by what he saw: "It was totally disorganised. The first sight was probably the worst I have ever seen, that and the genocide. . . . I asked for a meeting with my commanders. I called them back from the field, told them to leave their subordinates in charge. The senior ones came back to meet. They were terribly demoralised—even that was an understatement."[76]

Kagame was, for a number of reasons, the natural choice to replace Fred Rwigyema. First, he was one of Rwigyema's closest friends, with unique insights into the preparations that had been made for the attack on Rwanda. Second, he could draw on an extensive network in Uganda. He had been one of the original "Kabamba 27" who had started Museveni's war against Obote. Thereafter he had served in military intelligence—where he could clearly still count on the friendship of many colleagues. This network was crucial for the RPF. If Uganda were to fully withdraw its support, even unofficial, from the RPF, then the movement would be finished. One of the best ways to prevent that was to have at the apex of the RPF organization someone whom Museveni knew and trusted. After the death of Rwigyema, Kagame was probably the only one who could fulfill that role. Finally, Kagame could count on his own reputation. Caesar Kayizari explains:

> They [the RPA officers and rank and file] knew him from before, as a tough one, you did not cross roads with him. Two, they knew his level. Someone can be tough, authoritarian, but without knowledge in what you are authoritarian of. . . . But if you are authoritative, and you have done your homework, then the end product is much better. So some of them knew him from previous wars, in NRA bush, where he went and found problems, and problems diminished. . . . Even in NRA they said "ah Kagame has come, it will be solved." That is why everyone was waiting for him after the death of commander Fred because they knew what he would bring on the table.[77]

FIGURE 5.1. The commander of the Rwandan Patriotic Army, Paul Kagame, being interviewed by Ndore Rurinda for Radio Muhabura. Courtesy of the Rwandan Ministry of Defense Archives.

Kagame understood that, since a quick victory was now impossible, it was imperative that what remained of the RPA be reorganized and prepared for the next phase of a war, which promised to be long. For that, several objectives had to be fulfilled. First, the RPA had to be extracted from its engagement with the FAR before making a strategic withdrawal to a place of safety. While Uganda might provide some small-scale and temporary sanctuary, it would not agree to the RPA establishing its base of operations there. With the RPA's main ally out of the running, only one safe haven remained: the rainforest-clad volcanoes of Virunga National Park in northwest Rwanda. Second, the logistics base would need to be vastly improved. Providing enough food and munitions for the soldiers had proven a major headache so far, and if the war was to be continued, this would have to change. Third, a method would have to be established to treat injured RPA fighters in the safety of Uganda or Tanzania, preferably in hospitals. Though frontline medical treatment already existed within the RPA, it needed to be improved. Most important, the strategic withdrawal had to take place without a total collapse in morale or the complete disintegration of the RPA. Here Kagame used an old trick. Ludoviko "Dodo" Twahirwa was sent west with about two hundred soldiers to attack the border post at Gatuna. A quick victory would help restore the battered morale of the RPA. It would also allow the gathering of key intelligence for a strategic relocation to the Virunga Mountains.

Meanwhile fighting raged on. On 22 October, the two sides locked horns just south of Gabiro. Once again, the FAR Gazelle helicopters took part in the fighting. They made themselves felt around Gabiro until one was shot down by the RPF. Another helicopter crossed the border and attacked suspected RPF targets in Uganda.[78] The British ambassador in Kinshasa reported to London that "according to French Military Attaché Rwandan aerial reconnaissance had located two RPF training camps in Ugandan territory, one west of Rwemhasha and the other north of Kagitumba. The latter was attacked on 22 October by Rwandan Gazelles firing 24 rockets."[79] The RPF suffered another setback when a large logistics convoy was captured by the FAR around Nyagatare.

To enable a strategic withdrawal to the volcanoes, order had to be established in the chaos that now reigned throughout RPA lines. Thus, it was doubly devastating when Chris Bunyenyezi and Peter Bayingana, two key members of the temporary command, were killed on 23 October. As with the death of Fred Rwigyema, there are many theories as to how they died. I will present the official—and, to my mind, most plausible—version. On the morning of 23 October, or possibly the day before, a significant FAR element managed to slip through a gap in the RPA lines and set several ambushes in the rear of the RPA positions.[80] While traveling to the frontline, both commanders were killed in separate ambushes. Then, the situation rapidly deteriorated. An RPF member notes that "the deaths of these leaders in a period of less than a month was a devastating blow to the month-old RPA. The force was thrown in disarray."[81]

Following these crushing two days, Kagame gave the order for his force to melt away. A staged withdrawal took place toward Kagitumba, where the force was reorganized into small mobile units.[82] Several of these moved west, following Dodo Twahirwa's unit. Others moved into Akagera National Park or slipped over the border into Uganda together with the most seriously wounded. However, though Kagame and the rest of the RPA High Command had been able to extricate most of their forces from Gabiro and Kagitumba, some had become detached. For example, a column was operating in Akagera National Park, out of touch with the High Command as it had lost its radio.

As the RPA withdrew from Gabiro, the FAR and Rwanda's political leadership thought the war was over. According to the British high commissioner in Kampala, his Rwandan peer was "claiming complete victory over the rebels. . . . It seems that the rebels have suffered a serious reverse, but I think the Rwandan Ambassador's claim of total victory is probably premature."[83] As Cullimore suspected, the Rwandan ambassador in Kampala was wrong. While the RPA had been dealt a serious setback, it was not defeated.

THE POLITICAL ASPECTS OF THE OCTOBER 1990 INVASION

Because political action ran concurrently with military operations, it is worth taking a closer look at the former, picking up the political thread where we left it, just after 5 October. On 8 October Rwandan Foreign Minister Casimir Bizimungu briefed the diplomatic corps in Kigali for the first time since the start of the invasion. During the briefing, the Ugandan ambassador mentioned the actions that had been taken by his government to prevent the RPF from being reinforced, but "complained that he had not been received at the Foreign Ministry until [then]."[84] Similarly, the Tanzanian ambassador noted that the frontier with Rwanda had been "secured" in order to stop RPF sympathizers from infiltrating across the border. Clearly, the Tanzanians were playing the same double game as the Ugandans. In fact, the RPF column cut off in Akagera National Park was able to escape the FAR by slipping into Tanzania. The Rwandan foreign minister was also pressed by the Vatican, as well as the United Nations Development Programme and Swiss representatives, about the human rights situation of those arrested on 5 October. The Belgian press also wrote that "the Rwanda government are using the incursion to deal with their political opponents within Rwanda and that there have been executions."[85]

However, while the Belgian press might have been putting pressure on Kigali, Prime Minister Martens let it be known that he was not at all pleased with President Museveni and Uganda. Museveni had visited Brussels on the weekend of 6–7 October to explain his position in the affair. In discussions with the prime minister, Museveni emphasized two points: first, that the Rwandans who had deserted from the NRA were experienced "bush warriors," and second, that a political solution was needed as quickly as possible.

He also warned that if no political solution was reached, the situation in Rwanda could escalate.[86] However, the Belgians had been left with the feeling that Uganda was responsible for much more than Museveni would admit.[87]

In a meeting with the heads of mission of the European Community on 9 October, the Rwandan foreign minister went a step further and claimed that the government of Uganda was actively working with the RPF. According to Bizimungu, entire units had been equipped and recruited by Uganda to reinforce the RPA. The minister also indicated that Rwanda would take up the matter with the UN Security Council and with the Organisation of African Unity.[88] After his visit to Belgium, Museveni cut his European tour short and flew back to Uganda, where he gave a one-hour press conference upon landing. Although the president seemed fatigued after what must have been a hectic week, he still spoke at length about the Rwandan situation. The conference showed the ambiguity Museveni felt toward the RPF. He explained how, after hearing from Army Commander Mugisha Muntu that the RPA had attacked Rwanda, he had immediately warned the Rwandan authorities. In fact, so Museveni continued, he had warned Habyarimana on several occasions that "those boys are very dangerous for you. They are disgruntled. They have acquired skills. Of course we will police it, but if a faction of the Rwandans comes and says join us they can desert in big numbers."[89] Despite these actions, which indicated a sense of responsibility from one head of state to another, High Commissioner Cullimore noted that "[Museveni] doubted whether Rwigyema's troops could be defeated, and ruefully indicated that they included 'some of our best people.' . . . Indeed he made no attempt to conceal his sympathy for Rwigyema's cause and referred to him throughout as 'Fred.'"[90]

Despite this ambiguity, the Ugandan government continued to maintain that it had not been involved in the execution of the attack on Rwanda. When High Commissioner Cullimore spoke with Ugandan Minister of State Ateker Ejalu, the latter

> was adamant that, as the President had said at his press conference, it was not always possible to know who was a Rwandan. Those who had been here for 30 years or more now spoke fluent Ankole or Luganda and had in many cases changed their names. The president lost over 20 of his personal staff from State House including his driver. . . .

> I said I remained puzzled as to why so many Rwandese should now want to return to an overcrowded and poor country having survived a number of hostile regimes in Uganda especially that of Obote II. Ejalu said that although official NRM [National Resistance Movement] policy towards the Rwandan refugees had always been sympathetic there had nevertheless continued to be considerable harassment at grass roots level especially in Ankole country.[91]

The French government, closely allied to Habyarimana, was not buying the Ugandan explanation. Two French diplomatic communications reveal France's peculiar position. On 13 October, Gilles Vidal, an adviser to President Mitterrand, told the British ambassador in Paris that he was sure that Uganda had structurally helped the RPF and that Museveni must have been in the know. After all, how could the Ugandans not have noticed when the RPF drove off with much of their military arsenal? The ambassador then "asked what Museveni could hope to gain from the violence which was embarrassing for him as OAU [Organisation of African Unity] president. Vidal thought that Museveni might see the invasion as a way of getting rid of the Tutsi refugee population in Uganda."[92] Vidal added that he did not believe a negotiated solution would be possible in the short term: "A Tutsi victory would lead to Hutu rebellions against what they would see as minority rule. . . . The best solution would probably be for President Habyarimana to stay in office under new political arrangements which included guarantees for the Tutsis."[93] What is interesting is the particular emphasis on ethnicity. While British diplomatic communications indicate an awareness of the ethnic factor, Vidal puts it at the center of his analysis.[94]

The French ambassador in Rwanda, Georges Martres, did the same in a cable dated 15 October and entitled "Analysis of the situation by the population of Tutsi origin." His message concerns the reaction of the Tutsi population within Rwanda to the invasion by the RPF. As it is the first diplomatic communication that speaks of genocide, four years before the events of 1994, it is worth quoting in full:

> The Rwandan population of Tutsi origin believes that the military action has failed in its psychological consequences, as it has not led to results rapid enough to prevent the mobilisation of Hutus against the prospect of a return to the former monarchy.

> It is still counting on a military victory, thanks to the support in men and means from the diaspora. This military victory, even partial, would enable it to escape the genocide. By holding part of the east of the country, General Rwigyema would present a sufficient threat to force President Habyarimana to negotiate. . . .
>
> The Tutsi are convinced that if the current authorities were to enjoy total victory, the departure of the French and Belgian troops would result in an exacerbation of the repression and persecution, and would lead to the total elimination of the Tutsi. Failing a military victory by General Rwigyema, the Tutsi, who do not believe in President Habyarimana's promises of openness and dialogue, would welcome a coup d'état within the Hutu clan that would bring a more moderate leader to power. Such a person still needs to be found. But some people remark that President Habyarimana took power in similar circumstances in 1973 and that he was totally unknown at the time.[95]

Like Vidal, Martres places ethnicity at the heart of his understanding of the situation. This is most likely a reflection of the opinions of the circle of Rwandans with whom the French had the most contact. The French military-technical relationship with Rwanda meant that its diplomats and soldiers often communicated with the FAR High Command. As many senior FAR officers were later implicated in the Genocide, this is probably one of the sources of information through which the French internalized the importance of ethnicity. However, Martres's knowledge of Rwandan history allows him to take his analysis one step further than Vidal. In 2014, in an interview about his cable, he explained that he "talked about genocide from the start because a reading of the history of Rwanda and more recent events convince me that the risk of genocide was on everyone's minds. . . . I myself used the term genocide without imagining that it could take such a shattering form. I envisaged instead a renewal or aggravation of some massacres."[96] While Martres underestimated the severity of the genocide he predicted, his report proves the exceptional access and capability of the French diplomatic staff in Rwanda.

In Uganda, however, the French were less welcome. The relationship between France and Uganda, the most important allies of the Rwandan government and the RPF, respectively, is well illustrated by an anecdote by High

Commissioner Cullimore. A few weeks after the start of the invasion, the French minister for overseas development visited Uganda and had a meeting with President Museveni to which Cullimore was invited. The French minister confronted the Ugandan president and asked: "Why did you not prevent it?" before adding, "What on earth are all these people going into Rwanda for, I mean they don't even speak French?" Museveni "said, with very large eyes which would get very big when he was a bit cross, first of all, 'I didn't think I was supposed to be the jailer of the Rwandans. Uganda is not a prison.' And secondly he said, 'It may have escaped your notice, but they all speak Kinyarwanda. That's their mother tongue.'"[97]

THE START OF CEASEFIRE NEGOTIATIONS

With France and Uganda at loggerheads, the first serious peace proposal came from Belgium. Prime Minister Martens, Defense Minister Guy Coëme, and Foreign Minister Mark Eyskens traveled to Nairobi on 14 October to meet President Habyarimana. The trio assured the press that rather than interfering in the affairs of another country, this was a "sounding out [of] opinions to see if it was possible to bring conciliation among the different groupings within the country."[98] While this might have been true, part of the motivation was probably to hand over the initiative in the peace talks to Habyarimana. Choosing Nairobi as the meeting place was in itself mildly provocative. Kenya and Uganda were in troubled diplomatic waters at the time, and President Arap Moi had never had any sympathy for the RPF. Thus, it cannot have come as a surprise that the Kenyan government tried to use the talks between the Belgian delegation and Habyarimana as a stick with which to beat Uganda.[99] In addition, Martens made several negative remarks about Uganda while in Nairobi. While it would seem that the Belgians heavily favored Habyarimana, this is probably not the whole truth. The Belgian decision not to intervene militarily and to more or less withdraw the support of their military training mission was seen as a betrayal by many FAR officers, even though the Belgian troops remained in-country.

As a meeting of regional presidents was scheduled to take place in Mwanza, Tanzania, on 17 October, Museveni decided to reassert himself before the talks. At a press conference held a day earlier, he reiterated that the Ugandan government had had no prior knowledge of the plan to attack Rwanda. While there had been rumors that the refugees would try to organize something soon, these had been passed on to the relevant Rwandan authorities. He also responded to criticism that the Ugandan army had been ineffective at closing the border, arguing that it was almost impossible to close due to the terrain and the sympathy of the local population for the RPF's cause. Besides these protestations of innocence, the Ugandan president also dwelt on the upcoming talks. Cullimore reported that, in Mwanza, Museveni planned to renew his offer to Habyarimana

> to use his good offices to try to persuade Rwigyema and the rebels to accept the ceasefire and commit themselves to not attempting to overthrow the Rwandan government if Habyarimana would commit himself to finding a political solution to the refugee problem. . . . At some stage the Rwandan government would have to talk directly to the refugee leaders. They were high calibre people. He had spent many hours with Rwigyema before the incursion trying to encourage him to lead a refugee delegation to talk to Habyarimana.[100]

The press conference also laid bare signs of increasing animosity between Uganda and Rwanda. Toward the end, the Rwandan ambassador, who was sitting next to Museveni, explained that Rwanda now considered itself "as the victim of 'foreign aggression.' Museveni responded with a smile that he thought it difficult to categorise the return of one's own people after 30 years in exile as 'foreign aggression.'"[101]

At Mwanza, Museveni and Habyarimana met their Tanzanian counterpart, President Hassan Mwinyi. The conference was surprisingly successful, and the "Mwanza Communiqué" was published at its close. Habyarimana pledged that his government would open discussions with "the internal and external opposition under the auspices of the OAU Secretary General."[102] In return, both Museveni and Mwinyi pledged that they would try to convince the RPF to observe a ceasefire. It had taken the two presidents all their powers of persuasion to convince Habyarimana to talk to the RPF, without which there would be no chance of a ceasefire.[103] It is unclear whether an explicit plan was drawn up for the next steps of the peace process, but the agreement seems to have been that Museveni and the Belgians would use their good offices to contact the RPF and encourage them to agree to, and implement, a ceasefire.

Immediately after returning from Mwanza, Habyarimana left for another round of international diplomacy. First stop, Paris. There, he spoke with President Mitterrand and several other government advisers on 18 October. After receiving pledges that he would continue to receive political support, as well as ammunition and weapons from France—albeit in a smaller quantity than he would have liked—the Rwandan president headed back to Africa.[104] However, before returning home, he first visited Mobutu at Gbadolite, his extravagant jungle palace compound. Despite the problems encountered by the Zairian detachment in Rwanda, the relationship between the two presidents appeared intact. Indeed, the two were known to be close personal friends, and this would remain the case until the death of Habyarimana in 1994.[105]

Meanwhile, the Belgian delegation headed to Kampala for the next act in the first ceasefire attempt. Museveni informed the Belgians that he had sent an emissary to the RPF and that the reply he had received on 22 October stated that they accepted an immediate ceasefire.[106] Exactly what followed is unclear, but no ceasefire materialized on 22 or 23 October. Indeed, as the two sides never met, and due to a general lack of sources, it is difficult to determine whether both sides had actually agreed to a ceasefire being implemented on either of these dates. What exactly did the RPF mean by an "immediate ceasefire"? Was this message properly communicated to Habyarimana by Martens?[107] And in view of the battlefield chaos, could a ceasefire have been successfully imposed by either side? Two facts are nonetheless certain: First, that for the RPF a ceasefire would have come at the ideal moment. It would have allowed Kagame and his officers to reorganize their battered force in relative tranquility. Second, that on 23 October, when Bayingana and Bunyenyezi were killed, the campaign swung definitively in favor of the FAR.

Although fighting raged on, further diplomatic efforts were also made. On 25 October, Habyarimana, Mobutu, and President Pierre Buyoya of Burundi met at a Communauté économique des pays des Grands Lacs (CEPGL) summit of regional presidents held in Gbadolite. Mobutu and Buyoya tried to impress upon Habyarimana that the best course of action was indeed to sit down with the RPF, organize a ceasefire, and start negotiations. Naturally, as relations between Zaire and Belgium were less than amicable at the time, a senior government official told the British Embassy that "the GOZ [government of Zaire] would not play any part in peace negotiations if the Belgian government had a representative at the summit. He said that this was 'diplomatic reciprocity' as Zaire had not been included in the Belgian-organised talks to resolve the Rwandan Crisis."[108] The CEPGL heads of state went even further, when both Habyarimana and Buyoya encouraged an initiative by Mobutu to make him a middleman between concerned parties in the Rwanda Crisis.[109] Almost at a stroke, and perhaps to the relief of the Belgian government, the CEPGL summit put the diplomatic process back into African hands. The importance of the OAU had been confirmed in Mwanza, and now Mobutu, who had infinitely better regional contacts than the Belgians, had maneuvered himself into a key position, as a result of which further negotiations would be held in Zaire.

President Buyoya's involvement at this stage of the process deserves further scrutiny. Buyoya was a Burundian soldier, ethnically Tutsi, who had come to power through a coup d'état in September 1987. While he claimed to be an ethnic moderate, and did occasionally act as one, his government strongly supported the RPF. Burundi was the second biggest supporter of the RPF after Uganda. Not only did the RPF eventually open an office there, but it also had strong networks among the Rwandan refugees in the country, including some within the military intelligence services. The close relationship between the RPF and Buyoya can be largely explained by the fact that the ethnic Hutu-Tutsi dynamics that were so important in Rwanda were mirrored in Burundi. However, Burundi had not had the equivalent of Rwanda's Social Revolution, and the army and government remained dominated by Tutsi.

The Belgian delegation also continued to push for some kind of solution to the crisis, with secretary-general of the OAU, the Tanzanian Salim Ahmed Salim, and Martens meeting in Frankfurt in late October. Gradually the idea had crystallized that a peacekeeping force needed to be put in place between the two warring parties. The OAU indicated it could provide the troops if the European Community agreed to fund them. OAU assistant secretary-general Ahmed Haggag thought a force consisting of North Africans would be best. "Zaire was ruled out: off the record, he said their troops had done a lot of indiscriminate killing. In light of previous bitter experience, the force would not be put together until funding had been obtained."[110] However, by this point, negotiations were overtaken by events on the ground. With the defeat of the RPF now imminent, the efforts of the Belgians were in vain. Nonetheless, the round of blitzkrieg diplomacy conducted by Martens did give birth to many of the ideas that would eventually be taken up in the Arusha Accords years later.

* * *

Before moving on, let us determine where the main protagonists of this chapter stood in late October 1990. As the RPA and the FAR will be covered in detail in the next chapter, a few words on Habyarimana and Museveni will suffice. The RPF invasion created both problems and opportunities for Habyarimana. On the one hand, he now faced two concerted threats to his rule. First, there was the increasingly vocal domestic opposition. Doubts about his rule had circulated for some time prior to the attack. These had become serious when President Mitterrand had insisted in his La Baule speech that aid to African countries would be tied to democratization. Habyarimana had been able to contain the domestic opposition by promising reform of the governance system. Second, he was now also burdened with the RPF military challenge to his rule. Though neither of these threats were insurmountable, an alliance between the RPF and the domestic opposition might well prove fatal to him.

On the other hand, the invasion by the RPF had also offered Habyarimana opportunities. France had rushed to Rwanda's aid, even though no reforms of any kind had yet been implemented. This suggested that Mitterrand's new La Baule doctrine mattered more in theory than in practice: if Habyarimana called, France would answer. The invasion had also allowed Habyarimana to move against the domestic opposition, with the mass arrests of 5 October being justified by the need to eradicate internal RPF collaborators. While there had been a backlash in the international media and his government had had to answer difficult questions as a result, the fallout had been contained.

The end of the immediate threat posed by the RPF did not spell the end of Habyarimana's problems. The short war had depleted the already meager government treasury, and the Rwandan president would soon have to go cap in hand to the International Monetary Fund for a new loan. Securing this loan, which would undoubtedly come with strings attached, would be Habyarimana's priority for the next couple of months.

As for Museveni, what can we conclude about his relationship with the RPF? In 1998, he himself said that "faced with a *fait accompli* situation by our

Rwandan brothers," the Ugandan government decided "to help the Rwandese Patriotic Front (RPF), materially, so that they are not defeated because that would have been detrimental to the Tutsi people of Rwanda and would not have been good for Uganda's stability."[111] In this case, the elusive Ugandan president seems to be telling the truth. Indeed, evidence suggests that although Museveni knew that the Rwandan element in his armed forces was interested in returning home, he had neither known the exact date nor anticipated the scale of the desertion. The RPF's decision to go ahead put Museveni in an acutely embarrassing position during the year in which he was the chairman of the OAU. It also made him look impotent in the eyes of those Ugandans who thought the Banyarwanda enjoyed too much influence in the country. On top of that, the RPF took a staggering amount of weapons, and their replacement would not come cheap. These factors probably provoked Museveni's initial anger toward the RPF, including his public condemnation of the invasion and the closing of the border to reinforcements and supplies.

However, as October passed, Museveni seems to have slowly changed his position. He was, after all, very close to the RPF High Command; both Fred Rwigyema and Paul Kagame were personal friends, and he did not want to see their organization destroyed in a military confrontation. This was probably why he favored a negotiated solution from the very start of the conflict. In addition, Habyarimana's response to the invasion likely alienated Museveni. Not only did Rwandan, French, and Belgian diplomats heap the blame for the invasion on Uganda, but FAR troops also violated Ugandan sovereignty repeatedly. Gazelle helicopters and FAR mortars hit targets in Uganda, and infantry repeatedly crossed the border.[112] In this context, Museveni increasingly turned a blind eye as his NRA commanders helped their former comrades. As one Ugandan officer remarked: "I have fought side by side with these chaps not only against Obote but later in the North. One of them saved my life when we were fighting against Alice. Would you expect me to refuse them now when they come to me because they haven't any more ammunition?"[113] This frame of mind is confirmed by Senator Tito Rutaremara: "Our most important support was our relationship with each and every soldier in the Ugandan Army. . . . We had spent years fighting and living together. When we needed to slip out of Rwanda, we would always find an army officer who would say, 'Cross here. Pass here.' At the time Museveni was saying he was not helping us, they were letting us pass."[114]

Other RPF cadres also remember that the "NRA commanders in the bordering region of Rwanda were a constant supply of heavy artillery, ammo, ammunition, other supplies and cover. Of course this was done with complicity with the senior leadership of Uganda."[115] Yet this did not mean that the aid Museveni distributed to the RPF was unconditional or always forthcoming. Museveni had to make sure he did not draw the ire of the international community at a time when Uganda was still rebuilding from its own long civil war. Rwanda had powerful allies in the West and sanctions could have been disastrous. There were also elements within the NRA and the Ugandan intelligence services who were less than keen on the Banyarwanda. Yet even for this anti-Banyarwanda group the decision to help or not was not straightforward. While they might feel reticent about arming the RPF, the more support they gave, the more likely the Banyarwanda in Uganda would be able to go home. In the following years, Ugandan support for the RPF would be crucial and it is doubtful the organization could have survived without it.

6

Forging the RPA

November 1990–January 1991

FOR THE FAR GARRISON STATIONED AT THE GATUNA BORDER post, the arrival of Ludoviko "Dodo" Twahirwa's column, on 3 November 1990, must have been a nasty surprise. Only days before, the Rwandan ambassador in Uganda had proclaimed a total victory over the RPA, but the attack now battering their position proved this was far from true.[1] Before the day was out, the RPA troops had driven the FAR from its position, inflicting numerous casualties on the defenders.[2] This victory, so soon after the retreat of its main body from Gabiro and Kagitumba, was an enormous boost to the morale of the RPA, just as its commander Paul Kagame had hoped. Twahirwa consolidated the victory the next day, when his troops ambushed the FAR company that had been sent to retake the border post, capturing large amounts of munitions and several heavy weapons.[3]

It is currently believed that the RPA redeployment to the Virunga Mountains took place through Uganda, and that there was a lull in the fighting between late October 1990 and January 1991, when the RPA captured Ruhengeri.[4] This stands to be corrected, since the RPA and the FAR were engaged in a series of skirmishes throughout the closing months of 1990—with the villages of Kiyombe, Cyumba, Kaniga, and Kivuye all being contested.[5] Usually initiated by the RPA, these skirmishes served several functions. First, they kept the FAR confused about the locations of the main RPA force as they moved to the Virunga Mountains. To amplify the confusion, RPA units would often move in small groups, and then reunite before an attack. Second, small-scale hit-and-run operations were carried out to scrounge for resources and capture key supplies.[6] These operations were not without risk, and the RPA suffered several stinging small-scale tactical defeats. For example, on 20 December 1990 the RPA's 6 Battalion was preparing a surprise attack in the area of Gatonde when they were discovered by the FAR. Acting aggressively, the FAR took the fight to 6 Battalion, which was forced to withdraw, losing its first aid station in the process. The next day the two forces, now well aware of each other's presence, fought a pitched battle over the same terrain.[7]

It was during this period that the RPA started its transformation from an uncoordinated and defeated rebel group to a formidable fighting machine. However, it must be kept in mind that the changes described below did not occur overnight and that it took many months for their full effect to become apparent.

DISCIPLINE AND COMBAT DOCTRINE

When Paul Kagame arrived at the front line in October, he had found a thoroughly exhausted and demoralized force. The situation was so bad that it remained one of his defining memories of the war, together with the Genocide: "There was nothing in its right place, not a single thing. Casualties were lying in the road, so many in such a short time."[8] It was from this shambles that Kagame, chairman of the RPA High Command, would have to rebuild his force, together with his fellow officers.

Many generals and soldiers have noted that an army without mental strength is at best a fragile tool. No matter how well armed a force may be, if it lacks "fighting power"—the "mental, intellectual and organisation foundations"[9] that manifest themselves as "discipline and cohesion, morale and initiative, courage and toughness, the willingness to fight and if necessary to die . . . the sum total of mental qualities that make armies fight"[10]—it will fail on the battlefield. The RPA High Command worked on this first. As Caesar Kayizari explains:

> He [Kagame] was God given. I am not being spiritual, but I am stating the reality. He brought in iron discipline . . . in operations from the day he arrived. . . . [This] was not limited only to military operations . . . even . . . within civilian operations within RPF. . . .

> When he comes in the Struggle he raises the bar, beyond shooting . . . and the bar is for everybody, for small men: soldiers know their bar, NCOs know their bar, as well as for the commanders and our civilian support group. . . . There were benchmarks, or you had to explain why you could not meet them: more than "sorry I got lost." Because you are dealing with lives of Rwandans, you cannot afford that luxury. . . . Kagame was very articulate on that. . . . Of course he is a good manager: he can hit you hard but give you another chance. After being hit hard, you will get it. Then later sometimes he will manage you, except if you become impossible, unmanageable, ungovernable. . . .
>
> This is a war which is fought, seriously fought. If you ask me what was your biggest weapon . . . I would say discipline . . . because that was our center of gravity. He told us . . . "Discipline is the foundation stone upon which we build our liberation." He said it in Swahili: "What I would like you to understand is that discipline . . . will bring fundamental change in our country of Rwanda. . . . I want your behavior, your acts, to be different from those we are fighting."[11]

According to Kayizari, Kagame viewed self-control as the most important part of discipline. Everyone in the RPF and RPA, from the senior officers to civilian cadres, was expected to fully commit to the liberation of Rwanda. To achieve this, the RPA High Command used two methods. The first and preferred method was to have members—military and civilian—internalize the values of the RPF and the reasons for their armed struggle. Officers and political commissars explained to the rank and file why the RPA was waging its struggle and how discipline would help ensure final victory. The second method, as in any army, was to make sure that those who displayed undisciplined behavior were punished.[12]

As long as the Struggle was being fought, it was considered unacceptable to give in to personal temptation or gratification—"Not just here [on the front line] but globally, [also] if you are Charles Murigande or Patrick Mazimhaka in New York."[13] Officers were expected to lead by example and shared the same food and accommodation as their troops. This attitude also extended to social contact among RPF members. Female cadres were well represented throughout the organization, but casual sex was strongly discouraged. As Christine Umutoni explained, "We don't want the men to think the girls are here for that, and we don't want people saying 'that girl slept with so and so in her last unit.'"[14] The result of this emphasis on discipline was remarkable. Lieutenant General Roméo Dallaire, the commander of the United Nations Assistance Mission for Rwanda (UNAMIR)—who would arrive in 1993, and about whom more will be said later—wrote that "the [RPA] soldiers we did see were clearly well-led, well-trained and motivated. They wore an idiosyncratic combination of East German summer uniforms and rubber boots, but were always clean and neat. The rank and file tended to be young, sometimes even boys; the officers too were young but clearly knew how to work their troops. When not training, soldiers had lectures to attend and equipment to clean and maintain."[15] Similarly, veteran BBC journalist Fergal Keane noted how "they were lanky and thin and most looked like teenagers. But as we got closer I noticed that their uniforms were neat, and that the troops themselves were not slouching, but instead seemed to be standing to attention. . . . There was no sign of the usual detritus of beer bottles and discarded clothing that follows so many African guerrilla armies."[16]

Another of Kagame's strengths was his ability to build an effective command structure. When he arrived, and despite the deaths of Paul Rwigyema, Chris Bunyenyezi, and Dr. Peter Bayingana, the RPA could still count on several excellent commanders. Steven Ndugute and Sam "Kaka" Kanyemera already held key positions and were soon joined by outstanding battlefield commanders like Dodo Twahirwa, Thaddeus Gashumba, Fred Ibingira, Charles Muhire, Charles Ngoga, Theogene Bagire, and Charles Musitu. Younger soldiers who displayed aptitude for command were also quickly promoted to positions of significant responsibility. Good examples are James Kabarebe, Charles Kayonga and Caesar Kayizari. Other important posts relating to military intelligence, the RPA medical services, and political education were held by Faustin Kayumba Nyamwasa, Karake Karenzi, Dr. Joseph Karemera, and Frank Mugambage, respectively. Together with this group of officers, Kagame was able to project his vision and will throughout the RPA, as Kabarebe notes:

> The role of the leader was central and the sole reason for our success. Remove him from the equation and the Struggle would not have been successful. His style of leadership was involving. His intent was passed to everyone, cadres, soldiers, commanders. We lived among meetings, even during heavy fighting. His intent was communicated.

> He understood the strength and the weaknesses of his people.
>
> You could never tell him a lie because he knew everything. He knew what was going on on the battlefield, and his own intellectual understanding was very strong.
>
> Sometimes he took risks we were not convinced of. But then, when they worked out, we would understand. For him nothing was impossible. With him on our side we knew we were psychologically stronger than the others.[17]

Communicating the commander's intent was especially important for the way Paul Kagame decided the RPA would henceforward wage its war.

Regardless of whether Rwigyema had intended to wage a protracted guerrilla struggle or not, Kagame had no choice but to wage a guerrilla war. The mauled RPA he found upon arrival could not stand up to the French-supported FAR out in the open. However, he did not wage his guerrilla campaign along standard lines. To understand the distinction, it is worth looking at two examples of these "conventional" unconventional wars: the Vietnam War (1955–1975) and the fight conducted by the Taliban against the Coalition-supported central government in Kabul, Afghanistan (2001–2022). In the first case, the North Vietnamese and Vietcong guerrillas operated on several levels: "Guerrillas operate within and around their hamlets and villages. District companies move within their district and the province battalions operate within their province. Main force units operate across province boundaries."[18] In this system, the hard-core guerrillas who do most of the fighting move from region to region, where they link up with the district- and village-level units. These low-level groups supply the main-force units with shelter, guides, and local information on enemy deployments. When the United States armed forces questioned village-level groups on their reasons for supporting the Vietcong, one of their replies was that the guerrillas were better for the people than the government: "The struggle for social justice aims also at putting an end to the abuses by GVN [Government of Vietnam] civilians and military officials. Members of the Front [Viet Cong] frequently refer to the venality and arrogance of the local government authorities, and compare the latter with the Front cadres whom they regard as honest, self-sacrificing, and gentle in their relations with the population."[19]

There is a similar story in Afghanistan. Lieutenant Colonel David Kilcullen, who served as counterinsurgency expert to General David Petraeus and US Secretary of State Condoleezza Rice, writes that "the Taliban's relationship with local tribal allies is important in this pattern of conflict, and arises largely from opportunities created by the Afghan government. . . . The Taliban exploited this, posing as defenders of the local tribes against misrule by unrepresentative appointed provincial and district governors, and seeking alliances with dispossessed and disenfranchised tribal power brokers."[20]

The Taliban alliance with local tribal leaders allowed their main-force units access to village-level support, as in Vietnam. "Taliban organisation structure varies between districts, but most show some variation of the generic pattern of a local clandestine network structure, a main force of full-time guerrillas who travel from valley to valley, and a part-time network of villagers who cooperate with the main force in its area."[21]

However, from the start of the Struggle for Liberation, the RPA faced an important obstacle to fighting this kind of war. The Hutu-Tutsi ethnic divide meant that most Rwandans were predisposed to work against the RPA, which they considered to be a Tutsi, as well as a foreign or specifically Ugandan, organization. This meant that the RPA would not be able to exploit local grievances against the central government. Where local grievances did cause disloyalty to the Habyarimana presidency, these grievances pushed the people into the hands of domestic opposition parties—as will be explained in the following chapters—rather than the RPF/A. On top of that, northern Rwanda, the most suitable region of the country to conduct a traditional guerrilla campaign, was also the most loyal to the central government. In short, Rwanda did not meet the criteria for a traditional guerrilla campaign.

Kagame's answer to this problem was that the RPA would fight a guerrilla war without explicitly relying on the support of Rwanda's population. Instead, his troops would use the natural terrain to their advantage and wage a war of maneuver against the FAR: "He brought serious manoeuvre warfare. . . . At first, . . . some senior commanders were doubting. But when it succeeded, they said, 'the old man, he knows.' . . . It was recently being applied in the USA army. . . . Command initiated fighting. So he brought it and he made our enemy dance on his head. And he [the enemy] was always tripping. So that brought confidence again among the commanders."[22]

This maneuvrist approach is a fascinating blend of strategies and tactics from different sources. The basic concept of maneuver warfare had first crystallized in the late stages of the First World War and in the interwar period. Theorists like Heinz Guderian, Basil Liddell Hart, and Mikhail Tukhachevsky saw it as a way to restore the advantage of the offense over the defense by harnessing the power of the internal combustion engine.[23] During the Second World War, these theories were put into practice by the German and Soviet armed forces. From then on, maneuver remained an important strand in both NATO and Warsaw Pact military thinking. One similarity among these various doctrines is that they were conventional par excellence. They were designed to be used by one conventional army against another, which is one of the reasons the US and the USSR ran into such problems in Vietnam and Afghanistan. Their troops had been training and preparing for a conventional maneuver war between NATO and the Warsaw Pact in Western Europe rather than for a fight against small bands of irregular troops conducting hit-and-run attacks.

Kagame would have been well aware of the latest developments in maneuver warfare as he had been attending the United States Army Command and General Staff College at Fort Leavenworth when the RPA attacked Rwanda on 1 October 1990. He might also have been influenced by high-level officers in the NRA—like Mugisha Muntu—who had received training in the Soviet Union. However, most of his operational experience had come from fighting with, or against, guerrillas or insurgents. Indeed, the NRA insurgency against the Obote II government had been fought like the insurgencies described above.[24] There are also rumors that Kagame received training in Cuba. As such, the RPA High Command chairman was in a good position to adapt a conventional warfighting doctrine to the unique circumstances the RPA faced in its war against the FAR.

Two key aspects borrowed from classical maneuver warfare were the decentralization of command and a focus on initiative. In a fast-paced, fluid battle, a single commander cannot control their forces in detail—especially when they are fighting many miles away. As a result, it would be up to local commanders to make their own decisions. As Kayizari explained to me in an interview:

> We sat only in the meeting to be briefed on where to go, what to do and how to do it. But also leaving you the room to do it another way even when you see the situation has changed on the ground.
>
> JBK: Ah ok, so he was happy to give trust to his commanders?
>
> Yes, yes, yes. He said if the situation changes—which it does in war—based on this maneuver warfare, put another maneuver approach to the situational problem on the ground. And some of us were very young, were busy, seriously making notes. Because while we had fought, he had also been in military schools, so we wanted to see what is he saying.[25]

However, unlike the US or Soviet Union, the RPA was not a conventional armed force. It could not count on the full support of a nation state and did not have the supply train or vehicles to conduct classical maneuver warfare. As a result, it conducted maneuver warfare on foot, as light infantry. Operations were characterized by night marches and infiltrations, after which attacks would be launched on surprised FAR detachments: "So, we are doing . . . highly mobile warfare. Making deep operations in enemy territory. If the enemy declares victory in Musanze, we attack the national park. . . . When he comes, he moves his forces to that sector, then overnight we have attacked where he has maintained a minimum force and we are not bothered to hold territory. Territory is not our issue; destabilizing our enemy psychologically and militarily is [at the] top of [the] agenda."[26] This forced the FAR to fight on the RPA's terms and made it impossible for the former to bring their force multipliers, like light armor, to bear on the latter.

However, the RPA could not fight its war without regard to the Rwandan population. The RPA High Command was adamant: "We were ordered: 'Do not harm the population!'"[27] Many RPA commanders who had fought during the NRA Resistance War understood that the internal opposition was key to destabilizing the Habyarimana regime. Any war crimes or massacres carried out by the RPA would be counterproductive, alienating the internal opposition and strengthening the position of the presidency. This did not mean that the civilian population of northern Rwanda was left entirely unmolested. For military and humanitarian reasons, the RPA encouraged the population of the north to move out of the combat zone and flee toward Kigali. This had several military benefits, as Kagame told British lieutenant colonel John O'Brien: "[Kagame] 'advised' the residents of the combat area to move out as he feared infiltration and did not want to commit any of his scarce manpower to internal security duties."[28] For the RPA, a battlefield with as few civilians as possible also presented other advantages. It meant the FAR would not be able to use the local population as guides or human shields, and it allowed the RPA to employ its heavy weapons without fear of causing collateral damage. In addition, the arrival in and around Kigali of the internally displaced population placed an additional strain on an already overtaxed Rwandan government. The strategy of pushing civilians out of the north did have humanitarian and political consequences. First, forcing people to leave their homes is traumatic and must have been accompanied by coercion. Second, the Rwandan government would prove incapable of taking care of the large numbers of internal refugees the war generated. Many would be forced to live in squalid refugee camps on the outskirts of Kigali where they would prove vulnerable to the extremist ideology of Hutu Power.

UNIT COHESION

While the Rwandan Patriotic Army could count on its members being either combat experienced or trained to an acceptable standard, the secretive nature of the attack on Rwanda had made thorough preparation impossible. Normally the men, women, and units that engage in war, in the British or French army, for example, have had time to prepare and exercise together. This allows procedures to be honed and the personalities within the units to bond. It is also of importance to the commander-subordinate relationship and trust. Officers, NCOs, and the enlisted troops have to become familiar with one another, simply to know how their peers think about a certain problem.[29] Operating procedures and small-unit tactics will have subtle differences between units, especially as operational experience starts to influence textbook drills.[30]

However, because the RPA units were only physically formed on the Ugandan-Rwandan border days or even hours before going into combat, they were lacking in unit cohesion.[31] Though many of the soldiers and officers would have known each other well, and in many cases would have fought together before, there would have been many new faces at the assembly stations and jumping off points. Crucially, their NRA comrades were also absent, creating a key missing link within the RPA. This problem was exacerbated by the fact that, though the core of the RPA came from Uganda, many recruits and volunteers had grown up in Congo, Tanzania, or Burundi. Others had come from as far as the United States and Europe.[32] Though they were "Rwandan," the cultural backgrounds and experiences of this variety of recruits would have been broad. One of the expressions of this heterogeneity was the many languages spoken within the RPA. This was an advantage in the diplomatic sphere, where RPF diplomats could switch seamlessly between English, French, Swahili, and Kinyarwanda, but in combat it could be a significant drawback. Under stress, everything becomes more difficult, including clear communication. It is telling that the RPA used Swahili as its battle command language, while Kinyarwanda was used during the pre-operation briefings.[33]

As in any field of human endeavor, in combat, practice makes perfect. However, as the RPA was already engaged in a life-and-death struggle, the practice would have to be obtained on the battlefield itself. This meant that if the RPA was to grow its unit cohesion, one of the most important objectives for its High Command was to avoid large-scale defeat. Small-scale victories, like that of Twahirwa's column at Gatuna, showed the troops that they could defeat the FAR and gave them self-confidence. But it is impossible to conduct a war without suffering setbacks, and local defeats, if properly analyzed, could also be instructive. For example, in early December 1990, an RPA unit attacked the FAR garrison at Rwempasha. The attack proved a failure: the FAR defenders fought tenaciously, and several RPA units accidentally started shooting at one another as the situation deteriorated. The lesson learned by the High Command was that the RPA would have to work on its coordination before launching large-scale operations; no such attacks were attempted again until January 1991.[34]

The combat doctrine that the RPA chose, with its emphasis on maneuver and decentralized command, was difficult to master. Troops were expected to endure long marches, carrying weapons while on minimal rations—often at night. In such situations soldiers must be taught that basics like light and sound discipline are key. A carelessly used flashlight or rattling rifle magazines might give away one's position to the enemy. Learning to trust in commanders and comrades is just as important. The German military philosopher Carl von Clausewitz notes that only through continuous action and emphasis on these elements "does the soldier learn to know his powers. The more a general is in the habit of demanding from his troops, the surer he will be that his demands will be answered. . . . It is only in the soil of incessant activity and exertion that the germ [of fighting spirit/unit cohesion] will thrive, but also only in the sunshine of victory."[35] As we will see in the next chapters, the learning process was long and the RPA did not always bathe in the sunshine of victory. It had some close scrapes: the attack on Ruhengeri in January 1991 had to be postponed because of the difficulties encountered on the march to the town. On this occasion, the RPA was lucky: as the FAR was slow to react, they did not lose the element of surprise. But there also were real reverses. The March 1991 Nyagatare Offensive was defeated by the FAR because, among other reasons, RPA soldiers accidentally fired on the night march toward the objective.[36] However, these setbacks did not destroy the RPA as a fighting force, and as the war progressed the fighting spirit, unit cohesion, and combat power of the RPA would steadily grow.

RELATIONS BETWEEN THE RPF AND THE RPA

The logistical weakness of the RPA during the October campaign suggests that the RPF had not been able to prepare its civilian cadres in Uganda and abroad to their full potential. This was probably, as with the military preparations, a result of the need for tight secrecy in the run-up to the invasion. However, when it became clear that the war would be a protracted one, cooperation between the RPA in the warzone and the RPF civilian cadres behind the front became increasingly important. In this sense, the attack on Rwanda had been a success. It had loudly announced the existence of the RPF/A and shown that they were not only talk. This had been particularly important to gain the support of the Banyarwanda refugees who were still sitting on the fence. Nonetheless, it took time to convince some of the older refugees that the RPA would not end up like the Inyenzi of the 1960s.[37]

Women played an important part in this process. Aloisea Inyumba was appointed commissioner of financial mobilization in 1988, which made her one of the first top-level female RPF cadres. When the RPA arrived in the Virunga Mountains, she made strenuous efforts to set up crucial supply routes. At the grassroots level she mobilized RPF sympathizers in Ugandan refugee camps. "Wherever Inyumba went to raise money she brought photos and videos of the suffering Inkotanyi [a moniker for the RPF/A, inspired by the name of one of the famous precolonial regiments]."[38] When I asked Ndore Rurinda if he had known Aloisea, his answer showed profound respect for his late comrade. "I knew her personally? You bet. She trained me on the cadreship programme, supervised my initial internship, and I later worked fulltime with her as a junior cadre. . . . Can't exhaust this person in few words; humility, loyalty and clarity of intent characterised her dealings and appearance. RPF cadre to the core."[39]

Refugees in Uganda baked food and donated other supplies. These were then transported in secret to the hideouts among the volcanoes.[40] These same supply lines were also used to bring new recruits to the main force.

> We were working [behind the front line]. . . . The military men who were there from the army, they had to be transported to Rwanda. . . . We had to do it clandestinely. . . . People passing here and there. Looking for the way for people who are . . . in the East of Congo, and bring them. The Rwandese were found outside in Europe, where they could come to Uganda, and we had to hide them and pass them through to Rwanda. Then the ways to bring the people from Burundi and Tanzania. . . . We had to transport them, feed them, bring others, find them and so on.[41]

Christine Umutoni was one of the top female leaders in the RPF who helped mobilize abroad. Before the invasion, she had traveled to Burundi via Tanzania carrying a letter from Fred Rwigyema for RPF supporters there. Generally, the RPF could count on a good deal of support from Burundi, where many Banyarwanda refugees had settled. Besides the refugees, there were also sympathetic elements in the Tutsi-dominated security forces. In Kampala, a neighbor of Fred Rwigyema was the Burundian ambassador and the two maintained regular contact.[42] Umutoni continued these trips once the war had started and worked hard on mobilizing support in southern Africa. She visited RPF cells in Lesotho, Swaziland, Botswana, Mozambique, South Africa, and Zimbabwe and maintained contact with FRELIMO, ZANU-PF, and the African National Congress. Though these countries did not contribute directly to the RPF coffers, they allowed the organization to fundraise and helped envoys, like Umutoni, achieve their objectives.[43]

Besides her work mobilizing international support, Umutoni also helped with the political education of the troops. Though many had followed courses at the RPF schools in Uganda, not all had been able to attend. To make sure they absorbed the RPF ideology, Umutoni led two-week courses from makeshift classrooms in the Virunga Mountains. Most of her pupils were military intelligence officers and political commissars. The curriculum was composed of Rwandan history, a bit of Marxist-socialist economic theory, African liberation struggles, the reasons for the Struggle, and the RPF eight-point political program. It also included special sections on the importance of youths and women in the Struggle. Once they had completed the course, it would be the responsibility of military intelligence operatives and political commissars to pass on what they had learned to the rank and file.[44]

The mobilization of the RPF civilian support was especially important between November 1990 and February 1991. While Rwanda is close to the equator, the high altitude of the volcanoes (4,000–5,000 meters) means it can get surprisingly cold. Several volcanoes are almost permanently shrouded in a thick, humid, fog that makes the low temperatures even more difficult to bear. As Kagame himself admitted, "I'd not studied well the conditions of the mountains. You'd wake up in the morning and find soldiers frozen to death."[45] Yet it was the only place where the RPA could regroup in relative safety from the FAR.

Just as supply lines had to be established, so did medical care. While the RPA had excellent frontline medical care, it had to be integrated with hospital-level attention. This meant bringing wounded RPA troops into Uganda or, sometimes, Tanzania, and finding sympathetic doctors and nurses to operate on them. Caesar Kayizari's injury is a good illustration of this system in action. In 1991, he was shot through the jaw while leading his soldiers:

> I was operated [on] in the grass. . . . With the whole mandible gone, the bullet hit here. And shattered the bone—jaw. . . .
>
> JBK: So the [RPA] doctors were good?
>
> They were good. They were able to save life. At any cost. Even at the cost of hurting you extremely. Because if they didn't do it, I would be dead. Because I was bleeding like a pipe of water.

> I was evacuated through our short lines to the initial treatment. . . . Then it was decided [by the RPA doctor who had provided the initial treatment] mine was fatal, I had to be taken clandestinely to Mulago Hospital [in Kampala], and then they had to manage how to treat me clandestinely. . . . We had to find one managing emergencies, so that the story is falsified.[46]

After receiving treatment at Mulago, Caesar was flown to Belgium, where he was given a bone transplant to restore function to his jaw. Peter Kalimba, who was himself injured by gunfire but recovered, notes that "this [medical care] was one of our biggest weapons besides our discipline."[47] The knowledge that lifesaving treatment was readily available in case of injury was an important morale boost for the RPF.[48]

The emphasis on medical care shows the profound importance the RPA High Command placed on the welfare and lives of its troops. According to Kayizari, "[We were] lucky that our initial commanders loved their men. Loved their soldiers. They loved their people and they loved their nation."[49]

FIGURE 6.1. A forward aid station for Rwandan Patriotic Army battlefield casualties, probably in the Virunga Mountains. Courtesy of the Rwandan Ministry of Defense Archives.

This attitude among the commanders is exemplified by a story told of Adam Wasswa. After seeing an overzealous RPA attack on a FAR position, he is said to have commented that "to fight a lion with your bare hands is brave, but also stupid."[50] This caring attitude was felt throughout the organization. As a former officer explains, "It is very important to recognize the value of a soldier. As long as you communicate and they respect you, you cannot fail."[51] Foot soldiers were also aware of this attitude and adopted it in their relationships to one another. "We ate sorghum porridge every day. When there were beans, we saved them for our injured comrades."[52]

WORKING TOWARD A CEASEFIRE

While the RPA was regrouping in the Virunga Mountains, political maneuvering continued. As he now felt he had the upper hand, President Habyarimana became increasingly recalcitrant in his position on negotiations with the RPF. On 29 October, he announced in a radio address to the nation that he would "not negotiate with the rebels until they left the country."[53] This attitude was confirmed when Charles Nyandwi, the Rwandan minister for higher education who had been sent to Brazzaville, told Congolese president Denis Sassou Nguesso that the government of Rwanda would not negotiate with the RPF.[54] Thus, it was surprising when, on 31 October, it was the RPF that failed to turn up for negotiations in Zaire. Rwandan foreign minister Casimir Bizimungu arrived at Gbadolite to find that no RPF delegation was present. According to the latter, they had not come because the FAR had broken the 23 October ceasefire brokered by the Belgian prime minister. Bizimungu still met with his Zairian counterpart, who pressed that the government of Rwanda should negotiate with the RPF. In response, Bizimungu explained that this was no longer necessary because the RPA had been pushed out of Rwanda.[55]

Zairian diplomats, supported by their Ugandan colleagues, hoped to get negotiations back on track by putting pressure on Habyarimana, but their plan was complicated by the arrival of a French diplomatic mission to the region.[56] Minister of Cooperation and Development Jacques Pelletier and Jean-Christophe Mitterrand, the son of the French president, visited both Kampala and Kigali before stopping to meet President Mobutu in Gbadolite. While Pelletier and Mitterrand told Mobutu that they had urged Habyarimana to agree to a ceasefire and to change his one-party political system, it is difficult to believe they did so forcefully.[57] When the Canadian ambassador to Zaire, Claude Laverdure, visited Habyarimana a few days later, Habyarimana "was adamant that he would not talk to the RPF who, he said, were not refugees but professional Ugandan soldiers. He was quite convinced that Museveni was personally responsible for the incursion. Habyarimana recognized the need for a regional conference but said that arranging one was 'Mobutu's responsibility.'"[58]

The next round of diplomatic wrangling took place on 20 November, when Habyarimana and Museveni met for bilateral talks at Cyanika, in northern Rwanda. On the same day, the Rwandan president also met with Mobutu and Buyoya in Goma. Initially, it seemed as if both meetings had gone well, and Mobutu announced that in the plan for peace negotiations, "the accent will be placed particularly on the ceasefire and its strict application."[59] However, the next day, Radio Rwanda announced that in the bilateral meeting Museveni had told Habyarimana that the RPF were regrouping in Uganda. The government of Uganda immediately released a press statement explaining that this was "very unfortunate and highly irresponsible and consistent with the Rwandan propaganda of hoodwinking the world into believing that the armed conflict in Rwanda is an external aggression which the Rwandan Government has now repulsed. The truth of the matter is that a war is taking place on Rwandan soil as Rwanda herself admitted."[60] High Commissioner Cullimore met Museveni on 22 November to hear his side of the story. The Ugandan president explained that while the meeting had proceeded smoothly, he was under the impression that Habyarimana still thought that "Uganda could solve his problems for him." He then explained that

> he had tried to persuade Habyarimana that he should negotiate with the rebels now while the going was good. They were not seeking to overthrow Habyarimana but there had to be some kind of power-sharing and an arrangement which would allow some of them to be absorbed into the Rwandan army. If Habyarimana waited the rebels would only become stronger as their new leadership became better established and they attracted more sympathisers to their cause.[61]

Museveni also told Cullimore that while talks were taking place in Goma between the government of Rwanda and the RPF, under Zairian guidance, he did not think that they would amount to much in the face of Habyarimana's reluctance to concede anything.

Museveni's prediction proved prescient. On 10 December, the members of the US Embassy in Bujumbura had a meeting with the director general for African affairs of Burundi's Foreign Ministry, M. Niyungeko. In the meeting, Niyungeko told the Americans that even though the key parts of a regional peace plan were in place—ceasefire and observation force, regional refugee conference, direct communication between the RPF and the government of Rwanda—the plan had been rejected by the government of Rwanda delegation. The warring parties had met twice in Goma on 22 November, with President Mobutu presiding. However, the government of Rwanda delegation was unwilling to agree with a set of RPF conditions, which included public records of the proceedings, the presence of neighboring state delegations at the talks, and a formal recognition of the RPF.[62] According to US diplomats, "the GOR [Government of Rwanda] is no longer interested in a diplomatic solution."[63]

Between 11 and 14 December, General Jean Varret, who was in charge of all French military cooperation missions, visited both Burundi and Rwanda. While in Burundi, President Buyoya told him the same as Niyungeko had told the Americans: It was important that Habyarimana redouble his efforts to find a way to unite all Rwandans.[64] Buyoya was not so much concerned with the well-being of Rwandans as afraid that the violence in Rwanda would spill over into Burundi. The country was in the middle of a sensitive period, as Buyoya was seeking to mend damaged ethnic relations, and violence in Rwanda might put that process in jeopardy. Indeed, Varret noted that while Buyoya was steering a moderate course, this could not be said for significant elements of the, mostly Tutsi, Burundian armed forces.[65] When Varret met Habyarimana, the latter was still not interested in talks with the RPF. The RPF, he insisted, was being supported by Museveni, who wanted to annex Rwanda and make it "the Kuwait of Uganda" (the first Gulf War was then taking place in the Middle East).[66]

THE RPF'S STRATEGY FOR THE WAR—THE ATTACK ON RUHENGERI

It is difficult to reconstruct the RPA's grand strategy. The main problem is that it is difficult to distinguish the degree to which the RPA had a set strategy to win the war from late 1990 onward, and the degree to which RPA veterans imposed a strategic vision on the past following the end of the war. Keeping this caveat in mind there is a set of ten "Strategic Assumptions of the Struggle for Liberation" that RPA veterans and the Rwanda Defense Force (RDF) consider to have been the basic assumptions of the RPF/A throughout the war:

1. Most of the diaspora will support the RPF/A war effort.
2. The RPF will maintain its cohesion throughout the conflict.
3. The Ugandan government, and especially the National Resistance Movement (NRM) and the NRA, will provide political and military support.
4. The UN and the OAU will recognize the RPF.
5. The RPF campaign will crystallize the domestic opposition to Rwanda's ruling MRND party.
6. The Government of Rwanda will be forced to negotiate due to internal, regional, and international pressure.
7. The MRND will have domestic support through ethnic propaganda.
8. The economy of Rwanda will not survive a protracted war.
9. There will be no direct regional military involvement/support for the MRND.
10. France will support the MRND.[67]

If these strategic assumptions were drawn up before the start of the Struggle, they were indeed prescient. Of the ten, only number nine proved incorrect. Zaire did directly intervene in October 1990 and played a key role in the defeat of the RPA at that time. However, the obvious conclusion of the strategic assessments is that time would be on the side of the RPF. As long as it remained in the field, destabilized Rwanda's economy, and made enough noise to make its presence felt in both Kigali and the other African Great Lakes capitals, the Habyarimana government would eventually crumble.

By early January 1991, Paul Kagame had decided that the RPA was strong enough to attempt a major coup. The target Kagame had chosen for the attack was the town of Ruhengeri. This was one of Rwanda's most important towns because it was the heartland of the northerners who dominated the Rwandan government. It also housed a large prison, where many of the most important political prisoners were kept, and was home to a commando training center. Kagame later explained: "There were these political prisoners

MAP 6.1. The Attack on Ruhengeri and the Strike to Gabiro. (1) On 23 January the RPA (Rwandan Patriotic Army) attacks Ruhengeri and holds the town for a day. (2) From January to March 1991 the FAR (Forces armées rwandaises) and the RPA engage in a series of battles as the former try to dislodge the latter from the Virunga Mountains. (3) At the beginning of May, two RPA battalions strike toward Akagera National Park in order to relieve the pressure of the FAR attacks on the Virunga Mountains. The fighting would last until 28 May. Map by Brian Balsley.

in Ruhengeri. We understood that if we had them in our hands, it would also hurt Habyarimana's government politically and create some kind of new dynamic."[68] Another key objective was the town's bank, as the RPF was keen to use the money in the vaults to finance its war effort.[69] On 20 January, Kagame called a meeting of the High Command, where the necessary dispositions were discussed. About six hundred RPA soldiers, divided into five battalions and commanded by Fred Ibingira, Camile Ntambara, Edward Karangwa, "Maligenya," and John Gashugi, would take part in the attack. Overall operational command was in hands of Vedaste Kayitare and Ludoviko Twahirwa.[70] The next day, the rank and file were briefed by their commanders and the leading elements began moving to their designated jumping off points. Initially, the plan had been to attack Ruhengeri on 22 January, but traveling through the jungles of the Virunga Mountains was so tough that progress was slow. Small skirmishes were fought with FAR outposts at the Kinigi Guest House which was part of the gorilla trekking infrastructure. Moving as a unit was also difficult: "Our linear movement had started to break up due to darkness under the bamboo canopy, we even tried to hold onto each other's shirts in order to keep the linear movement, but this too proved very difficult and each time the line broke, we had to halt and start whistling to re-locate each other."[71] By the end of the day, Kagame realized that his troops would not be able to attack Ruhengeri that night. Instead, he ordered a halt, and it was decided that the town would be attacked the next day at dawn.

Had Kagame known what his opponents knew he might not have waited. By the end of the evening of 22 January, the FAR accurately guessed that about 400 RPA troops were heading for the region of Ruhengeri town. That afternoon the local commander had already told the sisters of the Sint-Vincentius missionary hospital to prepare for combat casualties and had declared a curfew at 13:00. Apparently, the commander also called for reinforcements from Kigali and Gisenyi.[72] The Para-Commando Battalion was in reserve in the capital as were the Gazelle ground attack helicopters. Both could be prepared for action and sent north in a matter of hours. Had his calls been heeded and the Para-Commando Battalion sent north from the capital, the RPA would have had a very hard fight on its hands come morning. However, for some unknown reason, no action was undertaken.

The attack started at 05:30 on 23 January. By 08:00 Ruhengeri was in the hands of the RPA.[73] As at Gatuna, most of the FAR garrison was quickly routed, though some posts offered heavy resistance, beginning with the gendarmes at Camp Muhoza, who were practically wiped out.[74] Those who put up the heaviest resistance were probably partly garrisoned with French troops who had been training their FAR counterparts.[75] After gaining control of the town, the RPA set about releasing political prisoners from the jail and collecting any weapons and supplies they could get their hands on. At the jail there was an unexpected setback, as the RPA were unable to find the keys to the cells. While the idea was broached to shoot the locks, it was decided that it would be too risky for the prisoners. Meanwhile, the warden had been given the order to kill the most important prisoners. They were saved by Colonel Charles Uwihoreye, who refused to carry out the executions.[76] Out of a total of about one thousand freed prisoners, three stood out for their importance: Colonel Theoneste Lizinde, formerly one of Habyarimana's closest allies; Captain Muvunanyambo; and Commander Stanislas Biseruka.

As news of the attack reached Kigali, the FAR Para-Commando Battalion was immediately dispatched to retake the town. It was followed closely by two sections of the French 8e régiment de parachutistes d'infanterie de marine (8e RPIMA), whose orders were to evacuate any Europeans in town. Habyarimana had hoped that the French paratroopers would take an active part in the fighting, but the request was turned down by Ambassador Martres. By the time the FAR para-commandos and the French arrived at Ruhengeri, the bulk of the RPA had withdrawn, their objectives achieved, to the protection of the Virunga Mountains. However, some actions did take place as the para-commandos started clearing the town of the RPA rear-guard.[77] The French paratroopers advanced closely behind the FAR in order to evacuate the European population. Martres reported the next day that "the unit commanded by Colonel René Galinié stayed within the limits of the mission parameters they were given, intervening in the residential zone immediately after the city had been recaptured by the Rwandan para-commandos. Staying within the mission parameters did not exclude a certain audacity which the French paratroopers had to display in the last two hours before nightfall."[78]

Despite the concern for expatriates, none were harmed, and the French soldiers returned to Kigali in two columns at 23:00 on the night of 23 January and at 01:00 the next morning. Besides a motley group of French, Canadians, Belgians, Egyptians, Omanis, Americans, and Austrians, the convoys were also carrying fifty-two Rwandans, including the district judge and two *sous-préfets.* The flight of these last three was, according to Martres, "a disturbing sign of the loss of confidence in the upper-echelons of the Rwandan administration."[79]

The attack on Ruhengeri was a spectacular coup for the RPF and RPA. It signaled to the world that it had not been vanquished during the October 1990 campaign and that they were able to strike at the heart of the Habyarimana regime. Within three months of his arrival, Kagame had laid the groundwork for the transformation of the RPA from a defeated force to one that could fight with confidence against the FAR. It is worth noting here that Paul Kagame's role in leading the RPA, and the RPF, to victory is more than a postwar myth. Besides the testimonies of the former RPA commanders presented above, there are also contemporaneous foreign observers who stressed the importance of his leadership. For instance, the British defense adviser who succeeded Lieutenant Colonel Molyneux-Carter wrote that Kagame

> arrived in the area of operations to find chaos; the army in disarray, morale rock bottom, the three senior commanders dead and the area of operations unfavourable, being open and devoid of cover. . . . From this mess, he marshalled his troops, identified a modus operandi, caused the RPA to rethink its battle plan and launched an intensive training programme in guerrilla warfare and tactics. . . . Kagame is clearly a charismatic leader who in the face of extreme adversity pulled his army together and has gained both territorial and political successes.[80]

* * *

Between November 1990 and January 1991, Paul Kagame and the RPA High Command laid the foundations for eventual victory by reforging a broken force. This was achieved both by adapting various existing combat doctrines to the circumstances of the Struggle and by ensuring close cooperation between the RPA and the RPF.

This chapter shows the folly of military historians who have regarded African military organization as nothing more than "tribal" or who posited that the Western way of war is the surest way to victory. Although the RPA's combat doctrine drew inspiration from a broad range of Western and Eastern military thought, the RPA High Command molded foreign theories to suit the circumstances in Central Africa. In the process it developed its own way of fighting, which relied on a combination of daring operations and guerrilla warfare, while surviving on a shoestring budget—as would be showcased in its most extreme form during Operation Kitona during the Second Congo War in 1998. Especially important is that the RPA managed to do this without relying on foreign advisers, building instead on the experiences of its own commanders in Uganda and, later, Rwanda. In the next chapter we will look at the fighting power of the FAR, and how even French support proved insufficient to make up for the sheer determination and motivation of the RPF/A.

7

The FAR

"Only Slightly Interested in the Profession of Arms," January–October 1991

SHORTLY AFTER THE FALL OF RUHENGERI, THE BRITISH DEFENSE adviser in Uganda, Lieutenant Colonel George Molyneux-Carter, was invited by the Rwandan Embassy in Kampala for a tour of the frontline in northern Rwanda. The invitation was also extended to Brigadier Mohamed Abdelramin of Sudan and Colonel Shaban of Tanzania. Between 16 and 21 February 1991, the group spoke to high-level FAR officers, including the minister of defense and the former head of military intelligence. They also visited the battlefields where the fighting had taken place in October, as well as the more active frontline around Ruhengeri, and spoke to RPA prisoners of war. After the tour was completed, Lieutenant Colonel Molyneux-Carter wrote a long report for the high commissioner in Uganda.

Any wonder about the FAR's inability to defend Ruhengeri in January quickly evaporated:

> The Rwandese military bases we saw this day [in the northeast of the country] were pathetically amateur in their positioning, tactical layout, camouflage and concealment, mutual support, state of preparedness, protection, and so on.
>
> Their tactics are incredibly poor. They do not patrol; they do not operate at night; there was no (operational) map in the infantry positions; there were no trenches, only bulldozer scrapes; there was no scrape to scrape communications trench or string/wire; there was no defence in depth. There were no radios for platoon commanders; ammunition (for

> different small arms) was heaped centrally in some shell scrapes with no identification system to assist resupply in haste at night; Machine gun fields of fire were limited to in one case 10, but normally not more than 100 metres. Only one Rwandan officer had a compass; there were no field defences beyond the circle of scrapes. No range cards were in evidence; . . .
>
> Most of the commanders drank beer during the mid-day lunch break, and many empty beer bottles lay around the positions.[1]

Nor was the disarray limited to a small sector of the front:

> At Ruhengeri town [two days later] we met Major Bizimunga who is the Commander of Operations in the Ruhengeri sector. . . . All defensive positions are situated in or near the town because it is too difficult he told us, for Rwandese soldiers to operate in the forest area. . . . GOR [government of Rwanda] officers pointed out how easy it had been for the RPF to infiltrate through their forces and therefore attack Ruhengeri prison. The GOR forces had been deployed in firm defensive bases, about a kilometre apart, in a thin line. No patrolling had been done between the positions.[2]

Whereas the previous chapter examined the basis for the remarkable recovery of the RPA under the leadership of Paul Kagame, this chapter looks at the fighting power of the FAR. It begins with a discussion of the structural problems faced by the FAR and the attempts by the French military training mission to address them. Then it will look in some detail at the fighting that took place between February and March 1991—for two reasons. First, this fighting deep in the Virunga National Park has been utterly ignored until now, despite the fact that it gives a good idea of the continuous low- to midlevel combat that went on during all the combat phases of the Struggle for Liberation. Second, this was the moment in time when the FAR and the RPA were most closely matched. The chapter will then move on to discuss some of the early, abortive attempts at peace. It will end on an analysis of the FAR officer corps.

THE FIGHTING POWER OF THE FAR

Before the start of the war, the FAR had been considered a competent force by the standards of the region.[3] It was a small professional army that did not—like the Zairians, for example—prey on the local population. Belgium had remained the main military partner of the FAR after Habyarimana took power in 1973. Their advisers continued working in Rwanda, and FAR officers would regularly receive training at the École royale militaire in Brussels.[4] Emmanuel Neretse, a senior FAR soldier, had undergone a typical path for someone of his stature. He had completed basic officer training at the École supérieure militaire de Kigali in the 1980s and then, after serving as instructor at Camp Gako, was sent to Belgium for a six-month course at the Centre des transmissions et de l'électronique at Peutie. A couple of years later further courses followed at the École d'infanterie de l'armée belge in Arlon and the Institut royal supérieur de défense in Brussels, leading to the coveted Brevet d'état-major (BEM).[5]

Yet this varnish of respectability obscured internal rot. Until Habyarimana came to power, officers in the FAR had not been allowed to have other off-duty employment. After the president changed this regulation, the quality of the FAR started to decline. Many officers took the afternoon off to work on the side, and ethically dubious businesses soon flourished. Among other outrages, FAR rations and equipment intended for soldiers were sold privately. The resulting lack of equipment made regular training impossible. Other business opportunities were also enthusiastically explored, which meant that over the course of the 1980s many in the officer corps became businessmen who were only marginally interested in soldiering. Still, considering that both France and Belgium maintained military training missions in Rwanda, one would have expected the FAR to be more capable than it was in 1990. While the internal corruption of the force must have been an important contributor, Western militaries also have a record of failure when it comes to building the structural military capacity of Third World allies.[6]

Unlike their French counterparts, Belgian advisers did not swing into action after the outbreak of hostilities, probably because of their government's reticence to get involved in what they considered a civil war. A French officer stationed in Rwanda was not impressed: "Before NOROIT was deployed [see below], the training was done by the Belgians, and honestly it was a mess. The most unprofessional, peace-time TTPs I've ever seen. Complete battalions had been slaughtered by the FPR [RPF] and the FAR units had widely lost their self-confidence."[7] The Belgian Parliamentary Inquiry concurred and found that, once the war broke out in October 1990, "'the relationship [between the Belgians and the Rwandans] cooled.' The Belgian technical and military cooperation was reduced to a secondary role. Colonel Vincent even added that the officers and NCOs did nothing ('nothing or practically nothing')."[8] Had Belgian trainers been as invested in the cause as their predecessors during the First Rwandan Civil War or Habyarimana's coup d'état of 1973, they would have pushed their training mandate to the limit. In that sense the outbreak of the war completed a process that had been underway for a long time, as France replaced Belgium as Rwanda's main military partner.

The start of the war exposed many of the problems within the FAR. James Gasana, who would hold the post of minister of defense from April 1992 to July 1993, later wrote that "a large part of the credit for the victory of the war of October 1990 really lies with the foreign troops (Belgian, French, Zairian), both by their psychological impact, and, for the Zairian troops, by their role in combat."[9] As the impact of the Zairians and Belgians has already been discussed, we will now turn to the French. From the start of the RPA attack, the role of the French Mission d'assistance militaire (MAM) changed from "instruction in time of peace to the preparation and support of forces in times of war or crisis."[10] This was well within the parameters of the treaty governing French military assistance to Rwanda. A 1983 modification of the original 1975 treaty had removed "the ban on French military to be associated directly or indirectly with any preparation or execution of military operations."[11] This change in stance also meant that at the outbreak of war several additional French officers arrived to advise the highest FAR echelons. The most important of these was Lieutenant Colonel Gilbert Canovas, of the 1er régiment de parachutistes d'infanterie de marine (1er RPIMa), who advised the Rwandan government and the chief of the FAR General Staff.[12] The Rwandans were exceptionally grateful for the help provided by the French. Colonel Léonidas Rusatira wrote on behalf of the Rwandan Ministry of Defense that "during the most difficult moments, their presence, their support and friendly counsel were particularly effective and appreciated. They played a decisive role as effective advisers."[13]

As the war went on, the FAR increasingly relied on French support. After the debacle at Ruhengeri, the French government decided to substantially raise the number of military instructors attached to the FAR. By January 1991, their presence in Rwanda was split into two elements. The first part consisted of the French soldiers of Opération Noroît. They were charged with the protection of the expat community and the French Embassy. The Noroît units had strict rules of engagement and were not supposed to fight the RPA. Nonetheless, as Colonel Thomann, commander of Noroît between 21 October and 6 December 1990, points out:

> To these . . . aspects of the mission, we must add the stabilising effect of the presence, even if not active, of a foreign intervention contingent, to bolster a power threatened by external aggression and confronted with a non-negligible risk of internal disorders, of ethnic or political origin.[14]

The tasks of Noroît units ranged widely throughout the country, from securing supply convoys to Ruhengeri and Gisenyi, to escorting the French ambassador and training the FAR at Camps Kanombe and Gako.[15]

The second part of the French contingent was the MAM, which was there specifically to increase the effectiveness of the FAR. It was subdivided into four detachments.[16] The first three were the *détachements militaires d'assistance technique* to the Gendarmerie, the army, and the air wing. Each of these consisted of about twenty officers, NCOs, and soldiers who were scattered throughout the FAR and provided training and technical expertise—especially to the FAR helicopter unit. These detachments had been in place in Rwanda since the first military cooperation agreements between Rwanda and France in 1975. In 1991 a new element was added that would become the fourth component of the MAM. The Détachement d'assistance militaire et d'instruction (DAMI) arrived in Rwanda on 22 March 1991. It was composed of about thirty officers and soldiers, many drawn from the 1er RPIMa, and was tasked with the training of FAR troops and the stabilization of the key sectors of Gisenyi and Ruhengeri. As with Noroît and the rest of the MAM, the rules of engagement for the DAMI were tight and its members were not supposed to be engaged in direct combat with the RPA. However, the spirit of the DAMI mission was different to that of the rest of the MAM. The MAM did not normally leave Kigali, but the DAMI trained FAR units in their camps and bases around the country.[17] As the DAMI was mostly composed of special forces—selected for their initiative, aggression, and endurance—it could be counted upon to push the limits of its mandate and thus formed an important part of the FAR military machine.

The additional training that the DAMI could provide was in short supply. From the start of the war, the FAR increased considerably in size. Casualties needed to be replaced, and the small peacetime force that had numbered about 8,000 soldiers was insufficient to hold back the RPA. Emmanuel Neretse—the aforementioned FAR officer who had trained in Belgium—wrote that "after 1 October 1990, in order to cope with emergencies, there was need to urgently swell the ranks to counter the RPF invasion. The training of a soldier was often done over a short period. From 15 days at the height of the crisis in October 1990, it took about 3 months in 1992."[18] He went on: "Instead of training new recruits at Gako Training Centre alone, from November 1990, a cohort of three battalions was trained in less than one month at Bigogwe Commando training centre, Gisenyi. . . . Other recruits were trained at Gabiro. . . . Unlike Bugesera Training Centre, which accommodated a maximum of three battalions only, the size of the area allowed to train many recruits at the same time."[19]

In just a couple of years, the FAR grew from 8,000 to 31,000 soldiers.[20] Most of that expansion, from 8,000 to 21,600, took place in the first five months of the war.[21] These shortened mass trainings caused the collapse in the quality of both soldiers and officers, which Lieutenant Colonel Molyneux-Carter observed on his visit to Rwanda. Therefore, one of the most important jobs of the DAMI was to retrain certain units and bring them up to a higher standard.

Thanks to the several reports sent from Lieutenant Colonel Gilles Chollet, commander of the DAMI, to Colonel Galinié, the French military attaché, detailing the progress of the different battalions, it is possible to give an overview of the problems faced by FAR units throughout the war. The commander of the Gitarama Battalion, which was the first to be retrained, was Major Singirankabo. According to Lieutenant Colonel Chollet, Major Singirankabo was an amicable officer who was not particularly interested in leading his unit. Like many battalion and company commanders, he lacked a regular staff for the battalion administration and was as a result chronically overworked.[22] Similarly, the commanding officer of 63 Battalion, Commandant Nkundiyaremye, "did not attend a single tactical training session. He did not show up in the field to check the work of his officers and soldiers and seems on the whole to show little interest in his battalion, at least as regard to their training."[23] On the other hand, Captain Ngendahimana, who commanded the 1st company of 32 Battalion, was considered both a friendly and intelligent officer whose military experience allowed him to lead his company confidently.[24] Even within the same unit, the quality of the officers could vary a great deal, as the following comparison between two lieutenants of the 41 Commando Battalion shows:

> [Second Lieutenant Ngilinshuti] Company commander . . . completed the entire officer training course in Kigali. . . . While this officer has some tactical and technical knowledge, he does not have the stature of a leader. Little aware of his role and responsibilities as a leader, he seems to be only slightly interested in instruction or in the profession of arms in general.
>
> He puts up with more than he commands, by doing and demanding the minimum.
>
> His lack of rigor in the management of his personnel and material was flagrant and revealing from the very first days of instruction. He is certainly the most incompetent and unpleasant company commander we have had to train in the past five months as intellectual honesty is not one of his qualities either.[25]

However, Ngilinshuti's direct subordinate, Second Lieutenant Nzabalinda, who had not completed his officer training, was considered "intelligent and dynamic, . . . wholly satisfactory during these two weeks. Conscious of his role and assiduous at work, he has good tactical knowledge and is appreciated by his men who he commands with a firm hand but also good cheer."[26] Despite the presence of officers like Captain Ngendahimana and Second Lieutenant Nzabalinda, Lieutenant Colonel Chollet's verdict on the officers of the Gitarama Battalion can probably be extended to most of those serving in the FAR: "In general, the officers are not very good, not very motivated and especially, don't lead by example."[27]

The tasks of the officers within the FAR were complicated by the inadequacy and general lack of equipment. There were insufficient radios, binoculars, compasses, and maps, which meant that it was difficult for several battalions, or even companies, to conduct coordinated operations. This also explains why FAR units who engaged with the RPA were unable to regularly and effectively call on their heavy artillery, sometimes as far as 10–15 kilometers away, as that requires both a map and a radio.[28]

Another problem the FAR had to cope with was its bewildering complement of small arms. Most FAR battalions were equipped with weapons that used the 7.62×39 mm Soviet round (AK-47, AKM, RPD) and those that were chambered for 7.62×51 mm NATO (Vektor SS-77, FN MAG, FN FAL, HK G3). While these rounds are of a similar caliber, they are not compatible with each other. Having both in one unit puts a strain on supply and causes confusion in the heat of combat. The practice of mixing different kinds of weapons and calibers was not limited to small arms. The support platoon of the Ruhengeri Commando Battalion was, for example, equipped with 81 mm mortars made in South Africa and the United States and 82 mm mortars made in China. The effort to consolidate these arms per unit, while blindingly obvious, seems to have only been pushed by the DAMI, rather than by the FAR itself.

However, what really worried Lieutenant Colonel Chollet and the other French officers was that the officers and soldiers of the FAR lacked any notion of gun safety. Basic safety drills, like checking whether a bullet was chambered, were unknown. This led to regular negligent discharges during training sessions that resulted in a steady stream of casualties.[29] In the worst cases this could have tragic consequences like when a FAR captain did not handle a grenade properly, killing himself and severely injuring five of his comrades.[30] Most soldiers trained by the DAMI were also unaware of how the sights on their rifles worked, or of how to carry out basic weapons maintenance. Some units had no weapons oil, while others were issued it in spray cans that were both expensive and prone to break in Rwanda's tropical climate.

As one of my informants explained, these problems were a constant drain on the morale of FAR troops:

> [Their morale was] very different according to the units. Some units, including the French-trained units, had developed a high morale [by 1992]. But the bulk was low morale, albeit disciplined and there were not so many deserters. Most battalions were [torn] between the fear they had for the FPR [RPF], the low confidence they had in their chiefs—you commonly saw units without their commanding officers, who were brown-nosing in Kigali instead of commanding their units, the poor training they had received—it was a small peace-time army that had been hastily increased with poorly trained draftees and launched in war

> operations against the FPR [RPF], whose soldiers were better trained, whose chain of command was far more involved, who acted by hit and runs, and enjoyed a wide support including artillery from Ugandan forces. So, except of some tough units, the FAR had lost the initiative, developed few [*sic*] and poor reaction and a loser's morale.[31]

THE ENGAGEMENTS OF FEBRUARY–MARCH 1991

Following the attack on Ruhengeri, the FAR was ordered to clear the Virunga National Park and its volcanoes of RPA forces. The terrain the two belligerents would spend the next several months fighting over was extremely tough. The sector of the national park that straddles the Rwanda-Uganda border is dominated by three dormant volcanoes. The westernmost is the Sabyinyo, a gnarled, craggy old mountain 3,669 meters high filled with deep caves. Then there is Gahinga, the smallest of the three, reaching only 3,478 meters. Finally on the eastern end of the park there is Muhabura. Known in Kinyarwanda as "the guide" or the "beacon" because it can allegedly be seen from everywhere in Rwanda on a clear day, it rises to 4,127 meters. These high mountains are all covered in thick jungle and are connected to each other by ridges, the most prominent being that between Gahinga and Muhabura. The tropical vegetation means that vision is limited to a dozen meters at best and navigational skills are key. There are no roads suitable for motor traffic in the national park, which meant that all the necessities to keep a fighting force operational, from food to medicine to ammunition to mortars, machine guns, and artillery, had to be carried on the backs of the RPA and FAR soldiers.

The two FAR battalions selected for the operation were the Ruhengeri and Huye Commando Battalions. They were to jump off from Ruhengeri—which at 1,845 meters is dwarfed by the volcanoes—and clear RPA troops from the two valleys between Sabyinyo and Gahinga, and Gahinga and Muhabura. This mission was considered critical because the RPA used these valleys to bring in reinforcements from Uganda.[32] On 7 February 1991 the FAR soldiers started their long, uphill climb to take the fight to the RPA.[33] It was not long before small skirmishes with RPA outposts and the difficult terrain slowed the advance to a crawl. Nonetheless FAR morale was lifted when they saw the poor state that many RPA troops were in: Kagame's men were then inadequately clothed for the cold conditions in the mountains and poorly fed.[34] This was the time before the RPF organized proper supply lines, and despite the success of the raid on Ruhengeri, the RPA was still in the process of rebuilding itself.

Over the next couple of weeks, the FAR and the RPA played a cat-and-mouse game. By 12 February, the FAR had reached the Gahinga and Muhabura volcanoes and launched several operations to find and destroy the RPA with the support of their heavy weapons. However, despite several contacts, they were unable to bring a large RPA force to battle.[35] The next day, probably to show that they were still very much alive, the RPA launched several 122 mm Grad rockets at the FAR from a position about a kilometer to the south of the peaks of Mount Sabyinyo. Normally, these 122 mm Soviet-manufactured rockets come on trucks mounted with a 40-barrel launcher. However, in this case, it seems more likely the RPA was using Grad-P single-tube launchers. Nonetheless, it was a considerable achievement for the RPA to have carried these rockets and their launchers all the way up into the mountains. The FAR responded with counterbattery fire from its 120 mm mortars.[36] On the following day, 14 February, the FAR sent out a patrol to see whether the counterbattery fire had been effective, or whether it had to hunt down the 122 mm rocket launchers and the teams carrying them. However, the RPA seems to have expected such a move: as the FAR infantry began moving up, they were exposed to heavy flanking fire and forced to withdraw to the edge of the national park.[37]

On the same day, fighting also took place on the ridge between Gahinga and Muhabura. This ridge was one of the key tactical positions in the area, and both sides wanted to control it. Because of the difficult terrain and the relatively small number of forces deployed, neither side was able to effectively dominate the crest. However, by 15 February, the FAR had had enough and ceased any further attempts to seize or maintain its positions between Gahinga and Muhabura.[38] While this technically signaled a victory for the RPA, its troops were in a very poor state. The high tempo of operations and poor supply lines were steadily taking their toll. This meant that despite their victory they would be unable to carry out any operations against Ruhengeri or Gisenyi in the near future—something the FAR was well aware of because it could occasionally listen in on RPA radio communications.[39] So for the rest of February both sides continued fighting in much the same way. The FAR still patrolled in the jungle but were limited by the RPA, which prepared ambushes.[40] Occasionally one of the sides would launch a larger operation; the FAR, for example, tried to position observation posts on the peaks of the three volcanoes while the RPA launched hit-and-run attacks to keep their opponents off-balance.[41]

At the beginning of March, the RPA was ready to resume major operations. On 4 March, the FAR position at Nyagahinga, just east of Muhabura, was overrun by an RPA attack. However, as per their combat doctrine, the RPA abandoned the position shortly afterward, presumably having captured some weapons and ammunition.[42] Between 6 and 9 March, the RPA launched several other hit-and-run attacks and 122 mm rocket strikes on FAR forces operating in the national park.[43] However, the main RPA blow fell in Eastern Rwanda. On 5 March, Yankee and Charlie Mobile Forces launched an attack on Nyagatare, an important logistics center for the FAR. The objective of the RPA High Command was to repeat the success of the January attack on Ruhengeri. The plan of attack was also similar: a night march followed by a dawn attack. As with the attack on Ruhengeri, the approach march caused problems. Careless soldiers, fumbling around in the dark, accidentally fired their weapons several times, alerting the FAR garrison to the impending attack. The FAR response was mixed. Its artillery observers acted quickly and called down a strike on the advancing RPA columns. But the RPA kept coming, pressed home the attack, and overran the first FAR lines. One of the reasons the RPA was able to push back the FAR was that many of the FAR's rank-and-file troops were too drunk to properly organize themselves. Having recovered from the initial shock, the FAR garrison counterattacked along the length of the frontline the next day. They were supported by reinforcements with armored personnel carriers who attacked the RPA in the flank. As Charlie Mobile tried to conduct a fighting withdrawal it was caught in the crossfire and lost between 80 and 145 soldiers.[44] Defeated, the two RPA units spent the rest of the day hiding in the tall grass and marshes by the Muvumba River, before slipping out of the area under the cover of night.[45] Over the next couple of days the FAR would carry out several sweeps in an attempt to find the RPA and force an engagement, but Charlie and Yankee Mobile were able to escape.[46]

While these continuous operations had military objectives, they were closely related to events on the political scene. Both sides synchronized military operations with diplomatic efforts. On 17 February, for example, the RPA's High Command exhorted its troops to keep up their efforts for just two more days. Indeed, negotiations were taking place in Tanzania at that very moment (see the next section). At practically the same moment, the General Staff of the FAR ordered its officers to explain the importance of the peace talks to the troops and the reason they were taking place.[47]

THE N'SELE CEASEFIRE AGREEMENT AND ITS COLLAPSE

Early February 1991 saw Habyarimana under pressure from several quarters. He had been embarrassed by the ease with which the RPA had raided Ruhengeri and realized that changes had to be made—despite a defiant speech made to the Rwandan parliament, the Conseil national de développement (CND), in which he declared that the FAR had the situation under control. The ministers of justice and of civil service, as well as the minister of general affairs at the presidency, were all fired and replaced. Commander Uwihoreye of the Ruhengeri sector—on whom more later—was also sacked and replaced by Major, later General, Augustin Bizimungu.[48] But the most important change was that Habyarimana distanced himself from the portfolio of security, which was now handed over to Colonel Augustin Ndindiliyimana as minister at the presidency charged with defense and security.[49] Ndindiliyimana's appointment, together with the arrival of the French DAMI, was intended hopefully to help stiffen the resolve of the FAR.

Military defeat also changed Habyarimana's mind on negotiations with the RPF. While the FAR had seemed to be on top of the situation, the attack on Ruhengeri clearly showed the balance of power was not decisively in their favor. So on 17 February 1991, on the occasion of another regional summit in Zanzibar attended by Tanzanian president Ali Hassan Mwinyi and Ugandan president Yoweri Museveni, the Rwandan president changed his bullish attitude and agreed to reaffirm the Mwanza Communiqué, which prescribed a ceasefire agreement and talks with the RPF.[50] This was confirmed two days later, during another meeting in Dar es Salaam.[51] To sweeten the deal for Habyarimana, it was also agreed that his good friend President Mobutu of Zaire would remain involved in facilitating peace talks.[52]

About a month later, the first sustained negotiations between the RPF and the government of Rwanda took place at N'Sele, in Zaire. After five days of negotiations, the two parties agreed to a ceasefire formula. The ceasefire would be monitored by a multinational African neutral military observer group, and all prisoners of war, or people jailed in relation to the war, were to be released. Furthermore, a political dialogue, which presumably would lead to a permanent peace settlement, was scheduled to start within fifteen days. Although the "N'Sele Ceasefire Agreement between the Government of the Rwandese Republic and the Rwandese Patriotic Front" was signed on 29 March, the FAR and RPA clashed violently at Mutara on 30 March.[53] Next, Pasteur Bizimungu and Jacques Bihozagara met with British ambassador Robert Cormack in Kinshasa on 1 April. During the talk, they indicated that the RPF was still willing to take part in a political dialogue, but that they did not believe the same could be said of the Rwandan government. In his report to the Foreign Office, Cormack concluded that

> Bizimungu was highly critical of the French role. . . . In fact they were guarding key points in Kigali including the PTT [postal, telegraph, and telephone service] and the Radio Station. They were also giving Rwandan troops based in Ruhengeri practical instruction in how to attack RPF positions, the French could obviously not be trusted to give disinterested advice to the GOR and he was therefore counting on countries such as Britain to put pressure on GOR to rectify the internal political and social situation. I said we had little direct influence with the GOR but had been, and would continue to be, indirectly involved through the European Community. . . .
>
> There was little in this encounter to make one optimistic about the likelihood of an early solution to Rwanda's problems. The RPF is highly suspicious of the GOR and it will take a good deal of arm twisting before the latter agrees to recognise the RPF.[54]

The RPF's motives for this visit were clearly self-serving. On the one hand, by showing willingness to proceed with the N'Sele agreement, Bizimungu implicitly denied any RPA complicity in ceasefire violations. On the other, by complaining about French operations in Rwanda, he was highlighting the bad faith of the Rwandan government. As the RPA was itself conducting long-range reconnaissance patrols into the east of Rwanda at the time, this was not entirely justified. Nonetheless, the RPF had good reason to be worried about French operations around Ruhengeri.

The arrival of the DAMI, together with the aforementioned appointment of Colonel Augustin Ndindiliyimana, reinvigorated the FAR. Toward the end of April, only one month after the deployment of the DAMI, the FAR

FIGURE 7.1. A Rwandan Patriotic Army commanders meeting in the field, ca. 1992. Courtesy of the Rwandan Ministry of Defense Archives.

launched a number of concerted efforts to flush the RPA out of the Virunga Mountains.[55] They attacked Mount Sabyinyo but were met by the RPA's Delta Battalion under the command of Charles Kayonga.[56] After hard fighting, the FAR was repulsed, but the RPA High Command decided that a distraction was needed on another section of the frontline to relieve the pressure.

Two battle-hardened battalions were selected to range deep into FAR territory and strike at targets in and around the Akagera National Park. To make sure these two units would manage to avoid detection as they descended from the Virunga Mountains, an array of diversionary attacks was launched at FAR positions around the park.[57] On 30 April, several RPA units attacked the border post at Cyanika and the surrounding area. Heavy fighting took place throughout the day, and the French suspected that the RPA was receiving artillery support originating in Uganda.[58] By 2 May, the FAR had repelled the RPA attacks and organized several *ratissages* during which they counted sixty enemy dead. As the fighting around Cyanika was taking place, the FAR noticed "numerous rebel concentrations opposite Gatuna,"[59] leading the FAR General Staff to believe an attack against the Byumba sector was imminent.

On the night of 2–3 May, the FAR in Ruhengeri started showing worrying signs of indiscipline. In their quest to quickly expand the armed forces, the general staff had promoted a large number of soldiers to the ranks of corporal and sergeant over the heads of more seasoned colleagues. The latter, many of whom had been fighting on the frontlines since October, promptly mutinied and started firing their weapons into the air to express their anger at the injustice.[60] Two soldiers were seriously injured in the fracas.[61] The trouble soon spread to Gisenyi and to Camp Kanombe in Kigali. There the mutineers detonated grenades and started pillaging the houses of ordinary Rwandans that bordered on the camp.[62] On the night of 4 May, Ambassador Cormack witnessed similar scenes:

> While I was in Gisenyi, there were explosions and gunfire which went on for about 2 hours between 7:30 and 9:30 pm. This turned out to be Rwandan troops firing in the air in some cases to celebrate promotions and decorations and in other cases to protest against not being promoted/decorated. . . . There were a good many military roadblocks between Gisenyi and Kigali and between Kigali and Gahini, but fewer between Kigali and Butare. The soldiers were reasonably polite but not always sober and were certainly lacking in military bearing.[63]

According to the Belgian Embassy, the background to this small mutiny was that FAR troops had been operating almost continuously against the RPA since October 1990. While small successes had been achieved, these had not been of a permanent nature, causing considerable stress among the FAR rank and file.[64] The situation was restored when President Habyarimana personally visited the mutineers on the night of 4–5 May. Having heard the demands of the protestors, 671 promotions were canceled on his express order.[65]

Under cover of these battles and the FAR mutiny, the two RPA battalions set out toward Akagera National Park. An RPA veteran remembers that "for the first time in our struggle, we were supplied with tinned beef and beans and plastic jerrycans for drinking water. . . . All combatants, rank and file, were very excited by this change of diet. . . . This boosted our morale as we felt that we were now treated like other contemporary world armies."[66] While the FAR suspected that the RPA were infiltrating through their lines toward Akagera National Park, they were unable to verify their information despite helicopter reconnaissance flights and foot patrols.[67] On 16 May, however, a

FAR helicopter did spot the RPA battalions close to Lake Rwanyakizinga and attacked them with its 68 mm SNEB rockets.[68] This spotting, together with other intelligence, must have given the FAR a good idea of the locations of the RPA battalions.[69] Logan Ndahiro recalls that "as night fell, on 20th May 1991, the enemy had come close to where we were hiding and besieged us. He had completely surrounded us and had mobilized Gabiro barracks for a dawn attack."[70] However, the RPA command decided to preempt the FAR and attacked in the middle of the night, catching many FAR troops sleeping in their tents. Fierce fighting continued the next day as the RPA moved back toward the northwest. In the chaos of battle, the RPA was also able to ambush several FAR resupply convoys.[71] While the FAR informed the French that the fighting had gone their way, they felt compelled to reinforce with an additional battalion the Akagera sector, which, they now believed, was the theater of operations the RPA was focusing on.[72] By 28 May, the fighting died down as both sides retired to lick their wounds.

From the available testimonies and reports, it is difficult to determine whether the battle for Akagera National Park had a definitive winner. Both sides fought hard and neither was defeated. However, the RPA was the strategic victor of the engagement. It had initiated the fight with the goal of drawing attention away from the Virunga Mountain sector and keeping the FAR off-balance. It had succeeded on both scores. The battle also shows the progression of the RPA as a fighting force. Its units could now count on more properly organized supplies and were able to go toe-to-toe with the FAR over the same terrain where they had been defeated only six months earlier. At the same time, the battle for Akagera National Park was the first time that FAR units, though seemingly not those directly engaged in combat, started showing blatant indiscipline. Instances of indiscipline reoccurred on 28 and 29 May, when FAR units protested against a new promotion system. At the same time, a Gendarmerie company in Ruhengeri protested against certain replacements.[73] Considering the divisions within the officer corps, to which we now turn our attention, it is no wonder that the troops were on the brink of open mutiny.

REGIONALISM WITHIN THE FAR

The relationship between officers in the FAR and their conduct was at the core of the organization's problems. Under Habyarimana's presidency, whatever esprit de corps had survived from colonial times was slowly eroded, as officers jockeyed for positions and privileges. The 1973 coup d'état had opened up the possibility of political power for soldiers. As there were no military threats to Rwanda until 1990, for twenty years FAR officers had little else to do but to think about how to advance their own position. Some, like Colonel Stanislas Mayuya and Colonel Laurent Serubuga, decided it was best to stick loyally to Habyarimana, while others, like Major Theoneste Lizinde and Colonel Alexis Kanyarengwe, tried to seize power for themselves.[74] However, there were many shades of gray between these two extreme positions—loyalty and coup—and by attaching oneself to a strong group of like-minded officers from the same region, or by eliminating a rival, it was possible to increase one's own chances. This is probably what happened to Colonel Stanislas Mayuya, then commander of Camp Kanombe and of the Para-Commando Battalion, when he was murdered in April 1988. According to an anonymous ICTR (International Criminal Tribunal for Rwanda) witness:

> Prior to the death of Colonel Mayuya, there was a, sort of, indiscipline in one of the companies of the paracommando battalion. Colonel Mayuya had been sick and had been taken to Belgium. He was operated on, treated and brought back, and he found that there was a rumour circulating that he had been poisoned. And while convalescing, he opened an inquiry himself. And while he was questioning people, the NCO who had circulated the rumour fled outside the country, and those who were suspected were taken to justice. And in the meantime, Colonel Mayuya was assassinated and the chief of staff decided to dissolve the unit in which that rumour had been circulating [3 company].[75]

According to Gérard Prunier, Colonel Mayuya was murdered on the orders of Habyarimana's wife, Agathe Kanziga. "Colonel Serubuga, one of the most powerful *akazu* members, organized Mayuya's murder. The sergeant who actually pulled the trigger was later murdered in jail and the prosecutor in charge of the file was murdered during the inquiry."[76] During testimony before the ICTR, Laurien Uwizeyimana—a professor at the National University of Rwanda—explained that those investigating the murder found out that it was Habyarimana's family who had been responsible, but that the president "did not dare to act against the murderers, and it was the investigators who were [jailed]."[77] Several military inquests were also launched into the death of Colonel Mayuya, and two officers were arrested, Colonel Anselme Nkilikibona and Déogratias Ndibwani, though they were eventually released without charges in 1993.[78] It is difficult to know how much credence to give to this murky tale, but what it does show, mainly because no one seems to have doubted that the murderers had come from inside the established circles of power, is that relations among FAR officers were extremely poor.

Regionalism had been important in internal politics since independence. Indeed, just before the start of the war, the then-head of military intelligence of the FAR, Anatole Nsengiyumva, wrote that

> this ill [regionalism] NEVER disappeared from the country. It is currently in full swing. It is sometimes "NORTH-SOUTH," or else "GISENYI-RHENGERI," or else "BUGOYI-BUSHIRU." . . . The NORTH-SOUTH problem is currently being exploited by certain minds who always want to create disturbances. The demands of "Southerners" are still UNCLEAR, although they consider themselves victims of a certain injustice towards people of the South. . . . From the point of view of the "Northerners" the regime is instead courting the people of the SOUTH, who are insatiable and UNGRATEFUL, while those of the NORTH are victims of this situation. They believe they should have more than they receive at present.[79]

The outbreak of war gave the perfect cover for groups of officers working together, or individuals trying to get rid of rivals. In the analysis of former Minister of Defense James Gasana:

> The mess in managing this war situation disorganised the FAR and reduced its performance. Deputy chief of staff Colonel L. Serubuga, sometimes in complicity with Colonel E. Sagatwa, took advantage of the war to marginalise officers from the South, such as Colonel Rwanyagasore, who perished in a mysterious accident, and Majors A Nteziryayo, Sabakunzi and F. Niyonsaba. He also took the opportunity to expose to death brilliant young rival officers from the north, feared for their more developed sense of the state, for their popularity among the troops . . . such as Lieutenant Colonel D. Nsabimana and Major Rwendeye.[80]

In total more than 250 officers and troops were still in jail in April 1991. Most of them were being held in the Kigali prison where they staged a strike to protest their conditions in May.[81]

Matters started coming to a head when seven officers were court-martialed in July 1991.[82] The first was Major Sabakunzi of 64 Battalion, who had been arrested for conspiracy on 2 October 1990 and was facing the death penalty. His story neatly shows how the FAR treated its own. According to Gasana, Major Sabakunzi had been accused by a FAR captain who had attempted an insurance fraud that Sabakunzi had prevented; he had not been involved in any conspiracy at all.[83] The Belgian Embassy also doubted the major was involved in nefarious activities. Despite misgivings about his guilt, Sabakunzi was beaten so badly during his arrest that he spent several days in a coma before being jailed in Ruhengeri while awaiting trial. He was in the town when the RPA attacked in January and liberated everyone being held in the prison. After he too was freed, he did not join the RPA but returned voluntarily and placed himself at the disposition of the Rwandan judicial authorities. In spite of this act of loyalty, he was only assured an adequate defense after the intervention of Professor Filip Reyntjens and the Belgian military prosecutor's office.[84]

The other six officers included Major Mutambuka, of the antiaircraft battalion, who was also accused of conspiracy, Commanders Habyarimana (unrelated to the president) and Munyagatanga, who were prosecuted for failing to carry out orders, and Gendarmerie Lieutenant Colonel Uwihoreye, who had been in command of Ruhengeri when the RPA attacked and had refused to execute the prisoners. Uwihoreye was accused of cowardice and conspiracy. Only one of the two remaining officers has been identified: Commander Kanamugire of the Gendarmerie. While all of these officers were eventually acquitted, none of them were allowed to re-join the FAR, and thus lost their salary.[85]

A couple of months later, a regional lobby group, the Amicale de Byumba, wrote to President Habyarimana to summon his help against the regionalism within the FAR. Several officers were part of the Amicale and in an astonishingly bold letter explained that

> Major Emmanuel Mugabo and Major Evariste Nyampame were sidelined from their career through incomprehensible transfers carried out arbitrarily and in an illegal manner. Some others, such as Commander Gaspard Mulindahabi and Commander Godfroid Butare, who were summarily dismissed on the eve of their retirement, Captain Pierre

> Canisius Hitimana, Lt. Evariste Bizimana, as well as Second Lt. Mukuralinda, were arbitrarily and illegally side-lined in very confusing circumstances, clearly motivated by hatred. . . . Lt. Colonel BEM Anselme Nkuliyekubona and Major BEM Gaspard Mutambuka were arbitrarily arrested and detained respectively for more than two years and more than 11 months and finally released without any formal charges being brought against them, before they were dumped on the street.[86]

The letter goes on to explain that, in several cases, life had been made impossible for these soldiers and their families after they were thrown out of the army, as they now "live in a situation of total material isolation and are deprived of their elementary social rights."[87] Some of those who had been arrested had even fought against the RPA. One of them was

> Commander BEM Emmanuel Habyarimana, who was illegally and arbitrarily arrested, although he had proven his qualities on the battlefield during almost the entire month of October 1990 in Mutara. . . . Your excellency, we believe that it is within your authority and power to find a remedy to this situation . . . which is only bringing shame to our country. Also we would like to point out that Byumba is not the only prefecture that has suffered from such injustice at all levels both within the Military and the Civil Service.[88]

The settling of personal scores by FAR officers was debilitating to the force as a whole. It meant that the energy required to command soldiers in battle against the RPA was being wasted on fighting internal opponents. It can be surmised that this caused problems on the battlefield itself, as certain commanders would have been unenthusiastic to support, or take orders from, certain factional antagonists. Parallel networks of patronage developed within the FAR, as junior officers stuck close to those who could protect them from arbitrary dismissal, undermining the official chain of command. These networks became even more pronounced and important as President Habyarimana embarked on the transition from a single-party state to what was supposed to be a multiparty democracy.

* * *

When the FAR was called to war in October 1990 it carried on its back the accumulated weight of regionalism, corruption, and indiscipline that had been building up since 1973. Although Zairian, Belgian, and later French military aid could camouflage this deficiency to some extent, the inescapable conclusion was that the majority of the FAR officer corps—the brain of any army—was, indeed, only "slightly interested in the profession of arms." The rank and file could hardly miss the fact that many of their commanders did not care about their plight. Not only were officers regularly absent, but the mass promotion that led to the mutinies of 2–6 May showed that even the general staff lacked a true understanding of the feelings of soldiers on the frontline.

While the regular FAR troops often fought well and could beat the RPA on occasion, the trajectories of the two organizations were fundamentally different. The main weakness of the RPA was material: it lacked supplies, weapons, and proper clothing for its troops. As the RPF increased its mobilization and established supply routes to RPA camps on the Ugandan-Rwandan frontier, this weakness would slowly disappear. However, the FAR faced a more difficult problem. It was able to count on plenty of matériel but lacked the "mental, intellectual and organisation foundations"[89] of a proper fighting force. This was a more existential challenge, one that would have taken a motivated officer corps years to remedy under ideal circumstances. But, as this chapter has made clear, the FAR lacked both a motivated officer corps and the luxury of time.

8

Multiparty Politics and the Battle of Agasentimita

August 1991–July 1992

ON 10 MARCH 1992 THE BELGIAN AMBASSADOR IN RWANDA, Johan Swinnen, was visited by a "Rwandan officer, charged with an important function at the general staff." The officer, whose identity the ambassador kept confidential, had come to give his opinion on the politico-military affairs in the country. Getting straight to the point, the officer explained there could be no military solution to the conflict with the Inkotanyi (a nickname of the RPF/A); the only way forward was a negotiated settlement and that would only be possible if real political change took place in Rwanda. If a legitimate multiparty democratic system was put in place, the RPF would lose much of its appeal, he argued. The sine qua non for successful peace negotiations with the RPF was internal political reform in Rwanda.[1] This chapter shows that the unnamed officer's analysis was largely correct but also that it was not shared by most of the FAR High Command. To do so it looks at the process of democratization that had been underway when the war broke out, the formation of Rwanda's first true multiparty government, and the interplay of these events with the ebb and flow of battle. It also examines two important military turning points: the Battle of Agasentimita and the RPA's Byumba Offensive.

TRANSITIONING TO MULTIPARTY POLITICS

President Habyarimana had been promising political reform since he formed the Commission nationale de synthèse sur les réformes politiques au Rwanda on 21 September 1990, and remarkable progress had been made under pressure from the war. On 28 December 1990, the commission had published its initial recommendations for a new political charter, to allow for comments from the Rwandan public. The recommendations were discussed at the MRND party congress four months later. While the intention had been to put the new charter to a referendum, it was agreed instead to pass it on to the Conseil national pour le développement (CND, Rwanda's parliament) for ratification.[2] The main change proposed by the commission was political pluralism and thus an end to the one-party state. Other clauses aimed to ensure the country's stability. Political parties had to "seek and consolidate the cohesion of the Rwandan people"[3] and were not allowed to discriminate on the basis of ethnicity, region, or religion. They were also banned from forming "militias or other similar organisations,"[4] as maintaining security was the role of the state. Habyarimana signed the charter into law on 10 June 1991.[5]

The first serious political party to emerge in this confusing climate—in which political change was promised, while thousands were arrested and jailed due to the war—was the Mouvement démocratique républicain (MDR), which published its manifesto in March 1991.[6] Harking back to President Kayibanda and his MDR-PARMEHUTU party, the MDR drew on regional opposition to the Habyarimana presidency.[7] Yet the association with Kayibanda was not merely ideological: Faustin Twagiramungu, leader of the MDR, was married to one of the daughters of the former president, and Emmanuel Gapyisi, another prominent member, to another.[8] The MDR appealed to such early successes as the abolition of the monarchy and independence and could count on strong support in many parts of Rwanda that had been neglected throughout Habyarimana's rule.[9] However, the party was divided at the core. While "PARMEHUTU" had been dropped in order to signal that the party was no longer committed to exclusionary ethnic politics, many members undoubtedly remembered that independence and the abolition of the monarchy had gone hand in hand with enormous anti-Tutsi violence. Considering the situation in the country in early 1991, and the fact that the RPF was often identified as a Tutsi organization, the MDR attracted many people with strong anti-Tutsi views.[10]

The second party to appear, mainly based in the south of the country around Butare, Rwanda's university town, was the moderate Parti social-démocrate (PSD). At its core, it had two veteran politicians, party president

Frédéric Nzamurambaho and executive secretary Félicien Gatabazi, who had both served as ministers in past governments. The party was liberal on the ethnic issue, believed in a moderated free market, and was one of the opposition groups that were not disturbed by the prospect of cooperating with the RPF.[11] Another important party was the Parti libéral (PL), a mostly urban party headed by Justin Mugenzi and his brothers. There are rumors this party was conceived by President Habyarimana himself as a pro-business outfit that would help develop Rwanda. But its liberal credentials and the membership of Landoald Ndasingwa, who owned the well-frequented Chez Lando bar in Kigali, made it popular among the Tutsi business community.[12]

For the FAR, the transition from a single- to a multiparty state was a disorienting experience. As the US ambassador in Rwanda pointed out:

> During the period 1973 to 1990 the armed forces were an organ of the one-party state. The role of the military was to protect that state, the MRND party and its President MGen. Juvénal Habyarimana. . . . The creation of new parties, for the most part in opposition to the MRND and Habyarimana, was a shock to the system. The change of the army's role from that of support and protection of Habyarimana and the MRND to apolitical protector of a multiparty state is not well understood by either the military or the civilian opposition. MRND hard-line officers see the opposition parties as a threat to the MRND, as collaborators with the RPF, and thus, as a threat to the armed forces. The opposition parties see the military as a tool of the president and his party.[13]

The importance of regionalism both in the FAR and in Rwanda's political scene meant that it was only a matter of time until they intermingled, exacerbating each other. Officers and soldiers who felt disenfranchised in an army dominated by officers from Ruhengeri and Gisenyi were automatically drawn to parties like the MDR and the PSD. This created yet another layer of tension and mistrust within the military. In a letter to the FAR chief of staff, the head of military intelligence, Anatole Nsengiyumva, makes it clear that he has been spying on soldiers with different political affiliations (note that this letter was written in July 1992, a year on from the events described here, but the dynamics it reveals probably started immediately after the advent of multiparty politics):

> In my previous memo, I talked about a subversive movement led by the *Parti Liberal* and some members of other opposition parties. . . . Commander Donat Habimana has been recruited by the PL and was said to be the leader of the team in Gisenyi. . . . [He] often attends meetings one of which was held in Lando's house. . . . Warrant Officer Ndoli . . . received a Mazda car offered by Landoald Ndasingwa (the car belongs to him). It is now driven by former Corporal Rurangwa of the Recce Battalion.[14]

After naming several more sections, which, he feels, have been infiltrated by the PL network, Nsengiyumva moves on to the second part of his report, which considers infiltrations carried out by the RPF. However, he does not make a link between the subversive movements of the PL network and the RPF. In fact, what exactly the PL network is planning remains unclear, though Nsengiyumva points out that they were printing counterfeit money and distributing pistols. The head of military intelligence concludes:

> Our soldiers have been contacted by the PL and by other opposition parties, and they are involved in demobilizing good soldiers. Those identified as such should be dismissed from the Rwandan Armed Forces [FAR]. I will strive to find tangible evidence. . . . Major Ngirumpatse and Ntezilyayo should be kept on a close watch. The G4 service of the R.A.S.H. should be streamlined, because it has been infiltrated by Major Ngirumpatse. The case of Commander Donat Habimana should be followed up closely, while Commander Bahizi should be closely watched.[15]

In sum, the introduction of multipartyism with its end goal of a democratic Rwanda complicated the already strained relations between officers in the FAR. In mid-August 1991, the French Embassy started hearing rumors of a possible coup attempt planned for the night of 15–16 August.[16] By 15 August, Colonel Bernard Cussac, who had replaced Colonel Galinié as military attaché, reported that a coup attempt would not be carried out by the RPA who, "as things stand, cannot reach the capital,"[17] nor would it come from the internal opposition, who were neither armed nor properly organized. Rather, Cussac suspected that such an attempt would come from either "young officers who can no longer stand the geographical recruitment imposed by the staff of the FAR and the incompetence of its leaders,"[18] or from elements within the army who saw the movement toward a democratic Rwanda as a threat to their privileged position.[19]

CROSS-BORDER WARFARE

After two months of relative calm following the heavy fighting in Akagera National Park in May 1991, both sides stepped up the tempo of operations in the Virunga Mountains. The FAR had managed to build a position on the ridge between two of the dormant volcanoes that dominate Volcanoes National Park. Nestled between the cragged Sabyinyo and the smaller Gahinga, the strongpoint hindered movement over the Uganda-Rwanda border, limiting the RPA's freedom of maneuver. On 21 August 1991, the RPA launched a serious attack to dislodge the FAR from the same ridge. After a bombardment by 120 and 82 mm mortars, two companies of attackers advanced through the thick foliage, which was defended by the newly DAMI-retrained 41 Commando Battalion. As the jungle in this part of the Virunga Mountains is incredibly dense, fighting took place at close quarters. By 10:00, the two platoons that had been guarding the FAR flank closest to Gahinga broke, and the RPA occupied the position. In an afternoon counterattack, the FAR managed to retake the position.[20] A week later, the RPA were back for another attempt. While the Sabyinyo/Gahinga ridge was subjected to a series of punishing bombardments and attacks, another RPA element moved around Sabyinyo in an attempt to outflank the position. Outmaneuvered, the FAR units gave up their strongpoints without a fight. However, the RPA might not have intended to force a breakthrough, since after capturing substantial amounts of material, they conducted a tactical withdrawal, allowing the FAR to retake the positions it had lost earlier in the day.[21]

After a short breather, the RPA returned for round three. The FAR on the Sabyinyo/Gahinga ridge were mortared relentlessly throughout 2 September and the following night. At daybreak the attack went in and managed to surround the FAR positions. The trapped soldiers were saved by the arrival of an additional company that proved able to cover their retreat out of the encirclement. After regrouping, the FAR counterattacked and succeeded in retaking the ridge by 17:00.[22] On the night of 5–6 September, the RPA carried out two more attempts to take the Sabyinyo/Gahinga ridge, but this time the FAR managed to repulse the attacks. Perhaps encouraged by this success, they mounted a big sweep of the area between the two volcanoes on 7 September and were able to surprise an RPA company. The latter was forced to retreat after a sharp engagement.[23]

This episode shows that, even by mid-1991, the FAR had not yet been beaten. Despite the troubles of its officer corps, French-trained units could still face off the RPA, especially when in entrenched positions. Even when pushed back, the FAR were usually able to rally and carry out a counterattack. As Caesar Kayizari put it: "While they were defeated, the FAR were good fighters. . . . You defeat him and he does counterattack."[24] The FAR were not exclusively on the defensive either and would regularly try to push the RPA out of strategic volcanoes: "Yes they did [dislodge us] not once, but several times. But we would counterattack immediately. We were determined to see who would be the winner. . . . Sometimes they would dislodge you tactically because if you hold on to territory you will have many casualties. So we would go back. Because [the FAR] . . . are getting supplies from the government and you are a guerrilla so you have to use your resources efficiently."[25]

What is clear is that RPA commanders were more creative and used maneuver to their tactical advantage, as the flanking movement around Sabyinyo and the attempt to surround the FAR on 2 September show. The problem for the FAR was that these intense bouts of fighting wore down its most effective troops. As a French officer explains:

> The units trained by the French DAMI . . . performed very well. . . . We (I mean the DAMI) taught them manoeuvre, use of battalion and company fire support, and it worked very well. But, as soon as the training was completed, the units used to be sent as "patches" or "firefighters" all over the frontline, and their routine mission was to re-gain terrain the other battalions had lost. They suffered terrible losses: I have personally seen the 33rd in April 92, it had been trained six months earlier and its remaining strength was under 300, instead of the initial 600. By our standards, a unit with 50% losses is no longer used in offensive operations but the FAR high command had no real choice and continued tasking them to heavy offensive operations.[26]

The battles in the volcanoes also prove beyond reasonable doubt that the RPA did have rear bases in Uganda, at least in the Virunga Mountains, although probably along the frontier. The Ugandan border is simply too close to the Sabyinyo/Gahinga ridge for the RPA to have been operating exclusively from Rwandan territory.[27]

Just like the RPF, the FAR did not only operate exclusively within Rwanda's borders either. From the beginning of the war, Rwandan troops had regularly violated Ugandan sovereignty.[28] While these violations seem to have been limited to bombardments or fighting relatively close to the border, the FAR eventually became bolder and also moved operations into Zaire as the war progressed. On 15 February 1991, a cable was sent from the UNHCR office in Kinshasa. Concerned with the protection of refugees on the Rwanda-Zaire border, the report stated that UNHCR personnel had heard from

> a considerable number of unrelated sources . . . that on various occasions armed Rwandese elements, both in uniform and in civil have entered Zaire over the last few weeks in search of refugees they would claim to be actually rebels. In a number of instances (four cases were cited a number of times) persons who were probably refugees were actually taken back to Rwanda by force. Mission saw on various occasions Rwandese Army vehicles with soldiers driving slowly past refugee reception centre. Various sources, including Zairean civil servants implicitly or explicitly accused Zairean army of being accomplice in this exercise, having been paid to identify and/or arrest such persons.[29]

It makes sense that the FAR, or the various Rwandan intelligence services, would have been interested in what was happening across the border in Goma, where quite a few RPA deserters, often from Burundi, had sought shelter, fleeing the fighting and hardships of the Virunga Mountains. And it is entirely possible that there were RPF cadres in Goma recruiting for the RPA or looking for information across the border in Rwanda. However, it can also be hypothesized that the FAR and the Zairian Armed Forces (FAZ) were working together, abducting refugees and then demanding ransoms for their release. Either way, the report from Lieutenant Colonel Molyneux-Carter, who was in Gisenyi only a couple of days after the above UNHCR message was sent, confirms that FAR/FAZ cross-border operations were likely being carried out:

> He [the sector commander] said there was close cooperation with Zairean troops at their common border. Indeed we met 4 Zairean officers

> in the barracks, before touring the border area. Later when I mentioned this point to Major Nzabanita, he became extremely agitated—he was remarkably angry at my allegations, but the other liaison officers with us admitted their presence and he grudgingly agreed that perhaps there were Zairean officers, but they were probably off-duty or on leave. Quite what he had to hide I do not know.[30]

Another interesting snippet comes from a confidential French cable sent by Colonel Cussac to Paris. During the fighting for the Sabyinyo/Gahinga ridge, he reported that Uganda's National Resistance Army was massing around Mbarara and Gisoro, which the FAR High Command interpreted as a sign of an upcoming RPA offensive. While the main source of this information had been a diplomat in Kampala, the intelligence had also been confirmed by a FAR special missions unit called the Commando de renseignement et d'action dans la profondeur (CRAP). The text reads: "During the night of 4–5 September, vehicles were observed on the Mbarara-Gisoro road (40 km north of Ruhengeri). (This information is confirmed by FAR CRAP)."[31] As the Mbarara-Gisoro road is at about 10 kilometers from the border, the obvious conclusion is that a FAR CRAP, probably from the Para-Commando Battalion, had snuck into Uganda undetected and gathered intelligence deep inside the country.

In mid-September 1991, the RPF and the government of Rwanda met for another round of negotiations in Gbadolite, Zaire. While both parties agreed to some modifications of the earlier N'Sele Ceasefire Agreement, there was no realistic chance of a cessation of hostilities. The RPF argued that the political situation in Rwanda had changed with the advent of multiparty politics and that they would not negotiate with a delegation composed solely of MRND members.[32] One of the reasons the RPF took such a strong stance was to help strengthen the internal opposition in Rwanda. Had the RPF agreed to officially negotiate with an exclusively MRND delegation, it would on the contrary have conferred legitimacy on the ruling party and undermined the opposition. This was a clear case of "The enemy of my enemy is my friend": although the opposition parties, especially the MDR, were not pro-RPF, they were indeed anti-Habyarimana.

By this point, both France and the United States had lost faith in Zairian President Mobutu as a mediator. There were also suspicions that Habyarimana was trying to keep the talks in Zaire alive to buy himself more time to deal with the turbulent internal political situation in Rwanda.[33] In response, the United States and France started taking on an active behind-the-scenes role to get the Habyarimana regime and the RPF talking. The US oversaw some talks in Harare, Zimbabwe, while the French invited the two parties to Paris.

Between 17 and 23 September 1991, an RPF delegation visited France to lay the groundwork. It met with Jean-Christophe Mitterrand, son of the French president and an adviser on African affairs, and Paul Dijoud, the director of African affairs at the French Foreign Ministry. The French wanted to kick-start peace negotiations between the two parties, convince the RPF that a military solution was not the best possible outcome, and "dispel any possible misunderstanding concerning the mission of the French soldiers currently stationed in Rwanda [by demonstrating] that we are friends of all Rwandans without exclusion."[34] Naturally, Kagame took exception to the last point, as his troops could hear French soldiers advising FAR units by radio intercepts. Nonetheless, he was open to a secret meeting in Paris to see if peace talks could progress to the next stage.[35] Delegations of the government of Rwanda and of the RPF would meet up to start talks in Paris 13–14 January 1992.

THE BATTLE FOR AGASENTIMITA—SECTOR CENTIMETER

RPA operations changed toward the last quarter of 1991. So far, the High Command had not been concerned with taking and holding terrain. But as the war went on and peace negotiations became increasingly serious, it was clear that having a permanent base of operations in Rwanda would significantly add to both the strength and legitimacy of the movement. The Virunga Mountains were a good place to hide and rebuild but could not be used for the new purpose.

Paul Kagame was faced with a choice of where the RPA should decide to capture territory, and then stand and fight to protect it. While the battle for Akagera National Park showed that the RPA could now face the FAR in the open, it was close, and the RPA columns had fought a mobile battle. This time that would not be possible, as the lightly rolling hills of Akagera National Park were prime terrain for the FAR armored units and helicopters. Enlarging the area of operations around the Virunga Mountains would also be highly problematic, as it would require capturing Ruhengeri permanently.

And not only would capturing the town be harder now that the DAMI was in place, but supplying such a large population on a permanent basis was probably beyond the logistical capacity of the RPF. On top of that, any permanently captured territory in this sector would be flanked in the west by the Zairian border, a strategic liability considering the close ties between the FAR and the FAZ.

This left only one option: the swath of land bordered on the east by Nyagatare and on the west by Butaro. For the RPA High Command, this was familiar ground. Its units had traversed the hilly terrain both during the strategic maneuver to the Virunga Mountains and during the preparations for, and the aftermath of, the fighting in Akagera National Park. It was also an important part of Rwanda, as it dominated one of the two main roads into Uganda. Finally, it was a formidable natural defensive position, crisscrossed as it was by small rivers, ravines, and thick banana groves.

By October 1991, the RPA had infiltrated and firmly established itself in a narrow strip of land that the troops called Sector Centimeter (Agasentimita in Kinyarwanda). Four or five battalions had reinforced the already imposing natural position. The narrow gorges were obstructed with antitank traps and riverbanks cleared of cover. Several belts of well-camouflaged foxholes and trenches were sited among the banana plantations and forests. In front of these positions, killing zones were designated that were covered by heavy machine guns and mortars.[36] The RPA again made a concerted effort to get the civilian population to leave. The High Command decided this was necessary for three reasons. First, the RPA could not feed them. Second, the RPA wanted to deny the FAR the bonus of a friendly population that could be counted on to act as guides. Third, the RPA wanted to be able to use its heavy weapons without fear of causing civilian casualties. This last point is important, for by removing the local population the RPA also exposed itself. It removed the risk for the FAR heavy artillery—which was much more numerous and potent than that of the RPA—of hitting Rwandan civilians.[37]

It had been a grave strategic mistake for the FAR to give up Sector Centimeter without a fight. Whereas it could have fought an attritional battle from an advantageous defensive position, its commanders were now forced to attack a prepared position. Considering the political importance of the sector, it was also impossible to ignore it. Despite its disadvantage, the FAR

MAP 8.1. Agasentimita and Byumba Offensive. (1) In October 1991 the RPA (Rwandan Patriotic Army) infiltrates "Sector Centimeter" and fortifies the area. (2) Between October 1991 and early January 1992, the FAR (Forces armées rwandaises) launches the "Rukokoma" Offensives with the objective of driving the RPA out of the sector. (3) From February the RPA are able to take the initiative and launch an offensive of their own. First the FAR fortifications (such as Kabuga) around the sector are dismantled one by one. (4) Then the RPA strikes toward Mulindi and Byumba, capturing Byumba on 5 June 1992. Map by Brian Balsley.

prepared "several very heavy offensives."[38] Colonel Déogratias Nsabimana was dispatched to personally lead the preparations. All the big FAR combat multipliers were deployed, including the reconnaissance battalion with its light armor, helicopters, and artillery. The latter was especially hard on the RPA soldiers. Until now, the FAR had often fired in the blind, but now that the RPA was in fixed positions, FAR gunners, supported by their French mentors, were able to zero in on their targets. Throughout October, November, and December and on New Year's Day 1992, the FAR launched a number of coordinated attacks to push the RPA out of Sector Centimeter.[39] Collectively these attacks are known as the Rukokoma offensives.

While they were all eventually repulsed, the offensives pushed the RPA to the limit. On 9 November Colonel Nsabimana's forces attacked along the frontline forcing the RPA to deploy its reserves. Then, with the bulk of the RPA now engaged in battle, several FAR units managed to force a breakthrough that threatened to outflank all of Sector Centimeter. At the last moment the RPA's reserve of last resort, the headquarter protection units, were thrown into action and managed to avert the mortal threat.[40]

Gérard Prunier, who was once with the RPF when they were caught in combat, described the FAR in the following way:

> They were heavy and sluggish. Their officers were stupid and poorly trained. The one time I was caught in combat, their tactics were idiotic; they came at us uphill, through the bush, crashing through the undergrowth, making a hell of a noise, we knew exactly where they were; their confidence, verging on stupidity, had to do with the French artillery support they had. But the French artillery was imprecise and we did not get hit. When the poor FAR came within range, they were slaughtered in one minute flat by heavy machine gun fire. They ran back downhill, leaving lots of corpses behind.[41]

While they were now on the strategic defensive, the basic combat doctrine of the RPA did not change. They conducted as mobile a defense as possible.[42] Logan Ndahiro explains:

> The battles to maintain Agasentimita were a mixture of conventional, positional and guerrilla mobile warfare. At the beginning of the fighting, we opted to be defensive (positional warfare). We could let the enemy attack us in our trenches, under pressure from their Commander-in-Chief's orders.
>
> This made him vulnerable and exposed him to our positional fire, and then when he is retreating, we would waylay him in ambushes that caused him many casualties. The objective was first to destroy and

> demoralize him while in our defensive positions with minimal losses on our side.
>
> Apart from ambushes, we used night sniping into his defences but quickly fall back to ours, sieging him, cutting his food supply routes and a number of times sending mobile forces through his defences to attack him far and behind his positions.[43]

To minimize the effects of the FAR artillery, the RPA would try to "hug" FAR troops so they could not call on their heavy guns without hitting their own troops. Another tactic involved withdrawing to secondary defensive positions after repulsing a FAR attack to avoid the retaliatory bombardment that was sure to follow. Nonetheless living under constant artillery bombardment saps morale even if there are only light casualties. During these times, RPA commanders and RPF political cadres worked overtime to maintain the morale of the troops and explain the reasons for fighting and for enduring the tireless hammering of the FAR artillery. Paul Kagame and the rest of the High Command also led by example, establishing their headquarters in Sector Centimeter to show the troops they shared their hardships. What also helped with morale was an increasingly improved supply situation. Because the RPA was now in a static position, regular supply lines could be established and maintained.

By January 1992, the FAR had proved incapable of dislodging the RPA from Agasentimita. As the FAR and RPA regrouped, Colonel Cussac summed up the just-ended year:

> The behaviour of the FAR continued to deteriorate, the serious abuses committed by "uniformed armed men" multiplied, and the repeated appeals of the French technical advisers to improve discipline and security had little effect on the ground, especially within a Gendarmerie whose deputy chief of staff appears to suffer from a permanent incapacity to improve the service of his army, unless this is the effect of a deliberate choice.[44]

RWANDAN INTERNAL POLITICS AND THE FIRST SUCCESSFUL CEASEFIRE (JANUARY–JULY 1992)

While the fighting raged on in northern Rwanda, talks had resumed in Paris 13–14 January 1992, under the supervision of the French Foreign Ministry.

The government of Rwanda delegation was led by its ambassador to Uganda, Pierre-Claver Kanyarushoke, while Pasteur Bizimungu headed the RPF team.[45] However, the RPF took exception to the attitude of Paul Dijoud, the director of African affairs at the French Foreign Ministry, and little progress was made.

The solution to the impasse came from the internal Rwandan opposition. When the new constitution had been accepted in mid-1991, President Habyarimana had appointed Sylvestre Nsanzimana to form a new government. Nsanzimana was part of the old guard: he had been a member of the PARMEHUTU and had served as foreign minister and rector of the University of Rwanda. Since February 1991, he had been minister of justice and, in this capacity, had been "instrumental in discreetly releasing the victims of the October 1990 mass arrests."[46] Because of this background, the French and Belgians hoped (vainly, as it turned out) that he would be seen as a compromise candidate.[47]

In late 1991, Nsanzimana did negotiate with opposition parties to try to form a multiparty cabinet, but they refused to join his government.[48] The MDR, PL, and PSD had formed the Comité de concertation de l'opposition to coordinate their actions. In response to Nsanzimana's overtures, they argued that the president and territorial administration still retained too much power in the new constitution. On top of that, they felt that they were operating from a position of strength. When Nsanzimana was forced to present a mostly MRND cabinet, the opposition parties organized several large demonstrations. The most important, held on 8 January 1992, drew as many as fifty thousand people to the streets of Kigali.

By mid-January, Rwandan intellectuals and the Church had made it clear that they also expected a proper multiparty government in the near future.[49] The Catholic and Protestant churches cooperated and acted as intermediaries between the Habyarimana presidency and the opposition parties.[50] Negotiations lasted throughout February and March, when a compromise was reached. The constitution would not be changed and the presidency would retain its power. However, Dismas Nsengiyaremye, an MDR member, was appointed to form a new government. On 7 April, his government was sworn in—the first truly multiparty government in Rwanda's history.

At this crucial juncture, James Gasana was made minister of defense in the new government. Gasana was a Hutu MRND man who had studied in the United States and served as minister of agriculture, livestock, and the environment in 1990–1992. He had gained a reputation as a smart, efficient manager untainted by corruption. More important, and perhaps because he was from Byumba and not from the northwest, he was a moderate. All these attributes made Gasana a threat for the FAR High Command, which was corrupt, regionalist, and incompetent. Gasana had only been in the job for two days when the first volley was fired of what would become a hostile relationship between the minister and the hardliners in the FAR. Chief of Staff Colonel Laurent Serubuga tried to divert operational information that would normally be shared with the ministry, probably to cover the setbacks being suffered by the FAR, but was caught red-handed.[51] Gasana then set a plan in motion to rejuvenate the FAR High Command.[52] The president was pressured into giving the good example, and he retired from the army on 22 April.

However, Gasana's first real test came on 29 May, when the Minister of Information M. P. Ndengejeho announced plans on the national radio for a reduction in the size of the FAR. These plans were only supposed to be put into practice at the end of the war, but the minister's address did not make that clear. This announcement, combined with the sharp defeats the RPA had inflicted on the FAR as they broke out of Sector Centimeter (see below), meant that the already fragile discipline and cohesion in the FAR snapped. Different sections of the FAR started shooting at each other in Ruhengeri, killing at least five.[53] The next day the same happened in Gisenyi, where at least seventeen more people were killed. A section of French troops had to be sent in to protect the expatriate community, one of whom was robbed in their house by mutinous Rwandan troops.[54] There were also indications that mutinies might break out in Camp Kanombe, Kigali's largest military base, and the French put the troops of Opération Noroît on highest alert. By 1 June, the mutiny had spread to the south of the country. In Butare, FAR troops sacked the stocks of the OPROVIA parastatal company, while in Kibuye other FAR soldiers robbed the local bank. "Sixteen million Rwandan francs were taken. The president of the republic asked the French Ambassador for the intervention of Noroît, but he refused."[55]

Gasana would later write that "conservative officers and politicians seized this as a golden opportunity and wanted to exploit these military mutinies to overthrow the [first multiparty] government. Aware of what was at stake I went to Ruhengeri to listen to the mutineers."[56] When he arrived in Ruhengeri, Gasana found that the local commander, Lieutenant Colonel

Bizimungu, and Chief of Staff Colonel Serubuga were unable to calm the mutineers. In the pouring rain, and without an umbrella as the troops did not have any either, Gasana listened to the problems of the soldiers. They explained that the management of the army was poor and that certain groups were discriminated against; "they even touched on basic problems such as why (and for whom) the war [was being fought]."[57] The minister of defense held several such meetings with discontented soldiers over the next couple of days, and, together with targeted arrests, these measures restored discipline throughout the FAR. Naturally, Gasana was now convinced that the entire FAR High Command ought to be sacked, and he got his opportunity on 6 June. The day before, the RPA had launched one of the decisive offensives of the war and captured Byumba (see below). Knowing that he could now count on the support of President Habyarimana, the moderates within the FAR, and the French military advisers in Rwanda, Gasana sacked Colonel Seruguba, chief of staff of the FAR, and Pierre-Célestin Rwagafilita, chief of staff of the Gendarmerie. To save face, these old-timers were technically retired for having reached the military age limit for their ranks. They were replaced with two enigmatic officers.

Colonel Déogratias Nsabimana was promoted as the FAR's new chief of staff. The US Embassy in Rwanda described him as "a complex figure. He is celebrated as one of the true heros [*sic*] of the ongoing war with the RPF, having been in command of troops in the Mutara sector since the outbreak of the war in October 1990. He is highly respected by his soldiers and, in this time of decreasing army discipline, is known as an officer to be obeyed."[58] Nsabimana had also been one of the officers in command during the fighting in Sector Centimeter, and though he had been unsuccessful, the RPA regarded him as a tough adversary. The US report did add as a final note that "he is known as a man who gives no quarter, believed to have tortured prisoners to death and instituted summary executions on the battlefield."[59] Pierre-Célestin Rwagafilita was replaced as chief of staff of the Gendarmerie by Colonel Augustin Ndindiliyimana, who was moved from his position as minister at the presidency charged with defense and security. Ndindiliyimana was "well respected in and out of the armed forces, and generally considered to not have used his positions of power to enrich himself."[60]

Gasana did not rest with the sackings of Serubuga and Rwagafilita. He also set his sights on the other two officers of the old guard: Colonels

Théoneste Bagosora and Elie Sagatwa. Nevertheless, these two officers still enjoyed the support of the president and managed to extend their contract by one extra year. However, Gasana made sure that Bagosora did not hold another operational command. Instead, he was employed as a civilian as chief of staff in the Ministry of Defense.[61]

The relationship of Colonels Nsabimana and Ndindiliyimana with the president and with the hardliners in the army is difficult to pin down. Both seem to have enjoyed the support of President Habyarimana, Prime Minister Nsengiyaremye, and Minister of Defense Gasana.[62] By promoting two younger officers, Habyarimana was able to sideline two members of the old guard who had built their own networks within the FAR and might pose a threat now that Habyarimana had himself fully withdrawn from the armed forces. Gasana would have preferred to have Colonel Gatsinzi as FAR chief of staff, but Habyarimana refused.[63] Regionalism might have played a role here. Nsabimana was from Ruhengeri, in the northwest, whereas Gatsinzi was from the south of the country. Having one southern officer might have been acceptable to the president, but two—Ndindiliyimana was also from the south—would have been too much. Despite his best efforts, Gasana was unable to make an immediate impact on the fighting power of the FAR (as we will see below), but by sidelining several of the most hard-core elements he had made an impressive start.

The change in government did make a real and immediate difference to the peace negotiations. The new Foreign Minister Boniface Ngulinzira traveled to Kampala to meet vice chairman Patrick Mazimhaka, one of the RPF's top political cadres, on 24 May. They agreed that formal negotiations would open in Paris two weeks later. There were two major differences between the negotiations conducted in Paris on 6–8 June and those that had taken place in January. First, the government of Rwanda was now represented by Ngulinzira instead of Kanyarushoke. Second, the French facilitators and US observers stayed out of the details of the talks. We are, however, privy to the details because of a report that the British ambassador in Paris, Ewen Fergusson, wrote to the FCO:

> The French and Americans left the Rwandans, speaking Kinyarwanda, to it, after the opening ceremony. . . .
>
> Although the talks did not produce much in terms of substance, they effectively launched the peace process. The mechanics of talks are now established, the next round being scheduled for 10–12 July in Zaire

> or Tanzania. . . . Equally although Mobutu (still in France) formally remains the mediator, his role is not active at this point.[64]

Fergusson added an interesting note on the French take on the situation in Rwanda:

> The Quai [d'Orsay, the headquarters of the French Ministry of Foreign Affairs] added that the RPF would, in any case, never accept to share power with Habyarimana: he had been forced to join these talks by growing pressure and the RPF had seized the chance as part of a two-pronged approach—the other prong being military. . . . The Quai stressed that the different interest groups within Rwanda and even inside the GOR and armed forces were numerous and it was impossible to know who was plotting with whom.[65]

It is worth briefly discussing why the July 1992 ceasefire was the first to be successful. While an extensive literature has developed on the point at which belligerents are ready to negotiate, German military philosopher Carl von Clausewitz was among the first to get to the heart of the issue: "There are two considerations which as motives may practically take the place of inability to continue to contest. The first is the improbability, the second the excessive price, of success." He continues, "As war is no act of blind passion, but is dominated by the political object, . . . the value of that object determines the measure of the sacrifices by which it is to be purchased. . . . As soon, therefore, as the required outlay becomes so great that the political object is no longer equal in value, the object must be given up, and peace will be the result."[66]

Unlike many others, including perhaps President Habyarimana himself, the new multiparty government understood that the chance of success in the war against the RPF was too small to continue the conflict. In part this was precipitated by the RPA's success in the field, which had become obvious by spring 1992. This had dispelled the idea, brought about by the RPA's defeat in October 1990, that the FAR could win the war. However, more important, before Nsengiyaremye, Gasana, and Ngulinzira took up their respective roles, there was no one within the political establishment who grasped that reality and could drive it home.

For the RPF a peace agreement made sense on several levels. It was now on the front foot militarily and negotiating from a position of strength. The

RPF was now also talking with a different partner, not the Habyarimana regime as such, but the multiparty government that also included the political opposition. Leaving these new interlocutors with a good impression would be key in the quest to depose Habyarimana. Finally, there was the constant specter of French military intervention, which could swing the balance of power from the RPA back into the hands of the FAR.

However, we should not underestimate the possibility that previous ceasefires had probably failed partly because they had been implemented too soon after having been agreed upon by diplomats. In a war where communications of both sides were far from perfect, it took time for the FAR and the RPA—especially maneuvering or forward units—to receive news from their respective high commands. So, matters were handled differently this time. A temporary truce would go into effect on 19 July at midnight; the ceasefire itself would follow on 31 July. This left both sides a good three weeks to inform all units and soldiers of the impending ceasefire and wind down combat operations. It was also agreed that if the ceasefire held, both sides would meet to start proper political negotiations in Arusha at the start of August.[67] With a clear path to a ceasefire followed by proper negotiations now mapped out, both sides redoubled their efforts on the battlefield to gain as favorable a position as possible.

THE RPA'S BYUMBA OFFENSIVE (JANUARY–JULY 1992)

While complicated internal political maneuvers were going on behind the front line, the war entered a crucial phase. It is important to keep in mind that the internal rivalries and mutinies within the FAR described above directly impacted its fighting power vis-à-vis the RPA.

With the FAR on the back foot after its failed offensives on Sector Centimeter in late 1991, it was the turn of the RPA to launch a series of attacks. The first objective was to break out of Sector Centimeter and the ring of defenses the FAR had thrown up around it. This defensive line consisted of a series of mutually supporting fortified hills that were supposed to keep the RPA hemmed into Sector Centimeter and prevent any breakout. Crucially, while the hills were well protected, they were not physically linked by a continuous belt of trenches or fighting positions. This meant that the RPA was able to infiltrate through the defensive line under cover of darkness, a key weakness that Kagame and his staff would ruthlessly exploit.[68]

After making the necessary preparations, the RPA started its attack around the end of February. The linchpin of the defensive line was a position on a hill close to Kabuga. It was surrounded by land mines, and the FAR had created killing grounds by using bulldozers to clear anything that might serve as cover to an attacker. Realizing that a frontal attack on such a strong position would cause heavy losses, the RPA decided to envelop the strongpoint and starve out the defenders.[69] At first, RPA patrols, conducted under the cover of night, infiltrated past Kabuga with the mission to scout approaches that were not under the guns of FAR positions on neighboring hills. They would then lay ambushes for supply convoys headed for the garrison. Gradually the noose was tightened until an iron ring surrounded Kabuga. Meanwhile, other RPA troops continuously harassed the defenders on top of the hill with mortars and small arms fire. While the RPA was able to replace the troops surrounding and harassing the strongpoint, the defenders did not have the same luxury. After a couple of days, the conditions in the strongpoint became hellish. Water and food ran out. The troops were forced to stay in their foxholes all day and all night, under the hot equatorial sun, relieving themselves where they stood. Injured soldiers could not be evacuated, their cries and groans demoralizing their impotent comrades. The dead could not be buried. Slowly, individual soldiers started deserting their positions.

Three attempts were made by the FAR to relieve the position from the outside, but only one managed to get through to Kabuga. While the relief brought in fresh troops and some supplies, they did not manage to significantly alter the tactical situation as the corridor that they had opened to push through to Kabuga was quickly sealed off again by the RPA. After seven days, the RPA, which was listening in on FAR communications, heard the High Command pass on the message to the commander of the Kabuga garrison that they would not be relieved from the outside and that their only chance was to attempt to break out themselves. Instead of surrendering, the garrison did try, with great bravery but against common sense, to break out. Most of them were killed trying to fight their way out of the encirclement, but a few did manage to get through.

Over the following month, the RPA systematically rolled up the rest of the FAR defensive positions. The positions around Gashenyi, Bushara I, Bushara II, Mutojo, Runyinya, and Mabare fell one after the other.[70] Bounding forward from this success, the RPA launched two more offensives in quick succession. The first, at the end of May, extended the western flank of Sector Centimeter. By attacking here, the RPA cut off one of the main roads from Rwanda to Uganda and also captured the Mulindi Tea Factory and Plantation. On 2 June, the tea plantation, which is situated on a hill overlooking the Kigali-Katuna road, was captured. From then on, it would become the permanent headquarters of the RPA.

Only three days later, the RPA High Command unleashed one of the most decisive attacks of the war. Advancing out of Sector Centimeter, several RPA battalions moved on Byumba, which was captured on 5 June 1992. As with the capture of Ruhengeri eighteen months earlier, the RPA raided the town before withdrawing back onto the surrounding hills. The next day, two FAR battalions reoccupied the town and started to thoroughly pillage it. French troops from Opération Noroît, which had been sent to evacuate expatriates, noted in their operational diary that "Byumba is occupied by the FAR who plunder the city centre. . . . The FAR continue to sack the downtown stores despite the presence of Noroît."[71] Two days later, on 8 June, heavy fighting was still taking place around the town, with the FAR Para-Commando Battalion trading blows with the RPA along the entire Kiyombe-Mukarange line.[72] Even though their comrades were engaged only kilometers away, "the looting of the city centre by the FAR continued."[73]

For the rest of the month there was heavy fighting as each side tried to improve their position. By 19 June, the FAR was on the edge of total collapse. The Ruhengeri Battalion, one of those sent to reinforce Byumba, which had been holding a position to the west of the town, started retreating toward the hamlet of Base. It was rallied the next day by the intervention of the FAR General Staff, but the situation remained critical.[74] Once more, it was the French who helped stabilize the situation. Colonel Jacques Rosier, the commanding officer of the 1er RPIMa, had helped conduct an assessment of the FAR on behalf of the French État-major des armées (EMA). He had concluded that it was lacking in three aspects. First, the FAR did not possess a capable cadre of commanders. Second, it did not possess mobile reserves that could be quickly deployed to threatened sectors to bolster defenses or conduct counteroffensives. Third, it lacked the firepower to stop RPA attacks in their tracks.[75]

Days after handing in this report, Rosier was made operational commander in Rwanda. His top priority was to get a battery of 105 mm howitzers, which France had donated to the FAR, operational. Between 22 and 25 June, twenty-five French advisers from the 35ᵉ régiment d'artillerie parachutiste arrived together with two 105 mm howitzers and at least 10 tons of ammunition to set the process in motion.[76] The advisers also helped to bring the other Rwandan field artillery battery up to fighting trim. It consisted of the heaviest guns in the FAR arsenal: 122 mm Soviet-designed D30 howitzers.[77] Rosier also supported the promotions of capable officers, like Nsabimana and Ndindiliyimana, to replace their notoriously incompetent colleagues.[78]

While the French worked desperately behind the scenes, the RPA maintained its high tempo of operations. On 26 June, it attacked on the Mukarange-Miyove axis but was pushed back. By 1 July, there were rumors that the Ruhengeri Battalion had again broken.[79] The next day, 51 Battalion, which had suffered such heavy casualties that it was combat ineffective, was dissolved and its remaining elements distributed over other units.[80] On 4 July, the troops of Opération Noroît reported a "worrying situation around Byumba. The RPF is present within a 3 kilometre radius north of Byumba. The FAR authorities in the area request the intervention of French troops, especially the 105 mm guns."[81] Shortly thereafter, on 6 July, the Para-Commando Battalion, which was still holding its positions to the north of Byumba, was attacked at dawn. Reinforcements were rushed up at the end of the day, and the situation was again stabilized.[82]

By 8 July, Rosier judged the 105 mm battery to be capable enough to be committed to the fight and it started bombing RPA positions around Byumba.[83] The effect was immediate. One of the first targets to be hit was the headquarters of Delta Mobile Force, the RPA unit that had been fighting against the FAR Para-Commando Battalion. An RPA officer who was present described the bombardment:

> It was during one of these meetings taking place at Delta Mobile Force headquarters at Mukarange that, at around 5 pm, the enemy started shelling our position. This shelling [was] the first of its kind in terms of intensity and the heaviest we had ever encountered so far. . . . Every one of us, including our commanders was thrown into panic. The shelling caught us by surprise and . . . targeted our combatants' trenches/*handakis.* As there was no cover to go to, some of us who were in the meeting, thus not in trenches, found ourselves prone to the shells shrapnel. . . .

> All Senior Officers present wondered what type of medium range artillery had been used in this shelling. . . . Later on, we learnt that it was 105 mm medium range artillery piece operated in batteries by the French. . . . We later nicknamed this medium-range artillery "*dimbahasi*" due to its impact on explosion that caused earth tremors.[84]

Colonel Rosier felt that a limited counterattack in the Byumba sector, with the support of the heavy guns, would help restore the morale of the buckling FAR.[85] However, he had overestimated the FAR's fighting power:

> On D-day everything went well in the morning (after the snack) until noon (soup time).
>
> Thereafter, the momentum was broken under the pretext of a lack of ammunition. . . . I drew the conclusion that any lost ground would be irretrievable and that, were we to leave, the worst was to be feared militarily. The FAR were undergoing war rather than waging it. The organisation remained desperately frozen despite my advice. I had to impose that the batteries would not be dispersed all over the front. And I indeed felt that the idea of a reserve, although politely welcomed, struggled to establish itself.[86]

* * *

On 30 July 1992 both sides ceased fire for the first time since the start of the war. The RPA held the upper hand, though its troops and commanders must have been exhausted after a long period of combat. It had accomplished its objective of conquering an important part of Rwanda and would thus be able to conduct the forthcoming negotiations from a position of strength. One of the moments most symbolic of the RPA success was when its political leadership crossed into Rwanda on 7 June and settled in at the Mulindi Tea Plantation. It was the first time that the RPA High Command and the RPF political leadership were unified on Rwandan soil. The FAR, on the other hand, had been defeated. It had been unable to push the RPA out of the country and faced enormous internal problems. However, it was now led by a capable minister of defense and two new chiefs of staff. How successful their attempts at reform would be is the subject of the next chapter.

9

A Struggle for Peace

July 1992–March 1993

SINCE THE START OF THE WAR, RWANDAN TUTSI HAD BEEN subjected to ethnic violence. As had occurred during the Social Revolution and the lead-up to Habyarimana's 1973 coup d'état, political instability was used by extremists within the government to kill thousands of Tutsi in local massacres throughout the country. The Genocide itself started on 7 April 1994, but ethnic violence was a regular occurrence from October 1990 onward. The first recorded ethnic attack after the outbreak of war occurred on 11 October 1990 at Kibilira, between Gitarama and Ruhengeri. Using the recent invasion to stoke the fires of fear, the *bourgmestre* (mayor) pointed to the local Tutsi as accomplices of the RPF. At his instigation, the *commune* secretary, the local head of the MRND, and various other Hutu notables of Kibilira killed "at least 348 people," burned fifty houses, and destroyed or pillaged "nearly all the farm animals, food reserves and household furnishings."[1] In some "sectors," roughly the same as a rural municipality, people stood up to the killers. Sector leaders in Ntaganzwa and Longi protected their people, and in the sector of Rugarama, the Tutsi organized themselves on the crest of an uninhabited hill and managed to keep their attackers at bay.[2] A local priest telephoned the papal nuncio and the French and Belgian embassies for help. According to the human rights association ADL (Association rwandaise pour la défense des droits de la personne et des libertés publiques), the Belgians responded first, informing the presidency of the slaughters.[3] In turn, the presidency sent the prefect of Gisenyi to stop the killings. When he arrived on 13 October, together with four gendarmes, the killings immediately ceased. While some people were arrested, the Gisenyi public prosecutor later told investigators that he did not have the resources to investigate the killings. Those who had been arrested for the murders were released after four weeks.[4] Although it is unclear whether the public prosecutor truly lacked the resources to investigate the massacre or he was told not to pursue the matter, the outcome is that those responsible for the 350 deaths walked free.

This chapter deals with two interwoven themes. One is the use of ethnic violence since the start of the Struggle for Liberation on 1 October 1990. The other is the start of the Arusha peace negotiations. Normally peace talks are carried out between two parties to end a war, but those held at Arusha were atypical. As previously noted, the "game was not two-sided as the later tragic events in Rwanda have tended to make onlookers believe, but in fact three-sided, between the Habyarimana regime . . . the internal opposition . . . and the Tutsi exiles [RPF]."[5] Within this three-sided struggle, there were two main conflicts: the military confrontation between the RPF and the Rwandan government, and the wrangling over the path to multiparty democracy between the domestic opposition parties (MDR, PSD, PL) and Habyarimana's MRND. Although these two conflicts had different origins, the objective of the Arusha peace negotiations was to solve both in one fell swoop.

For the extremists in the MRND and the new Coalition pour la défense de la République (CDR)—a mix of reactionary army officers and ethnic hardliners—the success of multiparty reform was as much of a threat as the RPA's military challenge. However, because of the strength of the internal opposition parties and international pressure, there was little the extremists could do to prevent political change. So they followed Clausewitz's dictum and continued their politics by other means. Their weapon of choice was ethnic violence.[6] Initially ethnic violence was used as it had been during the Social Revolution. It was a method for punishing the RPF—caricatured in Rwanda as an external force of invading Tutsi hellbent on restoring their "feudal" monarchy—by killing Tutsi within the country. However, this rather crude, though historically familiar, pattern changed as it became clear that it would not stop the RPF. As time went on, the killings were increasingly used to undermine the process of political change in Rwanda and, by extension, the Arusha negotiations. In this sense the Tutsi in Rwanda were used like an enormous pool of hostages, to be killed and abused in the pursuit of the political goals of an extremist segment of the Rwandan elite. However, the moderates were not helpless in the face of this violence. Dismas Nsengiyaremye's multiparty government tried to use its influence to push for a successful conclusion of the peace negotiations, which would open the door to democratic elections. While such an election might not have spelled the end of the MRND, it would at least have allowed mechanisms to be put in place that would have severely curtailed the power of the extremists.

To set the scene the chapter starts with a brief overview of ethnic violence from the start of the war, before moving on to the Arusha peace negotiations. My account will help disprove the widely held belief that Rwanda was a country of "systematic, centralised and unconditional obedience to authority."[7] In this view, President Habyarimana, and Kayibanda before him, are seen as figures with absolute authority whose will invariably became policy.[8] The main problem with this characterization is that it robs all other elements of Rwandan society of their agency. A close reading of existing sources shows that agency and individual initiative were present throughout Rwandan society, both for good and ill. The internal opposition, led by Prime Minister Nsengiyaremye, tried to change the country for the better. Hundreds of thousands of people joined the MDR, PSD, PL, or other opposition parties. Rwandan human rights organizations carried out daring research that rejected the government's official narrative time and again; and dozens of journalists, among them the Catholic Priest André Sibomana, defied the message of hate spread by their Hutu Power colleagues.

ETHNIC ATTACKS

The second bout of large-scale killings also took place in the northwest of Rwanda. The Bagogwe are a Tutsi subgroup who were harassed from the first days of the war.[9] Already in late 1990, local authorities had stripped many of them of their possessions or else arrested them without reason.[10] However, when, on 23 January 1991, the RPF attacked and briefly captured Ruhengeri, one of the most important cities in the area, the Bagogwe were targeted for their supposed role as RPF accomplices. Immediately after the attack Ambassador Johan Swinnen reported, "There are rumours of ethnic violence in the prefectures of Ruhengeri and Gisenyi." During both the counterattack on Ruhengeri and the mopping up operations the next day, "the Rwandan para-commando battalion took no risks when it came to real or alleged rebels."[11] Eric Gillet and André Jadoul, two Belgian lawyers who investigated the attacks in 1992, wrote in their report that the "killings were rapidly of such a magnitude that it was possible to speak of massacres or even genocide. Very soon, numerous lists of victims were circulated."[12] In Mukingo commune, the police and forest guards, with the assistance of the teachers and director of a local school, were ordered by the burgomaster to round up the local Bagogwe, whom they then "killed . . . with stones, spears, sticks and guns."[13] One eyewitness explained:

> At that time, around 1991, it was mainly soldiers and senior officials like Kajelijeli [the burgomaster] who would say they are taking these people [Bagogwe] for detention but actually they took them for massacres. . . . When they were taken away, we were there. We watched it happening, as they were taken to the *communal* detention cells. They disappeared afterwards. And anyway, people like Kajelijeli said that these people have to be killed. And they—first of all, they were taken into detention but at night they would take them, massacre them, and throw them into big pits.[14]

The houses and possessions of the dead were pillaged. Around the same time, on 27 January 1991, the burgomaster of Kinigi, Thaddeé Gasana, had his henchmen kill between thirty and sixty Bagogwe, some of whom were buried in a mass grave behind his house, which was later found by the International Commission of Investigation on Human Rights Violations in Rwanda.[15] Just days later, on 2 February, another sixty people, this time residents of Gaseke and Giciye, were killed by gangs encouraged by the authorities and supported by the police. Only one perpetrator was arrested and brought before a judge.[16] There were similar attacks in the northwest around 4 February, in Mutara, Kanama, Rwerere, and the city of Gisenyi, as well as in Kanzenze, in the south. The attacks on the Bagogwe lasted about a month and a half but because of the region where they occurred, close to the frontlines and in the heartland of the northern clique, it took a long time for news to get out. It is unclear how many Bagogwe were killed, though most estimates count at least three hundred. The International Commission of Investigation on Human Rights, the report by Gillet and Jadoul, and the Associations rwandaises de défense des droits de l'Homme all agree that the anti-Bagogwe violence was genocidal in intent.[17]

The speed with which the ethnic killings started after the outbreak of war is one of the strongest indicators that the popular memory of the Social Revolution—the acceptability of killing Tutsi and the associated impunity—was still alive in Rwanda. Kibilira was about 100 kilometers from the frontline and after only eleven days of war there was no reason to target Tutsis in the commune other than as an echo of the traditional reaction to Inyenzi. These attacks were in essence revenge for the reverses suffered by the Rwandan government. We will now look at a different, premeditated attack, with a clear objective: to undermine the development of a multiparty system in Rwanda.

On 1 March 1992, a large Parti libéral (PL) rally took place in Nyamata, the main city of the Bugesera region, to the south of Kigali. Justin Mugenzi, the founder of the party, and François Gahima, the local leader, were both in attendance and accused the MRND mayor, Fidèle Rwambuka, and the subprefect of various misdeeds. At the end of the rally, both the mayor and the subprefect made it clear that they would seek revenge. The next day an anonymous pamphlet was distributed that attacked the PL leaders and "called the local population, especially youngsters, to be on guard against these 'bandits who hold you hostage under the pretext of democracy.' The tract concludes 'they may not escape us.'"[18] On 3 March 1992, Radio Rwanda broadcast a report which warned that Tutsi were going to kill notable Hutu.[19] The night after this warning, attacks and killings started throughout Kanzenze; over the following five days, about three hundred people were murdered.[20] A further fifteen thousand fled their homes. The authorities had been apprised of events as early as the afternoon of 4 March, when Monique Mujawamariya, a human rights activist working for ADL, called the commander of the local military base at Gako to warn him that people were being killed.[21] By 6 March Belgian ambassador Johan Swinnen had been informed of events by the White Fathers, a missionary society operating in the region. The missionaries told the ambassador that local authorities were doing nothing to stop the killing, and that gendarmes were trying to force people who had taken refuge in churches to return to their homes, "back into the arms of the agitated Hutus." That evening Swinnen called the FAR chief of staff, Colonel Serubuga, no fewer than four times, "to encourage him to take effective actions such as deploying Rwandan soldiers or gendarmes." He was told by the duplicitous colonel that "orders had been given to the military Camp Gako . . . to actually intervene."[22]

The next morning Swinnen headed for Nyamata, where he arrived on 7 March. He first stopped at the Nyamata church and as the most important missionaries in the area were his compatriots, he was able to get a great deal of information on the situation:

> At the moment of my visit (from noon to around 17H00) the refugees kept streaming in, many with mattresses, personal belongings . . . in total one could already estimate around 4,000 to 5,000. . . . In the apothecary dozens of heavily and less badly injured were being treated. I could count 15 bodies, including two women and a boy of about eight. Most of the dead were the elderly who had not been able to flee. All victims had been horrifically attacked with machetes, sticks . . . mostly to the head.[23]

According to Swinnen, there was no doubt that the provocative anonymous pamphlet had been written by the municipal authorities themselves. Both he and the French ambassador, Martres, were shocked by the slow response of the FAR and the Gendarmerie.[24] Most of the witnesses he spoke to explained that, on the night of 6–7 March, gendarmes and soldiers had stood by impassively or had even acted in concert with the killers. After the ambassador returned to Kigali, he spoke with several opposition figures. On 8 March, he was visited by PL leader Mugenzi himself. Mugenzi claimed that the attack had not been a spontaneous outbreak of violence by Hutu peasants against their Tutsi neighbors, but that elements of the MRND youth militia, the Interahamwe, had been specially mobilized from Kigali.[25] Swinnen would later be told by a FAR colonel with MDR sympathies, Anselme Nhizirungu [Nshizirungu], that soldiers had taken active part in the killings, some dressed in civilian clothes and wearing MRND hats.[26] Again, as with the cases in northwestern Rwanda, no one was prosecuted for the killings. Although the French soldiers of the 2^e^ RIMa launched a two-day relief operation for the Tutsi refugees following the Bugesera massacres—during which they distributed food and blankets to six hundred people in the parishes of Nyamata and Rilima—they had not intervened during the massacres themselves.[27] Yet the French had several hundred troops in Kigali that could have swung into action on 7 March, the day Ambassador Swinnen reached the area.[28]

Following the killings in Nyamata, Ambassador Swinnen became increasingly concerned about the situation in Rwanda. On 8 March, he warned that the troubles should be rapidly brought under control to prevent them from spreading throughout the country.[29] He also sent several cables to Brussels, explaining that informants were communicating knowledge of a "secret general staff charged with exterminating the Tutsi in Rwanda."[30] Besides several people close to the president, this "general staff" was alleged to have close contacts with the Rwandan secret service, the Service central des renseignements (SCR), and the National Academy of the Gendarmerie in Ruhengeri. According to Swinnen's informants, this secret body could count on special teams made up of selected gendarmes in training, a hard core of Interahamwe who had received military training, as well as the Interahamwe's rank and file.

THE ARUSHA NEGOTIATIONS

Following the July 1992 ceasefire, the RPF and the government of Rwanda conducted protracted peace negotiations in Arusha, Tanzania. The negotiations centered around five topics: the rule of law, power sharing in a broad-based transitional government, the resettlement of Banyarwanda refugees currently outside of Rwanda, the integration of the FAR and the RPA, and miscellaneous issues, which would be discussed one by one. Once consensus had been reached on the different matters, they would all be combined into the final peace treaty.

The Tanzanians acted as facilitators throughout the Arusha negotiations, with Ambassador Ami Mpungwe taking the lead. Moving the negotiations out of the sphere of influence of President Mobutu of Zaire changed the atmosphere of the talks. Tanzania was a stable country, and its troops had not been involved in Rwanda during the war. In addition, while sitting president Ali Hassan Mwinyi was not sympathetic to the RPF, former President Julius Nyerere, a giant of African liberation movements and still influential behind the scenes, was squarely in its camp. The Tanzanians were also experienced with this type of negotiations. They had been involved in conflict or conflict mediation in Nigeria, Mozambique, Angola, Namibia, Zimbabwe, and South Africa. They prepared properly, as Ambassador Mpungwe explains: "We did a lot of studying about Rwanda, the conflict, the historical and contemporary dynamics of what was happening."[31]

The international community played an important role during the Arusha negotiations, as it had during the fighting. Especially interesting are the roles of France and Uganda. Both had observer status at the talks and supported their allies. However, both were also growing tired of the war and used their leverage to cajole the RPA and the Rwandan government into agreements.[32] Other observers were the Organisation of African Unity, the United States, Belgium, Germany, Zimbabwe, Burundi, Zaire, and the United Kingdom.

While the negotiations were straightforward for the RPF—whose aim was to obtain as advantageous a peace deal as possible—that was not the case for the delegation sent by the government of Rwanda. Within the multiparty government, three men were fully committed to the stipulation of peace with the RPF: Prime Minister Dismas Nsengiyaremye (MDR), Minister of Defense James Gasana (MRND), and Foreign Minister Boniface Ngulinzira (MDR).[33] All three envisaged a peace encompassing not only an agreement with the RPF but also a normalization of relations with Uganda.[34] The US ambassador in Kigali noted after a meeting with Gasana and Ngulinzira that "the intention to sign a peace treaty with the RPF and to negotiate separately with Uganda are two important departures from the position of the former government that should open new avenues of discussion for all parties."[35] The problem faced by the "doves" was that significant factions within their government, the MRND, and the FAR supported neither the idea of talking with the RPF nor that of normalizing relations with Uganda.

The first part of the negotiations, on the rule of law, was concluded soon after the ceasefire agreement came into effect. On 18 August 1992, Foreign Minister Ngulinzira and Pasteur Bizimungu, a member of the executive committee of the RPF, signed the Protocol of Agreement between the Government of the Republic of Rwanda and the Rwandan Patriotic Front on the Rule of Law. The protocol stipulated that both sides agreed that postwar society would be based on national unity, democracy, pluralism, and human rights. National unity implied "that the Rwandese people, as constituent elements of the Rwandese nation, are one and indivisible." As such, it also entailed "the rejection of all exclusions and any form of discrimination based notably, on ethnicity, region, sex and religion."[36] This protocol paved the way for the rest of the negotiations, because it enshrined the fundamental idea that both sides would form a broad-based transitional government (BBTG) until elections could be held at a later date.

This early success had been one of Ambassador Mpungwe's goals. By starting with the noncontentious issues, he hoped to build trust between the negotiating parties.[37] However, the next phase of the negotiations would not go so smoothly. Between September 1992 and January 1993, the RPF and the government of Rwanda delegation struggled to find a compromise on how power would be shared in the BBTG. Which ministries would go to which party, and how many ministries would each party have? Both President Habyarimana and certain members of the RPF delegation were responsible for the slow pace of the progress.

On 22 September 1992, Prime Minister Dismas Nsengiyaremye wrote a withering letter to President Habyarimana to try to unblock the negotiations. After explaining that the multiparty government had made good progress in several fields, especially in bringing about an enduring ceasefire with the RPF and in signing the Protocol on the Rule of Law, the prime minister pointed to the existence of "blockages found at the level of government." These—he contended—"could be quickly corrected if the constitutional powers of the President of the Republic, judged excessive by some, were deployed to unblock certain situations unnecessarily crippling the functioning of the administration."[38] Nsengiyaremye, for instance, berated the attitude of MRND ministers in the multiparty government who, at this crucial time, had sulked through a cabinet meeting instead of cooperating. Rather than forcing the ministers of his party to cooperate, Habyarimana had proposed another meeting to be scheduled for a later date. Nsengiyaremye also informed the president that his personal chief of staff had disrupted negotiations on 17 September, when he had demanded that the government of Rwanda delegation return to Kigali from Arusha, even though the negotiations were proceeding along the agreed lines.

In addition to his anger at the president's lackadaisical attitude toward the Arusha negotiations, the prime minister also called him to account for several other ongoing problems in Rwanda. First, the cabinet had unanimously agreed that a review should take place of all civil servants at the communal and prefecture levels. However, at a meeting on 18 September 1992, MRND ministers had refused to even look at the resulting report, which, according to Nsengiyaremye, might lead some "to conclude that this is the complicit protection of some mayors, especially those involved in the Murambi and Bugesera troubles, as well as the Bagogwe massacre."[39] Second, the cabinet had yet to discuss the reintegration of soldiers who had been unjustly evicted from the FAR. Third:

> The perpetrators of growing and blatant insecurity are still roaming and sowing terror and desolation everywhere. The interventionism of some authorities destroys any initiative of the public prosecutor's office, the Gendarmerie and the administrative authorities.
>
> As the Interahamwe is the only organisation that accepts soldiers into its ranks, and this "youth" is more supervised by police officers than by politicians, it should be called to order and should stop terrorizing the population. During the demonstrations of 28/07/1992 in Gitikinyoni, the active presence of elements of the Presidential Guard was noted. The Gendarmerie formally identified two who participated in this event. This is, to say the least, a strange situation, which needs to be normalised quickly.[40]

Finally, the prime minister concluded his long missive by pointing out that:

> It follows from the foregoing that you bear a double responsibility for blocking the action of the government, first as President of the Republic . . . then as President of the MRND Party, which occupies half the ministerial positions in government and is the principal obstacle to the proper functioning of the cabinet. . . . I urge you to put an end to these outdated and antidemocratic practises, which unnecessarily impede the implementation of the government programme. Also, in the superior interest of the nation I ask you to make a positive commitment to the process of democratization of Rwandan political life.[41]

This bold letter to Habyarimana aptly illustrates the main problems confronting the multiparty government as it tried to negotiate peace and advance the democratic process in the country. However, the government of Rwanda was not the only actor suffering from internal disagreements.

At a conference held twenty-five years after the events, the Tanzanian facilitator Mpungwe reminded Patrick Mazimhaka, one of the RPF negotiators, that he had on occasion weighed on the RPF team to keep it in check. "Patrick . . . will recall, we pushed heavily on the RPF." The Tanzanians wanted a peace that would last, so "we told them [the RPF] . . . You may be stronger and smarter than the government on such and such a point, but we do not agree with you. We went to RPF headquarters in Mulindi and had direct discussions with Paul Kagame. I said, 'Paul, your people in Arusha are being difficult, please assist.'"[42] And, sometimes, the RPF did reprimand its negotiators. For instance, the British defense adviser in Uganda, Lieutenant Colonel Johnny O'Brien, was told that, even though two negotiators had been clearly briefed by Kagame and Museveni on how far they were allowed to push for Habyarimana to make concessions, they had gone too far "in their strong stands demanding Habyarimana's stepping down and the degree of power sharing in the coalition."[43] Both Kagame and Museveni had been unpleasantly surprised when they heard about the positions the two had taken. After the negotiators returned to RPF-held Rwanda, they were arrested "and were told that they would not be released unless they toed the line—which they subsequently agreed to do."[44]

Three articles of the proposed protocol (14, 21, and 46) posed especially intractable problems.[45] Article 14 stipulated that the BBTG would consist of the organizations included in the multiparty government of 16 April 1992, as well as the RPF. However, this meant leaving out a new political party, the Coalition pour la défense de la République (CDR), which had only come into being after the swearing in of the multiparty government. This new extreme right-wing party was, according to Joyce Leader, the US deputy chief of mission in Kigali, "particularly feared by members of the opposition for its Ku Klux Klan–like approach to ethnic relations."[46] Because of its fanatical stance on the ethnic issue, the RPF did not want the CDR to have a ministerial portfolio. Conversely, the MRND saw it as a valuable ally against a possible MDR, PSD, PL, and RPF coalition.

The other two articles revolved around an issue that Prime Minister Nsengiyaremye had also highlighted in his letter to Habyarimana, namely the role and prosecution of local authorities implicated in massacres or human rights abuses. Article 46, in particular, stipulated that the BBTG government would get rid of all "incompetent elements as well as authorities who were involved in the social strife or whose activities are an obstacle to the democratic process and to national reconciliation."[47] As many of those implicated in the massacres were MRND party members, Habyarimana was keen to find ways of shielding them from prosecution, which is where Article 21 came in. In general, Article 21 governed how the BBTG cabinet would function, and how a majority of two-thirds would be sufficient to pass a decision. Yet it also outlined a number of exceptions to this rule, where decisions made by the cabinet had to be unanimous. The most important of these was the "exercise of the prerogative of mercy and mitigation of sentence."[48] Considering the MRND would not command a majority in the cabinet, the chance of clemency for those who had been involved in ethnic killings or other human rights abuses was very small indeed. Taken together, Articles 21 and 46 would ensure that the MRND would lose control of many civil service posts and that at least some of its members would be imprisoned.[49]

Despite objections to these articles, which continued to be raised until January 1993, the government of Rwanda delegation signed the first part of the Protocol of Agreement on Power-Sharing within the Framework of a Broad-Based Transitional Government on 30 October 1992.

HABYARIMANA REACTS

While President Habyarimana had never been particularly keen on the idea of negotiations and had dragged his feet in any matter relating to the Arusha peace talks, he particularly balked at the power-sharing framework. Such a framework not only left many of his MRND party members open to prosecution for past crimes but also severely curtailed the powers of the presidency itself.[50] Speaking to an MRND rally in Ruhengeri on 15 November, a mere two weeks after the signing of the Protocol of Agreement, Habyarimana called the Arusha peace talks "a scrap of paper"[51] and a "civil coup d'état."[52] Two days later, Prime Minister Nsengiyaremye sent him another long letter demanding an explanation:

> The positions you have expressed on the Arusha Accords and on the security problems within the country, as well as the assistance to the Forces armées rwandaises and the Interahamwe to support your electoral campaign, have raised many questions on the future of the peace process and of the democratic process in our country. . . .
>
> Regarding the peace process, you said that the Arusha Accords are but a scrap of paper . . . and as such do not commit the Rwandan people. Such a declaration by an official of your rank, who calls into question the commitments of the government, constitutes a barely veiled disavowal of the Arusha Accords and opens the way for a resumption of hostilities. Therefore, it is my duty to remind you that such a move is contrary to the letter and spirit of the governmental program to which

> you and your party, the MRND, subscribed on 16/4/1992, as well as to the higher interests of the Rwandan nation. . . .
>
> The main objective of the government's programme is to negotiate a peace agreement with the Rwandan Patriotic Front. This approach meets the aspiration of all Rwandans concerned about the future of their country. As there is no military solution to the fratricidal war that Rwanda has been experiencing for more than two years, a negotiated solution is the only way out for all the protagonists of this conflict.[53]

The prime minister went on to explain that the negotiations being carried out by the government delegation led by Foreign Minister Ngulinzira were based on documents and discussions from within the Rwandan cabinet. As such, the president would have been aware of the substance of the talks. More important, no other members of the cabinet, including the MRND ministers, had disavowed any of the protocols signed at Arusha so far. Thus, the president's latest U-turn was unfounded, and the signed documents did "fully commit this government [to the peace process]."[54] Then Nsengiyaremye asked "whether, like your ally, the CDR, the MRND also publicly denounced the Arusha Accords and therefore called into question the peace process."[55] If so, "you will have to take responsibility before the Rwandan people and history, and assume, alone, the disastrous consequences of this position."[56]

The prime minister also took umbrage with another part of the president's speech, in which the latter expressed pride in the fact that FAR soldiers and officers supported his electoral campaign. Nsengiyaremye remarked that soldiers were obliged by law to remain neutral; besides, he stressed, the electoral campaign had yet to be officially opened. "It is therefore regrettable that the country's top official is bragging, and publicly, about breaking the law."[57] As Habyarimana had heaped praise on the Interahamwe in the very same speech, Nsengiyaremye finished his letter by explaining that "it has repeatedly been pointed out that these youths include armed elements and should as such be disbanded in accordance with the law on political parties in Rwanda."[58] The Rwandan prime minister was not the only person shocked at the president's public disavowal of the Arusha negotiations. Ambassador Mpungwe and the Tanzanians were also "particularly miffed"[59] and "most upset."[60]

On 22 November 1992, the prime minister and the Tanzanians received Habyarimana's answer to their outrage. Instead of taking a step back, the

MRND escalated the issue when Léon Mugesera, MRND vice chairman of the Gisenyi Prefecture, delivered the infamous speech introduced in the opening paragraphs of chapter 1. After expressing his support for Habyarimana's Ruhengeri speech, Mugesera informed his audience of what he had recently told a PL member:

> "The mistake we made in 1959, when I was still a child, is to let you leave." I asked him if he had not heard the story of the Falashas, who returned home to Israel from Ethiopia? He replied he knew nothing about it! I told him "So don't you know how to listen or read? I am telling you that your home is Ethiopia, that we will send you by the Nyabarongo so you can get there quickly!" . . . Do not be afraid, know that anyone whose neck you do not cut is the one who will cut your neck. Let me tell you, these people should begin leaving while there is still time.[61]

Negotiations resumed in Arusha on the very day that Mugesera gave his inflammatory speech. However, by this point, Habyarimana had lost faith in Foreign Minister Ngulinzira, whom he now described to US Ambassador Robert Flaten as "a servant of the RPF and the parties for change."[62] Because the government of Rwanda and the Tanzanians expected significant difficulties in the negotiation of the second part of the Protocol of Agreement, which would involve the actual division of ministerial portfolios among the political parties, it was suggested to change the subject to military integration instead.[63] For these two reasons, Habyarimana sent a delegation of FAR officers to join the government negotiating team. Composed of four colonels and a major, and lead by Colonel Bagosora, this delegation formed a parallel network through which the president could keep an eye on the foreign minister. Jean-Christophe Belliard, one of the French observers at the negotiations, remembers:

> I worked a lot with Ngulinzira who listened to me. But I also knew that Ngulinzira was powerless. It was not him who took decisions. The real decisions were taken elsewhere. We could see that Kanyarushoki [the Rwandan ambassador to Uganda, who also played a key role throughout the Arusha negotiations] was continually slowing things down and playing for time, while the third person, Bagosora, did not speak but seemed to think a lot. I had the sense that a lot of things got decided at his level.[64]

One of the biggest problems during the talks was the disagreement between the MRND and the opposition parties on the division of the ministerial portfolios. Mediation was conducted by an interdenominational religious council, as had been the case during the initial formation of the multiparty government. While neither President Habyarimana—representing the MRND—and the CDR nor Prime Minister Nsengiyaremye had initially wanted to budge, heavy pressure from the diplomatic community in Kigali and from the Tanzanians in Arusha eventually proved decisive.[65] On 9 January 1993, the two sides signed the second part of the Protocol of Agreement on Power-Sharing within the Framework of a Broad-Based Transitional Government. However, as the next section will show, there was significant opposition to the protocol back in Rwanda.

PROVOKING A RESUMPTION OF HOSTILITIES

Both the MRND and the CDR had already been upset by the first part of the Protocol on Power-Sharing. The second part sent them into a frenzy. Not only was the CDR excluded from the BBTG, but the RPF and the MRND were allocated the same number of ministerial portfolios. Resorting to violence was a way for the MRND and the CDR to sabotage the peace process without losing face before the international community in Arusha. Writing to Geneva, a UNHCR employee explained that "since Monday [18 January] incidents have broken out in Kibungo, Butare, Gikongoro, Cyangugu, Gisenyi and Kigali. . . . [The] political class appears to be badly split over protocol on power-sharing signed at Arusha on 09/01/1993."[66] Two days later, the violence spread to Kigali, and the situation spiraled out of control:

> MRND supporters erected roadblocks in all entry and exit points to Kigali, thus preventing people from entering or leaving. In downtown Kigali numerous roadblocks brought the city to a virtual standstill. Shops, banks, schools and offices, public and private, were closed and traffic was almost non-existent as all vehicles with exception of those holding diplomatic plates were prevented from circulating. Authorities report fierce clashes between opposing political parties resulting in scores of people injured amid passive and sometimes complacent attitudes of security forces. More than 100 injured people were reportedly taken to hospital. Moreover ugly scenes of looting and rampage

> in Kigali shantytowns by uncontrolled mobs and heavily armed thugs were the order of the day thus creating a climate of widespread panic amongst the powerless population. . . . Both MRND and CDR have announced that they will continue their opposition campaign against the Arusha Protocol of agreement by staging further demonstrations in the coming days. Their latest demand is that the Prime Minister should step down. In sum, the test of wills between the ruling MRND party and the opposition parties is engaged in earnest.[67]

Another important development on the Rwandan political scene occurred on 20 January 1993. A letter was circulated around Kigali announcing the existence of the Alliance des militaires agacés par les séculaires actes sournois des Unaristes (AMASASU), in translation, the "Alliance of Soldiers Annoyed by the Underhand Secular Acts of the Unarists." In Kinyarwanda, *amasusu* means "bullets" which explains why the unwieldy name was chosen. The authors of the letter remained anonymous, but they purported to be a group within the military animated by the intention to "thwart the malicious plans of the members of the UNAR [Union nationale rwandaise] party who have been aggressing us from 1959 to the present. We support political pluralism and democracy with all our might because we want to see real justice established in Rwanda."[68] In other words, AMASASU wanted to make sure that the RPF, which it equated with the old UNAR monarchist party, would not be able to return to Rwanda. The next sentence invoked another memory from the Social Revolution, namely that real democracy and justice in Rwanda would always favor the Hutu majority of the country. The letter then turned even more sinister:

> We know, as you do Mr. President, that we are fighting on the borders of our country whilst on the inside there are individuals who support our aggressors publicly and with impunity. If these blackmailing *Inyenzi* start the war once again, how do you plan on preventing us from teaching these inside traitors the lesson they deserve? After all we have already identified the most virulent among them and we shall act with the speed of lightning![69]

This message was right in line with Mugesera's speech just a few months before. It is difficult to follow the logic of AMASASU. By this point, it was already clear that for the FAR there could be no military solution to the war: it was too weak to hope to fight and prevail against the RPA. More important, the FAR's weakness had nothing to do with treacherous elements within Rwanda, and everything with the corruption and incompetence of its officer corps. However, AMASASU, which was probably composed of elements inside the military intelligence services of the FAR, does not seem to have fully understood this reality.

By the end of the month, it was clear that it was not just opposition party members who were being targeted by MRND and CDR militias. An ethnically motivated attack on USAID employees provoked a scalding reply from the State Department, which ordered its ambassador to give Habyarimana a dressing down.[70] Prime Minister Nsengiyaremye also insisted in a letter to the president that the massacre of civilians had to stop.[71] On 28 January, an open letter signed by all the major domestic and international human rights groups denounced the ethnic massacres that had recently taken place in the north of the country. Over 250 people had been killed over the preceding weeks just because they were Tutsi. The letter presented two examples. In one instance, the aggressors had put up an illegal roadblock and stopped a bus. They had forced the passengers to get off and show their identity cards for an ethnicity check. Then, having picked out four people, they had proceeded to kill them, dumping their bodies in a common grave. In another instance, an old Tutsi couple had been burned alive in their house. When their son returned home for the burial, he too was set upon by "aggressors."[72]

Considering these massacres took place in the very region where Habyarimana and Mugesera had renounced the Arusha Accords and, in the case of the latter, called for genocide, there is little doubt that local MRND authorities, supported by their colleagues at the national level, were behind the murders. As a French Embassy councillor who had traveled to the northwest told Belgian Ambassador Swinnen: "The attacks against the Tutsis appear methodical and organized. They are not spontaneous reactions of the population. The MRND and the CDR have been identified as the instigators of the unrest."[73] The Ugandan government, for its part, was even convinced that the president was "personally implicated."[74]

The RPF was now faced with a difficult situation. On the one hand, they confronted a recalcitrant president who had personally disavowed the Arusha peace talks, followed by Mugesera's call for genocide. On the other, they had established a working relationship with opposition parties that were genuinely committed to the peace process. To make matters worse, Tutsi were now being killed in the immediate proximity of the RPA forward positions. These killings were a clear breach of the July 1992 modified N'Sele Ceasefire Agreement, whose Article VII had stipulated that "'cessation of hostilities' shall mean the end of all military operations, all harmful civil operations and denigrating and unfounded propaganda through the mass media."[75]

SI VIS PACEM, PARA BELLUM

As Roessler and Verhoeven point out, the motto of Paul Kagame throughout the Struggle for Liberation was *Si vis pacem, para bellum,* "If you want peace, prepare for war."[76] This meant that the RPA had not been idle during the seven-month ceasefire (July 1992–February 1993). Inter-unit sports events had kept the morale and physical fitness up, as the different battalions competed in football, basketball, and volleyball leagues. Paul Kagame and other officers also visited the units, laying out why the decision had been taken to negotiate with the government of Rwanda at Arusha. "It was explained why are we asking this percentage [of government ministries and], why [we do] not take it all since we are the better guys. They were all explained that this was nation building. It was not eating the cake. We are not dividing the cake; we are nation building."[77] Occasionally, the RPF politicos who were at Arusha would come and explain the process to the troops themselves. RPA members who had not visited the political schools in Uganda, but had gone directly to the front, followed classes organized by the RPF, or by the RPA political commissars, in which they were taught the history of Rwanda, why the Banyarwanda were refugees, and some Marxist theory. The syllabus also included a chapter on the indispensable role of women and youths in the Struggle.[78]

Besides investing in the mental well-being of the troops, the RPA also reorganized its fighting units. Eight combined mobile forces (CMF) were created from various battalions and columns. Each consisted of between 1,000 and 2,000 soldiers and carried enough heavy equipment—mortars, recoilless guns, and heavy machine guns—to be able to operate independently. Each CMF was led by capable, and by now experienced, battlefield commanders who were well versed in the RPA combat doctrine of mobile warfare. An all-female unit led by NRA-veteran Nuriat Nambaje, Yankee Mobile, was also formed. While women had until now been spread throughout RPA units, it was decided that, considering the length of the ceasefire, it would be better if the force were generally—although not stringently—segregated: "Women empowerment was preached from the highest levels of command. Both in the political wing and the military wing women were well organised and had a voice."[79]

As the ceasefire meant that the RPF/RPA were now stationary in Mulindi, regular supply lines were set up that brought food and weapons to the front. Christine Umutoni explains that the division of labor between the RPF and the RPA was important in this respect. In many guerrilla movements, tensions arise between the frontline troops, who are considered heroes, and those who organize their supplies, whose contribution tends to be belittled. However, the RPA saw, and the High Command explained to the troops, that it was the political wing of the organization, the RPF, which organized the Banyarwanda community, bought supplies, and then transported them to the frontline. The mutual respect between the two branches is shown by the fact that RPA troops were required to salute their RPF comrades, even though the latter were not soldiers, "and they all did, such was their discipline."[80]

In deciding how they would react to the ethnic killings in northern Rwanda, the RPF had to take several factors into consideration. Both sides had earlier violated the N'Sele Ceasefire Agreement by expanding their military arsenals.[81] However, the murder of Tutsi in the open, following the provocations by the president, could not be ignored. The opposition in Rwanda was in no position to stop these killings, or to make sure they would not resume in the future as the Arusha Accords were being implemented. Perhaps more important was that these killings represented everything the RPF was against. What would its supporters, inside and outside Rwanda, and its soldiers, some of whom might have had family members who were being killed, feel if the RPF sat on its hands? Faced with these facts, the RPF felt it had no other choice but to resume hostilities. Other reasons for the RPF attacks have been put forward. Both Linda Melvern and Bruce Jones argue that the RPF wanted to ensure that when negotiations resumed, they would be able to demand a larger share in the postwar Rwandan army.[82] This may well have been an additional reason to resume hostilities; however, the topic of troop levels, which had indeed briefly come up at Arusha, was not being discussed when hostilities resumed.

8 FEBRUARY 1993 OFFENSIVE

Once the decision was taken, the RPA was ready to swing into action at a moment's notice. As Caesar Kayizari explains: "Our leadership could not hold its arms and see everything going in smoke. So immediately quick attack. . . . All forces were to attack in their sector. To tell these guys that . . . if you want to fight as you have always insisted, we are available for a fight. And what we did, we made a deep attack. . . . We bypassed their trenches, we bypassed their front units and attacked their rear forces."[83]

On 8 February 1993, all RPA units attacked simultaneously. Charlie Mobile, under the command of Willex Kiiza, moved through the Virunga Mountains and attacked Ruhengeri, which was captured on the same day, with the exception of Lieutenant Colonel Bizimungu's command post.[84] Caesar Kayizari, who was in command of one of the companies that took the town, remembers: "I was in the town, on the airfield, that is where my company . . . went in, others went on the hills overlooking the city."[85] In response, the FAR brought in extra troops from Gisenyi and Gitarama and launched a counterattack, which was repulsed after eight hours of fighting. The next day the FAR continued their counterattack.[86] The fighting was intense and, on 10 February, the RPA decided to pull out of the center of town: "The briefing we had got from the command in chief had said . . . 'Go fight to punish the enemy that is killing the Rwandese people. Don't waste a lot of your personnel on capturing territory, fight punchy, and if you see you have done the punishment, pull back to better strategic positions.' The purpose was to force him . . . back to Arusha."[87]

On the eastern flank of Charlie Mobile, three CMFs—Alpha, Bravo, and Delta, commanded by Sam Kaka, Ludoviko "Dodo" Twahirwa, and Vedaste Kayitare, respectively—pushed through the gap between Lake Ruhondo and Byumba. Further east, 7 Mobile, led by Theogene Bagire, struck around Nyagatare.[88] On every front, the RPA pushed back the FAR, inflicting heavy casualties. Only around Ruhengeri and Byumba did the FAR mount a tenacious resistance. A major advantage of the RPA during the fighting was its combat doctrine, which was understood throughout the force. As Caesar Kayizari explains, "While it was centralized command, it was decentralized execution on our part. The commander-in-chief is commanding it, but he allows freedom of maneuver to the lower commanders as they assess the

MAP 9.1. The February 1993 Offensive. (1) The extent of the zone held by the RPA (Rwandan Patriotic Army) from July 1992 to February 1993. (2) On 8 February 1993 RPA troops attack all along the line. The most important attacks are those toward Kinihira, which threaten to cut the Kigali-Ruhengeri road, and the brief capture of Ruhengeri for the second time. (3) The FAR (Forces armées rwandaises) launches strong counterattacks which force the RPA out of Ruhengeri on 10 February. Following the end of the fighting on 20 February 1993 the RPA withdraws to its pre-offensive positions. The areas it vacates are designated as a demilitarized zone. Map by Brian Balsley.

territory."[89] This flexibility allowed commanders to react quickly to developments on the battlefield without having to refer back to the High Command for their every move.[90]

On 15 February 1993 Bruno Delaye, an adviser on African affairs to President Mitterrand, reported that the RPA was "militarily in a position to take Kigali."[91] The news came at a moment of heightened tension between President Habyarimana and Prime Minister Nsengiyaremye. The president wanted to fight to the end and told Delaye that it was "better to die than to submit to the Tutsi."[92] The prime minister, on the contrary, wanted to negotiate. With the FAR crippled on the battlefield and Rwandan politicians unable to take control of the situation, the French were left in a tight spot:

> We are at the limit of the strategy of indirect support to the Rwandan Armed Forces. . . . Their degree of motivation is too uneven (because of differences between northern and southern Hutus) to contemplate with equanimity a stabilisation of the military balance of power. If the front were to cave in, **we would have no other** choice but **to evacuate KIGALI** (the official mission of our two infantry companies is to protect expatriates), **unless we become cobelligerents.**[93]

On 20 February, now only thirty kilometers from Kigali, the RPF announced a unilateral ceasefire and stopped major offensive operations.[94] According to Caesar Kayizari, the RPA stopped on the brink of total victory "because the international mood was in Arusha, so if you begin capturing Kigali it is too much . . . and that is Kagame's uniqueness in studying the situation."[95]

The French reaction to the RPA offensive was to increase support to the FAR. First, large amounts of ammunition were flown to Rwanda, especially for the FAR's artillery. Second, Opération Noroît was reinforced with two companies, bringing its strength up to several hundred.[96] The top brass of the RPA and the RPF might also have factored this into their decision to stop the offensive, as a direct confrontation with French troops would carry enormous risks. Third, a detachment from 1e RPIMa was sent to help the FAR stabilize the situation. Colonel Didier Tauzin, who was in command of the assistance mission (Opération Birunga), and his team from the 1e RPIMa took off from Biarritz in their Transall C-160 at 06:00 on 21 February. They arrived in Kigali the next day around noon, after a short stop in Bangui, Central African Republic. Colonel Tauzin was also immediately given command of the French troops who made up the DAMI (Détachement d'assistance militaire), most of whom were also members of the 1e RPIMa.[97] Tauzin quickly decided that to reverse the tide of battle, a parallel command structure, in which French officers advised their FAR colleagues at all important headquarters, would have to be put in place.

> As soon as I returned to Kigali, I visited Colonel Nsabimana. . . . This true warrior had not given up, but the way he greeted us showed that our arrival represented his last chance to turn around a disastrous situation. He is clearly prepared to accept anything I ask. He will de facto place himself under my command and will execute without fail all the orders drawn up for him by Chéreau [full name and rank unknown] who will take charge of his general staff with two or three officers.[98]

Besides the general staff, French officers were also embedded in the three frontline sector commands: Lieutenant Colonel Gégou, supported by a team of twelve specialists from the 1e RPIMa, was sent to Byumba to fight alongside Lieutenant Colonel Gratien Kabiligi; Lieutenant Colonel Gilles Chollet, who had been in command of the DAMI, was sent with his team to support Lieutenant Colonel Bizimungu in the Ruhengeri sector; and the team of Lieutenant Colonel Étienne Joubert was deployed to the central sector around Rulindo. Besides these advisers, there were two other teams. One supported the FAR heavy artillery batteries, while the other, composed of engineers, roamed the frontline helping to construct defensive positions.[99]

Although the RPA had declared a unilateral ceasefire on 20 February, Tauzin's account suggests that heavy fighting continued after that date. The fighting around Ruhengeri and Byumba was not going the way of the FAR, but the mortal threat was in the central sector around Rulindo, Base, and Tumba. There, during the main stage of the offensive, Sam Kaka's Alpha Mobile had pushed the FAR back and was only thirty kilometers from the center of Kigali. Crucially, the RPA was also threatening to cut the Kigali-Ruhengeri road, which would mean that moving reinforcements from sector to sector would become much harder for the FAR.[100] It is unclear if Alpha Mobile had already occupied this key position before 20 February and was just conducting minor operations to improve its frontline, or whether it was actually still attacking.

As is the habit of special forces, selected for their aggression and initiative, Colonel Tauzin set about organizing a counterattack. The plan was for the FAR to attack from the Byumba salient and capture Kissaro, cutting off the RPA spearheads and exposing their rear.[101] It took until 27 February to assemble the 3,000 men who were to carry out the offensive, code-named "Miyove." But difficulties in assembling the required munitions and lack of transport meant that the offensive was repeatedly postponed. Toward the end of February, with negotiations set to resume at Arusha, the French government decided that the offensive would be detrimental to diplomatic efforts to reimpose a ceasefire and canceled Opération Miyove.

Eighteen years later, when Colonel, by then General, Tauzin wrote his book on Rwanda, he argued that Opération Miyove might have been a turning point in the war. He believed that, under French command and with the massive support of its heavy artillery, the FAR would have been able to break the RPA.[102] However, this assessment seems overly optimistic. Tauzin and his team had only been on the ground for a week, and they could only have restored the fighting power of the FAR by so much. In early February, and despite the long ceasefire, the FAR had been smashed by the RPA attack, and by the end of the month, its troops would still have been disorganized and demoralized. Nor—contrary to what Tauzin seems to think—would the FAR and the French have found an RPA with a weakened impetus or morale. After all, it had not been the FAR that had stopped the RPA offensive, but Paul Kagame himself.[103] Indeed, Tauzin's analysis clashes with that of Pierre Joxe, the French minister of defense at the time, who wrote to President Mitterrand on 26 February:

> The Rwandan army no longer fights. . . . I struggle to see why the RPF would abandon such a close victory, which would, no doubt, not even require a general offensive on its part. . . . He [Habyarimana] is, by his political intransigence, and his incapacity to mobilize his own army, largely responsible for the current fiasco. If the RPF retakes the offensive, our soldiers could, in a matter of hours, find themselves face to face with the rebels.[104]

On 7 March, the RPF and the government of Rwanda met in Dar es Salaam to sign a new ceasefire agreement that would enable both parties to return to the negotiating table at Arusha. One of the clauses of the ceasefire obliged the RPA to withdraw to its pre–8 February offensive positions in northern Rwanda. This caused a serious internal debate within the RPF, and was seemingly one of the few occasions in which grave doubts were raised about Kagame's decisions throughout the organization. Tito Rutaremara clearly remembers that

> Kagame had [to do] a lot to convince us to go behind [the original frontline]. He worked very hard. . . . The civilians wanted to keep [the captured territory] . . . and there were even some military people who were behind us. . . . At the end we understood that we could not have the international community against us. We had to bend a bit. . . . He understood it before us. And he fought it, to make us understand it. . . . It was only one or two days, and then we understood it, and then we went on mobilising the others. . . . He gave the order to go and explain it to our members outside Rwanda. To go out and start telling our cadres in Burundi, Zaire, Uganda, Tanzania and we went on explaining. . . . I was given that work to go and explain to our cadres and our political organisation outside.[105]

James Kabarebe, who was Kagame's aide-de-camp at the time, remembers that all the important officers assembled for a meeting in territory that had been captured during the 8 February offensive. Once there, Kagame asked them three questions: "First, 'How did you get here?' The assembled officers answered, 'On our feet.' Well, Kagame replied, 'You still have both your feet.' Second, 'What equipment did you have?' The answer was 'Guns.' Well, the chairman of the High Command concluded, 'Now you have more guns because we captured many.' Third, 'Considering all this, could you come back if you so willed?' To which the officers answered, 'Yes we could.'"[106] Besides meeting with the High Command, Kagame went to all the CMFs to personally explain to the soldiers why he was asking them to give up the ground that many of their comrades had died to capture. In Caesar Kayizari's view, the authority Kagame had accrued by leading the RPA from victory to victory allowed him to convince the soldiers of the need to give up the territory they had captured and permit negotiations to resume.[107]

At this point, and since this chapter has had much to say about the FAR's complicity in war crimes and ethnic killings, it is worth briefly examining the human rights record of the RPA. There were accusations of sporadic RPF and RPA's human rights abuses from the start of the war.[108] The March 1993 International Federation for Human Rights (FIDH) report stated that the RPF had been "guilty of attacking civilian targets, of summary executions, forced expulsions of populations, injuring civilians, and pillage and destruction of property."[109] The report also notes that abuses and the plunder of cattle and other foodstuffs were especially common after the RPA had suffered defeat in late October 1990. It is undoubtedly true that the RPA lived off the land to an important degree throughout the war. Health care centers were often raided for medicines and bandages. Similarly, FAR positions were attacked to capture weapons. Other raids would undoubtedly have been carried out for cattle and other foodstuffs. There are also persistent rumors that the RPF kidnapped people from the frontline, presumably to hold them ransom.[110]

According to Prunier, the RPA committed war crimes during the 8 February Offensive.[111] His assessment is backed up by CLADHO (Comité de liaison des associations rwandaises de défense des droits de l'Homme), an association of Rwanda's five most significant human rights associations.[112] As CLADHO was fearless in its criticism of the FAR and the Habyarimana government, its assessment is above suspicion.[113] Both Prunier and CLADHO estimate the number of arbitrary executions at 50 to 150. The exact causes of these killings—were they revenge acts for the ethnic killings the MRND had committed in previous weeks?—and the reaction of the RPA High Command remain unknown.

Onerous as these killings may have been, the RPF's most important role in the humanitarian crisis in Rwanda was its policy of pushing the population out of its zone of control (though it should be noted that a large portion of the internally displaced people in Rwanda were not from the zone the RPA occupied). While the RPF's policy was logical—the organization could not feed or care for the population, or control it—the hundreds of thousands of refugees housed in atrocious conditions in camps throughout Rwanda certainly contributed to the destabilization of the country. It should also be noted that the small population that remained in the RPF zone was well treated, although certainly tightly controlled.[114]

The political effects of the 8 February offensive were negative, as Prunier and Gasana have pointed out.[115] For many within the opposition, the military superiority of the RPF was driven home for the first time. Following shortly on the heels of this revelation came the realization that the RPF could take power by force. The influx of internally displaced people and the reports of RPA human rights violations added to the fear of the RPF. As a result, many opposition parties began to split into moderate and "Hutu Power" wings. Those who were part of the latter were close to the MRND and CDR on the ethnic issue and became convinced that the Tutsi and thus the "Tutsi-RPF" were a mortal enemy of the Rwandan Hutu.

* * *

Once they had started, the Arusha negotiations could only have one outcome: the definitive end of Habyarimana's presidency and of the one-party MRND state. In their place would come elections and a multiparty system in which the RPF would have a say. Habyarimana had started the process of constitutional change in 1989, so these developments did not come as a surprise. However, now that the threat to the president and other vested interests of the MRND from northwestern Rwanda was around the corner, accompanied by the specter of accountability for past crimes, this elite balked. To derail the negotiations, they turned to the old trick of ethnic violence. The massacres in Bugesera, Habyarimana's rejection of agreed-upon protocols, Léon Mugesera's violent hate speech in Gisenyi, and the violence that followed were "the continuation of politics by other means."[116]

Because the multiparty government of Nsengiyaremye was unable to prevent the ethnic violence, the RPF felt it had no other option but to force the intransigents back to the negotiating table. This choice was driven by several factors, including sympathy for the plight of the victims, the RPF's standing within the diaspora if it failed to act, and the need to show Habyarimana and his clique that a return to open conflict would not end well for the FAR. The RPA's lightening campaign was successful in two ways. Militarily, it showed that the RPA was now a formidable fighting force that could carry out complicated offensive operations. And politically, it forced Habyarimana and the elite from the North-West back to the negotiating table.

However, the offensive also polarized members of the opposition parties and fractured their internal unity. In this respect, the losers of this period were undoubtedly the moderates. The Nsengiyaremye-Ngulinzira-Gasana triumvirate, the engine for peace within the Rwandan government, was still in power and still had the support of the international community. However, their position was much weakened within Rwanda because of the splits within their own political parties.

10

"Cry 'Havoc!'"

February 1993–March 1994

On 18 May 1993, toward 20:00, Emmanuel Gapyisi, a popular but highly controversial MDR politician, was shot dead outside his house in Kicukiro, Kigali.[1] In the aftermath of the assassination, the leaders of the three main opposition parties—Faustin Twagiramungu (MDR), Dr. Théoneste Gafaranga (PSD), and Justin Mugenzi (PL)—came together to discuss the deteriorating security in the country. On 24 May they issued a letter to President Habyarimana in which they blamed him and his supporters for Gapyisi's death: "Everyone notes with bitterness that the only categories of people whose security is ensured are on the one hand the president, his family and entourage, and on the other, the expatriates who are the object of particular attention on the part of French troops stationed in Kigali."[2]

After pointing out that ethnic pogroms and other unrest had killed "thousands of people" since the start of the war and that the president had done nothing to stem the tide of violence, its authors explained that they "are indignant that insecurity is orchestrated or encouraged by those who want to exploit this situation for the benefit of the regime."[3] After listing the instances in which the president or the MRND were implicated in human rights violations, and explaining that Habyarimana was using his influence to ensure that the perpetrators would not be punished, the letter moves on to the MRND party militia, the Interahamwe:

> The dictator used elements of law enforcement either to execute his plans or to give cover to his other civil forces, in particular the militias

> of the MRND–CDR parties. . . . Thus acts of looting, rapes, killings . . . carried out by certain elements of the Rwandan armed forces have not been punished; soldiers and gendarmes responsible for multiple crimes have never been worried and remain present in the ranks of the security forces. . . . The moral and material support that elements of the presidential guard provided to the Interahamwe and CDR militias in their murderous expeditions has been repeatedly decried but the head of state has never taken the complaints of the parties and the population seriously.[4]

This chapter will cover two main themes. First it will look at the parlous state in which Rwanda found itself after the 8 February 1993 offensive. Because it does so thematically this section often reaches back to events in 1990, 1991, and 1992. Under the combined pressures of economic collapse and the war, Rwandan society began to break at the seams. From 1991 onward, violence spread throughout the country: assassinations, terrorist attacks, and banditry became everyday occurrences. In many cases this violence was not ethnic but political, based on disagreements between the ruling MRND and the CDR, on one hand, and the MDR, PL, and PSD, on the other. Naturally, regionalism also played an important part. The chapter will then turn to the continuation of the Arusha peace negotiations and highlight the role of the Nsengiyaremye-Ngulinzira-Gasana triumvirate, the driving force behind the search for peace on the side of the government. Without them it is unlikely that the Arusha Accords would ever have been concluded. The final sections of the chapter will bring these two themes together and show how the accords were structurally undermined.

POLITICAL ASSASSINATIONS

One of the other main complaints in the letter of the opposition parties to Habyarimana was that, besides the murder of Gapyisi, there had been dozens of political assassinations since the outbreak of war. One of the first significant incidents was an attack on the second home of Judge Joseph Kavaruganda, the head of Rwanda's Supreme Court. The house was located about 600 meters from the presidential residence at Kanombe and on 11 September 1991, Joseph and his wife, Annonciate, were planning to spend a couple weeks there. Joseph arrived early in the evening after a session at the court. Their youngest daughter was about to return to her studies abroad, and the two parents realized that if they took her to the airport, they would not make it back to Kanombe before curfew set in. They decided to spend the night in Kigali instead. Around 8 p.m. they left for the airport with their daughter. At 2 a.m. their house staff in Kanombe heard noises in the garden and saw soldiers—men in uniform—moving around. Shortly thereafter, the men opened fire on the home with anti-tank rockets.[5] The following morning, the tire tracks of the assailants' jeep were traced back toward the presidential compound. It is unclear who was responsible for the attack, although neither Joseph nor Annonciate thought it was ordered directly by President Habyarimana.[6]

The attack on Kavaruganda's house was followed by the assassination of David Gatera in October of the same year. Gatera was a founding member of the PL and an important business partner of his brother, Justin Mugenzi, who was in turn a founding member and chairman of the PL.[7] Within the PL, the assassination was seen as "a persecution against Mr Mugenzi" and an attempt "to cut down his right arm in business . . . and to weaken him mentally so that he couldn't advance as he had been doing . . . in the political arena."[8] According to the official version, the assassin, a soldier named Kuzungu, was taking revenge on Gatera, who was said to have murdered his father after an extortion attempt.[9] On 26 December 1992, Mugenzi was again targeted through his family, when a grenade attack was carried out on the home of his sister, injuring several children.[10]

Matters did not improve the following year. According to André Sibomana, one of the most important human rights activists in Rwanda, "the whole of 1993 was marked by massacres, killings, abductions and all kinds of odious crimes."[11] Sibomana himself was threatened and several European missionaries were shot dead by Rwandan security services.[12] There were also attempts on the lives of Stanislas Mbonampeka and Donat Murego, the vice chairman of the PL and executive secretary of the MDR, respectively. In his testimony to the international tribunal, Joseph Ngarambe, a leader of the PSD and human rights activist of the ADL (Association rwandaise pour la défense des droits de la personne et des libertés publiques), explained that the murderous insecurity he feared had become "quite ordinary. . . . They were killing on a daily basis in Kigali."[13]

Journalists were also often targets for arbitrary arrest, torture, or assassination.[14] On 6 December 1991, Belgian ambassador Johan Swinnen was visited by Boniface Ntawurushintege, who worked for the *Umurangi* newspaper. He had "swollen feet, bleeding toes and scars on the right arm. He had been tortured with iron wire [helical cutting cable] by . . . Captain Simbikangwa of the Presidential Intelligence Service, who had repeatedly yelled that other journalists would suffer the same fate ('*parce que nous tenons à notre Général, à notre Président*')."[15]

Later the same day Ntawurushintege was arrested. Swinnen was also visited by André Kameya, editor-in-chief of the opposition newspaper *Rwanda Rushya,* who had come to show the ambassador a death threat that he had received on Ministry of Defense letter-headed paper and that was signed by a group of "comrades in arms of a fallen hero." Swinnen tried to intervene with the Rwandan authorities, hoping that the assassins would be scared off by the personal involvement of the Belgian ambassador, but to no avail. Kameya was arrested toward the end of February 1992.[16] Arrest and torture were not the only threats journalists faced. On 29 November 1992, Straton Byabagamba, a columnist for the Rwandan Catholic Church and PL leader for the Kanombe Commune, was shot dead in his house. A few months later, on 6 April 1993, Callixte Kalisa, a journalist for TV Rwanda, was shot dead when entering his house in Remera. He had worked on the film *Gorillas in the Mist* and had been a witness in the murder case of Dian Fossey.[17]

TERRORIST ATTACKS

Between October 1991 and September 1993, at least fifty-two terrorist attacks using mines or other explosives were carried out in Rwanda. Mines were placed along roadsides, at bus stations, bars, markets, and post offices, killing those who drove or walked over them. Sometimes the mines were used as improvised explosive devices. Having been set with a time delay, they were not triggered by someone stepping on them, but rather exploded after a set amount of time, turning the mine into a more or less conventional bomb.[18] This spate of attacks remains shrouded in mystery, because their objective and perpetrators are impossible to pin down.

A report emanating from the French Embassy sums up the confusion. After stressing that, from December 1991 onward, terrorist attacks had spread beyond the frontline, the report suggests two alternative explanations for them. The first is that these mines were being planted by the RPF in an attempt to destabilize the Rwandan political scene or hinder FAR logistics. At the site of one of the terrorist attacks, French troops had recovered remnants of an anti-tank mine and had sent it to the Army Laboratory in Paris, which concluded that the mines had been produced in a Warsaw Pact country and sold to Uganda at some point during the previous three years.[19] The Rwandan Centre de recherche criminelle et de documentation (CRCD), which worked closely with the French Gendarmerie training mission, reached the same conclusion, as did in part at least one RPF source, a colonel who told a Ugandan journalist that the RPF was responsible for some of these bombings.[20] The second possibility was that the attacks were being carried out by those who wanted to specifically destabilize the new multiparty government. Belgian Ambassador Swinnen espoused this reading of events. The source who had warned him about the existence of a secret general staff had also written that "this clandestine general staff disposes of cells at the level of each prefecture and each commune. It is also this group which has been planting anti-tank and anti-personnel mines and spreading terror in urban centres, especially Kigali."[21] This latter theory was also supported by both the MDR and the PL, including Prime Minister Sylvestre Nsanzimana and Minister of Justice Stanislas Mbonampeka.[22]

Besides the structural lack of investigative skills in the Gendarmerie, another problem was that the mines were often planted by improvised hired assassins, rather than by members of the organization behind the attack. This could lead to bizarre situations. In one case, a Burundian living in Rwanda was caught planting mines, but this—according to the French Embassy—was of little help to investigators who were forced to conclude that "according to the side you support, you can use this affair to (hastily) claim: That the sponsor was a Tutsi of the RPF; or that the sponsor is an officer very close to the president."[23] Another difficulty faced by investigators was that, even though they could track the origin of mines, this did not automatically lead to the guilty party. First, a bewildering array of mines were used, ranging from Warsaw Pact anti-tank to Belgian-made anti-personnel mines.[24] Second, mines can easily be sold or dug up from their original location and reused.

It is possible that both the RPF and the hardliners within the Rwandan government/FAR, and perhaps even the opposition, were all planting mines. Some devices that targeted assets of strategic value, such as Rwanda's petroleum infrastructure and power plants, point to the RPF. However, others, such as the two anti-personnel mines found in the banana plantation of an agronomist, or the two mines that went off on 12 March 1992 in Nyanza—a place of no military value, but indeed the former royal capital of the Mwami—do not seem to have been the work of the RPF. Regardless of who planted them, these bombs greatly contributed to the atmosphere of insecurity that settled over Rwanda toward late 1991 and early 1992. As the chief of staff of the Gendarmerie wrote on 8 May 1992, "With the war launched by the FPR [RPF] against our country in Oct 1990, the insecurity characterized by armed robberies with the use of firearms and grenades, as well as the laying of mines and bombs on public roads and in places with a high concentration of people, has not stopped growing."[25]

BANDITRY AND CRIMINALITY

Before the outbreak of the war, Rwanda had not experienced substantial violent organized crime. Yet, by the eve of the Genocide, the country was awash with heavily armed, more or less organized gangs. The significant difference between this banditry and the other forms of violence discussed in this chapter is that the former was uncontrolled and undirected. Though hard facts and figures are difficult to come by, the best guess is that many of these bandits were army deserters, internally displaced persons, or young men squeezed by the social tensions caused by the economic malaise. They became more adept and numerous as the war went on and more people suffered from its consequences. As early as 1991, some businessmen had started asking the Ministry of Defense for weapons licenses because they were afraid of being attacked in their homes.[26]

By 1992, these gangs had become a real problem. Because the Gendarmerie and police were either implicated in the crimes or outgunned, they "locked themselves by night in their compounds (there had been several attacks with hand grenades against them), and the bad guys were on the verge of controlling the town, every night as of midnight."[27] This meant that security, especially in Kigali, was in the hands of the foreign troops: first the French and, later, the United Nations Assistance Mission for Rwanda (UNAMIR). While the French troops of Opération Noroît did not have a mandate to intervene in the case of intra-Rwandan trouble, they still made concerted efforts to make the town a safer place. Not only did they want to maintain the initiative, but the Europeans were subject to the same banditry as the average Kigalian.[28] The 2ᵉ RIMa seemed particularly active in this regard, almost always sending out a patrol following reports of gunfire or grenades going off in town.[29] High-alert squads mounted in pickups could quickly reach the scene of a crime and were often successful in apprehending suspects.[30] The French soldiers would then hand over the suspect to the French gendarmes stationed at the embassy. However, while these gendarmes were trained police officers, they had no jurisdiction and would therefore turn over all suspects to their Rwandan colleagues.

For example, on 10 May 1992 at 1 p.m., a section of French troops from the 2ᵉ RIMa had to intervene after a Belgian couple was attacked by four machete-wielding criminals. Later that day, around 9 p.m., a Gendarmerie deserter attempted to rob another Belgian couple but was stopped by two FAR soldiers. An off-duty, and therefore unarmed, French officer happened upon the scene and was soon confronted with a situation in which the detained deserter tried to convince the soldiers to release him, rob the couple, and kill the French officer. The discussion between the deserter and the FAR soldiers was ongoing when a squad of French soldiers arrived and took control. On 18 May there was an attempted robbery of a grocery store by "three men dressed in military uniforms and two civilians" armed with grenades.[31] French troops responded but were unable to make any arrests on this occasion. Roughly a month later, on 22 June, French troops were again scrambled, this time to the house of a French expat in Kigali who had been attacked in his home by a dozen men armed with machetes and grenades.[32] In addition, between 1 and 22 June, French forces in Kigali logged no less than eight incidents in which grenades or firearms were used in the city.[33] While Westerners were frequent victims of attacks and robberies, it seems they were not specifically targeted because of their ethnicity: "I don't think the *musungus* [whites] were targeted as Westerners, more probably as criminal opportunity targets because they were richer than the average Kigalian."[34] However, as French troops were not supposed to interfere in Rwandan affairs, but could legitimately protect expatriates, it was more risky for criminals to target Westerners.

Nor was this banditry confined to Kigali and surroundings. As the commander of the Gendarmerie company in Cyangugu explained: "The Cyangugu-Gikongoro road has along its bank a forest that stretches over 50 kilometres, and bandits will lay ambush along that road. I was a victim of such an ambush once at around 8 p.m. on my return from a meeting. We ran into one of those ambushes, and the bandits would waylay, so to speak, vehicles in order to steal their property. . . . In Cyangugu *préfecture*, . . . armed banditry . . . was raging."[35]

After the FAR mutiny in 1992, the army itself became, in many instances, not much more than a group of bandits. When the mutiny started on 29 May, five people were killed in Ruhengeri, and seventeen more the following day. By 19:00 on 30 May, French troops in the capital had been put on red alert in case the mutiny spread to Gisenyi and the Kanombe military camp in Kigali. By 20:50 a French detachment had intervened in Gisenyi and order was more or less restored. However, even the presence of French troops could not prevent a French citizen from being robbed in his house by "uncontrolled FAR elements."[36] On 1 June the mutiny spread: FAR troops in the south robbed the bank of Kibuye, taking 16 million Rwandan francs, while more "uncontrolled FAR elements" plundered an OPROVIA warehouse in Butare.[37] Nor were these isolated incidents. According to the International Commission of Investigation, another bank was robbed in Ruhengeri on 5 June.[38] While the mutiny was an explosion of discontent within the army that was eventually brought under control, it became increasingly common for the FAR to terrorize the Rwandan people it was supposed to protect. Soldiers abused their position of power to force internally displaced people to work on their farms for starvation wages and raped women throughout the country. Rape was not confined to the aftermath of heavy fighting or the frontline. The International Commission, for instance, reported in March 1993 that around military barracks "dozens of young girls, some as young as twelve or thirteen, are pregnant as a result of rape" and that "at military barriers, it has become practice to demand a '*contribution en nature*' from passing women."[39] A Rwandan newspaper summed up the situation, writing that "soldiers are the biggest cause of insecurity. When they have had too much to drink they will do anything: shoot at people, ransack houses, rape girls and women. . . . The civilians have had enough and will defend themselves with their traditional weapons. In several places bad soldiers have been found dead."[40]

By 1993, the Rwandan National Security Council was reporting that

> for some time now, the usual banditry we had become accustomed to has rapidly developed into organized crime especially involving firearms and grenades. . . . Gangs armed with machetes, clubs, guns and grenades

> operate at dusk and sometimes even in broad daylight. . . . It has been demonstrated that the perpetrators of such attacks are mainly criminals with remarkable skill in the use of firearms and explosives. In fact, these gangs include former soldiers, deserters and even undisciplined soldiers, who are still on active duty.[41]

The United Nations peacekeepers (on whom more later) agreed.[42] When the head of the Rwandan Gendarmerie, Colonel Ndindiliyimana, first met Roméo Dallaire, the general commanding UNAMIR, these bandits were the colonel's greatest concern.[43] A local gendarme reported on them in the following terms in early 1994:

> In all commune sectors the population have been subject of grenade attacks from bandits who excape [*sic*] after their crime. The population organised themselves and carried out night patrols in order to fight off the bandits but since they have none [*sic*] arms they invited the gendarmes to assist. . . . Armed banditry have [*sic*] grown again in the past few weeks because they learnt that the gendares [*sic;* gendarmes] have not enough arms and only a few of transport-possibilities. . . . Though armed robbery is the most ruthless and dangerous there are also pickpockets and thieves.[44]

One report from the Kicukiro Gendarmerie company stated that in the neighborhood of Nyanza a major problem was the "erection of roadblocks accompanied by robberies or all armed attacks even during daylight."[45] Several other neighborhoods, like Karambo, Sosoma, and Sahara, were also noted as especially dangerous. The main cause of insecurity in Sahara was "armed and grenade assassinations even in broad daylight."[46] Nor did banditry subside as 1993 turned into 1994. In fact, quite the opposite. By 1994, in many parts of Kigali, "villagers had to leave their homes and seek accommodation elsewhere in a bid to find peace and security."[47]

DESERTERS, IDPS, AND POLITICAL MILITIAS

In the summer of 1993, when a UNHCR official visited the RPF-occupied zone of Rwanda, he wrote that the "civilian population have been removed from all FPR [RPF] areas, except for two protected settlements at Gishambashayo (7,000) and Butaro (3,000). Most of the displaced people have been in the camps since June 1992."[48] As outlined above, the RPA's military strategy included pushing civilians out of the areas they occupied. There were several reasons for this modus operandi. First, a large, hostile population posed a security threat to the RPA. Locals could guide FAR troops to RPA positions or pass on important intelligence. Second, the RPA did not have the resources to properly look after a large population. Often, especially at the beginning of the war, the RPA barely had enough supplies for its own troops. Third, the RPA did not want Rwandans to be killed during the fighting or used as human shields. Last, it seems likely the RPF counted on the fact that large groups of internal refugees would further burden the government.

While this strategy had its advantages when the RPA operated from the Virunga Mountains, it became problematic after the 8 February offensive. Due to the large gains made by the RPA, almost 350,000 Rwandans became internally displaced persons (IDPs) and were forced into refugee camps around Kigali and Ruhengeri.[49] This brought the total number of IDPs in the country to 900,000.[50] These refugee camps were cesspits, and despite the best efforts of the International Committee of the Red Cross (ICRC) and the UNHCR, nutrition, education, and shelter were inadequate. However, these camps did contain a valuable resource that many within Rwanda were eager to exploit: idle young men. Minister of Defense James Gasana wrote to the prime minister that

> the recruitment [for the FAR] must focus on youth from combat zones for two reasons;
>
> 1. To save them from poverty in the displaced persons' camps where they suffer from idleness and hunger, whereas they have the strength to work.
>
> 2. As they have encountered the problems of the war, they are mentally more motivated than most people.[51]

However, the FAR faced the problem of holding on to its recruits. Regular soldiers suffered as a result of internal rivalries and politics within the officer corps. Not only were they likely to die fighting the more combat-proficient RPA, but life in the FAR was, quite simply, horrible. In addition, there were several attractive reasons to desert from the FAR. As Gasana himself would explain, the "value of their rifle and other personal equipment represented five years of salary for a soldier. You only had to steal one or two weapons, or recover them from the battlefield, to supply yourself for several years."[52] Military skills were also in high demand among political parties in Kigali.

From the onset of multipartyism, and in direct contradiction to the constitution, all the important political parties had formed "youth wings," which were in effect militias. The most infamous was that of the ruling MRND party, the Interahamwe, which would be responsible for the majority of murders during the Genocide. However, the MDR and PSD also had their own youth wings: the Inkuba (thunder) and the Abakombozi (the liberators), respectively. The CDR, the new extremist Hutu Power political party, followed suit with its Impuzamugambi (those with a single purpose). These militias could be called up if a demonstration was needed somewhere, or to intimidate or harass the supporters of other political parties.[53]

In the case of the Interahamwe and Impuzamugambi, these processes combined to create a particularly vicious kind of political rent-a-mobs. While many militia members were recruited from among the general population, the hard core consisted of those who had been forced to flee from the war and those who had served in the army.[54] Not only were these groups more naturally inclined to hate the Tutsi—and the RPF was invariably presented as a Tutsi organization—but former soldiers brought weapons with them as well. A report by the National Security Council pointed out that "some of our politicians have surrounded themselves with former soldiers armed with firearms and grenades allegedly for their own protection and that sometimes results in violent clashes."[55] Thus motivated, and heavily armed, this hard core were used as shock troops: they would be brought to the countryside, like in Bugesera, to jump-start ethnic killings, and would also be asked to intimidate or attack members of the opposition.[56]

The rewards for militiamen usually consisted of beer, food, status, and impunity.[57] There seems to be little doubt that many of them doubled up as the bandits who terrorized Rwandans at night. While the National Security Council did not make an explicit link between bandits and militiamen, it did note that both groups included deserters and discharged soldiers and that "most of these people at present, have taken to armed robbery."[58] As the victims of these bandit attacks were mostly ordinary, mainly Hutu, Rwandans, it is clear that the backers of these militias—the extremist anti-Tutsi, pro-MRND/CDR elements in the government and security forces—were ultimately uninterested in the plight of the people they purported to represent.

THE REACTION OF THE AUTHORITIES

The fusion of banditry, armed deserters, political militias, and state-sponsored ethnic killings was no mistake, and many were quite aware of the fact. Philippe Colyn, one of the staffers at the Belgian Embassy, reported to Brussels at the end of 1992 that

> the president asks the justice system and the intelligence services to carry out investigations but he refuses to clean up the administration and retains the troublemakers thanks to the arsenal of the MRND. Indeed, in the exercise of their duty, some authorities are guilty of or accomplices in carrying out crimes and acts of insecurity (massive arrests of October 1990, genocide of the Bagogwe, massacres at Kibilina, Bugesera and Kibuye, the military mutiny of 21.10.92, and the current ethnic and political troubles).[59]

The power of this group of extremists and the at least passive support they received from President Habyarimana made it difficult and dangerous for honest law enforcers to do their job. Not only were they faced with colleagues who actively opposed their work, if necessary through violence, but many of their services were also chronically underfunded. Minister of Justice Mbonampeka had, for example, complained to the Belgian ambassador as early as March 1992 that his work was being undermined by "incompetence" and "obstruction." Even though he had created several investigation teams consisting of members of the intelligence services, known as the Service central de renseignement (SCR), the Gendarmerie, and the office of the public prosecutor, they had not made any progress in identifying the culprits of the many bombings.[60]

The judiciary suffered so severely under budgetary restrictions that it was practically unable to fulfill its task. Highly symptomatic of the predicament of the Ministry of Justice is that it did not have its own dedicated building and transport and was forced to rely on infrastructures that officially belonged to other ministries. Almost 80 percent of the staff were unqualified, and office equipment was insufficient. Of the 659 judges in Rwanda, only 34 had law degrees. For public prosecutors, the figure was 18 out of 84.[61] In this environment, it was difficult to bring suspects to trial and even harder to get convictions. Compounding these problems was the deplorable state of the penitentiary system. According to a report compiled by the Rwandan National Security Council, which included all the important crime-fighting agencies in the country, prison turned petty criminals into dangerous gangsters. To make matters worse, "almost every day, the escape in droves of the most dangerous prisoners is reported in the prisons." This was possible because of the low numbers and corruption of the guards and the poor state of the prison buildings. The result was that "tough criminals, even those prisoners who have been sentenced to death, manage to escape from the prisons and go to organize new criminal gangs."[62]

Nor could the judicial authorities ensure the safety of their own staff or of inmates. For example, Innocent Munyemana, a criminal investigations officer, was assassinated by hand grenades "thrown by unknown persons through the window into his bedroom" on the night of 15–16 September 1993.[63] As the judiciary did not enjoy a strong independent position, it could not enforce the law with regard to people in a position of political influence. This meant that crimes carried out by anyone related to the regime, or belonging to an influential patronage network, could not be prosecuted. While interference in murder cases is particularly undermining for the justice system, seemingly subtler kinds of interference also took their toll, especially after the introduction of multipartyism, when several different political parties controlled different ministries and a phalanx of people interfered in trials and investigations in the hope of securing partisan outcomes.

From mid-1992, Rwanda also became increasingly saturated with weapons. On the one hand, there was an uncontrolled proliferation of weapons coming from "the front [that] . . . were sold by some unruly soldiers who were deserting their units to join forces with criminals. . . . In June 1993 for example, the Ministry of Defense made an inventory of more than 137 weapons stolen including machine guns."[64] On the other hand, weapons were being distributed through various civilian self-defense programs. Since the start of the war, civilians had carried out auxiliary operations to free FAR and Gendarmerie units for frontline duties.[65] However, from January 1992, the Ministry of the Interior also started handing out weapons to civilians along the frontline. At the start of the program, most of these weapons were Second World War–vintage MAS 36 bolt-action rifles, but as the war went on, the equipment became progressively more lethal. French military advisers in the country had questioned this program from the start. Colonel

Cussac wondered whether the weapons would "be used only against the RPF? Might they not be used for vengeance of a personal, ethnic or political nature?"[66] Colonel Rwagafilita, who was the head of the Gendarmerie until June 1992, was a particular fan of the program and wrote to James Gasana that the "population should be better informed, trained and organised to ensure, or contribute to their own security. The civil self-defence system should be rigorously applied to detect criminals and prevent acts of sabotage and terrorism by means of checks and searches."[67] It is obvious that these civilian self-defense units, especially as they were made up mostly of MRND party members, constituted a mortal danger to any Tutsi or opposition party member in the hills of Rwanda. In this sense, it is fair to conclude that some members of the security forces actively undermined security in the country.

Despite these difficulties, there *were* some who tried to curb the violence. Colonel Ndindiliyimana consistently worked on professionalizing the Gendarmerie from the time he was put in command of the force in June 1992. The US ambassador reported to Washington that Ndindiliyimana

> has made significant progress in revamping the image of his force. While there still are several thousand rank and file Gendarmes with no specialized training after boot camp, a good portion of the 7,000-strong force has been given specific police training, with the goal of changing their mentality from one of "destroy the enemy" to that of "protect the population." The Chief of Staff is having some success in removing his men from combat duties at the front and re-instituting discipline, and is perhaps the most prominent senior military officer to be generally trusted by opposition parties.[68]

However, despite the best efforts of Rwandan law enforcement and UNAMIR, Rwanda was by 1993 "awash with guns; grenades were readily available in the local market for about three U.S. dollars."[69] A Belgian intelligence report reached similar conclusions: "There were already reports of grenades being available in markets for 20 Belgian francs. Today, it is reported that in certain 'red-light' districts, prostitutes even agree to be paid in grenades."[70]

THE CONTINUATION OF THE ARUSHA PEACE TALKS

After the ceasefire was re-established at Dar es Salaam on 7 March 1993, the talks at Arusha resumed. The next item on the agenda was the Protocol of

Agreement on the Integration of the Armed Forces of the Two Parties, and it would prove to be the most contentious issue at the negotiations. The first question to be addressed was the strength of the postwar Rwandan army. By 20 March, an impasse had been reached. "The GoR [government of Rwanda] was proposing a total of 25,000; army of 17,000 and a Gendarmerie of 8,000. The RPF seeks a total military not exceeding 15,000 personnel, but are somewhat flexible concerning the sizes of the Army and the Gendarmerie within that ceiling."[71] In response, the Tanzanians called a meeting for the observers to listen to the proposal of each side. After the government of Rwanda had set out their position, the US representative noted that it could not understand why the government was interested in an army larger than the prewar FAR. The representative of the OAU also noted that a large, possibly unpaid, military would itself constitute a threat to peace.[72] When his turn came, the RPF's negotiator, Pasteur Bizimungu, also argued that a small army was preferable. Why spend excessively on defense with money that could otherwise be used to develop Rwanda?

After internal discussions, the RPF decided that they would be willing to accept an army of around 12,000 soldiers and 6,000 gendarmes. However, the RPF wanted the Gendarmerie and the local and communal police forces to be put under the authority of the Interior Ministry in the broad-based transitional government (BBTG). This demand did not come as a surprise, as the minister of defense in the BBTG was to come from the MRND, and the minister of the interior from the RPF. The eventual compromise called for a 13,000 strong army and a Gendarmerie of 6,000. Both would be under command of the Ministry of Defense. However, the post of chief of staff of the Gendarmerie would go to the RPF. By 3 April, both sides were busy working out the details of the command structure of the new army.[73]

The real sticking point for the negotiations was the distribution of troops in the postwar army. Both Minister of Defense James Gasana and Foreign Minister Boniface Ngulinzira had been thinking about this since at least November 1992. The former had traveled to Nicaragua to familiarize himself with similar processes in Central America and had then gone on to Washington, DC, to meet Lieutenant Colonel Anthony Marley, who would later prove to be one of the key neutral observers at Arusha, making several positive contributions when the talks were deadlocked.[74] The Americans reported on the 14 November 1992 meeting that

> the Minister and Director General seemed serious about solving the integration questions, but very concerned about the percentage of participation the RPF might demand at Arusha. The Rwandan military has yet to come to grips with the fact that they may have to give the RPF more than 12–15 percent participation in the army. On the other hand, they have clearly thought about the importance of integrating senior RPA Officers into the decision-making process (perhaps on a 50/50 basis) and the helpful impact this participation could have on security issues.[75]

The government of Rwanda indicated that they would be willing to offer up to 18 percent of the posts in the postwar army. The reasoning behind this offer was that that was the percentage of Rwandan refugees the RPF represented compared to the total Rwandan population.[76] The facilitators and observers had also already discussed the issue of percentages on 20 November 1992; High Commissioner Matogo of Uganda had noted that his country would try to convince the RPF to "accept a formula substantially less than 50–50; 30 percent would be adequate and a better expression of their actual numbers."[77]

When these percentages were proposed to the RPF in March or April 1993, they were refused outright. Indeed, the integration of forces was supposed to achieve security in postwar Rwanda. Therefore, the RPA's share of the postwar army would have to be strong enough to prevent and stop ethnic massacres or a repeat of the 1959 Social Revolution. Close to 50 percent would be necessary. Clearly, no refugees—the main constituency of the RPF—would return if their safety was not guaranteed. The other important aspect that must be taken into account is that, following the 8 February 1993 offensive, the RPA was the more capable fighting force. Offering them between 12 and 30 percent of the postwar military was not consistent with military reality. The issue proved so contentious that the two sides agreed to discuss it at a later date. Instead, they resolved to continue working on the rest of the practicalities of demobilization. In early June, with the outline of the Protocol on the Integration of the Armed Forces completed, except for the percentages question, the two sides moved on to the next item on the agenda: the Protocol on the Repatriation of the Rwandan Refugees and the Resettlement of Displaced Persons.

The Tanzanian facilitators hoped that, with the rest of the Protocol on Integration of the Armed Forces now complete, the two sides would be able to come to an agreement on the division of personnel in the postwar army. Ambassador Mpungwe met with the two delegations on 1 June 1993 to lay out the Tanzanian government's plan to break the stalemate on the issue: a 35–40/65–60 split of the army for the RPA and the FAR, respectively. To the horror of hard-line Colonel Bagosora, who wanted to stick to the 18 percent quota, Ngulinzira announced he was ready to negotiate from this baseline. The RPF delegation, however, told Mpungwe they could not accept that division of forces either.[78] Predictably, two days later, when the Tanzanian Minister of Defence Abdulrahman Kinana proposed the 35–40/65–60 formula, the RPF rejected it out of hand.[79]

This refusal angered most observers. Mpungwe insisted that the rejection showed "contempt and arrogance."[80] The Ugandans and Senegalese "argued for mounting as much pressure as possible to 'bring reality home to the RPF,'"[81] and the US observer relayed the "astonishment" of the rest of the observers to the RPF.[82] However, the Tanzanians were not about to give up and, on 7 June, Prime Minister John Malecela himself flew to Rwanda for discussions with President Habyarimana and the RPF. By the end of the day, the Protocol on Repatriation of the Rwandan Refugees and the Resettlement of Displaced Persons had been completed.[83] With only the protocol regarding the integration of the armed forces still outstanding, both sides hoped that they would have the entire package finished and ready to be signed by the end of the month.

In the course of the month, the Tanzanians also managed to convince the RPF to accept an integration formula lower than 50/50. The compromise that was reached divided the private and NCO ranks 40/60. In regard to officers, the ratio would be 50/50, with the caveat that if the unit commander belonged to one group (FAR or RPA), the second-in-command would always belong to the other. The peace agreement was supposed to be signed on 24 June 1993, but President Habyarimana refused. He had hoped that by putting Gasana in charge of the negotiations at Arusha, he would be able to have more influence on the process but, "in discussion with the GoR delegation, the two government ministers [Gasana and Ngulinzira] have been open to the idea of compromise, while Ambassador Kanyarishoke and the military members have been hardliners."[84]

THE DEFEAT OF THE MODERATES AND THE SIGNING OF THE ARUSHA ACCORDS

It was now obvious to the president that Prime Minister Dismas Nsengiyaremye, Minister of Defense James Gasana, and Minister of Foreign Affairs Boniface Ngulinzira were the driving force behind the Arusha negotiations. Their combined portfolios gave them a unique position with regard to political information, relations with external governments—especially France, Tanzania, and the United States—and the forces of order. These three were not interested in peace because they harbored a hidden sympathy for the RPF. Rather, they understood that peace was in the best interest of the Rwandan nation. Unlike many in the MRND and the CDR, Gasana also understood that a continuation of the war was unlikely to end in victory for the FAR. Despite his best efforts, the army remained a brittle instrument. In that sense, negotiating a peace settlement was preferable to a continuation of hostilities. Habyarimana and the hardliners in the MRND, CDR, and FAR were caught in a difficult position. They had never been genuinely interested in peace negotiations, but the talks at Arusha had now advanced so far that it was impossible to withdraw without incurring the wrath of the international community. It was equally clear that it would prove difficult to sabotage the implementation of the Arusha Accords in the face of the Nsengiyaremye-Gasana-Ngulinzira triumvirate.

President Habyarimana responded decisively and effectively. He suddenly objected to two points that had already been agreed upon in Arusha. First, he refused to accept that Dismas Nsengiyaremye would be the prime minister in the BBTG. Second, he opposed the 50/50 split of officer posts in the postwar army. Habyarimana's tactic was well understood by a British diplomat in London: "As the areas of contention which have resurfaced have all previously been regarded as settled it would appear that Habyarimana has decided to stall. . . . We would value French and American comments on what appears to have been a deliberate attempt to scupper the Arusha process."[85]

Prime Minister Nsengiyaremye immediately wrote to Habyarimana demanding an explanation. The letter was particularly fierce as the president had not only jeopardized the peace agreement again but also personalized the issue by demanding Dismas's resignation:

> It is imperative that the real motives for this last minute failure to sign the long-awaited Peace Agreement can be clarified. Those motives are part of a logic of rejection of a negotiated solution. Throughout the negotiations, you have constantly developed that rejection and you have even publicly voiced it on November 15, 1992 in Ruhengeri. Your supporters have implemented it in January 1993, more particularly through the disturbances they created in Gisenyi, Ruhengeri and Kibuye prefectures.
>
> Even presently, small terrorist groups are staging attempts against political leaders and creating dissensions throughout the country, in order to incite a new resumption of hostilities.
>
> In other words, it is necessary for you to find an excuse that would allow you to reject the signature of the Peace Agreement, to ask for the resignation of the current Government, to install a war-prone Government at your disposal, to incite the resumption of hostilities . . . and call for renegotiations of some clauses of the already signed protocols.[86]

However, Nsengiyaremye was outmaneuvered. The fact that the mandate of his multiparty government ran out on 16 July 1993 opened up several possibilities for Habyarimana,[87] who immediately designated Agathe Uwilingiyimana, of the MDR, as the new prime minister. Foreign Minister Ngulinzira was also replaced in Uwilingiyimana's new cabinet. Thus two of the driving forces behind the Arusha negotiations—Ngulinzira and Nsengiyaremye—were sidelined in one stroke.

Amid the turmoil, Minister of Defense Gasana realized events were moving in the wrong direction and decided to resign. He had already sent his family to Switzerland and followed them soon afterward. On 20 July 1993, he wrote in his letter of resignation that his move was the result "of the persistent threats and sabotage that I face in my current duties. These threats which place me and my family in a situation of permanent insecurity are the work of an anonymous political-military group which has given itself the name 'A.M.A.S.A.S.U.' and whose aims remain obscure."[88]

As we know (see chapter 9), AMASASU was probably made up of hardline, pro-Habyarimana and anti-Arusha elements within the military intelligence of the FAR. The grave implications of the fact that even the minister of defense could not count on adequate protection were not lost on Dr. Casimir Bizimungu, an MRND stalwart and former foreign minister, who privately told the US ambassador that "if Gasana cannot protect himself we are all threatened."[89]

Nsengiyaremye made one last attempt to regain his position as prime minister. He called an extraordinary congress of the MDR for 23–24 July 1993. However, the Interahamwe militia of the MRND blocked the entrance to the hall where the congress was to take place. Guichaoua writes that "it was finally the gendarmerie, on orders from Col. Theoneste Bagosora (then filling in for the Minister of Defence who had absconded), that was mandated to contain the clashes and maintain security."[90] Considering that Bagosora was known as one of the most hard-line anti-Arusha officers in the FAR, it seems much more likely that it was the chief of staff of the Gendarmerie, Ndindiliyimana, who sent in the gendarmes to maintain order. Once the congress got underway, it became clear that neither Uwilingiyimana nor party Chairman Faustin Twagiramungu enjoyed a majority; they were voted out of the party and Jean Kambanda was designated for the premiership.[91] Uwilingiyimana agreed to resign, but when she arrived home, she found Twagiramungu, Bagosora, PL chairman Justin Mugenzi, PSD president Frédéric Nzamurambaho, and MRND president Matthieu Ngirumpatse waiting. They proceeded to convince her that she should not resign. After some deliberation, Uwilingiyimana decided to stay on as prime minister. How Uwilingiyimana could continue without the support of her party and why the PSD and the PL backed such a move over the will of the MDR congress is unclear.

What is clear is that, within a month, President Habyarimana had, through a combination of clever politics, coercion, and the acquiescence of the now divided opposition, managed to remove the three ministers—Nsengiyaremye, Ngulinzira, and Gasana—who had been a thorn in his side since the swearing in of the multiparty government in April 1992. With them went their experience and the staff they had carefully cultivated in their ministries.[92] The new minister of defense, Augustin Bizimana, was a firm MRND man and quickly replaced most of the moderates promoted by Gasana. Nor did he use his power and influence to structurally support the Arusha peace process as Gasana had done, leaving any moderates who did vulnerable.[93] Nsengiyaremye, undoubtedly fearing for his life, fled to France. Of the three only Boniface Ngulinzira remained in Rwanda. He was killed during the Genocide.

The Tanzanian facilitators, international observers, and RPF all seem to have missed the importance of the changes summarized above. It could well be that the RPF was happy to see that James Gasana, an effective minister, was no longer in charge of the Ministry of Defense. By the same token, the Tanzanians might have been pleased that the end of the negotiations was in sight. On 26 July 1993 the Rwandan president announced that he was ready to sign the final text. The two sides met in Arusha on 3 and 4 August 1993 and signed the Peace Agreement between the Government of the Republic of Rwanda and the Rwandese Patriotic Front, also known as the Arusha Accords.

THE ARUSHA ACCORDS

There are many who are critical of the Arusha Accords.[94] They argue in particular that the accords gave too much power to the RPF, especially militarily. Alan Kuperman writes that "in light of the superiority of the rebels on a man-for-man basis by this time, the military integration protocol was tantamount to a negotiated surrender of the Hutu army to the Tutsi rebels."[95] While Kuperman is right that the RPA was the stronger fighting force, many of its advantages—which were based on unit cohesion, leadership, and doctrine—would have been lost once the two forces integrated. Many RPA soldiers would have come under the command of FAR officers, and as the two forces mixed, the well-oiled RPA Mobile Forces would have been broken up. Furthermore, the RPF would not be in control of the top ranks in the postwar armed forces. The minister of defense was earmarked for the MRND, while the chief of staff of the army would come from the FAR. The only top-tier position held by the RPF would be the chief of staff of the Gendarmerie. All things considered, the military aspects of the Arusha Accords were well balanced.

The same can be said for the political side of the accords. Each participant in the BBTG would get control over one or two consequential ministries. The MRND got the presidency and the Ministry of Defense, the RPF the Ministry of the Interior, the MDR both the prime ministership and the Ministry of Foreign Affairs, the PSD the Ministry of Finance, and the PL the Ministry of Justice. These were the only ministries of any real significance. While others existed on paper, Rwanda's financial situation meant they could exert little influence or control. In fact, the point could be made that the

MRND and the MDR were the two parties that did best out of the Arusha Accords politically.

To be sure, it can be argued that the MRND was losing the most compared to the prewar situation, when—thanks to the one-party dispensation then obtaining—it had enjoyed full control over politics and the military. Yet the MRND's losses did not come solely at the expense of the RPF. The implicit rejection of the one-party state, a process that had begun before the RPF attacked in October 1990, meant that the negotiations in Arusha were as much a renegotiation of the political status quo ante bellum as a peace agreement between the RPF and the government of Rwanda. Power was not only being transferred to the RPF, an external organization with historical ties to Rwanda, under the threat of force, but also to the internal opposition in continuation of the dismantling of the one-party state.

Another argument that has often been made is that the RPF would have stood no chance in the free elections to be held once the Arusha Accords had been implemented.[96] Usually, this contention is advanced together with the claim that the RPF shot down President Habyarimana's plane as part of a premediated plan to seize power by force. Proponents of this view stress that, in the polarized postwar climate of Rwanda, the majority of the population would have voted along ethnic lines. As 80 to 85 percent of the population were Hutu, most of the votes would have gone to the "Rwandan" political parties rather than the RPF. However, this fails to take two factors into account. First, the "Rwandan" parties consisted of the CDR, MRND, MDR, PSD, and PL. Of these the MRND, MDR, and PSD would probably have done best in any elections, but the chance of any of them gaining an outright majority would have been slim. Second, the RPF would have been able to count on the votes of the Banyarwanda refugees who were set to return to Rwanda from the surrounding countries once the Arusha Accords had been implemented. Not only were many of the returning refugees likely to vote for the RPF—as they had already been politicized—but the RPF would have been able to use its formidable political organization to mobilize support inside Rwanda. As Senator Tito Rutaremara explains:

> The people here did not understand. They thought the RPF was only Tutsi. Then they did not know we had that capacity for mobilization and sensitization. They thought we were suicidal when we said the

> transition will be 21 months. . . . All parties were saying the same thing. But we knew we had the capacity for mobilization. . . . The others said, these people, they will only use arms. But we knew we had the capacity for mobilization. . . . The cadreship had been working for seven years. . . . They had their relatives in Rwanda where they could start mobilizing.[97]

In such an electoral environment, it is doubtful any of the major parties would have been able to achieve an absolute majority. So some kind of coalition government would have been the most likely outcome. These factors mean that elections were not something the RPF was deeply worried about. All in all, the Arusha Accords were a well-balanced set of agreements that could have worked, had all the parties been committed to them.

UNAMIR, THE MURDER OF PRESIDENT NDADAYE, AND THE BIRTH OF HUTU POWER

In Tanzania both sides had agreed that the implementation of the Arusha Accords would be overseen by a United Nations peacekeeping force. Its goal was "to establish and maintain a climate essential for the secure installation and subsequent continuing operation of a broad-based transitional government."[98] Under the watchful eyes of the blue berets, the two forces would also integrate and demobilize their personnel. Once the BBTG was in place and the demobilization had been completed, the Arusha Accords would have been implemented and the peacekeepers would be able to go home.

One of the mistakes made at Arusha was that the negotiators had not factored in how much time it would take the UN to deploy a peacekeeping force to the country. This was particularly important, as the timeline set out for the implementation of the accords was tight.[99] The BBTG was supposed to be sworn in on 10 September, only a month after the talks had been concluded. However, it would be impossible for the UN to assemble a peacekeeping force in that time. Lieutenant General Roméo Dallaire, who had been put in charge of the UN force, arrived in Kigali for his reconnaissance mission on 19 August 1993. After this first preparatory stage he would have to write a report announcing how many troops he thought he would need. This report would then go to the UN secretary-general and Security Council; once their agreement had been secured, the troops to staff the mission would still have to be found.[100] All this would take at least three months. One US diplomat later said that "to put it uncharitably . . . the diplomats were handing a ticking time bomb off to the UN. This was not an agreement that was going to be workable in any realistic setting given the gross limitations of the UN."[101]

UNAMIR could hardly have come at a worse time for the UN, which was committed to two large peacekeeping missions in the former Yugoslavia and Somalia and dozens of smaller ones. The situation in Somalia was particularly worrying. On 5 June 1993, twenty-four Pakistani peacekeepers had been killed while searching for weapons in Mogadishu. A couple of months later, and only two days before the UN Mission for Rwanda was officially mandated, elite US forces went into Mogadishu on a mission to capture important lieutenants of Mohamed Farrah Aidid. During the ensuing battle—known as Maalintii Rangers to Somalis, and Operation Gothic Serpent or Black Hawk Down in the West—between two hundred and five hundred Somalis, eighteen US nationals, a Pakistani, and a Malaysian were killed. This catastrophe had important effects on the UN Mission that was about to be deployed to Rwanda, as British diplomat David Hannay explains:

> The depth of the shadow cast by Somalia cannot be exaggerated. It did not only apply to the United States, which had had a terrible experience in Somalia and had drawn, in my view, the wrong conclusions from it. It also applied to all the African countries who had troops in Somalia. . . . This had an appalling effect on everyone's reaction to Rwanda. Why did practically no African countries volunteer to send troops to Rwanda? Because some of them, the ones who were prepared to send troops anywhere, had got them in Somalia and were worrying a great deal about what happened when an operation started to collapse.[102]

After his reconnaissance mission, Dallaire thought that 5,500 well-equipped and well-trained troops with armored personnel carriers and helicopters would be able to carry out the mission. However, he was told that it was unrealistic to expect the countries that formed the UN to pay for or provide that many soldiers.[103] The next viable option was a force of 2,500 troops, but even securing that number was a problem. Eventually, on 5 October 1993, a watered-down version of this "next viable option" was mandated by the UN. Dallaire's force would be deployed with a minimal staff and then slowly built up to 1,200, before being expanded to 2,500 for a brief period. The countries that had been so important as observers during the Arusha Accords should have been the ones to step up and give Dallaire the 5,500 troops he needed. Germany, Belgium, the United Kingdom, Canada, and the OAU could easily have deployed the required numbers, especially if France and the United States had helped foot the bill and provided the necessary air-lift capacity.

In an unlucky historical coincidence, events in neighboring Burundi had a major impact on the political atmosphere in Rwanda.[104] Burundi has often been characterized as a twin of Rwanda because of the many shared political dynamics and sociological traits. The two countries had similar, although indeed distinct, precolonial histories. In addition, they were lumped together during the colonial period and were ruled by Germany and then by Belgium. As we have seen in chapter 3, events in Burundi often have an impact on Rwanda and vice-versa. The most obvious example is how the 1972 genocide in Burundi was a catalyst for the eventual overthrow of President Kayibanda one year later.

Burundi had been run by a mostly Tutsi army since the early 1960s when Michel Micombero seized power in a series of coups d'état. This dictatorial military regime was prone to outbursts of violence, especially against Burundi's Hutu population. On 29 April 1972 a group of Hutu supremacists rose in protest against systematic oppression at the hands of Micombero's government.[105] In Rumonge they formed bands and started killing "every Tutsi in sight, along with a number of Hutu who refused to join them."[106] Over the next couple of days these Hutu bands killed between 800 and 1,200 people.[107] The response of the Tutsi-dominated army was a campaign of selective genocide that lasted from April to September 1972. The general target was the Hutu, with a special emphasis on Hutu "civil servants, educated males, including the near totality of the secondary school population and university students."[108] In six months, between 200,000 and 300,000 Hutu were killed.[109]

President Pierre Buyoya was a product of Burundi's military-dictatorial system. He had seized power in a coup d'état in 1987. Shortly afterward, the army had killed almost 20,000 "unarmed Hutu civilians" in the north of the country. However, this became a turning point for his regime, due to international pressure. A "National Commission to Study the Question of

National Unity" was set up and over the next five years discrimination against Hutu in education and the civil service decreased.[110] This slow but deliberate liberalization quickly ushered in dramatic political change. In June 1993 free and fair democratic elections were held for the first time, and in another first, Melchior Ndadaye, a Hutu who had studied in Rwanda, was elected as president. Buyoya accepted the outcome of the elections, and Ndadaye appointed a broad government that included the Tutsi Sylvie Kinigi as prime minister. These changes were closely watched in Rwanda, where—due to the same Hutu-Tutsi dynamic—President Buyoya was automatically associated with the RPF. If democracy proved to be a success in Burundi, might it not also work in the framework of the Arusha Accords in Rwanda?

The first doubts regarding the democratic transition came on 11 October 1993, when the head of President Ndadaye's security detail received suspicious orders. Fearing a coup, he passed the information on to the head of the military court.[111] Ten days later it was clear that elements within the Burundian army were preparing to depose the president by force. Unbeknown to Ndadaye most of the army's High Command—the very people he relied on to protect him—were complicit.[112] On the night of 20–21 October the army surrounded the Presidential Palace, abducted Ndadaye, then murdered him.[113]

The intertwinement of Rwanda and Burundi became clear during, and immediately after, the assassination of Ndadaye. The night of the coup his wife, Laurence, called President Habyarimana. There was little the Rwandan president could do other than tell her that he had already been informed of the events.[114] That did not stop Habyarimana from trying. He telephoned his French allies and pushed for a military intervention in Burundi. In addition, he expressed his concern that ethnic massacres would soon follow in Burundi and that the "Arusha Accords would not withstand the overthrow of the President of Burundi."[115]

Habyarimana's analysis proved largely correct. Burundi's Hutu population was enraged that their democratically elected president had been assassinated by the predominantly Tutsi military.[116] Roadblocks sprang up throughout the country, and supporters of the late Ndadaye's political party took Tutsis hostage and started killing them: "In places where hostages were killed, the killing for the most part soon extended to all Tutsi women and children, as well as to the ransacking and burning of Tutsi homes. The massacre of Tutsis of both sexes and all ages then spread out in widening circles from these places. In some places the lives of the Tutsi women was [*sic*] spared, although they were often raped or kept captive."[117] In response the army started advancing from its barracks in the country's cities and towns to "restore order." It did this as indiscriminately as the Hutu killers: "As they reached places where massacres of Tutsis had taken place, they rescued survivors and for the most part engaged in the indiscriminate killing of Hutus, often aided by the survivors themselves."[118] It is difficult to estimate the number of people killed in the days and weeks following the coup. However, the intensity of the violence was extraordinary, and scholars estimate between fifty thousand and one hundred thousand dead, "roughly 60% Tutsi and 40% Hutu."[119]

As killings spread across the country people started fleeing en masse. General Dallaire, who had just arrived in Rwanda with a skeleton staff to prepare for the arrival of the bulk of UNAMIR's forces, wrote in one of his first sitreps that "tension due to Burundi situation is in evidence. . . . So far no less than 200,000 refugees in majority Hutu have crossed into Rwanda in the Kigali and Butare prefectures. Mostly women and children. . . . There is already some signs of ethnic frictions in the new refugee camps. Refugees have requested to be segregated by tribe."[120] Eventually the influx of refugees from Burundi reached about 300,000, which put a major strain on the already dysfunctional Rwandan government. In total, there were now around one million IDPs and refugees in Rwanda, or almost 20 percent of the population.

The impact on the Rwandan political scene was just as important, as Reyntjens wrote: "It is all too easy for Hutu extremists today to claim that 'we always told you that you cannot trust the Tutsi,' a belief that is now shared by many moderate Hutu."[121] The February 1993 Offensive had already made many moderates more skeptical of the intentions of the RPF and now, just eight months later, the Tutsi-dominated army in Burundi had launched a coup against a democratically elected Hutu president. In Rwanda wild rumors began to spread. One of them was that Paul Kagame had personally been in the Burundian capital of Bujumbura during the coup. MDR politician Pius Betabura gives a good account of how Ndadaye's assassination was seen in Rwandan political circles:

> One chooses a friend, but one never chooses one's neighbour, and no matter how, when something happens in your neighbour's home, it

> does affect you. The population of Rwanda monitored what was happening in Burundi because we could monitor the radio station and Burundian television, as well. So they followed the electoral campaign. They saw Ndadaye being sworn in, and immediately after the election when he began to work, he was assassinated. Assassinated by whom? A group of soldiers. But everybody knows that in Burundi at the time, the army was composed of just one ethnic group: the Tutsi. . . . People were demoralized. . . . The accords . . . made provision for, among other things, the joining of the two armies; that is, the RPF army and the government of Rwanda army [FAR]. They wondered "Let's say, tomorrow, if they [the RPF/Tutsi] are in all of the structures of government, . . . since their leader was in Bujumbura—if that happens in Rwanda as well, how will it be?" There was disquiet, people began to doubt the accords.[122]

The extremist wings of the opposition party seized this opportunity. On 23 October 1993 they organized a rally at the Nyamirambo Stadium and drew a large crowd of MRND, MDR, CDR, and (a few) PL members. Froduald Karamira, second vice chairman of the MDR and a sinisterly capable propagandist, "took to the podium to declare that the RPF, including specifically its leader General Kagame, were among the plotters who had killed Ndadaye." He continued his speech undermining the RPF and condemned anyone who was negotiating with them. Rather than negotiations, he said, action was in order: "The enemy is among us here [Tutsi in Rwanda]. We cannot sit down and think what happened in Burundi will not happen here, since the enemy is among us. . . . We must avoid. Avoid fighting other Hutu."[123] Reaching his crescendo Karamira shouted "Hutu Power!" And the crowd shouted back in unison, *Power, power, power.* Karamira cried "MRND Power!" Again the response from the crowd, *Power, power, power.* "CDR Power!" *Power, power, power.* "MDR Power!" *Power, power, power.* "Interahamwe Power!" *Power, power, power.* "JDR Power!" *Power, power, power.* "All Hutu Are One Power!" *Power, power, power.*[124]

Like all the other parties involved the French were well aware of the dangerous situation that had now been created. The Arusha Accords had been signed, but ethnic and political tensions were steadily rising: General Quesnot and Africa adviser Bruno Delaye wrote to Mitterrand that "a race is on between now and the arrival of the blue helmets in Kigali."[125]

It was in this environment that General Dallaire tried to get boots on the ground. He had a small staff in Kigali, but no countries had yet firmly committed to sending troops to Rwanda, even though the Belgians did have a reconnaissance mission in the city.[126] Dallaire's mission was also severely hampered by the lack of financial assistance from the UN.[127] Even though UNAMIR had no substantial forces on the ground, crucial milestones lay ahead. Most important was the installation of the BBTG, but a number of other objectives had to be achieved before that. First, General Dallaire wanted to establish a Kigali weapons secure area (KWSA), where all weapons would be placed under UNAMIR control. This would allow the peacekeepers to ensure security within the sector. Second, the French troops who made up Opération Noroît would have to leave. In turn, this would make it possible for the RPF political delegation to come to Kigali and take up its posts in the BBTG and Transitional Assembly. An RPA light battalion would accompany the RPF to ensure their security. It would be particularly important for UNAMIR to make sure that this battalion and the FAR troops stationed in the city did not clash with each other.[128]

Besides the worrying situation in Burundi, UNAMIR also had to deal with an increasingly fractured and complicated political scene in Rwanda. On 14 November 1993, the PL went down the same route as the MDR when it held a convention, "the result of which was a split right down ethnic lines within the party. The PL ministers in the current government fired the members of their personal staff who attended this unusual party meeting."[129] Another issue for General Dallaire was the constant and alarmist messages coming from the minister of defense that the RPA was about to restart the war with the help of Uganda. On 23 November he reported back to New York that "on two separate occasions this last week (Monday and Thursday), the head of mission was called by the Minister of Defence and the Minister of Foreign Affairs with information regarding the massing of NRA (Ugandan) troops and RPF elements in Kabale and Volcano areas with the aim of attacking Rwanda."[130] In both instances, UNAMIR sent military observers to verify the information and found nothing. When Dallaire questioned the foreign minister and the minister of defense, he found that the information on these so-called impending attacks originated from the cabinet of President Habyarimana. "Why the President with the seeming complicity of the Minister of Defense (same political party), is creating these potentially

FIGURE 10.1. 3 Battalion on the football field at Mulindi before departing for Kigali. Courtesy of the Rwandan Ministry of Defense Archives.

explosive scenarios is not quite clear except to possibly disrupt or slow down our deployments and thus affect the date of establishing the BBTG."[131]

Nonetheless, UNAMIR kept on working and by December 1993, General Dallaire felt his control over Kigali was strong enough to start the process that would lead to the swearing in of the BBTG. In keeping with the Arusha Accords, the first step was the departure of most French troops from Rwanda between 11 and 13 December.[132] Their withdrawal went off without a hitch and cleared the way for the RPF politicians to travel to Kigali. In the interim, it had been decided that the RPF delegation, who were to be escorted by an RPA light battalion, would be billeted in the parliament building known as the Conseil national pour le développement (CND).

On the morning of 28 December 1993, 3 Battalion lined up on the football pitch in Mulindi in their brand-new East German summer uniforms. Charles Kayonga, who was "only in his late twenties, but . . . obviously an experienced and able leader,"[133] commanded the unit. As its troops would be representing the RPF to the world, they had been handpicked and furnished with the best weapons and equipment the RPA's armories could supply. After a speech from the chairman of the High Command, the political delegation and the soldiers packed into the waiting buses and made their way to Kigali under the protection of a UNAMIR escort. Upon arrival, 3 Battalion immediately started to reinforce the complex around the building in case it was attacked. Dallaire witnessed the unfolding spectacle: "Once the RPF began digging, they never stopped for the next four months. From shell scrapes or foxholes, they dug full fire-trenches, then roofed the trenches for protection from artillery or mortar fire. They then dug full communication-trenches between the individual trenches and built bunkers that developed into caverns. By the time the war resumed in April, they had built an underground complex under the CND. It was clear that while the peace process was progressing, they were also prepared for the alternative."[134]

These field defenses reinforced an already strong building. The CND complex was one of the few buildings in Kigali built of reinforced concrete. Its position also commanded the surrounding area. Though located outside of Kigali city center, it was perched on a hill with a view over large parts of the city. The King Faisal Hospital, the Presidential Guard camp, and Mounts Kigali and Jali were all clearly visible from the roof of the multistory structure. It also overlooked the main road between the city center and the airport. Negotiating this building as the base for 3 Battalion in Kigali was a coup for the RPF politicians, and a major blunder on the side of the Rwandan government and the FAR. However, the strength of this position also came with a downside. Exposed on the ridge of its hill, and with few Kigalians living around it, the CND was an easy target for artillery fire. To further improve their position 3 Battalion skillfully placed its two heavy machine guns on the roof of the CND, overlooking the Presidential Guard camp in Kimihurura and the main road. These Soviet-designed 12.7 mm DShK's (Degtyaryova-Shpagina Krupnokaliberny) were potent weapons. Rugged and reliable, they fired a large caliber shell—also effective against lightly armored vehicles—to ranges of up to a kilometer. The RPF set up a first aid post in the basement of the CND.

As usual, the RPF pushed the boundaries. As the CND and 3 Battalion were resupplied from Mulindi in UNAMIR-escorted convoys that the FAR was not allowed to stop, the RPF was able to smuggle in ammunition, rotate troops, and increase the size of the garrison. This pathway also allowed for intelligence operatives to be brought to the CND from Mulindi before being infiltrated into Kigali, or, conversely, for long-serving agents in Kigali to be recovered and transported back to Mulindi.[135]

GOING AFTER THE OPPOSITION

It was at this point that the dynamics of chronic economic malaise, partial state collapse, and physical insecurity, combined with the memory of ethnic conflict dating back to the Social Revolution, coalesced to form a razor-sharp state of tension throughout Rwanda. Over a million refugees and IDPs, many on the brink of starvation, were camped out around Kigali and close to the border with Burundi. This environment favored those opposed to the Arusha Accords who used the confusion to their advantage to block the implementation of the agreement.

On 5 January 1994, the first attempt was made to swear in the BBTG in the CND under the protection of UNAMIR. As plainclothes members of the Presidential Guard whipped up the crowd outside, the ceremony broke down just after President Habyarimana had taken his oath. The list of ministers who were to be part of the government had been changed at the last minute and now included PL and MDR hardliners whose presence had not been previously agreed upon by the RPF.[136] Immediately the RPF let it be known that it would not go along with this sleight of hand and refused to continue with the swearing in. On 8 January, another attempt was made, but this time crowds, led by groups of militia and plainclothes Presidential Guards, harassed moderate MDR, PL, and PSD party members, making it impossible for them to reach the CND.[137] With some delegates already inside, the president made a last-minute decision not to attend and the ceremony collapsed.

The failure to install the BBTG made a bad situation even worse. On 19 January 1994, Justin Mugenzi, who had already been targeted before (see previous chapter), was ambushed again. While Mugenzi escaped unharmed, one of his bodyguards was killed in the incident.[138] Then, ten days later, someone unsuccessfully tried to kill the new RPA liaison to UNAMIR, Major Frank Kamenzi, by blowing him up with a hand grenade.[139] On 14 February, there was another attempt at installing the BBTG. However, as the PL and MDR remained split and could not decide on who would take up their allotted ministerial portfolios, none of the political parties showed up.[140]

On 20 February, a major diplomatic dinner attended by all political parties was held. UNAMIR general Roméo Dallaire has left the following account:

> The evening started well, with a lot of light hearted chatter. . . . There was some political discussion but it was all vague and optimistic. . . . Then something quite unexpected happened. I was sitting next to Félicien Gatabazi, the head of the influential (and still united) PSD party, and a well-known Hutu moderate from the south who was very pro-RPF, who had a few too many glasses of wine and got into an intense discussion with members of the MRND about their extremist views. The more drinks Gatabazi downed, the louder and more confrontational he became, until he was almost shouting. He started to insult individual members of the MRND, accusing them of manipulating the political process and causing the deadlock, and the whole room fell silent to listen. Gatabazi had already publicly accused the Presidential Guard of training militias at Kanombe barracks and had received a number of death threats; that night he was fearless.[141]

However, after the dinner, it was not Gatabazi but MDR president Faustin Twagiramungu whose car came under fire. While he survived unharmed, a gendarme bodyguard was shot dead.[142] The next evening Gatabazi's limousine was ambushed close to his house. The two gendarmes who were guarding him were killed on the spot, but Gatabazi, mortally injured, managed to get into his house and call UNAMIR for assistance. He died shortly after making the call.[143] Gatabazi was from the south, where the PSD was most popular and the response to his death was immediate. The next day, Martin Bucyana, chairman of the extremist CDR, who was traveling in the south close to Save, the home region of Gatabazi, was attacked by a mob and lynched together with his driver.[144] Thus, within the space of three days, assassins had targeted the heads of three political parties and succeeded in murdering two of them. Another attempt was supposed to be made at installing the BBTG on 22 February, the day after the lynching of Bucyana, but both Agathe Uwilingiyimana and the RPF refused to attend due to the killing of Gatabazi. The supporters and militias of the various political parties went out on to the streets of Kigali and "over the next couple of days 35 people died and a further 150 were injured."[145]

Throughout March, both sides tried to find a solution to the political impasse. With the help of Tanzanian mediators, both sides were able to agree, reluctantly, on which PL members would take up the allotted ministerial portfolios and seats in the national assembly. However, Habyarimana now insisted on the inclusion of the rabidly racist anti-Tutsi CDR in the new parliament.[146] In the RPF's view this issue had already been decided during the Arusha negotiations when the topic had come up and the CDR had been excluded. Habyarimana knew perfectly well that the RPF would not agree to a BBTG that included the CDR; unsurprisingly, the RPF delegation did not show up at the next attempt to swear in the government on 25 March. On 5 April UNAMIR's mandate was extended for six more weeks to give both parties more time to sort out their differences. The next day Habyarimana flew to Dar es Salaam to discuss the situation with regional leaders. After a long day of talks, he offered President Cyprien Ntaryamira of Burundi a lift in his new and comfortable airplane.

* * *

The activities of extremist anti-Tutsi, pro-MRND elements within the army and security forces, and of the militias of the MRND and CDR, as well as the existence of an enormous pool of potential recruits among IDPs and the structural weakness of the honest forces of order, caused the Rwandan state to lose its monopoly on violence. The whole country was impacted by the ensuing insecurity, which led to the "gradual unravelling of a social fabric"[147] and an early stage of state collapse. These developments can again be traced to the peculiar three-sided nature of the conflict in Rwanda. If the president and the MRND party had been focused on defeating the RPF, they would have preached national unity and maintained internal security. This would have entailed supporting the multiparty government of Prime Minister Nsengiyaremye. However, extremists within the MRND, who had at the very least the tacit support of Habyarimana, considered the internal opposition just as dangerous to their position as the RPF. To meet this internal challenge, they decided to unleash violence on their political opponents. While the extremists were strongly represented within the FAR, the army was technically under the command of the multiparty government and could not be used to hunt the opposition too openly. To surmount this obstacle, private armies and death squads were created from deserters and desperate youths who, in exchange for their service, were allowed to indulge in banditry as they pleased. The extremists do not seem to have recognized that the internal turmoil caused by these private armies fatally undermined their fighting chances against the RPF.

Three elements undermined the successful implementation of the Arusha Accords. First, the removal of the Nsengiyaremye-Ngulinzira-Gasana triumvirate by Habyarimana meant that the driving force for peace on the side of the government had disappeared. Their replacements were either unwilling or unable to properly support the peace plan. They could, for example, not count on the broad international support that Ngulinzira had skillfully built up. It remains a mystery how the international community supporting the peace talks and the RPF could have missed this factor. Second, the RPF's February 1993 Offensive and the murder of President Ndadaye of Burundi undermined the position of the moderate Hutu opposition. The latter was skillfully exploited by the "power" factions of the opposition parties. Third, the (Western) countries that had assisted effectively at Arusha did not provide troops for the UN peacekeeping force that the accords mandated. General Dallaire asked for 5,500 troops, a force that a coalition of the United States, Canada, the United Kingdom, Germany, Belgium, and various African partners could have easily furnished. Had the triumvirate remained in place and UNAMIR been a credible deterrent, the state might have regained its monopoly on violence and the Arusha Accords might have been successfully implemented. However, the non-implementation of the accords, which signaled the failure of negotiations, left only one place for the belligerents to settle their differences: the battlefield.

11

The Campaign Against Genocide

April–July 1994

AROUND 20:30 ON 6 APRIL 1994, PRESIDENT HABYARIMANA'S plane, a Falcon 50 given to him by the French government and flown by French pilots, started its descent to Kigali airport. On board were President Habyarimana and President Cyprien Ntaryamira of Burundi. With them were two Burundian ministers; chief of staff of the FAR major general Déogratias Nsabimana; Colonel Elie Sagatwa; Major Thaddée Bagaragaza; Juvenal Renaho, an adviser to Habyarimana; and Dr. Emmanuel Akingeneye, the president's physician. Finally, there were the three French flight crew: Jacky Héraud, Jean-Pierre Minaberry, and Jean-Michel Perrine. Moments later, the flight was shot down by one or two missiles fired from a handheld surface-to-air missile. The plane crashed just short of the runway in the garden of the president's house, killing all on board.

Only an hour and a half after the president had been shot down, a high-level meeting was convened by Colonel Bagosora, one of the most important Hutu Power leaders in the country. Present were the main commanders of the FAR and the Gendarmerie. We know what happened at the meeting because Roméo Dallaire, the general in command of UNAMIR, also attended. Following a short discussion, it became clear that the FAR was unwilling to hand over power to Agathe Uwilingiyimana, the designated prime minister according to the Arusha Accords. Instead, the FAR would take control of the country. In effect a faction of the FAR, headed by Bagosora, had committed a coup d'état.[1] Only a few hours later, FAR soldiers and Interahamwe militia set up roadblocks where they checked people's identity cards; Tutsi were immediately killed. At the same time troops from the Presidential Guards Battalion hunted down and assassinated the moderate opposition in the city. Over the next one hundred days about 800,000 people, mostly Tutsi, would be killed by the *génocidaires.*

As much has been written on it, the Genocide is not the crux of this chapter. Nor are the Western military interventions during this period, which are dealt with only briefly. Rather the chapter provides the first blow-by-blow account of the RPA's military campaign, which stopped the Genocide. To do so, it first provides a brief discussion of the evidence (or lack thereof) relating to the shooting down of Habyarimana's plane and of the first killings of the Genocide. Then it moves on to the crucial Battle of Kigali and the large flanking maneuver conducted by 157 CMF. The final sections of the chapter look at revenge killings conducted by RPA troops as they advanced.

THE START OF THE GENOCIDE

There has been an enormous amount of discussion, both by (semi)official inquiries and historians, over who shot down Habyarimana's plane.[2] There are two main theories. The first suggests that it was Hutu Power hardliners in the FAR who killed the president to take power and prevent the Arusha Accords from being implemented. The second argues that the RPF shot down the airplane to provoke the Genocide that it knew was being planned. Once the Genocide was underway—so goes the second theory—the RPF would be able to use its superior military might to seize full power in the country. This much-publicized hypothesis does not make sense on several levels. The RPA could have taken Rwanda by force in February 1993 but decided instead to return to the negotiating table. In addition, the Front had done well in the Arusha Accords. Though it had not secured total power, it had won enough guarantees that it would be in a good position to compete in elections in post-Arusha Rwanda. The movement was also supremely confident in its own abilities, not only militarily but also organizationally. Behind the RPA stood the formidable political machinery of the RPF, which kept it fed, clothed, and motivated. Once the war was over, this apparatus would be put in high gear to sell its program to Rwandans. Another problem with the conspiratorial theory is that it assumes clairvoyance on the part of the RPF, which would have relied on the CDR, MRND, and FAR hardliners to commit genocide. If the RPF did indeed shoot down the presidential plane, it is much more likely that it did so to eliminate what remained as the main obstacle to the implementation of the Arusha Accords. President Habyarimana had never wanted to negotiate with the RPF, as the previous chapters have shown. By removing him from the scene, the RPF might have expected to be able to push the implementation of the Arusha Accords without putting the peace process at risk. After all, the BBTG was ready to take office and only awaiting its official swearing in.

We will probably never know who shot down the plane because the hardliners within both the FAR and the RPA could have carried out the assassination. In addition, there is no evidence to speak of. The main facts are as follows. First, we know that both the RPA and the FAR had access to surface-to-air missiles. The RPA took several Soviet-made SA-7 Strela and SA-16/18 Igla surface-to-air missiles with them into Rwanda from Uganda and used them effectively against FAR helicopters. The FAR, though it did not officially have any portable surface-to-air missiles in its arsenal, could easily have obtained them from Egypt or found some on the battlefield. While much has been made of the fact that "white" mercenaries might have been hired because of their expertise with such weapons, this seems unlikely.[3] Portable surface-to-air missiles are designed to be used in the heat of battle, by conscripts, under high stress; they are not exceptionally difficult to operate. The mujahideen, for example, were able to deploy their Stinger missiles effectively against the Red Army in Afghanistan with minimal training. Considering the military experience of both the RPA and the FAR, there is no doubt that both had soldiers capable of effectively deploying these weapons. Third, they both would have been able to get their people in place near the flight path of the president's plane. As the wider area was under the control of the FAR, assassins from the army's extremist faction would have found easy access. This would have been harder, but not impossible, for the RPA.[4] A small, handpicked group could have evaded the—usually subpar—FAR patrols. As the previous chapters have outlined, the RPA had enormous experience with infiltration behind enemy lines. Fourth, any evidence collected in the area from where investigators think the plane was shot down is worthless because no proper chain of custody was established. The investigations were only carried out after the Battle of Kigali had been fought over the very places from where the missiles might have been fired. Equally, any eyewitness testimony on the launching of the missiles must be ignored. The flight time from launch to impact of an SA-16/18 missile is between 0.4 and 3.4 seconds, hardly enough time to get a proper look.[5]

However—and this is significant—the affiliation of those who shot down the plane is in fact irrelevant to the issue of the Genocide. Despite Habyarimana's demise, all the constitutional mechanisms were still in place to permit the swearing in of the BBTG, which was now planned for 7 April 1994. Rather, it was the actions of the FAR in the immediate aftermath of the death of the president that allowed the Genocide to take place. Instead of assisting UNAMIR in maintaining order, the FAR went on a killing spree, starting with the moderate political class.

The tragic story of Annonciate and Joseph Kavaruganda illustrates the method used. On the evening of 6 April 1994 Joseph, Annonciate, and two of their children were at home watching a football match when their eldest son, Jean-Marcel, called. He told his father, "Well, Daddy, they have just announced in Belgium that the presidential plane had been brought down, or that the news of his death will be announced later on."[6] Perturbed by the news, Joseph, the head of Rwanda's Supreme Court, went outside and asked the small UNAMIR contingent that was guarding the house to be on the alert. Soon after the phone rang again. This time, it was their neighbor Frédéric Nzamurambaho, chairman of the PSD and minister of agriculture. "Have you heard the news? It would appear President Habyarimana is dead. . . . I don't know, but it seems to me that we are being surrounded from nearby. And I don't know whether they're not going to kill people, carry out massacres during the night."[7] Though Kavaruganda had received death threats in the past, he hoped that UNAMIR would be able to protect both his neighbor and his own family.

Annonciate Kavaruganda remembers that in the early morning of 7 April, Jean-Marcel called again, relaying that the Belgian TV was reporting a political vacuum in Rwanda:

> My son asked his father, "If there really is a legal vacuum in Rwanda, what's going to happen tomorrow?" And his father replied and said: "There won't be a legal vacuum in Rwanda, because the Inkotanyi ministers are here, there are other ministers from other political parties, they're here, there are also MPs waiting to be sworn in. What we're

> lacking is a President. And if he's dead . . ."—At the time, we didn't know he was dead, we had no reliable information about his death. He said: "For this reason, I think that in the morning, all the parties will get together, and the MRND party, which must nominate the candidate for the presidency, so this party, they will tell me what I must do. And I will swear in the ministers. And if I'm not there, there will be a legal vacuum. But as long as the Constitutional Court is there, I can swear in the ministers, so there will not be a legal vacuum."[8]

After having hung up with his son, Nzamurambaho called again: "Mr. President, I've just heard that the neighborhood is surrounded, and no one can leave. I don't know what's going to happen." As Annonciate and Joseph became increasingly worried, there was a knock on their bedroom window. One of the Ghanaian peacekeepers was outside with a Rwandan soldier. Joseph went to the door and saw that there were about forty Presidential Guards around the house and that the UNAMIR contingent had been disarmed. Annonciate remembers what happened next:

> One of the soldiers came up from the group and gave him a military salute—he gave a military salute—and told him: "Mr President, I've been . . . we've been sent to fetch you. Our commanders told us to take you where other authorities have been put, to take you where Landouald Ndasingwa was taken, and where Faustin Rucogoza, who was minister of information, had also been taken. We were sent to fetch you. Come, let's go." He looked at them and said: "Why have you come to fetch me so early in the morning? 'Where' are you taking authorities very early in the morning, like this, or even during the night?" They said: "Our chiefs told us to look for you. If you don't come of your own accord, we will force you." And when he heard this, he became afraid. He told the Ghanaian soldiers that these soldiers wanted to kill him. He hurriedly closed the door, he locked it, but I think it was because he was very afraid; he was very afraid, he closed the door, he locked it, but he didn't take out the keys, he left them in the keyhole.[9]

Rushing through the house, Joseph locked every door behind him. When he arrived at the bedrooms, he told the kids to go to their washroom and lie flat on the floor. Annonciate goes on: "He found me in the bedroom, and he told me, 'There's a soldier who told me his name is Captain Kabera. He's an officer in President Habyarimana's office, and he's at the head of these soldiers who came to fetch me.' . . . He added: 'Let's go to our bedroom, let's go to our bathroom, we'll stay there.'"[10] Before hiding in the bathroom, Joseph called the Belgian and Bangladeshi UNAMIR detachments, who told him to stay put and that they would send soldiers. They hoped to be there within forty-five minutes. Jean-Marcel called for a third time and spoke to his father. He warned his father that he had heard that the neighborhood where his parents lived was going to come under attack and that the family should seek shelter. However, his father knew it was too late: "Soldiers are already here, there are very many of them. I've just seen them, they're outside. I don't know whether we will survive." During the conversation, the Presidential Guards lost their patience outside and started forcing their way into the house. Hearing the noise, Jean-Marcel asked: "'Dad. What's that?' And his father replied in French: 'I think it's the soldiers attacking. I think they're coming into the house, because I don't know what could . . . who else could be making that noise. It must be soldiers in the house.'" Annonciate remembers her husband's final words to his son: "He said to 'them': 'You and Juliette and Guillaume, look after yourselves, we may not see each other again. . . . You three might survive, be brave,' the phone went dead and communication was cut. They couldn't finish their conversation."[11]

As the soldiers searched the house, they found the children hiding in the other bathroom: "I heard our young daughter, Judith Kavaruganda, who was in her final year at secondary school, knocking on our door. She was calling out to us, saying: 'Dad, open the door! They're going to shoot me!'"[12] Once the soldiers had entered the room, Joseph made them wait while he got dressed. Annonciate used the opportunity to start packing a bag for her husband but was asked by one of the soldiers: "Do you believe that he needs any other clothes, that he needs to change?"[13] Joseph, Annonciate, and their two children were escorted out of the house and put in a pickup. Joseph sat in the front and the rest of his family in the back. As the driver started driving off, Captain Kabera noticed that the family was in the back of the truck and told them to get out and go back to the house. Once they were back at the house, Joseph returned with his captors one more time to give his wife some money, which was promptly stolen by one of the soldiers—who had now set about plundering the house. Then he was taken away. "And they left. That's the last day I saw him. They didn't come back. We stayed at home, and they hit us and looted us."[14]

For the rest of the morning and the early afternoon Annonciate and her children were beaten by the Presidential Guards while the small UNAMIR detachment looked on. While they did not intervene, their presence did probably prevent the family from being executed there and then. Some of the soldiers continued on their mission and went to the house of Ngango, the deputy chairman of the PSD, while others went to the neighbor's house. Annonciate heard the screams as Nzamurambaho and his family were massacred. In the confusion, one of the soldiers, probably a gendarme, came up to her and told her:

> I was part of Landouald Ndasingwa's escort, and I would like to inform you that they killed Landouald this morning, and his wife was killed, his children Patrick and Malaïka. And even his mother was killed. So I heard them say that they'll come and kill you after these UNAMIR soldiers leave. So I would advise you to run away. I'd advise you to take Julien and throw them [the children] over the fence and flee into the sorghum field, so he can tell your story afterwards. Otherwise, they said they intend to kill you so you won't testify to what you saw today.[15]

Later in the afternoon, another neighbor, MRND party member Dr. Casimir Bizimungu, arrived home with a military escort and Annonciate asked for his help. After some hesitation, Bizimungu took Annonciate, her two children, and the son of Nzamurambaho, who had managed to escape the slaughter at his father's house, to the Canadian Embassy.[16] Throughout the morning of 7 April, the above scene was repeated throughout Kigali, as FAR death squads went around the capital killing Tutsi and members of the moderate opposition. Joseph Kavaruganda, Frédéric Nzamurambaho (PSD), and Félicien Ngango (PSD) were killed in Kimihurura, and many others were also targeted. Luc Marshal, one of the Belgian officers with UNAMIR, was on the phone with Landoald Ndasingwa (PL) when Ndasingwa and his family were killed. Not content with the murders of the president of the Supreme Court, the leadership of the PSD, and the head of the moderate faction of the PL, the FAR also killed Prime Minister Agathe Uwilingiyimana (MDR), Faustin Rucogoza (MDR), Aloys Niyoyita (PL), and many others. As General Dallaire put it, "In just a few hours the Presidential Guard had conducted an obviously well-organized and well-executed plan—by noon on April 7 the moderate political leadership of Rwanda was dead or in hiding, the potential for a future moderate government utterly lost."[17]

Taking their cue from the FAR, the Interahamwe and Impuzamugambi militias set up roadblocks throughout Kigali where they forced people to show their identity cards. They too immediately killed any Tutsi. Traditional hiding places like schools and churches were assaulted, and the people who had taken shelter there were massacred with machetes, grenades, and clubs. Hutu who refused to join the slaughter or who were known to be moderate PL, PSD, or MDR members were also targeted. According to Alison Des Forges, by 11 April, 20,000 people, "the vast majority of them Tutsi," had been killed, as more people started joining the killers.[18] Over the next one hundred days, the figure would rise to around 800,000. How did the RPF respond to the unfolding massacres?

THE BATTLE OF KIGALI: FIRST PHASE

After Juvénal Habyarimana's jet was shot down, 3 Battalion, based in the CND, came under immediate attack from the FAR.[19] Recoilless rifles and mortars started pounding the structure from several directions. Despite the shelter afforded by its reinforced concrete walls and the trenches surrounding the complex, the CND was in a precarious position. To its direct north was Camp Kami, the base of the Military Police Battalion; to the east were Kigali airport and Camp Kanombe, which housed the Para-Commando Battalion; to the southwest were the Presidential Guards in Camp Kimihurura, while Camp Kacyiru, the headquarters of the Gendarmerie, was a couple of hundred meters west of the CND. Another infantry brigade, the reconnaissance battalion, artillery, mortars, and various second-line units were stationed throughout Kigali, with Camp Kigali, in the center of town, being an especially important base. In total, there were about 7,000 to 10,000 FAR troops facing the 600-strong 3 Battalion.

Throughout 7 April, as all parties tried to understand what was happening, the RPA in the CND did not leave the compound but returned fire, especially toward the Presidential Guard camp located nearby. At first, General Dallaire thought that the killings might be caused by elements of the FAR that had rebelled against their commanding officers. However, the scale of the massacres became clear to the RPF as people sought shelter around the

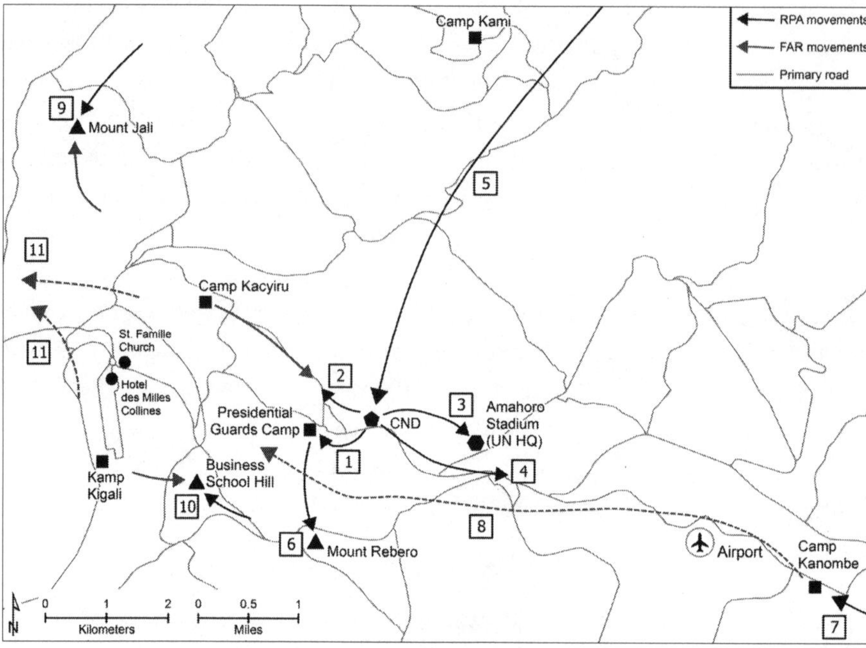

MAP 11.1. The Battle for Kigali. (1) Following the start of the Genocide the 3 Battalion of the RPA (Rwandan Patriotic Army) is engaged by the FAR (Forces armées rwandaises). RPA's four companies are immediately engaged. Leopard Company fights a close combat with the Presidential Guards around Kimihurura, while Lion Company moves to screen Camp Kami. (2) Tiger Company moves to attack the Gendarmerie around Camp Kacyiru. (3) Eagle Company advances toward the Amahoro Stadium to defend the Tutsi who have taken refuge under UN protection. (4) Part of Eagle Company is engaged by FAR Para-Commando Battalion troops who are stationed at Kanombe. (5) On 11 April the lead elements of the relief force (Alpha Combined Mobile Force, Bravo CMF, 59 CMF) arrive from the North. (6) Troops from 3 Battalion and 59 CMF capture Mount Rebero on 12 April and hold it against determined counterattacks. (7) 7 CMF arrives from the East and attacks Camp Kanombe, which is defended by the Para-Commando Battalion. (8) On 22–23 May the Para-Commando Battalion and other FAR units are forced to withdraw from Camp Kanombe. (9) 7 CMF and Bravo CMF engage in tough battles with the FAR on Mount Jali and are temporarily pushed back. They manage to capture the position on 20 June. (10) Business School Hill becomes a focal point for the fighting. (11) On 4 July, with the position in Kigali untenable, the FAR retreats from the city. Map by Brian Balsley.

CND. What also became clear was that UNAMIR was not strong enough to stop the unfolding Genocide. Though UN troops protected Tutsi and moderate Hutu who took shelter in their camps, their rules of engagement—and military weakness—prevented them from taking control of the situation.

No genocide has ever been stopped without the use of force, and the only armed group with the will and ability to intervene was the RPA. The RPA High Command had no other option but a full resumption of hostilities. Nor could there be any discussion of a ceasefire as long as the murder of Tutsis continued. This is an important point, since many did try to broker a ceasefire between the two parties.[20] However well intentioned, these attempts were unrealistic and uninformed: the only way to stop the killings was the unconditional surrender of the génocidaires and the FAR. As the genocidal extremists would not lay down their arms until they had completed the killing of Tutsi and moderate Hutu, the only solution was to defeat them by force of arms.

The RPA faced a daunting task. In total it could count on eight CMFs. Each CMF usually counted 1,000–2,000 troops but RPA units were understrength throughout the war.[21] A generous estimate would be about 1,500 soldiers per CMF. There was also 3 Battalion with 600 troops in the CND, several smaller reserve units with heavy weapons, and the High Command protection company. I estimate a maximum of 12,000 to 13,000 frontline soldiers for the RPA. Against this force stood the FAR and the Gendarmerie which could, together, count on 39,000 soldiers.[22] While the RPA knew it was the more competent military organization, these were still daunting odds. Especially when considering that the rule of thumb is that an attacker needs superiority in numbers against a prepared defense.

On 8 April, Chairman of the High Command Paul Kagame gave the commander of 3 Battalion, Charles Kayonga, the order to take action. All four of the companies of 3 Battalion were given different objectives. Eagle Company was to break out toward the Amahoro Stadium to defend the many Tutsis who had taken shelter there under UN protection; the RPF High Command did not trust that the Bangladeshi UN contingent would be able to protect the stadium from génocidaire extremists. The company split up and moved toward the stadium in a pincer movement. While the northern pincer made good progress, the southern pincer quickly ran into difficulties as it engaged elements of the FAR Para-Commando Battalion, which were advancing up the road from the Kanombe barracks toward the CND. Chui (Leopard) Company was ordered to contain the Presidential Guards stationed in their barracks in Kimihurura, with support from the DShK on the roof of the CND. Vicious fighting took place between Chui Company and the Presidential Guards, as Henry Anyidoho, the leader of the Ghanaian detachment of UNAMIR, recalls: "From dusk to dawn there were attacks and counter attacks mainly between the RPF and the Presidential Guards. . . . The Presidential Guards held on tenaciously and fought a pitched battle with the RPF. The frontlines between the parties were less than 100 meters. This situation, along the route from the Meridien Hotel to the Gendarmerie Camp in Kacyiru, remained the same for over three months during the civil war."[23]

Meanwhile, Tiger Company fought on the right flank of Chui and engaged the Gendarmerie in Kacyiru. The last company, Simba (Lion), engaged the military police barracks at Camp Kami. Despite seizing the initiative with these attacks, 3 Battalion would not be able to hold out against the FAR unless it was quickly reinforced.

THE RELIEF OF 3 BATTALION AND OPERATIONS AMARYLLIS AND SILVERBACK

The RPA offensive from Mulindi also began on 8 April. The main objective was to quickly relieve 3 Battalion. Alpha Combined Mobile Force, Bravo CMF, and 59 CMF were ordered to head straight for Kigali and bypass any pockets of resistance on the way.

> All these forces were infiltrating by passing enemy defences; not engaging because the end state was the capital city. Small forces would be left to hoodwink the very heavily barricaded enemy defences which had been there throughout the ceasefire period. This was to distract the enemy as the bulk . . . advanced to the capital. The enemy commanders were all in bewilderment when . . . they received communication that heavy fighting was going on very deep within the country, actually at the outskirts of the capital yet they were deeply dug in very far away.[24]

Captain, now General, Charles Karamba, stationed at the CND, remembers: "We were monitoring and in constant communication with the force that had been ordered by the Commander in Chief to link up with us. . . . At the same time engaging the enemy but aware that our reinforcement was coming."[25] Though 3 Battalion was on its own, its commanders and soldiers knew that they would not be forgotten and that they had a crucial role to play in the battle. Their aggressive actions around the CND were tying down three of the elite FAR battalions, keeping them away from other crucial sectors of the front.[26]

MAP 11.2. The Campaign Against Genocide. (1) On 8 April Alpha Combined Mobile Force, Bravo CMF, and 59 CMF are ordered to relieve 3 Battalion in Kigali as quickly as possible. They bypass FAR (Forces armées rwandaises) strong points, which are cleared by follow-up formations, and reach Kigali on 11 April. (2) 7 CMF and 157 CMF advance down the east of Rwanda. 7 CMF moves west after passing Lake Muhazi and joins the battle around Kigali. 157 CMF advances toward the south and reaches the border with Tanzania on 30 April. From there it advances to the west, threatening Kigali from the south. (3) The RPA (Rwandan Patriotic Army) fights a holding action around Ruhengeri, pinning FAR troops in the region that might otherwise be used in other sectors. (4) On 4 July the FAR starts its retreat from Kigali. Many of its units find refuge in Zaire. Map by Brian Balsley.

With Alpha Mobile, commanded by Sam "Kaka" Kanyemera, leading the way, the relief column moved south toward Kigali under the cover of night. By the morning of 9 April, they had reached Muyanza Mission Parish. Once there, however, Bravo CMF and 59 CMF were detected by the FAR and forced to fight off a counterattack.[27] The next day these units confronted the FAR again when they ran into an ambush at Zoko hill: "The two Commanding officers [Charles Ngoga and Ludoviko 'Dodo' Twahirwa for 59 CMF and Bravo Mobile, respectively] . . . held an urgent meeting where it was decided that to avoid further ambushes and unnecessary casualties, the forces should travel by day and confront the enemy during day light."[28] While this force distracted the FAR, Alpha Mobile had been able to slip through the net undetected and its lead company arrived at the CND from the direction of the King Faisal Hospital in the afternoon of 11 April. However, severe fire from the Gendarmerie in Kacyiru, which had a 37 mm cannon, prevented the rest of Alpha Mobile from reaching the CND during daytime. Later that night they were able to reinforce their comrades of 3 Battalion. Meanwhile, throughout 11 April, Bravo and 59 CMF, still trailing behind, fought running battles with FAR troops that were trying to stop them from reaching Kigali. Making steady progress, they joined the battle around Kigali the next morning.

Following the death of President Habyarimana, the international community immediately swung into action to save its own. Both France and Belgium launched closely coordinated missions to rescue their citizens, and those of allied nations, in Kigali. Considering the circumstances, this made sense. Ten Belgian peacekeepers had been killed while trying to protect Prime Minister Uwilingiyimana on 7 April, and the RTLM hate radio picked out Belgium and the Belgians as targets for its vitriol.[29] The Belgian Embassy also got several messages of Belgians being killed by the génocidaires. Though the threat to the French was less acute, due to the close working relationship between the French Embassy and military cooperants with their FAR and Gendarmerie counterparts, the French government was not taking any risks. They did not know how the situation would develop or how the RPA might treat French civilians it encountered.

On the night of 8–9 April, the lead elements of the French Operation Amaryllis landed at Kigali airport. Over 200 troops of the 3e régiment de parachutistes d'infanterie de marine (3e RPIMa) took control of the airport.

The next day, while reconnaissance operations were underway, they were joined by an extra company. On 11 April, the French started their operations, evacuating French citizens and the family of President Habyarimana. A further company from the 8e régiment de parachutistes d'infanterie de marine (8e RPIMa) reinforced the detachment, bringing total troop strength to well over 400. By 13 April, all French expats and diplomats, the family of Habyarimana, and other select Rwandans had been evacuated. The next day the last French troops left Rwanda.[30] The Belgians worked hand in hand with Amaryllis to evacuate their own people.[31] On 10 April, 250 Belgian para-commandos arrived at Kigali airport, and in cooperation with the Belgian troops in UNAMIR, started evacuating expatriates.[32] One day after the French, on 15 April, the last Belgian troops and civilians flew out of Kigali.

The reaction of the RPF to Operation Amaryllis and Operation Silverback (as the Belgian part of the evacuation was code-named) was pragmatic. On the one hand, the RPF wanted to avoid confrontation with foreign and especially French troops, as their intervention in the fighting could decisively turn the battle in favor of the FAR. On the other hand, the RPF wanted these foreigners out of the way as soon as possible. Neither the French nor the Belgians had shown interest in stopping the mass killings that were taking place, literally before their eyes. The longer non-UNAMIR foreign troops remained on Rwandan soil, the more likely they were to get involved. So, on 12 April, the RPF announced a sixty-hour window for foreign, non-UNAMIR troops to leave Rwanda, after which they would be considered co-belligerents. Both the French and the Belgians departed before the ultimatum ran out.

THE BATTLE OF KIGALI: SECOND PHASE

Kigali is overlooked by several important hills (Mount Rebero, Mount Kigali, and Mount Jali) that tower above the town. Anyone who holds them enjoys a decisive tactical advantage. Right after their arrival, troops of 59 CMF, supported by their comrades of 3 Battalion, launched an attack on Mount Rebero in the early morning of 12 April. This was typical of RPA tactics, as Henry Anyidoho observes: "The main tactics used by the RPF throughout the war was [*sic*] 'infiltration and encirclement.' They moved in small numbers mainly during the night and carried out dawn attacks. The RPF soldiers had a stubborn stamina. They had trained on the hills so well that they were always strong and battle ready."[33] The capture of Mount

Rebero was a key development, as it allowed the RPF to direct artillery and mortar fire onto Camp Kigali. Recognizing the danger of leaving this strategic peak in the hands of the RPF for too long, the FAR launched a series of determined and sustained counterattacks with its 73 and Muvumba Battalions, which the RPA succeeding in beating off. As Bravo Mobile moved up, it took over the position held by 59 Mobile on top of Mount Rebero, thereby allowing the latter to help Alpha Mobile and 3 Battalion in the urban fighting now taking place throughout Kigali.[34]

While these actions show that the RPA still possessed all the qualities that had made it a first-class fighting force, its troops started facing serious difficulties in the urban environment of Kigali. Throughout history, cities have swallowed up armies. Perhaps the most famous examples are the German 6th Army in 1942, as it tried to capture Stalingrad, and the Russian Army as it tried to occupy Grozny in Chechnya in 1994. Or more recently, the tough battles fought by the United States in Fallujah and Baghdad. In urban terrain, it is more difficult for units to communicate and work together, which reduces combat effectiveness. This proved a problem for the RPA, which had previously relied on its superior tactics and communications to overcome the more numerous FAR in the open. In addition, third-rate militias like the Interahamwe, which were worthless on an open battlefield, become deadly opponents when fighting on their home turf.[35]

The RPA and its commanders also faced another cruel dilemma. As Caesar Kayizari, who was intimately involved in the battles around Kigali as second-in-command, and later acting commander, of Alpha Mobile, explains:

> The commander in chief [Paul Kagame] gives us two missions . . . as much as possible rescue. And as you rescue you fight. The rescue will compromise a lot of the fighting capabilities. If you make deep rescues . . . it might mean vulnerabilities as you move to rescue instead of going for military objective after military objective. . . . Sometimes we have to scatter the forces for the humanitarian mission, rescuing people in danger of extermination. You would hear the news . . . that at location Z 5000 people are being butchered, and already you are under attack. So you have to take part of your force and as much as possible stop that carnage.[36]

At one point in the fighting, part of Alpha Mobile was withdrawn from the city center of Kigali and ordered to move to Bichumbi, where the local mayor was helping to organize the Genocide. "They were murdering people and when the force came here he ran away, and we saved quite a huge number of people, of course many were dead too."[37] Another rescue operation was launched on 16 April, when eight soldiers from 3 Battalion evacuated fifty people hiding in the St. André Parish, deep behind enemy lines. The problem of whether to prioritize military targets or humanitarian missions was a dilemma the RPA had to face throughout the hundred-day Campaign Against Genocide. On the one hand, the quicker the FAR were defeated, the quicker the Genocide would end: not only were the FAR defending the killers, but in many cases, they were active participants in the Genocide. On the other hand, the RPA did not have enough troops to attack the key FAR camps, the strategic hills around Kigali, and other military objectives *and* to mount humanitarian rescue missions throughout the country. This was a matter of numbers. And as we have seen, at the resumption of hostilities the RPA could muster eight combined mobile forces and 3 Battalion—a maximum of 15,000 troops—against FAR's 39,000 combat troops, not counting support units or the Interahamwe and Impuzamugambi militias.[38]

In the maelstrom of the ongoing war and Genocide, tensions within the FAR officer corps came to the surface. On 12 April, a group of moderate officers (Colonels Rusatira, Gatsinzi, Muberuka, Ntiwiragabo, Kanyamanza, Murasampongo, and Hakazimana, and Lieutenant Colonels Rwabalinda, Rwamanyma, and Kanyandekwe) signed a letter calling for a ceasefire and negotiations so that the Genocide could be stopped. However, these officers no longer commanded significant influence in the FAR. Their extremist colleagues, who were supporting or orchestrating the killings, now denounced them as traitors and forced the moderates' leader, Rusatira, into hiding.[39]

Chief of Staff of the Gendarmerie Augustin Ndindiliyimana, who was acquitted of charges on appeal before the ICTR, was known to be colorblind on the Hutu-Tutsi question and fled to Belgium in June 1994. Another important officer in the Gendarmerie, Paul Rwarakabije, who was also put on trial and found innocent, did not take part in the killings but kept fighting the RPA. He was frustrated, as a soldier, that the FAR joined in the Genocide: "The army deployed most of its forces to massacre civilians, diverting trucks, ammunition, and manpower to slaughter them. The genocide caused our resistance to crumble. It was a *cafouillage,* a real mess."[40] Yet he considered surrender out of the question. One of Rwarakabije's former comrades told Congo expert Jason Stearns that Rwarakabije "was a disciplinarian to the core. He never really asked why he was fighting; that was for the politicians to decide. And when the politicians ran, he just kept on fighting, like a robot."[41]

THE CENTRAL AND EASTERN AXES OF ADVANCE

While the RPA now had a significant force in Kigali, there still were strong FAR elements to their rear that had been bypassed in the rush to get to Kigali. It fell to the follow-up forces to deal with these pockets of resistance. Two forces, 21 CMF, under the command of Charles Musitu, and 101 CMF, under Charles Muhire, advanced on Kigali via Byumba, while 7 Mobile and 157 Mobile, under Theogene Bagire and Fred Ibingira, respectively, were tasked with capturing the east of Rwanda before swinging west to join the Battle of Kigali. Byumba was surrounded and fell around mid-April, and the FAR forces that had given it up headed for the relative safety of their comrades around Kigali, pursued by 21 Mobile. A crucial situation now developed, for if the RPA did not manage to prevent these retreating FAR elements from reaching Kigali, they would be in an excellent position to hit the RPF troops around the city in the rear. Though disorganized, this distraction might be enough to tip the balance in favor of the FAR. To prevent this development, several companies, reinforced by 21 and 101 CMFs, took up blocking positions at Mugambazi and managed to force the FAR to retreat toward Ruhengeri.[42]

Meanwhile, 7 Mobile had passed Gabiro in the east and swung west to join the fight in Kigali. Together with elements of Alpha Mobile, it faced the crack FAR Para-Commando Battalion. Brent Beardsley, one of General Dallaire's key officers in UNAMIR, remembers visiting the para-commandos before the outbreak of hostilities. The "troops appeared to be very tough field soldiers. They looked very fit, very physically fit, they were moving in formation under the command of NCOs, being briefed, their weapons appeared to be well-maintained, their boots, that type of thing."[43] Unlike the Presidential Guards, which were also considered an elite unit, the para-commandos had much frontline experience and had been one of the units that gave the RPA the toughest fight around Byumba in May 1992. For nine days, 7 CMF,

Alpha, and the paratroops fought tooth and nail around Kabuga before the latter were pushed back to Camp Kanombe.

THE BATTLE OF KIGALI: THIRD PHASE

With its rear now secure and 7 CMF coming in from the east, the RPA started to prize Kigali out of the hands of the FAR. On 22–23 May, 7 CMF finally pushed the para-commandos out of Camp Kanombe and their positions around the airport. The latter now found themselves close to being surrounded and had to fight their way out through a narrow gap between Mount Rebero and the RPA troops around the CND. The 7 CMF was immediately redeployed to help Bravo CMF with the fighting around Mount Jali.

Besides the continuous fighting around Camp Kacyiru and Camp Kimihurura, where the Presidential Guards had been contained even though they were still holding out, a focal point became the hill on which the University of Kigali's Business School is now located. This hillock, situated between the larger hills of Kimihurura and the center of town, was important because if the RPA captured it, the Presidential Guards would be cut off from the rest of the FAR.[44] It would also provide the springboard for an attack on Camp Kigali and the city center. Toward the end of May and early June the RPA would attack under the cover of night and push the FAR defenders back in vicious close-quarter fighting. However, come morning, the FAR, using their 37 mm antiaircraft guns and heavy artillery, would be able to push the RPA back. In this fashion, the hill switched hands multiple times.[45]

Following the capture of Camp Kanombe, the RPF stepped up the tempo of its rescue missions. On 2 June, two hundred people were saved at Kabgayi. Another raid was launched to save people stuck at the Sainte-Famille Church in the center of Kigali:

> Thousands of Tutsi had taken refuge in the Sainte Famille church, on the eastern side of central Kigali. One night in mid-June, the RPF sent a company two kilometres inside what was enemy territory, recovered six hundred Tutsis from Sainte Famille, and pulled them out to safety through RGF [Rwandan Government Forces] lines. The mission began as a clandestine operation and ended as a fully supported running battle with carefully planned artillery support—and, by the standards of any military force, ranks as a first class rescue.[46]

Sadly, the RPF was not able to save everyone at Sainte-Famille, as many people hiding inside the church did not believe that the RPF soldiers outside were their saviors, but rather génocidaires masquerading as RPF. A couple of days later, on 16–17 June, another rescue operation was mounted, this time to save those trapped at St. Paul. As during the Sainte-Famille raid, an RPA company went behind FAR lines under the cover of darkness and escorted several hundred people to safety. Yet the RPA could not be everywhere at once, and thousands of people were killed every day. On 10 June, for example, militias arrived at Nyamirambo Catholic Church in two trucks. Father Otto Mayer, sensing danger, managed to find a few gendarmes to confront the militia. However, as the militia had the support of the local FAR troops, the gendarmes were forced to back down. The militia took 170 Tutsis who were hiding in the church, walked them to a big pit nearby, and killed them.[47]

THE ADVANCE OF 157 COMBINED MOBILE FORCE

While the bulk of the RPA was fighting around Kigali, 157 CMF, under the command of Fred Ibingira, had advanced to the Burundian border, which it reached on 30 April, before swinging west. Advancing past Kigali to the south, it captured Nyanza on 29 May and started advancing north toward Kabgayi. By this point, it was clear to the High Command of the RPA that the intense and bloody fighting in Kigali was costing the lives of too many troops and that it seemed unlikely that the CMFs in the area would be able to force a breakthrough against the dug-in FAR. For example, 3 Battalion had been engaged in action continuously and lost about 250 of its 600 soldiers during the first couple of weeks of combat. So elements of 101 CMF and 51 CMF were redeployed to reinforce Ibingira's thrust. What brute force could not achieve, mobile operations would. On 2 June, Kabgayi was captured and, soon after, heavy fighting started around Gitarama. Dallaire reported at this time that the RPF was "containing RGF [Rwandan Government Forces, FAR] positions in Kigali . . . with a view to put maximum efforts around Gitarama."[48]

This hook put the FAR troops that were still holding out in Kigali in a difficult position: unless the situation changed radically, they might be surrounded and destroyed. Nonetheless, they kept on fighting, and on 10 June the RPA troops fighting in the Gatsata neighborhood in the shadow of Mount Jali were pushed back by the FAR.[49] On 13 June, after several failed attempts and heavy fighting, the RPA finally captured Gitarama.[50] With the town secured and the FAR almost wholly encircled, the RPA increased the pressure in Kigali. On 20 June, a breakthrough was achieved when Mount Jali was captured by Bravo CMF. The RPA also started pushing into the Kigali city center. Interahamwe and FAR troops were firmly entrenched in the area, and the Inkotanyi were forced to clear house by house and street by street as they advanced through the neighborhoods.[51]

On 3 July, after a six-hour fight, the RPA took the town of Butare in the south of the country and, at the same time, attacked all along the line in Kigali, with particularly fierce strikes directed against the Presidential Guards in Kimihurura and against Camp Kacyiru. Early the next morning, RPA sentries noticed that the positions in front of them seemed abandoned. As soon as they realized the FAR was withdrawing, the RPA attacked even harder to turn the retreat into a rout. Alpha Mobile entered the Presidential Guards Camp at 06:30 on the morning on 4 July.[52] Around the same time, Bravo Mobile overran Camp Kacyiru. By the end of the day Kigali was under control of the RPA.

THE LAST WEEK OF THE CAMPAIGN AND OPÉRATION TURQUOISE

In June 1994, the French government decided to intervene in Rwanda.[53] It remains unclear exactly why the French decided to take action when they did. Prunier suggests it was a rushed reaction to forestall other international initiatives and because it would look good domestically.[54] When the RPF heard of the French intention, Paul Kagame urged General Dallaire to "tell France that Kigali can handle more body bags than Paris."[55] This aggressive stance was based on France having supported the FAR before the outbreak of the Genocide, and having done nothing to stop it. Why would they mount an operation on Rwandan soil other than to rob the RPA of its victory? Gérard Prunier had been asked to act as an adviser for the French government and helped establish basic links between the latter and the RPF. In the first instance, however, the Quai d'Orsay was reluctant to open lines of communication with the RPF. Prunier changed tactics and told an official at the Ministry of Defense about the seriousness of the situation. After listening intently, the official exclaimed: "God dammit! It is our boys going in there. And if they get shot up because of those idiots at Foreign Affairs, there will be hell to pay."[56] The result was that two top RPF diplomats, Jacques Bihozagara and Theogene Rudasingwa, visited the French Ministry of Defense. Though the RPF was not wholly convinced of French intentions, the meeting helped break the ice; it showed the RPF that the French did not drink gasoline, and the French that the RPF did not eat barbed wire.[57] When the French entered southwest Rwanda there would be serious friction and several close calls with the RPA, but the two sides never came to blows.

When the French deployed to Zaire, where they staged before moving into Rwanda, they did so in a decisive manner. Following standard operating procedure, it was elite paratroops and Foreign Legion units that formed the spearhead. They were supported by fighter jets and helicopters. Many commentators have argued that this level of equipment suggests that the French were intent on supporting the FAR and fighting the RPA, rather than establishing a humanitarian safe zone.[58] While the motives behind the French intervention are murky, this criticism is incorrect. As has been mentioned before, Pakistani, Malaysian, and US peacekeepers had been killed in Somalia less than a year before. In former Yugoslavia, UN intervention forces had also suffered casualties, and finally, ten Belgian peacekeepers had been murdered in Kigali just months before. In each case, a lack of equipment and resolve had been the most important cause of death. The French High Command decided it would not risk the lives of its soldiers without ensuring they would be able to fight back if attacked.

Ruhengeri had been surrounded by Charlie CMF, commanded by Thaddeus Gashumba, since 6 May 1994. Now that the bulk of RPA forces were released from the Battle of Kigali, they could move north, in pursuit of the FAR, to reinforce Charlie CMF. Besides Ruhengeri, the last important town still in the hands of the FAR was Gisenyi. Though the advance to the northwest from Kigali was slow, with the RPF consolidating its position throughout Rwanda, the outcome of the war was no longer in doubt. On 14 July, Ruhengeri was taken; three days later, Gisenyi fell to the RPA, signaling the end of the war. This final phase of the war also saw the retreat of the FAR into Zaire. Thousands of troops accompanied by over a million civilians crossed the border into northern and southern Kivu by way of Gisenyi and through the zone occupied by Opération Turquoise. Normally, these troops would have been interned and disarmed by the Zairian armed forces. However, as President Mobutu was sympathetic toward the FAR, and Zaire was already becoming ungovernable, he allowed the retreating troops to set up base in

North and South Kivu. The mass displacement of ordinary Rwandans had many causes. Some had "been urged to flee by former Government civilians and military officials in their home areas, or . . . on their own volition they had decided to flee with or immediately ahead of former army soldiers because of a general fear of the RPA. . . . Many simply cited panic as their motivation."[59]

WAR CRIMES DURING THE CAMPAIGN AGAINST GENOCIDE (APRIL–AUGUST 1994)

One of the most controversial and contested topics of the Campaign Against Genocide is that of human rights abuses committed by troops belonging to the RPA. There is no doubt that, as the RPA advanced, some of its members killed civilians. As time went on, increasingly wild stories of this period were and continue to be put forward by journalists and academics. The sources used to justify their arguments are often problematic and should be avoided or, at the very least, handled with care.[60] There are two main exceptions to this: the Gersony Report and *Leave None to Tell the Story.* Both were written by knowledgeable, independent human rights activists, and this section is based on their work.

The first serious investigation that uncovered war crimes committed by members of the RPA was conducted by a small team led by Robert Gersony. By the time of the Genocide, Gersony was already a well-known expert on human rights abuses and had extensive experience in Latin America, Uganda, Somalia, and Mozambique.[61] His team had been tasked to study the situation in Rwanda to determine whether people who had fled abroad to escape the Genocide could return home. To this end, he received official permission to travel throughout the country from the UN, which commissioned the research, and from the RPF.

Between August and September 1994, Gersony and his team traveled through Rwanda counterclockwise starting in the northwestern provinces of Ruhengeri and Gisenyi. After a short detour to visit the large refugee camps around Goma in Zaire, they continued south to Butare, shortly crossed into Burundi and re-entered Rwanda, went through Kibungo, and ended in Tanzania. To be sure of their findings they also visited the refugee camps in Tanzania. During this journey the Gersony team interviewed around three hundred people one-on-one or in small groups in ninety-one different locations. Building on their human rights experience in other countries, the team made sure to go off the beaten track in order to speak to people who lived or were hiding there.

At the outset of the investigation, while in Ruhengeri and Gisenyi, the team realized that substantial numbers of Hutu were already returning home from Zaire.[62] When they interviewed people, "local residents . . . reported overwhelmingly that conditions in their area were secure, stable and peaceful."[63] In Gisenyi, the province bordering Ruhengeri, the situation was more concerning. People told the team that the RPA would abduct groups of between twelve and twenty-four people, take them to Gishwati Forest, and execute them.[64] However, the team was not particularly surprised. "Many hundreds of thousands of Tutsis had just been murdered by the Hutus. What I was hearing, given what had transpired, still fell into the category of revenge killings,"[65] Gersony told biographer Robert Kaplan.

When the team arrived in the provinces of Butare and Kibungo they realized something of a different order was going on there. Hutus who had fled a couple of months before, during the last stages of the war, were afraid of returning home lest they be killed by the RPF. At one village the Gersony team came across a school where they found a large group of corpses, recently murdered, hands tied behind their back. "On one wall, smeared in red, presumably in blood. . . . : 'Hutu can [*sic,* probably "come"] home to die.'"[66] Further in the village church they found unburied bodies of people who had been killed during the Genocide. Those bodies were in a more advanced stage of decomposition than those in the school, a sign that the people in the school had been killed after the territory came under control of the RPA. The evidence that Gersony and his team collected indicated that the revenge attacks were not solely the actions of low-level individuals but must also have included some coordination. For example, Gersony notes that the violence "includes . . . mass killings at meetings" where large groups were "invited to receive information about 'peace,' 'security' or 'food distribution' issues." Once the people had congregated the meeting would be "assaulted through sudden sustained gunfire; or locked in buildings into which hand-grenades were thrown; systematically killed with manual instruments; or killed in large numbers by other means."[67]

In total, Gersony estimated that between late April/May until July, "more than 5,000 and perhaps as many as 10,000 persons per month may have been killed."[68] Alison Des Forges writes, "Gersony himself reportedly estimated . . . the RPF had killed between 25,000 and 45,000 persons."[69] Gersony has always maintained that there was an important difference between the Genocide against the Tutsi and moderate Hutu and the revenge killings of the RPF, which he calls "mass murders." Nonetheless he believes that the "systematic and sustained killing and persecution of . . . [the] civilian Hutu populations"[70] was "organized and premeditated"[71] and that they "could not have occurred without senior officials in the army knowing."[72]

The only manifestation of the Gersony Report ever to have surfaced is a poorly detailed sixteen-page summary, in the form of briefing notes intended to be kept private.[73] In that sense, the work of Alison Des Forges is more complete. Des Forges was a Rwanda expert: she had written a PhD on the country's early colonial period and had spent time working for Human Rights Watch in Rwanda before the outbreak of the Genocide. Her work, *Leave None to Tell the Story,* meticulously details how Tutsi were systematically killed throughout Rwanda. While the bulk of her study deals with the crimes committed by the Hutu génocidaires, she also has a section on abuses committed by RPA troops. There she describes many specific incidents noting the different circumstances in which they occurred.

Like the Gersony team, Des Forges found evidence of massacres during public meetings. The best documented case happened on 19 June 1994 in Gitarama Province, when RPA troops assembled people from a refugee camp and locals in a field. Some hours later, RPA troops "opened fire on the crowd of hundreds of people. Some people fled down the road next to the field and were shot trying to escape by running through the woods on the adjacent hills." The RPA then started searching the hills for survivors, who "were caught and then killed with hammers, hoes, or other blunt instruments. The soldiers killed without regard to age, sex, or ethnic group."[74] Des Forges also identified two types of summary executions. First, there were those she calls "summary and arbitrary." It seems that these were directed against the former elite of the regime and had the objective of solidifying RPF rule. People targeted for execution included FAR officers, and in some cases their families, ministers, provincial prefects, and high-level administrators. The second, "Summary Executions of Persons Accused of Genocide," deals with the murder of people who the RPF thought took part in the

Genocide. Des Forges notes that there seem to be at least two variations. In some cases, the summary execution of people accused of Genocide seems to have taken place in a moment of anger, usually just after combat; "in some cases, RPF soldiers simply assumed that any people still alive in a community had killed Tutsi." During these massacres the RPF troops occasionally even disregarded ethnicity: "RPF soldiers decided that the people they found alive in the Bugeramanga sector of Murama commune, Gitarama prefecture, had all participated in the Genocide. They killed some thirty people by striking them with hoes and then throwing grenades into the house where they were gathered. Among those slain were some Tutsi as well as Hutu."[75]

Then there were much more systematic actions, often carried out by the Directorate of Military Intelligence (DMI), which was headed by Colonel Faustin Kayumba Nyamwasa.[76] In Byumba the DMI set up an interrogation post and started systematically questioning internally displaced people. Some were released but many were taken away and "disappeared." Another example of these operations started on 13 July when RPF soldiers "gathered several hundred displaced persons from Ntyazo, Ngenda, and Runyinya communes at a site near the town of Butare." The people were taken to the local Groupe scolaire where most of the women and some men were released. However, a substantial number of men were interrogated "and later 'disappeared.' Witnesses in the area declared that for two days they had heard the sounds of people being killed in the woods next to the school."[77]

One of the tragedies of these revenge killings is that, as explained above, Tutsi survivors or innocent Hutu, who had managed to survive the Genocide, were among the victims. Des Forges argues that

> revenge killings by soldiers—or other crimes of passion—as well as the unintentional killing of civilians in combat situations could never account for the thousands of persons killed by the RPF between April and late July 1994. . . . These killings were wide-spread, systematic, and involved large numbers of participants and victims. They were too many and too much alike to have been unconnected crimes executed by individual soldiers or low-ranking officers. Given the disciplined nature of the RPF forces and the extent of communications up and down the hierarchy, commanders of this army must have known of and at least tolerated these practices.[78]

She concludes that twenty-five thousand to thirty thousand is the minimum number of people killed by the RPF.

Trying to explain why war crimes were committed opens a researcher to the charge of justifying them. However, I believe that just as we look for clues to explain how the Genocide could have happened—ranging from the proverbial "cohesion of oppression" of (pre)colonial times to the slow but utter decline of the Rwandan state between 1990 and 1994—we must try to understand what motivations and causes were behind the revenge killings described above. The RPF does not deny that massacres took place. However, it contests their scope and believes that context is critical. A high-level adviser told Philip Roessler and Harry Verhoeven: "Of course there was revenge. But you need context. This is very emotional for us."[79] To explain the killings the RPF point to two factors. First, throughout the Campaign Against Genocide, the RPA suffered heavy casualties. The intensity of the fighting meant that the traditional sources of RPF manpower could no longer fill the gaps left in the RPA ranks. Faced with this dilemma, the RPA turned to the only source of readily available recruits: genocide survivors. In the months of the Campaign Against Genocide, thousands joined the ranks of the RPA. While commanders did their best to train the survivors as quickly and as well as possible, the exigencies of war demanded that the emphasis be placed on tactics and weapons training rather than on political education.[80] The result was that a large influx of troops who had survived the killings had often lost family, were highly motivated, but "not in a very forgiving mood."[81] The massive trauma of three months of continuous fighting amid a Genocide also took its toll on soldiers who had been with the RPA from the start. One veteran told me that "we became a bit contaminated." Another veteran remembered that "some Hutus couldn't afford to be bystanders. We essentially killed civilians."[82] Second, the RPF notes that the killings were never sanctioned at the highest level. Indeed, the fact that the Gersony Report highlights the differences between events in southwestern and northwestern Rwanda seems to indicate that local commanders were a crucial determinant in whether people were killed in their areas of responsibility. As the RPA spread across the country to secure remote towns, the tight control exerted by the stern disciplinarians of the High Command slackened, and "some commanders took advantage of this newly gained freedom of movement." The speed of the Campaign Against

Genocide, and the focus on the fight against the FAR, meant that individual commanders or soldiers could use the fog of war to commit atrocities unobserved by the High Command.

The RPF contests the claims by Des Forges and Gersony that the top brass allowed killings to take place with impunity. Every person I interviewed told me that, though abuses did indeed occur, the High Command cracked down on them when they got wind of it. "We had a military police, we had tribunals. Some were put in jail. Some were executed, some were even Genocide survivors."[83] Senior officers who had not been able to control their troops were also arrested.[84] However, due to the sensitive nature of this subject, which remains a taboo even today, the RPF is unwilling to explain how far these prosecutions went. Who was punished and were the punishments that were handed out commensurate with the crimes committed?

Another important factor is the general situation between April and August 1994, when the RPF was trying to establish control of the country. In areas liberated by the RPA, Rwanda had effectively ceased functioning as a state. Because the Genocide had been so extensive, thousands of the murderers who had taken part in the killings were still at large. There were no police officers or gendarmes to arrest them (the RPA had only a limited number of military police). There were no public prosecutors, judges, or supreme court to sentence them. And the only place to house those arrested on suspicion of participating in Genocide were a small number of utterly decrepit jails. For the ordinary people who had survived the massacres, there were no public utilities—no water, no electricity. The public health service had ceased to function. Crops rotted in the untended fields, and unexploded ordnance littered the hills. Hundreds of thousands were on the move through the country, either fleeing violence or on their way home. At the same time, thousands of Banyarwanda, the primary constituency of the RPF, came streaming back into Rwanda from Burundi, Uganda, and Tanzania, an exodus that would cause innumerable problems.[85] The ex-FAR had made away with the state coffers, so the country was bankrupt; there were no typewriters or other administrative necessities. To face this catastrophe, the RPF/A could only count on somewhere between 12,000 and 15,000 traumatized troops and its civilian cadres who were now arriving from Uganda and Burundi.

* * *

From a military perspective, the Campaign Against Genocide must rank as a successful campaign. Within one hundred days, the RPA vanquished a more heavily armed force three times its size without suffering any decisive defeats. This does not mean that the campaign was easy for the RPA. In Kigali's urban terrain, the RPA's initial success stalled in the face of heavy resistance by the Presidential Guards and FAR para-commandos.

Strategy, planning, and flexibility were the deciding factors. The RPA's battleplan was well thought out. Kigali was the single most important objective. It contained the trapped 3 Battalion together with the RPF's politicians, as well as the Ministry of Defense and the genocidal government. As such it constituted the center of the FAR's war-making capacity. To capture Kigali the RPA deployed the bulk of its forces (Alpha, Bravo, and 59, 21, and 101 CMFs). By concentrating so many of its troops to the key objective, the RPA was following one of the key tenets of war, but this left few troops for other operations. The High Command decided to favor the eastern (the advance of 157 CMF) over the western sector. While this was strategically correct, it was not an obvious choice. The ideological heartland of the génocidaires was northwestern Rwanda, and especially the cities of Ruhengeri and Gisenyi. This made the region a tempting target for the RPA. However, it was strongly garrisoned and easily defended. An attack here would risk the lives of many RPA soldiers and the chance of success was small. As such, Charlie CMF was the only unit detailed to attack in this sector, its likely objective being not the outright capture of the region but a holding action designed to keep FAR units occupied so as to prevent them from assisting their comrades in Kigali. In the eastern sector, 157 and 7 CMFs were tasked with striking south and surrounding Kigali from the east and south. Focusing on the east had another advantage: the RPA could count on Tanzanian neutrality which meant that it did not have to guard its eastern flank as it advanced. A similar advance in the west, had it been possible, would have risked a second intervention from Mobutu and the Zairian armed forces.

When it became clear that the RPA was unable to progress in Kigali, its High Command did not insist on redoubling efforts in the city. Instead, Paul Kagame ordered 101 and 51 CMFs to outflank the FAR's position, thus breaking the stalemate. There is no evidence that the FAR could count on its High Command and political leadership to make sound decisions throughout the campaign. Although the FAR was able to blunt the RPA's advance into Kigali, it was never able to gather up its reserves and to launch a determined counterattack in any sector. The lack of command is probably due to two factors. First, a large part of the FAR's officers were busy coordinating and supporting the Genocide, rather than fighting the RPA. Second, the FAR officers had become accustomed to leaning on French and Belgian advisers. In the absence of the foreign officers, they proved unable to withstand the pressures of war.

Conclusion

Debating the Struggle

1959–1964

Although many of the causes of the Rwandan genocide can be found in Rwanda's colonial, or precolonial past, the most important event for the combatants that remained within living memory was the Social Revolution. Habyarimana took part in the revolution as a young soldier of the Garde nationale, and while Kagame might have been too young to actually remember what happened, he certainly lived the events and was told what had taken place by his mother. Despite long debates, decolonization came to Belgian Africa very suddenly. In Rwanda, this meant that the limited elections that had taken place under Belgian supervision had in no way prepared the country for independent democracy; political parties had not had the time to grow and develop in peace. In turn, this meant that important questions could not be answered by working to consensus: Should Rwanda continue under the reign of the Mwami, as had been the case during colonialism, or should the country become a republic? What would the relationship between Hutu, Tutsi, and Twa be? Instead, the political parties were born in a crisis in which it quickly became clear that whoever had the most naked power would be able to capture the government.

In the ensuing civil war, the mostly Tutsi royalist faction never stood a chance. Its supporters comprised only 15 to 20 percent of the population and were forced to flee to Uganda, Burundi, Tanzania, and Congo. From there, several groups tried to continue their struggle against Kayibanda's MDR-PARMEHUTU, which had quickly become Rwanda's most important political party. Although these Inyenzi attacks launched from refugee camps just over the Rwandan border were unsuccessful, they were regularly followed by revenge killings. As would be the case between 1990 and 1994, these revenge killings did not usually occur close to where the attack took place. It was during this first civil war that the pattern emerged in which it became acceptable to punish Tutsi living inside Rwanda for the actions of refugees abroad. In effect, this turned the Tutsi population of Rwanda into a group of hostages. The revenge killings reached their peak in 1963 and 1964, forcing many of the Tutsi who had until then remained to flee abroad.

1964–1990

Three important historical episodes informed the lead-up to the outbreak of the Struggle. In 1972, violence along Hutu-Tutsi lines rocked Burundi and forced many Burundian Hutu to flee to Rwanda. With ethnic tensions already running high, President Kayibanda and several of his ministers decided to use the opportunity to reinvigorate their flagging rule. Tutsi were expelled from schools and businesses, and ethnic massacres took place throughout the country. To make matters worse, Kayibanda allowed Burundian refugees to attack their homeland from refugee camps in Rwanda. The Burundian response was aggressive and drew on the support of President Idi Amin of Uganda, who made it clear that he would intervene in favor of Burundi in the event of a military confrontation with Rwanda. Colonel Habyarimana, who had by now become the soldier in command of the Garde nationale, knew that in a war his troops would not stand a chance against a Ugandan-Burundian coalition. As such, he took on the role of leader of the moderate faction within the government, trying to defuse tensions and restore normality within the country. However, on the night of 4 July 1973, Habyarimana was summoned to the office of the president. Once he arrived, he was confronted with a letter addressed to himself and signed by several prominent northern politicians. In the letter, the politicians complained that they were being abused by the current regime and asked the commander of the army for redress. Precisely what happened next is unknown, but Habyarimana got into a fist fight with the president's aides and escaped fearing for his life. He immediately decided to seize power and was supported by the Garde nationale, the Belgian military assistants, and their ambassador.

The fate of the Banyarwanda in Uganda was intertwined with that of Milton Obote. Although the Rwandan refugees had initially been welcomed,

Obote resented the fact that they were generally pro-monarchist. Toward the end of his presidency (1966–1971), as he was busy making plans to eject them from Uganda, he was suddenly removed from power by Idi Amin. Under Amin the Banyarwanda enjoyed relative prosperity and many thought they would be able to stay for the long haul. This changed when Obote returned to power in 1980. Throughout his second presidency (1980–1985), he persecuted the Banyarwanda community. His repression peaked in 1982, when thousands of Banyarwanda were either forced into refugee camps or over the border and into Rwanda. In Rwanda, they were not welcome: Habyarimana was dead set against accepting these refugees of Rwandan origin in his country. Initially, they were corralled in squalid refugee camps, and soon after, they were pushed back across the border into Uganda. Trapped between Obote and Habyarimana, the Banyarwanda had no choice but to join the Ugandan rebel movement of Yoweri Museveni en masse. During the following years, many of their number, like Fred Rwigyema and Paul Kagame, rose to important positions within the National Resistance Army. When the NRA won the war and entered Kampala in 1986, a large portion of it was made up of Rwandans.

President Museveni immediately opened negotiations with Habyarimana over the possible return of the Rwandan refugees from Uganda. However, Habyarimana's position had not changed from the early 1980s, and negotiations dragged on for four years without any apparent result. This placed the Banyarwanda in a difficult position: although they were part of the inner circle of Ugandan power for now, their leaders knew this would not last indefinitely. The persecution under Obote had shown them that, for a large part of the Ugandan population, they remained unwelcome foreigners. Museveni faced a similar problem: on the one hand, he was grateful for the help of the Banyarwanda during his struggle and keen to assist his comrades in arms. On the other hand, it was clear that he would not be able to maintain the Banyarwanda in their posts if he wanted the support of the majority of the Ugandan people. With the situation in Uganda becoming increasingly untenable, and with Habyarimana stalling for time on both repatriation and internal political reform, the Rwandan Patriotic Front/Army saw they only had a small window in which they would be able to use military force to impose a return to their homeland. Although "option Z," an armed return, was considered to be a last resort, the RPF/A had prepared for the possibility.

Rwandans within the NRA had been recruited, other Banyarwanda had been brought to Uganda for military training, funds had been raised and supplies had been stockpiled. At some point in September 1990, Fred Rwigyema, the charismatic leader of the RPF/A, decided it was now or never.

1990–1994

On 1 October 1990, the RPA crossed the Rwandan-Ugandan frontier, signaling the start of the Struggle for Liberation. Throughout October, the RPA and the FAR (Forces armées rwandaises) were locked in close combat in the north of Rwanda. Although the RPA made initial gains, several factors turned the tide. General Fred Rwigyema, the inspirational leader of the RPA, was killed on 2 October. Three weeks later, his replacements, Major Chris Bunyenyezi and Major Dr. Peter Bayingana, met the same fate. In the meantime, the FAR received support from France, which supplied helicopters and sent a small intervention force that relieved the FAR from internal security duties. President Mobutu of Zaire also sent a detachment of troops who engaged in direct combat with the RPA. When Paul Kagame arrived toward the end of October, he found the RPA defeated and close to disarray. Together with the surviving commanders, he managed to organize a more or less orderly withdrawal along the Rwanda-Uganda frontier toward the Virunga Mountains.

Over the next four years, the RPA was transformed into a formidable fighting force. Recruits, usually already highly motivated, first received a political and military education. They were then slotted into battalions or, later, into combined mobile forces, led by increasingly experienced commanders working with an effective and well-understood military doctrine. The supply of the RPA also improved as the war went on: by 1991, the troops were receiving proper rations; in the course of the war, they would be equipped with former East German uniforms. RPA officers suffered the same hardships as their soldiers and ate the same food. The result was that the RPA rank and file had high morale, obeyed their commanding officers, and knew what was expected in combat. Naturally, none of this would have been possible without the support of the RPF, which raised money abroad, organized the Banyarwanda community in the refugee camps, and coordinated the political education of the recruits.

The FAR, by contrast, went from being a small and reasonably efficient force to a large, mostly incapable, and often parasitic one. FAR officers were unconcerned with the profession of arms and often spent time with politicians in Kigali rather than at the front line with their units. Other officers were actively corrupt and sold the rations and fuel meant for their troops. The result was that drinking on the job was tolerated, salaries often went unpaid, and training was lackluster. While French and Belgian military advisers tried to improve the situation, they were only partially successful: the casualty rates of newly trained units were so high that they quickly became combat ineffective. As a result, the morale of the FAR decreased throughout the war until it reached the point where there were regular open mutinies, *contribution en nature* was demanded from women living close to military bases, and bank robberies carried out by the FAR were not uncommon.

While the FAR and RPA fought on the battlefield, political change was taking place in Rwanda. In early 1991, Rwanda saw the birth of its first opposition parties since independence. Within a couple of months, the MDR, PL, and PSD became important players on the political scene. As Prunier has pointed out, this created a three-way conflict, as Habyarimana's MRND, which had led the one-party state for three decades, was now forced to share power with the opposition. The military success of the RPA in mid-1992 forced Habyarimana to the negotiating table. It also allowed a triumvirate of coalition politicians made up of Nsengiyaremye (Prime Minister, MDR), Gasana (Minister of Defense, MRND), and Ngulinzira (Foreign Affairs, MDR) to start working toward a peace agreement with the RPF. In the fourth quarter of 1992, Habyarimana openly showed his displeasure with the three ministers' progress and distanced himself from their program.

Ethnic violence at the start of the Struggle had mainly consisted of revenge killings, historically familiar from the days of the Social Revolution. This changed in 1992, when hard-line Hutu Power fanatics within the government started sabotaging political change by turning to internal violence. One example of their methods was the massacre of many Tutsi in Bugesera. As Habyarimana declared himself against the Arusha negotiations, he aligned with this group. His 15 November 1992 speech, followed by the hate-filled diatribe of Léon Mugesera, became the signal for more ethnic killings in northern Rwanda. To carry out these massacres, the MRND could count on some extremist elements with the FAR, the Gendarmerie, and the Interahamwe militia. By this point, the Interahamwe had no difficulty finding recruits. Many soldiers deserted the FAR due to the high casualty rates and poor working conditions. They often took their weapons with them as they left and looked for other ways to make ends meet. Some became bandits and terrorized motorists or townspeople. Others joined the Interahamwe. They were perfect recruits: young men with some military training, perhaps a bit of combat experience, and in need of money and political protection. While their value against an opponent like the RPA was limited, they were perfectly capable of intimidating the opposition or killing people who could not defend themselves. Another key source of recruits came from the refugee camps outside Kigali, formed when the RPF decided to systematically clear the zones under its control of people.

The killings in the north were a blatant breach of the ceasefire agreement between the RPF and the Rwandan government. To make matters worse, there was no doubt that they had been carefully organized by extremists in the MRND, probably with Habyarimana's support. The RPF decided that military action was the only means by which they could stop the massacres and force Habyarimana and the MRND back to the negotiating table at Arusha. The 8 February 1993 offensive was a significant military victory for the RPA and showed its superior fighting power vis-à-vis the FAR. It seems highly likely that the RPA could have pushed their attack and taken Kigali if they had wished to, but the offensive was stopped by Paul Kagame, who insisted that negotiations were the only way to reach a lasting solution to the conflict. Naturally, he was also reluctant to alienate the international community. The decision to stop the attack was met with disbelief by the RPA rank and file; many were so surprised that they refused to carry out the order immediately. Kagame responded to this breakdown in discipline by personally visiting each unit and explaining why they had to return to the negotiating table.

While the February offensive was a military success for the RPA and did indeed force Habyarimana to return to the negotiating table at Arusha, it had important domestic consequences for Rwanda. Within the MDR and PL "Hutu Power" wings split from the main bodies of the parties, scared by the RPA's display of power. This, combined with increasing internal security problems such as ethnic killings, banditry, mine and bomb attacks, and political assassinations, put Rwanda on a razor's edge. The moderates suffered a decisive setback when, within one month, July 1993, Habyarimana was able to remove the entire triumvirate from the picture. Nsengiyaremye and

Ngulinzira were sacked, while Gasana fled for his life under the threat of assassination. In this atmosphere, the Arusha Accords were finally signed on 3 and 4 August 1993.

Had the triumvirate remained in power, had Rwanda possessed an efficient police force and judiciary, and had UNAMIR commander Roméo Dallaire been given the number of troops he had asked for, the Arusha Accords might have been a success. Instead, the country entered a period of utter turmoil. Several attempts at installing the BBTG, as agreed at Arusha, failed. Then, in the early months of 1994, the leaders of several important political parties were either targeted or assassinated: PL chairman Justin Mugenzi (attempt, 19 January), MDR president Faustin Twagiramungu (attempt, 20 February), Félicien Gatabazi (killed, 21 February), and CDR chairman Martin Bucyana (lynched, 22 February). One month later, on 6 April, the plane carrying President Habyarimana was shot down when returning from Dar es Salaam.

APRIL–JULY 1994

The very night that Habyarimana's plane was shot down, Presidential Guard Battalion started the Genocide by killing all the moderate opposition in Kigali. At the same time, the RPF politicians, protected by the RPA's 3 Battalion in the CND, came under heavy fire from the FAR stationed throughout Kigali. As the Interahamwe set up roadblocks, the group of people who were being targeted broadened until it included everyone who was a Tutsi.

The RPF found itself in the same position as it had in February 1993. As the Genocide gathered steam, no one could do anything about it. Moderates within the FAR lost power within the first few hours, and UNAMIR did not have the mandate or the troop strength to restore order. As it became clear that force was the only way to stop the killings, the RPA launched the Campaign Against Genocide. Over the next hundred days, the RPA wrested control of Rwanda from the hands of the FAR. Throughout the campaign, the RPA had to choose whether to focus its limited resources on defeating the FAR—the surest way to end the Genocide as quickly as possible—or to redirect troops on rescue missions. While the rescue operations would save people in direct danger, they diverted valuable resources from the main objective of stopping the Genocide. In several places, the FAR put up fierce resistance but, in the end, its numerical superiority could not overcome the well-led veteran RPA CMFs. As the Campaign Against Genocide drew to a close, RPA troops, heavily affected by what they had witnessed, also committed many atrocities and war crimes.

A HISTORIOGRAPHICAL NOTE

The account presented in this book will undoubtedly be a starting point rather than the final say on the Struggle for Liberation. To paraphrase Mamdani, I hope other researchers can lean on my work and see beyond the horizon where my sights came to rest.[1] Nonetheless, it already has implications for existing scholarship. Tragically, more research has been done on the war crimes committed by RPA soldiers than on the Campaign Against Genocide. Several researchers have used the absence of scholarship to spread cynical and often untrue versions of events. Now that the reader is familiar with the history of the campaign, and the Struggle for Liberation more generally, the latter can be juxtaposed with three arguments frequently advanced by these researchers.

The first argument posits that "Tutsi refugee rebels, by pursuing an armed challenge against Rwanda's Hutu regime, provoked a retaliatory genocide."[2] It relies on two claims:

- The RPF decided to go to war in 1990 despite a breakthrough in the negotiations surrounding the return of the Banyarwanda to Rwanda.
- The RPF negotiated too well at Arusha and should have let the extremist CDR and other Hutu Power factions into the BBTG in early 1994.[3]

Both claims are dubious. When the RPF went to war in October 1990, the refugee issue had not been settled. Only slight progress had been made in a process that had been dragging on since the early 1960s. In the preceding thirty years the Rwandan government had never compromised on the issue. For the RPF, whose members remembered the brutal refugee pushbacks of the 1980s, there was not a single guarantee that progress would be made this time. The second claim is even more far-fetched. The idea that the people implicated in planning a Genocide—the extermination of all the Tutsi and moderate Hutu—would become more moderate or reasonable if they were allowed into government is preposterous.[4]

Judi Rever puts forward an even more extreme version of this argument in her *In Praise of Blood.* She argues that the RPF shot down President

Habyarimana's plane to provoke the Genocide. In her view, the RPF knowingly sacrificed the Tutsi in Rwanda in order to take power. Her theory is based on several wild assumptions. The most startling is that the RPF infiltrated the party militias, such as the Interahamwe, to provoke the massacres: "RPF technicians actively killed Tutsi villagers in staged attacks that were blamed on Hutu mobs or civilian defense units."[5] For such an accusation to be leveled the evidence would have to be compelling. Yet Rever bases her account on an investigation of the International Criminal Tribunal for Rwanda, whose evidence came solely from "political dissidents of the RPF and that of the deserters of the RPA."[6] This can hardly be considered ironclad. To complicate matters further, Rever, who made most of the classified reports in her book public, did *not* release the key sections of evidence that relate specifically to this accusation.[7] It is also clear that the ethnic extremists in Rwanda, who started killing Tutsi only eight days after the start of the war in October 1990, did not need encouragement to kill.

The second argument contends that the RPF/A did not do enough to save Rwanda's Tutsi population from Genocide. An early example of this kind of writing is Alan Kuperman's article "Provoking Genocide." Its important contention is that "the [RPA] battle plan was designed to conquer the country, rather than to protect Tutsi civilians from retaliatory violence. Had the rebels placed higher priority on protecting Tutsi civilians, they would have raced quickly to the country's southwest where most domestic Tutsi, some 86%, lived in the six prefectures of Kigali, Butare, Gitarama, Gikongoro, Cyangugu, and Kibuye."[8]

This argument, which posits that the RPF "sacrificed" the Tutsi of Rwanda to gain political power, ignores the military realities on the ground. The FAR strongholds of Kigali, Gitarama, and Ruhengeri blocked the route to the southwest. Though the RPA might have been able to infiltrate one of its combined mobile forces past these strongholds, the risk, as RPA commanders told Kuperman in interviews, was too great. Though the RPA held a military advantage over the FAR, the tide of a battle can—and does—swing quickly. The destruction of an isolated RPA CMF in the southwest could have been a crucial turning point with severe consequences. It might even have tipped the military balance to the advantage of the FAR, reinvigorating the force's sagging morale. For the RPA, this was an unimaginable risk: had they been defeated or even forced into a stalemate, this would not only have resulted in the end of their struggle, but it would also have left no one else to stop the killings.

Susan Thomson and Helen Epstein provide other examples of the genre. Epstein writes that "as soon as the plane [of President Habyarimana] hit the ground, the RPF began advancing. . . . Rather than heading south, where most of the killings were taking place, the RPF circled around Kigali. By the time it reached the capital weeks later, most of the Tutsi were dead."[9] Thomson notes that "RPF operations [during the Campaign Against Genocide] were not overtly intended to save Tutsi, although some did."[10] As explained above, the first main objective of the Campaign Against Genocide was to reach Kigali as soon as possible. The first elements of Alpha Mobile reached the capital on 11 April, only four days after the start of the Genocide. Furthermore, Caesar Kayizari's testimony shows that the RPA was torn between the need to end the war and its duty to the people about to be killed. The rescue operations launched at St. André, St. Paul, and Sainte-Famille were all specifically intended to save people from the slaughter. What makes Thomson's assertion especially misleading is that she must have known this: General Dallaire's *Shake Hands with the Devil,* required reading for anyone writing on Rwanda, mentions some of these actions.[11] Another example of Thomson's distortion of history comes when she argues that during the Campaign Against Genocide, the RPF's "troops encountered little in the way of opposition as they swept out from Kigali, to the south along the eastern side of the country towards the border with Tanzania, then west toward the border with Zaire."[12] The reader would expect this remark to come off the back of a discussion of the fighting in the city of Kigali, but Thomson never mentions anything of the sort. Again, this is especially problematic because Des Forges, whom Thomson relies on extensively, wrote in 1999 that "[the RPF's] troops encountered little opposition, *except around Kigali* [my emphasis], and they routed government forces in operations that began in early April and ended in July. As RPF soldiers advanced south down the eastern side of the country and then swept west, they even stopped the killers in the act of attacking or preparing to attack Tutsi at several churches or camps for the displaced."[13]

The third argument suggests that there was a double genocide. Judi Rever contends that while the FAR, Gendarmerie, and Hutu Power militias were committing Genocide against the Tutsi, the RPF and RPA were committing a concurrent genocide against the Hutu: "The RPF leadership was cognizant of history and appears to have studied the methods of the Third Reich."[14] Her argument is not new and had already been advanced during the late 1990s. In 2003, *fifteen years before* Rever's book was published, research carried out by Philip Verwimp had already rejected the double-genocide thesis for several regions of Rwanda. His study concluded that "for those prefectures in which we performed our fieldwork, the term *genocide* should be reserved for the killings committed by the Interahamwe and the FAR, and another should be used for the killings committed by the RPF. That word could be massacre or terror or another word, depending on the event."[15] Even Robert Gersony agrees with this assessment.[16] As Rever's book essentially revolves around the claim that her research exposed a hitherto unknown event, she, unsurprisingly, does not mention Verwimp's research even once.[17] In this light, it is impossible to disagree with Scott Straus, an expert on the Rwandan Genocide, who believes that Rever's tone is "breathless and conspiratorial, and her account of 'there is a conspiracy of silence that I broke, even if it destroyed my family,' is misleading and narcissistic."[18]

Why are these writers so keen to dismiss or diminish the accomplishments of the RPF/A during the Campaign Against Genocide? Thomson, Epstein, and Rever are highly critical of the RPF in general: critical of its human rights record in the Democratic Republic of the Congo, critical of its post-Genocide governance, and critical of the way the West interacts with the country. Whether such criticism is warranted is beyond the scope of this study, but what is clear is that it is much easier to be critical if the RPF can be framed as having done nothing right. By twisting and belittling the accomplishments of the RPF/A during the Campaign Against Genocide—and by emphasizing the human rights abuses the RPA did commit—such critics pave the way for the rest of their arguments. However, by doing so, they ignore the whole reality. The RPF did not provoke the Genocide, the RPF did not ignore the plight of Tutsi being killed, and the RPF did not commit a genocide against the Hutu. While hundreds of thousands of people, mostly Tutsi, were being killed with hoes and machetes, the rest of the world looked on. Heavily armed paratroopers were flown in with the sole mission of evacuating foreign nationals. The UN evacuated its civilian staff who could no longer be of any use. Susan Thomson, the critic mentioned above, was among the evacuees after she was forced to witness the murder of her UN Tutsi colleagues by militia members.[19] Those in UNAMIR who remained did what they could with the tools they had and saved thousands of people, but they could not stop the massacre. It was the RPA, advancing from its strongholds in the north, who defeated the FAR and the génocidaires by force of arms and so ended the Genocide.

Notes

INTRODUCTION

1. For example: Jacques Maquet, *The Premise of Inequality in Ruanda* (Oxford: Oxford University Press, 1961). The oeuvre of Alexis Kagame—*Un abrégé de l'ethno-histoire du Rwanda I* (Butare: Éditions universitaires du Rwanda, 1972) and *Un abrégé de l'ethno-histoire du Rwanda II* (Butare: Éditions universitaires du Rwanda, 1975), for example—is also relevant, as he acted as a key advocate for the role of the royal court in Rwandan history.
2. Claudine Vidal, "Le Rwanda des anthropologues ou le fétichisme de la vache," *Cahiers d'études africaines* 9, no. 3 (1969); René Lemarchand, *Rwanda and Burundi* (New York: Praeger, 1970); Alison L. Des Forges, *Defeat Is the Only Bad News: Rwanda under Musinga, 1896–1931* (Madison: University of Wisconsin Press, 2011); Catherine Newbury, *The Cohesion of Oppression: Clientship and Ethnicity in Rwanda, 1860–1960* (New York: Columbia University Press, 1988); David Newbury, *Kings and Clans: Ijwi Island and the Lake Kivu Rift, 1780–1840* (Madison: University of Wisconsin Press, 1991); Jan Vansina, *Antecedents to Modern Rwanda: The Nyiginya Kingdom* (Madison: University of Wisconsin Press, 2004); Jean-Pierre Chrétien, *The Great Lakes of Africa: Two Thousand Years of History,* trans. Scott Straus (New York: Zone Books, 2006).
3. Catherine Newbury and David Newbury, "Bringing the Peasants Back In: Agrarian Themes in the Construction and Corrosion of Statist Historiography in Rwanda," *American Historical Review* 105, no. 3 (June 2000): 840.
4. Colette Braeckman, *Rwanda, histoire d'un génocide* (Paris: Editions Fayard, 1994); Gérard Prunier, *The Rwanda Crisis: History of a Genocide* (London: Hurst, 1997); Human Rights Watch, *Leave None to Tell the Story: Genocide in Rwanda,* written by Alison Des Forges (New York, March 1999); Philip Gourevitch, *We Wish to Inform You That Tomorrow We Will Be Killed with Our Families* (New York: Picador, 2000); Linda Melvern, *Conspiracy to Murder: The Rwandan Genocide* (London: Verso, 2006); Linda Melvern, *A People Betrayed: The Role of the West in Rwanda's Genocide* (London: Zed Books, 2009).
5. Bruce D. Jones, *Peacemaking in Rwanda: The Dynamics of Failure* (Boulder, CO: Lynne Rienner, 2001); Mahmood Mamdani, *When Victims Become Killers: Colonialism, Nativism, and Genocide in Rwanda* (Princeton, NJ: Princeton University

Press, 2002); Scott Straus, *The Order of Genocide: Race, Power and War in Rwanda* (Ithaca, NY: Cornell University Press, 2006); Timothy Longman, *Christianity and Genocide in Rwanda* (Cambridge: Cambridge University Press, 2011); André Guichaoua, *From War to Genocide: Criminal Politics in Rwanda, 1990–1994*, trans. Don E. Webster (Madison: University of Wisconsin Press, 2015).

6. There are some exceptions: Omar Shahabudin McDoom, *The Path to Genocide in Rwanda: Security, Opportunity, and Authority in an Ethnocratic State* (Cambridge: Cambridge University Press, 2021); Marie-Eve Desrosiers, *Trajectories of Authoritarianism in Rwanda: Elusive Control before the Genocide* (Cambridge: Cambridge University Press, 2023).
7. Author's correspondence with Gérard Prunier, 24 January 2014.
8. Filip Reyntjens, *Political Governance in Post-Genocide Rwanda* (Cambridge: Cambridge University Press, 2013); Susan Thomson, *Whispering Truth to Power: Everyday Resistance to Reconciliation in Postgenocide Rwanda* (Madison: University of Wisconsin Press, 2013); Timothy Longman, *Memory and Justice in Post-Genocide Rwanda* (Cambridge: Cambridge University Press, 2017); Susan Thomson, *Rwanda: From Genocide to Precarious Peace* (New Haven, CT: Yale University Press, 2018). For the author's view on the subject, see John Burton Kegel, "Post-Genocide Rwanda," *Africa: Rivista semestrale di studi e ricerche* 1, no. 1 (2019).
9. Richard J. Reid, *War in Pre-Colonial Eastern Africa* (London: James Currey, 2007), 3.
10. For more on this, see Josefine Kühnel Larsen's outstanding "Peace by Peace: The Construction of National-Military Identity in Post-Genocide Rwanda" (PhD diss., University of Copenhagen, 2014); Marco Jowell, "Cohesion through Socialization: Liberation, Tradition and Modernity in the Forging of the Rwanda Defence Force (RDF)," *Journal of Eastern African Studies* 8, no. 2 (2014); Benjamin Chemouni and Assumpta Mugiraneza, "Ideology and Interests in the Rwandan Patriotic Front: Singing the Struggle in Pre-Genocide Rwanda," *African Affairs* (2019); and Frank K. Rusagara, *Resilience of a Nation: A History of the Military in Rwanda* (Kigali: Fountain Publishers, 2009).
11. Some interesting, but basic, early accounts do exist. See, in particular, Adrien Fontanellaz and Tom Cooper, *The Rwandan Patriotic Front: 1990–1994* (Solihull, UK: Helion, 2015); Laurien Uwizeyimana, *Octobre et novembre 1990: le Front patriotique rwandais à l'assaut du Mutara* (Ruhengeri: Éditions universitaires du Rwanda, September 1992). There is also a substandard "conspiracy theory" dissertation, which exculpates the parties most responsible for the Genocide: Barrie Collins, "The Rwandan War 1990–1994: Interrogating the Dominant Narrative" (PhD diss., SOAS, 2009). It was later turned into a book: Barrie Collins, *Rwanda 1994: The Myth of the Akazu Genocide Conspiracy and Its Consequences* (London: Palgrave Macmillan, 2014).
12. Besides the works mentioned above, see Daniela Kroslak, *The Role of France in the Rwandan Genocide* (London: Hurst, 2007), and Andrew Wallis, *Silent Accomplice:*

The Untold Story of France's Role in the Rwandan Genocide (London: I. B. Tauris, 2014).

13. Mark Moyar, "The Current State of Military History," *Historical Journal* 50, no. 1 (March 2007), 225; Martin van Creveld, "Thoughts on Military History," *Journal of Contemporary History* 18, no. 4 (October 1983), 549.
14. Prunier, *The Rwanda Crisis;* Prunier also covered the RPF in a chapter in Christopher Clapham, ed., *African Guerrillas* (Oxford: James Currey, 1998).
15. Guichaoua, *From War to Genocide.*
16. André Guichaoua, ed., *Les crises politiques au Burundi et au Rwanda (1993–1994)* (Paris: Karthala, 1995).
17. Claudine Vidal, "Les contradictions d'un lieutenant rwandais: Abdul Ruzibiza, témoin, acteur, faux-témoin," in *L'Afrique des Grands Lacs, annuaire 2008–2009,* ed. S. Marysse, F. Reyntjens, and S. Vandeginste (Paris: L'Harmattan, 2009), 43.
18. Interview with Ndore Rurinda, 3 January 2018.
19. The RPF's Pan-African-inspired, anti-neocolonial ideology is ably discussed by Philip Roessler and Harry Verhoeven, *Why Comrades Go to War: Liberation Politics and the Outbreak of Africa's Deadliest Conflict* (London: Hurst, 2016).
20. Stathis N. Kalyvas, "Warfare in Civil Wars," in *Rethinking the Nature of War,* ed. Jan Angstrom and Isabelle Duyvesteyn (London: Routledge, 2005), 89–90.
21. Gourevitch, *We Wish to Inform You;* Jean Hatzfeld, *A Time for Machetes: The Rwandan Genocide; Let the Killers Speak,* trans. Linda Coverdale (London: Serpent's Tail, 2008).
22. Reid, *War in Pre-Colonial Eastern Africa,* 9.
23. Timothy Stapleton, "The Importance of Operational Accounts in African Military History," *Journal of African Military History* 5, no. 2 (2021): 73–76.
24. Richard J. Reid, *Warfare in African History* (Cambridge: Cambridge University Press, 2012), ix.
25. Jeremy Black, *Rethinking Military History* (London: Routledge, 2004), 67.
26. Tami Davis Biddle and Robert M. Citino, "The Role of Military History in the Contemporary Academy," *Army History* (Summer 2015): 24–30. The authors identify that military history used to be about "mainly white men," but then fail to address the dearth of interest in African wars.
27. Geoffrey Parker, ed., *The Cambridge History of Warfare* (Cambridge: Cambridge University Press, 2009), vii.
28. Parker, vii.
29. Parker, vii.
30. C. G. Thomas and R. Doron, "Out of Africa: The Challenges, Evolution, and Opportunities of African Military History," *Journal of African Military History* 1, no. 1 (2017): 4; the thought is echoed by Reid, *War in Pre-Colonial Eastern Africa,* 3.
31. Martin van Creveld, *The Transformation of War* (London: The Free Press, 1991), 197.
32. For some very interesting, and counterintuitive, insights on civil-military relations in DRC, see Raul Sanchez de la Sierra, "On the Origins of the State: Stationary Bandits and Taxation in Eastern Congo," *Journal of Political Economy* 128,

no. 11 (2020), and his online presentation "State Capacity, Natural Resources and Conflict in the DRC," posted 17 June 2021, by Bocconi University, YouTube, https://www.youtube.com/watch?v=FKSNIwOYVeE.

33. A handful of Africanists, of course, have recently been championing the cause of African military history. Their work is a direct source of inspiration for this book. Particularly noteworthy in this regard are a series of books that are closely connected to my topic in both methodological and analytical terms. While Kennes and Larmer's and Roessler and Verhoeven's studies provide exceptional insight into the irrelevance of borders to warfare in Central Africa, Decker's book is an important start for understanding the role of fighting women in the Great Lakes throughout the 1980s and 1990s. Erik Kennes and Miles Larmer, *The Katangese Gendarmes and War in Central Africa* (Bloomington: Indiana University Press, 2016); Roessler and Verhoeven, *Why Comrades Go to War;* Alicia C. Decker, *In Idi Amin's Shadow: Women, Gender, and Militarism in Uganda* (Athens: Ohio University Press, 2014). See also Edward George, *The Cuban Intervention in Angola, 1965–1991* (London: Frank Cass, 2005); David Anderson, *Histories of the Hanged: Britain's Dirty War in Kenya and the End of Empire* (London: Phoenix, 2006); Daniel Branch, *Defeating Mau Mau, Creating Kenya: Counterinsurgency, Civil War and Decolonisation* (Cambridge: Cambridge University Press, 2009); Daniel L. Douek, *Insurgency and Counterinsurgency in South Africa* (London: Hurst, 2020); and Clapham, *African Guerrillas.*
34. Richard Reid, "Past and Presentism: The 'Precolonial' and the Foreshortening of African History," *Journal of African History* 52, no. 2 (2011).
35. Prunier, *The Rwanda Crisis,* 75.
36. For a recent alternative and insightful take that relies on some of the same diplomatic material used in this book, see Marie-Eve Desrosiers, *Trajectories of Authoritarianism in Rwanda.*
37. Christopher Clapham, "Rwanda: The Perils of Peacemaking," *Journal of Peace Research* 35, no. 2 (March 1998): 205.
38. Gérard Prunier, *The Rwanda Crisis,* 57, 141. Besides Prunier, see Filip Reyntjens, "Rwanda, Genocide and Beyond," *Journal of Refugee Studies* 9, no. 3 (1996): 245 ("The state is present everywhere and every Rwandan is 'administered.' The structure is pyramid-like and orders travel fast and well from top to bottom"); Peter Langford, "The Rwandan Path to Genocide: The Genesis of the Capacity of the Rwandan Post-Colonial State to Organise and Unleash a Project of Extermination," *Civil Wars* 7, no. 1 (2005): 12, 15; Leander Heldring, "The Origins of Violence in Rwanda," *Review of Economic Studies* 88, no. 2 (March 2021): 730–63; and René Lemarchand, "Disconnecting the Threads: Rwanda and the Holocaust Reconsidered," *Journal of Genocide Research* 4, no. 4 (2002). For earlier challenges to the notions of conformity and absolute authority, see Mahmood Mamdani, *When Victims Become Killers,* 199–200, and Timothy Longman, "Placing Genocide in Context: Research Priorities for the Rwandan Genocide," *Journal of Genocide Research* 6, no. 1 (2004): 37.

39. Peter Uvin, "Reading the Rwandan Genocide," *International Studies Review* 3, no. 3 (2001): 84–87.
40. See, in particular, Roessler and Verhoeven, *Why Comrades Go to War.*
41. Jan Vansina, *Oral Tradition as History* (Madison: University of Wisconsin Press, 1985). This is an expanded version of his earlier *Oral Tradition: A Study in Historical Methodology* (New Brunswick: Transaction Publishers, 1961).
42. RDF officer. I am paraphrasing from memory here, as this was an off-the-cuff remark.
43. Vansina, *Oral Tradition as History,* 35.
44. Roessler and Verhoeven, *Why Comrades Go to War,* 420.
45. Vincent Duclert, *La France, le Rwanda et le génocide des Tutsi (1990–1994)—Rapport remis au Président de la République le 26 mars 2021* (Paris: Armand Colin, 2021). There are some obvious criticisms of the report. The whole research team was French and did not include any Rwanda experts. For an analysis of the *Rapport Duclert,* see Camille Evrard, et al., "Dossier: Au-delà du rapport Duclert; Décentrer l'histoire du génocide des Tutsi du Rwanda," *Revue d'histoire contemporaine de l'Afrique* (November 2021).
46. Paul Quilès, *Rapport d'information par la mission d'information de la commission de la défense nationale et des forces armées et de la commission des affaires étrangères, sur les opérations militaires menées par la France, d'autres pays et l'ONU au Rwanda entre 1990 et 1994* (Assemblée nationale, Paris, 15 December 1998).
47. Catherine Newbury and David Newbury, "Bringing the Peasants Back In," 833. This is echoed in Marie-Eve Desrosiers and Aidan Russel, "Histories of Authority in the African Great Lakes: Trajectories and Transactions," *Africa* 90, no. 5 (2020).
48. France Génocide Tutsi, accessed 18 June 2019, https://francegenocidetutsi.org/.
49. Jacques Morel, *La France au cœur du génocide des Tutsi* (Paris: L'Esprit Frappeur, 2016).
50. National Security Archive, accessed 18 June 2019, https://nsarchive.gwu.edu/ and https://nsarchive2.gwu.edu/NSAEBB/NSAEBB117/index.htm.
51. Judicial Records and Archives Database, *United Nations International Residual Mechanism for Criminal Tribunals,* accessed 18 June 2019, http://jrad.irmct.org/.
52. *The Prosecutor v. Bizimungu et al.* ICTR-99–50-T; *The Prosecutor v. Bagosora et al.,* ICTR-98-41-T; *The Prosecutor v. Ndindiliyimana et al.,* ICTR-00-56-T. It should be noted that the ICTR material presents problems. First, the website is not particularly user friendly. Second, translations of ICTR material, when they exist, are not always accurate. Where I used translated documents or transcripts, I always checked that the translations convey the meaning of the original. See Transcript of 19 November 2002, Testimony of Alison Des Forges, Cross-examination by Mr. Degli, ICTR-98-41-T., 61, 104–105.
53. United Nations Archives Search Engine, United Nations Archive, accessed 18 June 2019, https://search.archives.un.org/.
54. Many World Bank documents on Rwanda can be found on the organization's website. Search for "Rwanda" under the Documents & Reports section: https://documents.worldbank.org/en/publication/documents-reports.

55. Access to Archival Databases, *US National Archives and Records Administration,* accessed 18 June 2019, https://aad.archives.gov/aad/series-description.jsp?s=4073.
56. FOI release: Rwanda 1992 to 1993, Government of the United Kingdom, accessed 18 June 2019, https://www.gov.uk/government/publications/foi-release-rwanda-1992-to-1993.
57. Johan Swinnen, *Rwanda: Mijn verhaal* (Kalmthout, Belgium: Polis, 2016).
58. Letter, Alexis Neviaski, Le chef de la délégation des patrimoines culturels, Direction de la mémoire, du patrimoine et des archives, Ministère de la Défense, to John Burton Kegel, 30 May 2016.
59. Bernard Lugan, *François Mitterrand: l'Armée française et la Rwanda* (Monaco: Editions du Rocher, 2005).
60. Letter, Nathalie Morin and Myriam Achari, Direction de la mémoire, du patrimoine et des archives, Ministère de la Défense, to John Burton Kegel, 6 February 2017.
61. Letter, Christelle Guichard, Secrétaire générale, Commission d'accès aux documents administratifs, to John Burton Kegel, 1 August 2017.
62. *Rapport Duclert,* 18 and footnote 22.
63. Henry Kwami Anyidoho, *Guns over Kigali* (Accra: Woeli Publishing Services, 1997); James K. Gasana, *Rwanda: Du parti-État à l'État-garnison* (Paris: L'Harmattan, 2002); Roméo Dallaire, *Shake Hands with the Devil* (London: Arrow Books, 2004); Abdul Joshua Ruzibiza, *Rwanda: L'histoire secrète* (Paris: Editions du Panama, 2005); Theogene Rudasingwa, *Healing a Nation: A Testimony* (North Charleston, SC: CreateSpace, 2013).
64. The problems that can arise if one does not rigorously verify the integrity of memoirs are amply demonstrated by the Ruzibiza affair. See Vidal, "Les contradictions"; René Lemarchand, "Controversy within the Cataclysm: Review of *Rwanda: L'histoire secrète* by Abdul Ruzibiza," *African Studies Review* 50, no. 1 (April 2007); Filip Reyntjens, "*Rwanda: L'histoire secrète* by Abdul Ruzibiza: Review of *Rwanda: L'histoire secrète* by Abdul Ruzibiza," *Africa Today* 54, no. 3 (2008).
65. The most important are Philippe Mahoux and Guy Verhofstadt, *Commission d'enquête parlementaire concernant les événements du Rwanda* (Sénat de Belgique, 6 December 1997); and Paul Quilès, *Rapport d'information.*

CHAPTER 1: THE ORIGINS OF RWANDA, CA. 1550–1959

1. Hearing held in Quebec on 28 and 29 April 2003, Judgement in Ottawa on 8 September 2003. *Leon Mugesera et al. v. The Minister of Citizenship and Immigration,* 23–24; for Alison Des Forges's well-informed take on Mugesera and on the speech, see Transcript of 19 September 2006, Testimony of Alison Des Forges, Examination-in-chief by Mr. Jegede, ICTR-98-41-T.
2. Rwandan precolonial history is complicated and contested. The Roman Catholic abbé Alexis Kagame was one of the first Rwandan historians to write the

country's history. His histories were written from the point of view of the Nyiginya royal court. Jan Vansina has disagreed with, or nuanced, much that Kagame wrote, although there also is a clear development in his thinking over his long career: *L'évolution du royaume Rwanda des origines à 1900* (Brussels: Belgian Royal Colonial Institute, 1962). This work, republished in 2000 with an additional chapter, was followed by *Antecedents to Modern Rwanda: The Nyiginya Kingdom* (Madison: University of Wisconsin Press, 2004). In this respect the introduction to the following work is also interesting: M. d'Hertefelt, A. A. Trouwborst, and J. H. Scherer, *Les anciens royaumes de la zone interlacustre méridionale Rwanda, Burundi, Buha* (Tervuren, Belgium: MRAC, 1962). For a very colonial—and outdated—take on Rwanda, see the oeuvre of R. Bourgeois.

3. Jean-Pierre Chrétien, *The Great Lakes of Africa: Two Thousand Years of History,* trans. Scott Straus (New York: Zone Books, 2006), 42; d'Hertefelt, *Les anciens royaumes,* 3.
4. David Newbury, "Precolonial Burundi and Rwanda: Local Loyalties, Regional Royalties," *International Journal of African Historical Studies* 34, no. 2 (2001): 255–314.
5. Vansina, *Antecedents,* 30.
6. David L. Schoenbrun, "Cattle Herds and Banana Gardens: The Historical Geography of the Western Great Lakes Region, ca AD 800–1500," *African Archaeological Review* 11 (1993): 48; Vansina, *Antecedents,* 23.
7. Vansina, *Antecedents,* 25–28.
8. Vansina, 39.
9. d'Hertefelt, *Les anciens royaumes,* 35.
10. d'Hertefelt, 34–35.
11. Chrétien, *The Great Lakes of Africa,* 145; see also René Lemarchand, *Rwanda and Burundi* (New York: Praeger, 1970), 12–13, and Newbury, "Precolonial Burundi and Rwanda," 286.
12. Vansina, *Antecedents,* 33.
13. Vansina, 33.
14. Vansina, 44–47, 207–8.
15. Vansina, 45–46.
16. Vansina, 5; David Newbury, "Precolonial Burundi and Rwanda." One of the other issues for which there is no room is the question of clan; see David Newbury, "The Clans of Rwanda: A Historical Hypothesis," *Africa: Journal of the International African Institute* 50, no. 4 (1980): 389–403; Marcel d'Hertefelt, *Les Clans du Rwanda Ancien: Eléments d'ethnosociologie et d'ethnohistoire* (Tervuren, Belgium: MRAC, 1971); and Chrétien, *The Great Lakes of Africa,* 88–94.
17. Vansina, *Antecedents,* 47.
18. Vansina, 60–61.
19. Vansina, 60–61.
20. Vansina, chapter 3.
21. Vansina, 95.

22. Vansina, 143.
23. Vansina, 152.
24. Vansina, 36–37.
25. Vansina, 134.
26. Vansina, 75.
27. Vansina, 135.
28. Vansina, 139.
29. Alison L. Des Forges, *Defeat Is the Only Bad News: Rwanda under Musinga, 1896–1931* (Madison: University of Wisconsin Press, 2011), 49.
30. Catherine Newbury, *The Cohesion of Oppression: Clientship and Ethnicity in Rwanda, 1860–1960* (New York: Columbia University Press, 1988), 12, 145.
31. Vansina, *Antecedents,* 134–35.
32. Vansina, 134.
33. Newbury, *The Cohesion of Oppression* 14; Vansina, *Antecedents,* 134–37.
34. Vansina, *Antecedents,* 136–38.
35. Des Forges, *Defeat Is the Only Bad News,* 16.
36. James J. Carney, *Rwanda before the Genocide: Catholic Politics and Ethnic Discourse in the Late Colonial Era* (Oxford: Oxford University Press, 2014), 24; Des Forges, *Defeat Is the Only Bad News,* 18.
37. See Jean-Pierre Chrétien and Marcel Kabanda, *Rwanda: Racisme et génocide* (Berlin: Alpha, 2016), and Jean-Pierre Chrétien, "Hutu et Tutsi au Rwanda et au Burundi" in *Au coeur de l'ethnie,* ed. Jean-Loup Amselle and Elikia M'Bokolo (Paris: La Decouverte, 2005) for good explanations of the weird—and often paradoxical and contradictory—world of racial classifications between 1850 and 1960.
38. Chrétien and Kabanda, *Rwanda: Racisme et génocide,* ch. 1.
39. John Hanning Speke, *Journal of the Discovery of the Source of the Nile* (London: William Blackwood and Sons, 1863), 246–47.
40. Speke, 247.
41. Speke, 247.
42. Another example of the genre is A. Pages, *Au Ruanda, sur les bords du lac Kivu: Un royaume hamite au centre de l'Afrique* (Brussels: IRCB, 1933).
43. Chrétien, "Hutu et Tutsi," 137, quoting from F. Menard, "Les Barundi" (Archives des Pères blancs, Rome).
44. Chrétien, "Hutu et Tutsi," 133; J. Hiernaux, *Analyse de la variation des caractères physiques humains en une région de l'Afrique centrale: Ruanda-Urundi et Kivu* (Tervuren, Belgium: Musée Royal du Congo Belge, 1956).
45. R. Bourgeois, *Banyarwanda et Barundi, tome 1 ethnographie* (Brussels: ARSOM, 1957), 64.
46. However, this is all rather contested. See Vansina, *Antecedents,* 20–21, 46, especially footnotes 14 and 21; Christiane Desmedt, "Poteries anciennes décorées à la roulette dans la Région des Grands Lacs," *African Archaeological Review* 9 (1991): 184–85.
47. Vansina, *Antecedents,* 18–21.

48. Chrétien, *The Great Lakes of Africa,* 69; see also Newbury, "Precolonial Burundi and Rwanda," 275–80.
49. M. le Ministre des Colonies, *Rapport sur l'administration belge du Ruanda-Urundi pendant l'année 1936* (Brussels: Etablissement Emile Bruylant, 1937), 97.
50. For an insider description of the Groupe scolaire, see R. Bourgeois, *Témoignages: Tome 1—Volume 2, Fonctionnaire territorial (1931–1961)* (Brussels: MRAC, 1987), 172–74.
51. Carney, *Rwanda before the Genocide,* 24.
52. Des Forges, *Defeat Is the Only Bad News,* 33–36.
53. Des Forges, 102.
54. Des Forges, chapter 5 and 131–42, 152–55.
55. Gouvernement Belge, *Rapport présenté par le gouvernement belge au Conseil de la société des nations de l'administration du Ruanda-Urundi pendant l'année 1924* (Geneva: Société des nations, 1925), 12.
56. M. le Ministre des Colonies, *Rapport sur l'administration belge du Ruanda-Urundi pendant l'année 1930* (Brussels: Etablissement Emile Bruylant, 1931), 74.
57. Newbury, *The Cohesion of Oppression,* 153–54.
58. Des Forges, *Defeat Is the Only Bad News,* 183.
59. Newbury, *The Cohesion of Oppression,* 167.
60. Catherine Newbury, "The Cohesion of Oppression: A Century of Clientship in Kinyaga, Rwanda" (PhD diss., University of Wisconsin–Madison, 1975), 282.
61. Leathern Dorsey, "The Rwandan Colonial Economy, 1916–1941" (PhD diss., Michigan State University, 1983), 218–19.
62. Newbury, "The Cohesion of Oppression," 282.
63. Dantès Singiza, "La famine Ruzagayura (Rwanda, 1943–1944): Causes, conséquences et réactions des autorités" (PhD diss., Université de Liège & Musée royal de l'Afrique centrale, Tervuren, 2011), 36–47.
64. Singiza, "La famine Ruzagayura," 36–47. See also Bernard Lugan, "Causes et effets de la famine 'Rumanura' au Rwanda, 1916–18," *Canadian Journal of African Studies* 10, no. 2 (1976): 349; and Roger Botte, "Rwanda and Burundi, 1889–1930: Chronology of a Slow Assassination, Part 2," *International Journal of African Historical Studies* 18, no. 2 (1985).
65. United Nations Charter, Chapter XII, Article 76.
66. Chrétien, "Hutu et Tutsi," 129.

CHAPTER 2: THE SOCIAL REVOLUTION AND INDEPENDENCE, 1959–1964

1. Stephen Kinzer, *A Thousand Hills: Rwanda's Rebirth and the Man Who Dreamed It* (Hoboken, NJ: John Wiley, 2008), 8. The point here is not whether the two-year-old Paul Kagame remembered this himself or heard it later from his mother. What matters is that this is how Kagame remembers it now, and probably how he remembered it before he became commander of the RPF.
2. Andrew Wallis, *Stepp'd in Blood* (Winchester, UK: Zero Books, 2019), 26–27.

3. "The Aftermath of a Massacre," *Sunday Times,* 9 February 1964, 3.
4. Atlantic Charter, 14 August 1941.
5. United Nations Charter, Chapter XII, Article 76.
6. Filip Reyntjens, *Pouvoir et droit au Rwanda: Droit public et evolution politique, 1916–1973* (Tervuren, Belgium: MRAC, 1985), 182.
7. Timothy Longman, *Christianity and Genocide in Rwanda* (Cambridge: Cambridge University Press, 2011), 67.
8. Carney, *Rwanda before the Genocide: Catholic Politics and Ethnic Discourse in the Late Colonial Era* (Oxford: Oxford University Press, 2014), 55. Its actual reach among the many nonliterate Rwandans was much higher, as the magazine was read to them.
9. Carney, 55.
10. Catherine Newbury, *The Cohesion of Oppression: Clientship and Ethnicity in Rwanda, 1860–1960* (New York: Columbia University Press, 1988), 192–93.
11. Trusteeship Council, *United Nations Visiting Mission to Trust Territories in East Africa, 1957: Report on Ruanda-Urundi* (New York: United Nations, 1958), 5.
12. R. Bourgeois, *Témoignages: Tome 1—Volume 2, Fonctionnaire Territorial (1931–1961)* (Brussels: MRAC, 1987), 173.
13. Trusteeship Council, *United Nations Visiting Mission to Trust Territories in East Africa, 1948: Report on Ruanda-Urundi* (New York: United Nations, 1948), 20.
14. Reyntjens, *Pouvoir et droit,* 210–18.
15. Trusteeship Council, *Visiting Mission to the Trust Territory of Ruanda-Urundi 1948,* 18; Gouvernement Belge, *Rapport soumis par le gouvernement belge à l'Assemblée Générale des Nations Unies au sujet de l'administration du Ruanda-Urundi pendant l'année 1949* (Brussels: Etablissements Généraux d'Imprimerie, 1950), 179.
16. M. le Ministre des Colonies, *Rapport sur l'administration belge du Ruanda-Urundi pendant l'année 1954* (Brussels: Imprimerie Fr. van Muysewinkel, 1955), 325.
17. The Belgian report to the UN of 1955 seems to suggest that the elections were scheduled to take place in 1957. Gouvernement Belge, *Rapport soumis par le gouvernement belge à l'Assemblée Générale des Nations Unies au sujet de l'administration du Ruanda-Urundi pendant l'année 1955* (Brussels: Imprimerie Fr. van Muysewinkel, 1956), 279.
18. Reyntjens, *Pouvoir et droit,* 192, notes that it is peculiar such a step could be taken on the basis of a simple letter, rather than through the passing of legislation.
19. Jacques J. Maquet and Marcel d'Hertefelt, *Elections en société féodale: Une étude sur l'introduction du vote populaire au Ruanda-Urundi* (Brussels: Académie royale des Sciences coloniales, 1959), 34; Bourgeois, *Témoignages,* 251.
20. Carney, *Rwanda before the Genocide,* 48.
21. Bourgeois, *Témoignages,* 253.
22. Maquet and d'Hertefelt, *Elections en société féodale,* 4–5.
23. René Lemarchand, *Rwanda and Burundi* (New York: Praeger, 1970), 83.
24. Trusteeship Council, *United Nations Visiting Mission to Trust Territories in East Africa, 1957,* Annex II, "Statement of Views," 42.

25. Trusteeship Council, *UN Visiting Mission, 1957,* Annex I, "Manifesto of the Bahutu," 39.
26. Trusteeship Council, 40.
27. Trusteeship Council, 40.
28. Trusteeship Council, 41.
29. Gérard Prunier, *The Rwanda Crisis: History of a Genocide* (London: Hurst, 1997), 50.
30. Trusteeship Council, *UN Visiting Mission, 1957,* Annex I, "Manifesto of the Bahutu," 7–8.
31. Trusteeship Council, *Visiting Mission to Trust Territories in East Africa, 1960: Report on Ruanda-Urundi* (New York: United Nations, 1960), 44.
32. Trusteeship Council, *Visiting Mission, 1960,* 43.
33. Jan Vansina, *Antecedents to Modern Rwanda: The Nyiginya Kingdom* (Madison: University of Wisconsin Press, 2004), 44.
34. Vansina, 48.
35. Pierre Rijckmans, *Rapport du groupe de travail pour l'etude du problème politique au Congo Belge* (Brussels: Chambre des Représentants, 20 January 1959).
36. Trusteeship Council, *Visiting Mission, 1960,* 49–50.
37. Trusteeship Council, 57. Quoting an analysis "made on 31 July by Mr. Vansina."
38. Trusteeship Council, *Visiting Mission, 1960,* 57.
39. Lemarchand, *Rwanda and Burundi,* 151.
40. Prunier, *The Rwanda Crisis,* 47; Carney, *Rwanda before the Genocide,* 84.
41. Miss Solesby to Foreign Office, "Indications of preparations for armed attack against Rwanda by refugees from Kivu Province of Congo, Burundi and Tanganyika," 23 July 1964, "FO 371/177022, JR 1821/3," NAUK; Lemarchand, *Rwanda and Burundi,* 176, 200, 205; Carney, *Rwanda before the Genocide,* 138; Trusteeship Council, *Visiting Mission, 1960,* 63; Frank K. Rusagara, *Resilience of a Nation: A History of the Military in Rwanda* (Kigali: Fountain Publishers, 2009), 143.
42. Trusteeship Council, *Visiting Mission, 1960,* 65.
43. Prunier, *The Rwanda Crisis,* 41.
44. This is in keeping with how contemporaries saw the events: Carney, *Rwanda before the Genocide,* 129; "Guerre civile au Rwanda," *Centre de recherche et d'information socio-politiques—CRISP,* no. 42 (27 November 1959): 15.
45. Trusteeship Council, *Visiting Mission, 1960,* 72; Lemarchand, *Rwanda and Burundi,* 162.
46. Trusteeship Council, 73.
47. Trusteeship Council, 73.
48. Donald L. Horowitz, *The Deadly Ethnic Riot* (Los Angeles: University of California Press, 2002), 7.
49. Trusteeship Council, *Visiting Mission, 1960,* 74.
50. Even Belgian colonel Guy Logiest wrote in his memoirs that "it was not uncommon for people to die if the Tutsi resisted." However, he immediately qualified this by insisting that "the Hutus were clearly not out to kill but only to drive out

the Tutsi." Guy Logiest, *Mission au Rwanda: Un blanc dans la bagarre Tutsi-Hutu* (Brussels: Didier Hatier, 1988), 39; MM. Fr. Peigneux, G. Malengreau, and S. Frédéricq, *Rapport de la Commission d'Enquête au Ruanda* (Brussels: 1960), 55.

51. Lemarchand, *Rwanda and Burundi,* 163.
52. Trusteeship Council, *Visiting Mission, 1960,* 74.
53. Jan Vansina, *Living with Africa* (Madison: University of Wisconsin Press, 1994), 81.
54. Lemarchand, *Rwanda and Burundi,* 164–65.
55. Trusteeship Council, *Visiting Mission, 1960,* 77.
56. "La Guerre Civile," *Centre de recherche et d'information socio-politiques—CRISP,* no. 42 (5 February 1959), 19.
57. Trusteeship Council, *Visiting Mission, 1960,* 76.
58. Kamer der Volksvertegenwoordigers, *Parlementaire Handelingen: Vergadering van dinsdag 17 november 1959* (Brussels: Belgisch Staatsblad, 1959), 3, "burgeroorlog op kleine schaal." A rather bizarre article by René MacColl, who was in Nyanza at the time, also argued that what was going on was a war. *Daily Express,* 13 November 1959, 1–2.
59. Logiest, *Mission au Rwanda,* 45.
60. *The Times,* 9 November 1959, 8; Trusteeship Council, *Visiting Mission, 1960,* 80.
61. Trusteeship Council, 77.
62. Peigneux, Malengreau, and Frédéricq, *Rapport de la Commission,* 66, 68. It is interesting to note how different people experienced events differently. On 9 November, a missionary wrote that "'the movement of [violence] is heard wherever the Hutu are numerous, except in the South and in the Territory of Biumba [Byumba].'" Quoted in Aya Tsuruta, "'It Is Difficult to Understand Rwandan History': Contested History of Ethnicity and Dynamics of Conflicts in Rwanda during Revolution and Independence" (PhD diss., University of Edinburgh, 2013), 150. This is strange as the Save hill episode happened just outside Butare/Astrida, the largest town in the south.
63. *The Times,* 10 November 1959, 12.
64. Trusteeship Council, *Visiting Mission, 1960,* 86; Carney, *Rwanda before the Genocide,* 127; Lemarchand, *Rwanda and Burundi,* 197; "Mission Criticisms of Ruanda Authorities," *The Times,* 7 December 1959, 8.
65. Trusteeship Council, 15.
66. Carney, *Rwanda before the Genocide,* 136.
67. Trusteeship Council, *Visiting Mission, 1960,* 15.
68. Trusteeship Council, 84; Tsuruta, "It Is Difficult," 157.
69. Trusteeship Council, 84.
70. Lemarchand, *Rwanda and Burundi,* 172.
71. Rusagara, *Resilience of a Nation,* 142.
72. Carney, *Rwanda before the Genocide,* 137.
73. James Jay Carney, "From Democratization to Ethnic Revolution: Catholic Politics in Rwanda, 1950–1962" (PhD diss., Catholic University of America, 2011), 275–76. For a discussion of the Belgian decision to postpone the elections, see Tsuruta, "It Is Difficult," 127–29.

74. Lemarchand, *Rwanda and Burundi,* 193.
75. Carney, *Rwanda before the Genocide,* 156.
76. "80 refugees flee Ruanda in new terror drive," *Chicago Daily Tribune,* 21 January 1962, 7.
77. No thorough study of the Inyenzi exists. Since very few of their number are still alive, it is almost impossible to write accurately about the organization.
78. Services d'information du ministère des affaires étrangères du Rwanda, *Toute la vérité sur le terrorisme 'Inyenzi' au Rwanda: Une mise au point du ministère des affaires étrangères du Rwanda* (Kigali: Services d'information du ministère des affaires étrangères du Rwanda, 1964), 12.
79. Barbey to Etat-Major General de la Défense Nationale, "Situation à Usumbura," 12 July 1962, "Burundi: Juillet '62–Mai '65," GR 6Q 50, SHD.
80. Services d'information du ministère des affaires étrangères du Rwanda, *Toute la vérité,* 13.
81. Lemarchand, *Rwanda and Burundi,* 219; "Rwanda Calm in Face of Civil War Threat," *The Times,* 19 June 1962; Carney, *Rwanda before the Genocide,* 157.
82. "Patrol Ambushed," *Daily Mail,* 9 July 1962, 5.
83. Emmanuel Coppieters, "Rwanda naar de Onafhankelijkheid," reprint from *De Standaard,* 23, 24, and 27 August 1962, 10.
84. High Commissioner for Refugees, *Report on the Situation of Refugees from Rwanda* (New York: United Nations, 1963), 1.
85. "Conjuration contre le Ruanda," 3/279, "Ruanda: Décembre '63–Septembre '64 GR 6Q 50," SHD; "Découverte d'un dépôt d'armes clandestines à Usumbura," *Le courrier d'Afrique* (Léopoldville, Belgian Congo), 3 December 1963, 1.
86. John Bennett to —, "Appreciation of the Rwanda Armed Forces as expounded by Col. Alexander, the U.S. Military Attaché," 14 February 1964, "FO 371/177017, JR 1201/3G," NAUK.
87. Barbey to Affaires Etrangères, "Evènements survenus à KIGALI," 23 December 1963, "Ruanda: Décembre '63–Septembre '64, GR 6Q 50," SHD.
88. Barbey, "Evènements survenus à KIGALI," 23 December 1963.
89. "The aftermath of a massacre," *Sunday Times,* 9 February 1964, 3.
90. "Genocide in the Heart of Africa," *Financial Times,* 7 February 1964, 7; *Le courrier d'Afrique,* 17 January 1964, 1. Despite what some have argued, there *was* widespread media attention given to the situation in Rwanda. See Kinzer, *A Thousand Hills,* 34.
91. "De sanglants incidents auraient lieu au Ruanda," *Le Monde,* 17 January 1964, 3.
92. "Rwanda Policy of Genocide Alleged," *The Times,* 3 February 1964, 10.
93. "Burgeroorlog Rwanda heeft nasleep van ellende," *Friese Koerier* (Heereveen, Netherlands), 14 February 1964, 15.
94. "Trois mille Tutsis réfugiés au Congo-Léopoldville lanceraient une 'attaque-suicide' contre le Ruanda," *Le Monde,* 6 February 1964.
95. Inyenzi attacks continued but would no longer pose a serious threat. P. Rijke to Ambassadeur, Kinshasa, "Onafhankelijkheidsdagviering 1 juli 1966, Rwanda," 2 July 1966, "Inv.nr.: 23 Archiefbloknummer: Z162," NL-NA. Another attack took

place on 20 July 1966, Ambassadeur Zeylstra to Minister van Buitenlandse Zaken, "Rwanda: Politiek," 27 July 1966, "Inv.nr.: 23 Archiefbloknummer: Z162," NL-NA. And again around 30 November 1966, P. Rijke to Ambassadeur, Kinshasa, "Rwanda Politiek," 30 November 1966, "Inv.nr.: 23 Archiefbloknummer: Z162," NL-NA.

96. Mahmood Mamdani, *When Victims Become Killers: Colonialism, Nativism, and Genocide in Rwanda* (Princeton, NJ: Princeton University Press, 2002), 130.

CHAPTER 3: FROM KAYIBANDA TO HABYARIMANA, 1959–1990

1. Baekelandt to Belext Bru, "situation intérieure," 5 July 1973, "18.888-III-1, Onlusten in Rwanda 1972–1973," FPFSA.
2. Etienne Ugeux, "L'armée a pris le pouvoir en douceur au Rwanda," *Le Soir,* 6 July 1973.
3. Etienne Ugeux, "Interview exclusive du président rwandais au 'Soir,'" *Le Soir,* 11 July 1973.
4. C. G. Verdonck Huffnagel to Minister van Buitenlandse Zaken, "Rwanda's nieuwe bewind," 29 November 1973, "Inv.nr.: 23 Archiefbloknummer: Z162," NL-NA, 2.
5. J. S. Bennett to West and Central African Department, "Elections in Rwanda," 28 July 1964, "FO 371/181948. JN 1018/2," NAUK.
6. Gérard Prunier, *The Rwanda Crisis: History of a Genocide* (London: Hurst, 1997), 80.
7. Filip Reyntjens, *Pouvoir et droit au Rwanda: Droit public et evolution politique, 1916–1973* (Tervuren, Belgium: MRAC, 1985), 481.
8. J. S. Bennett to West and Central Africa Department, FCO, "Bujumbura Despatch no. 9 of the 13th of November 1965: Elections in Rwanda," 13 November 1965, "FO 371/181948," NAUK.
9. René Lemarchand, "Rwanda: The Rationality of Genocide," *Issue: A Journal of Opinion* 23, no. 2 (1995): 9.
10. For more information, see Reyntjens, *Pouvoir et droit,* 493.
11. C. Th. R. van Baarda to Minister van Buitenlandse Zaken, "Aanbieding geloofsbrieven te Kigali," 18 April 1969, "Inv.nr.: 2 Archiefbloknummer: Z162," NL-NA, 3.
12. Huffnagel, "Rwanda's nieuwe bewind," 29 November 1973.
13. W. G. Zeylstra to Minister van Buitenlandse Zaken, "Rwanda: Politiek," 26 May 1967, "Inv.nr.: 23 Archiefbloknummer: Z162," NL-NA, 3.
14. Bennett, "Bujumbura Despatch," 13 November 1965.
15. W. G. Zeylstra to Minister van Buitenlandse Zaken, "Rwanda: Politiek," 26 May 1967, "Inv.nr.: 23 Archiefbloknummer: Z162," NL-NA, 3.
16. Philip Roessler, *Ethnic Politics and State Power in Africa: The Logic of the Coup–Civil War Trap* (Cambridge: Cambridge University Press, 2016), 54.
17. Bennett, "Bujumbura Despatch," 13 November 1965.
18. G. A. Vijgeboom to Ambassade der Nederlanden, Kinshasa, "Berechting ingevolge staatsgreep van 1967," 28 September 1971, "Inv.nr.: 23 Archiefbloknummer: Z162," NL-NA.

19. This is how the coup attempt was described to me by a Belgian military cooperant who had been in Rwanda at the time. For a slightly different version of events see Reyntjens, *Pouvoir et droit,* 500–501.
20. René Lemarchand, *Rwanda and Burundi* (New York: Praeger, 1970), 96–97.
21. Reyntjens, *Pouvoir et droit,* 502.
22. Algemene Directie van Politiek, Ministerie van Buitenlandse Zaken, "Nota: Onlusten in Rwanda," date unknown presumably March 1973, "18.888/III/1, Incidents au Rwanda 1972–1973," FPFSA.
23. Reyntjens, *Pouvoir et droit,* 503.
24. Huffnagel, "Rwanda's nieuwe bewind," 29 November 1973.
25. Algemene Directie van Politiek, Ministerie van Buitenlandse Zaken, "Nota: Onlusten in Rwanda," date unknown presumably March 1973, "18.888/III/1, Incidents au Rwanda 1972–1973," FPFSA. This document is a chronology, so while its date of publication is unknown it describes events day by day.
26. "Nota: Onlusten in Rwanda."
27. "Nota: Onlusten in Rwanda."
28. "Nota: Onlusten in Rwanda."
29. "Rwanda: Période du 24 février au 2 mars 1973," date unknown presumably March 1973, "18.888/III/1, Incidents au Rwanda 1972–1973," FPFSA.
30. Reyntjens, *Pouvoir et droit,* 503.
31. Baekelandt to Belext Bru, "Binnenlandse toestand," 6 March 1973, "18.888/III/1, Incidents au Rwanda 1972–1973," FPFSA; the author's additions in brackets are from a follow-up message. See Baekelandt to Belext Bru, "Binnenlandse toestand," 7 March 1973, "18.888/III/1, Incidents au Rwanda 1972–1973," FPFSA.
32. "Nota: Onlusten in Rwanda"; see also Baekelandt, "Binnenlandse toestand," 7 March 1973; this at least is the position Hitayezu held in 1969.
33. Reyntjens, *Pouvoir et droit,* 503.
34. Reyntjens, 503–4.
35. Baekelandt, "Binnenlandse toestand," 7 March 1973. See also: "Nota: Onlusten in Rwanda," emphasis mine.
36. US Embassy, Kigali, to Secretary of State, "Ethnic troubles," 7 March 1973, US-NA; US Consulate, Bukavu to Secretary of State, "Refugees from Rwanda," 7 March 1973, "ADD: Electronic Telegrams, 1973," USNARA.
37. Huffnagel, "Rwanda's nieuwe bewind," 29 November 1973, 3; More proof of the hard line of Munyaneza can be found in US Embassy, "Ethnic troubles," 7 March 1973. Emphasis mine.
38. US Embassy, Kigali, to Secretary of State, "Ethnic troubles: Request for emergency relief," 14 March 1973, "ADD: Electronic Telegrams, 1973," USNARA.
39. US Embassy, Kigali, to Secretary of State, "Kayibanda statement on recent troubles," 26 March 1973, "ADD: Electronic Telegrams, 1973," USNARA.
40. US Embassy, Kigali, to Secretary of State, "Rwandan Political Activity," 6 April 1973, "ADD: Electronic Telegrams, 1973," USNARA. Note there apparently was yet another coup attempt on 19 May 1973 that had also been stopped by

Habyarimana, see: Baekelandt to Belext Bru, "Ugeux au journal *Le Soir,*" 6 July 1973, "18.888/III/1, Coup d'état au Rwanda," FPFSA.

41. Something the US did not fail to exploit: US Embassy, Kigali, to Secretary of State, "Youth Para," 25 April 1973, "ADD: Electronic Telegrams, 1973," USNARA.
42. G. A. Vijgeboom to Ambassade der Nederlanden, Kinshasa, "Toestand in Rwanda," 28 mei 1973, "Inv.nr.: 23 Archiefbloknummer: Z162," NL-NA.
43. US Embassy, Kigali, to Secretary of State, "Barundi Refugee Activity," 14 May 1973, "ADD: Electronic Telegrams, 1973," USNARA.
44. US Embassy, Kigali, to Secretary of State, "Message to HCR Geneva," 14 May 1973, "ADD: Electronic Telegrams, 1973," USNARA.
45. US Embassy, Kampala, to Secretary of State, "General Amin declares he is ready to assist Burundi," 15 May 1973, "ADD: Electronic Telegrams, 1973," USNARA.
46. US Embassy, Kigali, to Secretary of State, "Burundi Situation," 16 May 1973, "ADD: Electronic Telegrams, 1973," USNARA.
47. US Embassy, "Burundi Situation," 16 May 1973.
48. US Embassy, Brussels, to Secretary of State, "Belgium may withdraw military technical assistance from Rwanda," 28 June 1973, "ADD: Electronic Telegrams, 1973," USNARA; "Belgian Diplomats Fear Burundi Clash with Rwanda Force," *New York Times,* 17 May 1973, 10.
49. Baekelandt to Belext Bru, "Priorite," 7 July 1973, "18.888/III/1, Coup d'état au Rwanda," FPFSA.
50. One of the former members of the Belgian military assistance mission described it to me as "just like the German operation in World War Two—operation Valkyrie." This is confirmed in Baekelandt to Elslande, Minister of Foreign Affairs, Brussels, "Staatsgreep," 10 July 1973, "18.888/III/1, Coup d'état au Rwanda," FPFSA.
51. Baekelandt to Elslande, Minister of Foreign Affairs, Brussels, "Staatsgreep," 6 July 1973, "18.888/III/1, Coup d'état au Rwanda," FPFSA.
52. Baekelandt to Belext Bru, "Situation interne," 5 July 1973, "18.888/III/1, Coup d'état au Rwanda," FPFSA; See also Baekelandt to Belext Bru, "Priorite," 7 July 1973, "18.888/III/1, Coup d'état au Rwanda," FPFSA.
53. US Embassy, Kigali to Secretary of State, "Rwanda Coup," 11 July 1973, US-NA; US Embassy, Brussels, to Secretary of State, "New Rwandan Government: Recognition Issue," 12 July 1973, "ADD: Electronic Telegrams, 1973," USNARA; This is confirmed in Baekelandt, "Situation intérieure," 5 July 1973. See also Baekelandt to Belext Bru, "Coopération militaire," 6 July 1973, "18.888/III/1, Coup d'état au Rwanda," FPFSA.
54. US Embassy, Kigali, to Secretary of State, "Rwanda Coup," 11 July 1973, US-NA; US Embassy, Brussels, to Secretary of State, "New Rwandan Government: Recognition Issue," 12 July 1973, "ADD: Electronic Telegrams, 1973," USNARA.
55. Telegram, US Embassy, Brussels to Secretary of State, "New Rwandan Government: Recognition Issue," 12 July 1973, "ADD: Electronic Telegrams, 1973," USNARA.

56. C. G. Verdonck Huffnagel to Minister van Buitenlandse Zaken, "Betrekkingen Rwanda met buurlanden," 13 July 1973, "Inv.nr.: 25 Archiefbloknummer: Z162," NL-NA; US Embassy, Kinshasa, to Secretary of State, "Zaire Radio Commentary on Rwandan Coup," 5 July 1973, "ADD: Electronic Telegrams, 1973," USNARA; US Embassy, Bujumbura, to Secretary of State, "Burundi Reaction to Rwanda Coup," 5 July 1973, "ADD: Electronic Telegrams, 1973," USNARA.
57. US Embassy, Bujumbura, to Secretary of State, "Micombero receives Rwandan Delegation," 11 July 1973, "ADD: Electronic Telegrams, 1973," USNARA.
58. I. Verkade to Minister van Buitenlandse Zaken, "Jaarrapport Rwanda," 30 January 1975, "Inv.nr.: 24 Archiefbloknummer: Z162," NL-NA, 6; US Embassy, Kigali, to Secretary of State, "Visit of Burundi President Micombero: Reconciliation at the top," 4 October 1974, *WikiLeaks,* accessed 9 January 2018, https://www.wikileaks.org/plusd/cables/1974KIGALI00543_b.html.
59. US Embassy, Kigali, to Secretary of State, "Generals Amin and Habyalimana [*sic*] meet at Kabale," 30 July 1973, "ADD: Electronic Telegrams, 1973," USNARA; This is confirmed in Baekelandt to Belext Bru, "Relations Rwanda avec Ouganda," 9 July 1973, "18.888/III/1, Coup d'état au Rwanda," FPFSA.
60. US Embassy, Nairobi, to Secretary of State, "Rwandan National Guard dismiss government and National Assembly," 5 July 1973, "ADD: Electronic Telegrams, 1973," USNARA.
61. Prunier, *The Rwanda Crisis,* 74–76.
62. Prunier, 82.
63. Paul Quilès, *Rapport d'information par la mission d'information de la commission de la défense nationale et des forces armées et de la commission des affaires étrangères, sur les opérations militaires menées par la France, d'autres pays et l'ONU au Rwanda entre 1990 et 1994* (Assemblée nationale, Paris, 15 December 1998), 80.
64. Andrew Wallis, *Stepp'd in Blood* (Winchester, UK: Zero Books, 2019), 73.
65. Le Comte J. F. de Liedekerke, Ambassadeur de Belgique, to Monsieur R. Van Elslandse, Ministre des Affaires Etrangères et de la Coopération au Développement, "Décès ex-président Kayibanda," 10 January 1977, "18.888-II, MRND-RPF 1988–1989," FPFSA.
66. Le Comte J. F. de Liedekerke, Ambassadeur de Belgique, to Monsieur R. Van Elslandse, Ministre des Affaires Etrangères et de la Coopération au Développement, "Récit de la mort de l'ancien Président Grégoire Kayibanda," 20 December 1976, "18.888-II, MRND-RPF 1988–1989," FPFSA.
67. Liedekerke, "Récit de la mort," 20 December 1976.
68. Prunier, *The Rwanda Crisis,* 45.
69. Prunier, 128.
70. Liedekerke, "Récit de la mort," 20 December 1976.
71. For example, in 1977 when Lieutenant-Colonels Aloys Nsekalije, Laurent Serubuga, and Buregeya ganged up on Habyarimana. While there were ideological issues at play (socialist-capitalist, this was in the middle of the Cold War), in the Belgian analysis a major problem was "the increasing corruption within

the high command. It is generally accepted that the head of state has integrity and demands the same difficult quality from his subordinates. However he is no longer managing and is making enemies because of it." R. van Crombrugge, Ambassadeur van België, to H. Simonet Minister van Buitenlandse Zaken, "Rwanda—politieke toestand," 31 October 1977, "18.888-II, Constitution Rwanda," FPFSA. There is also the Kanyarengwe Affair; see Prunier, *The Rwanda Crisis,* 115.

72. While this thesis does not subscribe to this Malthusian argument in its crudest form, the existing literature does make it clear that economic factors had a profound impact on the Rwandan population in the years leading up to the Genocide: Peter Uvin, "Reading the Rwandan Genocide," *International Studies Review* 3, no. 3 (2001).

73. World Bank, *Recent Economic Development and Prospects of Rwanda,* vol. 1, *The Main Report,* written by Attila Sönmez (Washington, DC: World Bank, 1974), 19. See also Philip Verwimp, "Development Ideology, the Peasantry and Genocide: Rwanda Represented in Habyarimana's Speeches," Yale Genocide Studies Program: Working Paper GS13 (1999), 1.

74. Val Percival and Thomas Homer-Dickson, "Environmental Scarcity and Violent Conflict: The Case of Rwanda," *Journal of Environment & Development* 5, no. 3 (September 1996): 278.

75. On this see also Marijke Verpoorten, "Leave None to Claim the Land: A Malthusian Catastrophe in Rwanda?," *Journal of Peace Research* 49 (July 2012); Catherine André and Jean-Philippe Platteau, "Land Relations under Unbearable Stress: Rwanda Caught in the Malthusian Trap," *Journal of Economic Behaviour and Organisation* 34, no. 1 (1998), in some ways the André and Platteau article shows extraordinary similarities with the classic on inequality in Bangladesh: B. Hartmann and J. K. Boyce, *A Quiet Violence: View from a Bangladesh Village* (Dhaka: The University Press, 1988).

76. Percival and Homer-Dickson, "Environmental Scarcity and Violent Conflict," 279.

77. André and Platteau, "Land Relations under Unbearable Stress," 37.

78. Isaac A. Kamola, "The Global Coffee Economy and the Production of Genocide in Rwanda," *Third World Quarterly* 28, no. 3 (2007): 578.

79. Richard L. Lucier, *The International Political Economy of Coffee: From Juan Valdez to Yank's Diner* (New York: Praeger, 1988), 122–24; "America Signs On," *The Economist,* 18 January 1964, 233.

80. Philip Verwimp, *Peasants in Power: The Political Economy of Development and Genocide in Rwanda* (New York: Springer, 2013), 85–87.

81. Johan P. Pottier, "Taking Stock: Food Marketing Reform in Rwanda, 1982–89," *African Affairs* 92, no. 36 (January 1993): 11; see also Reyntjens, *Pouvoir et droit,* 395–99.

82. Verwimp, *Peasants in Power,* 85–86; Philip Verwimp, "Agricultural Policy, Crop Failure and the 'Ruriganiza' Famine (1989) in Southern Rwanda: A Prelude to

Genocide?," Centre for Economic Studies Discussion Paper Series (DPS), Katholieke Universiteit Leuven, June 2002, 15.

83. "Green-Gum Booted Uganda on the Banana Standard," *The Economist,* 20 September 1986, 52; "Percolates Abroad," *The Economist,* 9 May 1981, 94; I. Verkade to Minister van Buitenlandse Zaken, "Rwanda," 19 November 1974, "Inv.nr.: 23 Archiefbloknummer: Z162," NL-NA, 2; World Bank, *Recent Economic Development and Prospects of Rwanda,* 13–14.
84. Peter Uvin, *Development, Aid and Conflict: Reflections from the Case of Rwanda* (Helsinki: United Nations University, 1996), 15; Peter Uvin, *Aiding Violence: The Development Enterprise in Rwanda* (West Hartford, CT: Kumarian Press, 1998), 40.
85. Jennifer Maria Olson, "Farmer Responses to Land Degradation in Gikongoro" (PhD diss., Michigan State University, 1994), 116; see also René Lemarchand, *The World Bank in Rwanda: The Case of the Office de valorisation agricole et pastorale du mutara (OVAPAM)* (Bloomington: Indiana University Press, 1982), and World Bank, *Mutara Agricultural and Livestock Development Project—Phase II, Staff Appraisal Report* (Washington, DC: World Bank, 1979).
86. *"The International Coffee Organisation 1963–2013: 50 Years Serving the World Coffee Community"* (International Coffee Organisation, 2013), 13.
87. Andy Storey, "Structural Adjustment, State Power and Genocide: The World Bank and Rwanda," *Review of African Political Economy* 28, no. 89 (2001): 365–85.
88. Nordic Africa Institute, *The International Response to Conflict and Genocide: Lessons from the Rwanda Experience, Historical Perspective; Some Explanatory Factors,* written by Tor Sellström and Lennart Wohlgemut (Uppsala, Sweden: Nordic Africa Institute, 1996), 37.
89. "Pointers: Rwanda fin de Régime," *Africa Confidential,* 20 October 1989. See also Ambabel Kigali to Belext Bru, "Politieke toestand Rwanda, begin 1988," 25 March 1988, "18.888-I-1 Télégrammes 'Sortie' Kigali 1985–1986."

CHAPTER 4: THE STORY OF THE RPF

1. The history of Rwandan refugees in Burundi is especially intricate and complicated. An article on it is currently in preparation.
2. Elijah Dicken Mushemeza, "Politics and the Refugee Experience: The Case of the Banyarwanda Refugees in Uganda (1959–1994)" (PhD diss., Makerere University, 2002), 106.
3. Mahmood Mamdani, *When Victims Become Killers: Colonialism, Nativism, and Genocide in Rwanda* (Princeton, NJ: Princeton University Press, 2002), 162.
4. M. le Ministre des Colonies, *Rapport sur l'administration belge du Ruanda-Urundi pendant l'année 1930* (Brussels: Etablissement Emile Bruylant, 1931), 91; M. le Ministre des Colonies, *Rapport sur l'administration belge du Ruanda-Urundi pendant l'année 1953* (Brussels: Etablissements Généraux d'Imprimerie, 1954), 152.
5. Interview with Vianney Shumbusho, 18 October 2018; general background was also given by Idi Gapardtui in an interview on 18 October 2018.

6. Interview with Vianney Shumbusho, 18 October 2018.
7. Interview with Ndore Rurinda, 10 September 2018.
8. High Commissioner for Refugees, *Report on the Situation of Refugees from Rwanda* (New York: United Nations, 1963), 3; Gérard Prunier, *The Rwanda Crisis: History of a Genocide* (London: Hurst, 1997), 65; Mushemeza, "Politics and the Refugee Experience," 137; interview with Ndore Rurinda, 10 September 2018.
9. High Commissioner for Refugees, *Proposal for Assistance to Refugees from Rwanda in the Kivu Province of the Congo* (New York: United Nations, 13 April 1964); UN support fluctuated over time. Refugee Policy Group, *Older Refugee Settlements in Africa—Final Report,* written by Lance Clark and Barry Stein (Washington, DC: Refugee Policy Group, November 1985), 126–29.
10. Interview with Vianney Shumbusho, 18 October 2018.
11. High Commissioner for Refugees, *1964 Programme—New Projects: Projects for the Settlement of Approximately 20,000 Refugees from Rwanda* (New York: United Nations, 10 April 1964), 14–15.
12. High Commissioner for Refugees, 14–15.
13. US Committee for Refugees, *Exile from Rwanda: Background to an Invasion,* written by Catherine Watson (Arlington, VA: US Committee for Refugees, February 1991), 8.
14. Author's correspondence with former RPF member, 27 August 2017.
15. Mushemeza, "Politics and the Refugee Experience," 141.
16. Mushemeza, 172; Philip Roessler and Harry Verhoeven, *Why Comrades Go to War: Liberation Politics and the Outbreak of Africa's Deadliest Conflict* (London: Hurst, 2016), 185–86.
17. Mamdani, *When Victims Become Killers,* 165–66. My interviewee Vianney Shumbusho, for instance, studied in Addis Ababa on a UNHCR scholarship.
18. Interview with J-L Denblynden, 24 August 2017.
19. US Committee for Refugees, *Exile from Rwanda,* 8–9.
20. US Committee for Refugees, 8–9.
21. Mushemeza, "Politics and the Refugee Experience," 132–33. This is a contentious issue. For instance, Clark and Stein state that the Rwandan refugees "also experienced difficulties in changing from being primarily pastoralists to becoming farmers, which many viewed as a lower status occupation." Refugee Policy Group, *Older Refugee Settlements in Africa,* 42. Another worthwhile piece on the history of the Banyarwanda in Uganda is Ogenga Otunnu, "Rwandese Refugees and Immigrants in Uganda," in *The Path of a Genocide: The Rwanda Crisis from Uganda to Zaire,* ed. Howard Adelman and Astri Suhrke (New Brunswick, NJ: Transaction Publishers, 1999), 3–31.
22. Mushemeza, "Politics and the Refugee Experience," 133.
23. US Committee for Refugees, *Exile from Rwanda,* 9. This is echoed by other Banyarwanda refugees. Interview with Ndore Rurinda, 10 September 2018.
24. Anonymous RPF member, as quoted in Mushemeza, "Politics and the Refugee Experience," 170.

25. UPC government employee, as quoted in Mushemeza, "Politics and the Refugee Experience," 118.
26. Refugee Policy Group, *Older Refugee Settlements in Africa,* 128.
27. Mushemeza, "Politics and the Refugee Experience," 118.
28. Mushemeza, 136.
29. Joshua Kato, "Fred Rwigyema, the Military Genius from Two Countries," *New Vision,* 10 April 2012, https://www.newvision.co.ug.
30. Pascal G. Ngoga, "Guerrilla Insurgency and Conflict Resolution in Africa: A Case Study of Uganda" (PhD diss., Lancaster University, 1997), 67, 212, 394–95.
31. Ngoga, 216–17.
32. There is some debate as to whether the elections were free and fair: US Committee for Refugees, *Refugees in Uganda and Rwanda: The Banyarwandan Tragedy,* written by Roger Winter (Arlington, VA: US Committee for Refugees, 1983), 3; US Department of State, *Uganda, 4 Annual Human Rights Report Submitted to Congress* (Washington DC: US Department of State, 1980); US Department of State, *Uganda, 6 Annual Human Rights Report submitted to Congress* (Washington DC: US Department of State, 1981); T. M. Unwin to UNHCR Headquarters, Geneva, "Evacuation to Third Country of Thousands of Rwandans," 24 June 1981, "100.UGA.RWA Refugees from Rwanda in Uganda [vol.1] (1979–1981)," UNHCR Archive.
33. US Committee for Refugees, *Refugees in Uganda and Rwanda,* 3; US Committee for Refugees, *Human Rights in Uganda: The Reasons for Refugees* (Arlington, VA: US Committee for Refugees, 1985), 10.
34. T. M. Unwin to R. Kalberer, UNHCR Headquarters, Geneva, "Discussion on various subjects," 6 May 1981, "100.UGA.RWA Refugees from Rwanda in Uganda [vol.1] (1979–1981)," UNHCR Archive.
35. Unwin, "Discussion on various subjects," 6 May 1981. Further talks between a Rwandan and Ugandan delegation were held in 1983. They led to nothing; see Ambabel Kigali to Belext Bru, "Réfugiés Ougandais. Réunion de Kabale," 11 March 1983, "18.888-I-1 Télégrammes 'Sortie' Kigali 1983–1984," FPFSA.
36. T. M. Unwin to UNHCR Headquarters, Geneva, "Evacuation to Third Country of Thousands of Rwandans," 24 June 1981, UNHCR.
37. Unwin, "Evacuation to Third Country," 24 June 1981.
38. Unwin, "Evacuation to Third Country," 24 June 1981; Similar sentiments in T. M. Unwin to UNHCR Headquarters, Geneva "More background—Rwandan Affairs," 8 May 1981, "100.UGA.RWA [vol. 1] (1979–1981)," UNHCR Archive; and also in Unwin, "Discussion on various subjects," 6 May 1981.
39. Peter Matovu, Fort Portal to T. M. Unwin, "Rwandese refugees serving in the Ugandan Army," 8 July 1981, "100.UGA.RWA [vol.1] (1979–1981)," UNHCR Archive.
40. T. M. Unwin to UNHCR Geneva, "Rwandan Refugees in Uganda," 8 February 1982, "100.UGA.RWA [vol. 2] (1982–1983)," UNHCR Archive.
41. US Committee for Refugees, *Human Rights in Uganda,* 19.

42. Patrick de Sousa, Uganda to UNHCR Headquarters, Geneva, "Mission to Mbarara District—21–22 October 1982," 26 October 1982, "100.UGA.RWA [vol.2] (1982–1983)," UNHCR Archive.
43. de Sousa, "Mission to Mbarara District," 26 October 1982.
44. de Sousa, "Mission to Mbarara District," 26 October 1982; and Dr. Robin Biellik, UNICEF to Thomas Ekvall, UNICEF, Kampala, "Displacement of Banyarwanda from Rakai District," 23 December 1983, "100.UGA.RWA [vol. 3] (1983–1984)," UNHCR Archive; US Committee for Refugees, *Human Rights in Uganda,* 19.
45. T. M. Unwin to UNHCR Headquarters, Geneva, "Welcome Speech by the Chairman of Mbarara District Councils to the Councillors assembled to hear the President's Message," 23 November 1982, "100.UGA.RWA [vol.2] (1982–1983)," UNHCR Archive.
46. Unwin, "Welcome Speech," 23 November 1982.
47. T. M. Unwin to UNHCR Headquarters, Geneva, "Summary of Trip Report, Mbarara, Kabale Districts, 27–31 October 1982," 8 November 1982, "100.UGA.RWA [vol.2] (1982–1983)," UNHCR Archive; W. Karango to UNHCR, Ottawa, "Re: CAN HCR264," 17 November 1982, "610.UGA.RWA [1972–1984]," UNHCR Archive; see also Ambabel Kigali to Belext Bru, "Troubles en Ouganda," 20 December 1983, "18.888-I-1, Télégrammes 'Sortie' Kigali 1983–1984," FPFSA.
48. Interview with Ndore Rurinda, 10 September 2018.
49. The degree to which the Rwandan government was unwilling to accept the return of refugees is shown by the Belgian report on the Rwandan-Ugandan ministerial meeting on refugees and displaced persons held 5–7 December 1984. The Rwandan government argued that of the thirty-one thousand people in the Kibondo Refugee Camp, only four thousand were Rwandans. The rest were Ugandans, and as such ought to be returned to Uganda as quickly as possible. Naturally the Ugandan delegation, bent on ejecting as many Banyarwanda refugees from Uganda as possible, argued that the majority of the refugees were actually originally Rwandans and thus ought to stay in Rwanda. The frustrated Belgian observer noted that "the impasse [was] complete." Ambabel Kigali to Belext Bru, "Réunion ministérielle rwando—ougandaise conc. Réfugiés et personnes déplacées," 14 December 1984, "18.888-I-3, Télégrammes Entrée Kigali 1974–1988," FPFSA.
50. The history of this episode is sketchy and deserves its own dedicated research. Many RPF members I spoke with told me that at least some of the Banyarwanda who fled back into Rwanda in the early 1980s were killed. It seems that most of the refugee camps were either in northern Rwanda or in Akagera National Park.
51. Interview with James Kabarebe, 16 October 2018. The interview with Kabarebe was not recorded, so I paraphrase rather than quote him directly.
52. Interview with James Kabarebe.
53. Interview with James Kabarebe; interestingly Kabarebe's account is supported by a Belgian diplomatic dispatch, according to which it seemed "that musseveni [*sic*]

men recruited a large number of refugees in camps in Rwanda in September." Ambabel Kigali to Belext Bru, "Recrutement réfugiés ougandais pour mnr/nra," 15 October 1985, "18.888-I-1, Télégrammes 'Sortie' Kigali 1985–1986," FPFSA.

54. Ambabel Kigali to Belext Bru, "Rapatriement réfugiés Ougandais," 1 October 1985, "18.888-I-1, Télégrammes 'Sortie' Kigali 1985–1986," FPFSA.
55. Ambabel Kigali, "Rapatriement réfugiés Ougandais," 1 October 1985.
56. Ambabel Kigali, "Rapatriement réfugiés Ougandais," 1 October 1985.
57. Ambabel Kigali to Delbel Geneve, "Message HCR à transmettre de toute urgence à HCR Geneve à l'attention de mr. Moussali," 9 October 1985, "18.888-I-1, Télégrammes 'Sortie' Kigali 1985–1986," FPFSA.
58. Ngoga, "Guerrilla Insurgency and Conflict Resolution," 220–21.
59. Ngoga, 221–22.
60. Ngoga, 222.
61. Ngoga, 243, 295.
62. Ngoga, 391.
63. Roger Winter, "Human Rights in Uganda: The Past, Present and Future," in *Three Papers Presented before the Commission of Inquiry into Violations of Human Rights* (Kampala, 15–16 February 1990), 40–41.
64. William Pike, "Conflict in Uganda" *The Times,* 24 August 1984, 4.
65. Interview with Ndore Rurinda, 10 September 2018.
66. Interview with Ndore Rurinda, 10 September 2018; interview with Jill Rutaremara, 7 September 2018.
67. Interview with Ndore Rurinda, 10 September 2018.
68. Interview with Jill Rutaremara, 7 September 2018.
69. Interview with Jill Rutaremara, 7 September 2018.
70. Cyrus Reed, "Exile, Reform and the Rise of the Rwandan Patriotic Front," *Journal of Modern African Studies* 34, no. 3 (September 1996): 485.
71. Interview with Tito Rutaremara, 9 October 2018.
72. "History," RPF, accessed 30 November 2018, http://rpfinkotanyi.rw/index.php?id=24.
73. Interview with Christine Umutoni, 14 May 2019.
74. Interview with Christine Umutoni, 14 May 2019.
75. Interview with Christine Umutoni, 14 May 2019.
76. Interview with Christine Umutoni, 14 May 2019.
77. Correspondence with former RPF member, 27 August 2017. See also interview with Jill Rutaremara, 7 September 2018; interview with Ndore Rurinda, 10 September 2018; interview with Tito Rutaremara, 9 October 2018.
78. Interview with Tito Rutaremara, 9 October 2018.
79. Frank K. Rusagara, *Resilience of a Nation: A History of the Military in Rwanda* (Kigali: Fountain Publishers, 2009), 175.
80. Correspondence with former RPF member, 27 August 2017.
81. Correspondence with former RPF member, 27 August 2017.
82. Interview with Vianney Shumbusho, 18 October 2018; interview with Jill Rutaremara, 7 September 2018.

83. Correspondence with former RPF member, 31 August 2017.
84. Correspondence with former RPF member, 31 August 2017.
85. Correspondence with former RPF member, 31 August 2017.
86. Interview with Ndore Rurinda, 10 September 2018.
87. Interview, 13 May 2017.
88. Correspondence with former RPF member, 27 August 2017.
89. Correspondence with former RPF member, 27 August 2017.
90. Interview with Caesar Kayizari, 14 October 2018.
91. Interview with Caesar Kayizari, 14 October 2018.
92. Cliff Ruhemba to Mr Chipman, UNHCR Switzerland, "Too much freedom is dangerous," 31 October 1989, "100.UGA.RWA [A]," UNHCR Archive.
93. Interview with Tito Rutaremara, 9 October 2018.
94. Anton Verwey to Haut-Commissariat des Nations Unies pour les Réfugiés, Genève, "Prise de positions du Comité Central du M.R.N.D. concernant le problème des réfugiés rwandais," 5 August 1986, "0.10 RWA [A]," UNHCR Archive.
95. Verwey, "Prise de positions," 5 August 1986.
96. S. S. Wijeratne, Senior Legal Advisor, to the Representative UNHCR Office in Japan, "Memorandum: Rwandan Refugee Policy (written by François-Xavier Doudou-Kiadila, Conseiller juridique pour l'Afrique)," 2 July 1987, "0.10 RWA [A]" UNHCR Archive.
97. Wijeratne, "Memorandum: Rwandan Refugee Policy," 2 July 1987.
98. Verwey, "Prise de positions," 5 August 1986.
99. François Ngarukiyintwali, Ministre des affaires étrangères et de la Coopération, to Chef Service Central de Renseignements, "Regain d'activisme des réfugiés rwandais," 5 March 1986, "Box: MIN—237 MINAFFET," National Archives of Rwanda; It seems both the Zairian and Rwandan embassies in Kampala were already keeping an eye on the Rwandan refugees since at least 1988. "Rwandan and Zairean colleagues in Kampala intend to send 'spies' to this 'inkotenyi' and will keep me informed of their conclusions." Ambabel Nairobio to Belext Bru, "Réfugiés rwandais," 10 June 1988, "18.888-I-3, Télégrammes Entrée Kigali 1974–1988," FPFSA.
100. UNHCR Kampala to UNHCR Geneva, "Re: uga/hcr/1062 hcr/uga/1065 and eth/uga/hcr/1005," 16 December 1987, "0.10 UGA [B]," UNHCR Archive.
101. "Joint Communique issued at the End of State Visit of H.E. Major General Habyarimana Juvénal President of the Republic of Rwanda and Founder-Chairman of the National Revolutionary Movement for Development (MRND) to the Republic of Uganda 4th February to 6th February 1988." "100.UGA.RWA [A]," UNHCR Archive; Anton Verwey, Délégué pour le Rwanda, Kigali, to UNHCR Genève, "Visite du Président Juvénal Habyarimana en Uganda," 15 February 1988, "0.10 RWA [A]," UNHCR Archive, 6.
102. République Rwandaise, Mission Permanente auprès de l'Office des Nations Unies, Berne, to UNHCR Geneva, 1 June 1989, "0.10 RWA [C]," UNHCR Archive.

103. Note pour Dossier: Solutions durables pour les réfugiés rwandais, Annex: "Mémorandum de la Partie Rwandaise sur le problème des réfugiés rwandais," 14 June 1989, "0.10 RWA [C]," UNHCR Archive, 13.
104. Marjon Kamara, Acting Representative UNHCR, Kampala, to Mr. E. Chipman, Head Desk V, RBA, UNHCR Headquarters Geneva, "Uganda/Rwanda Interministerial Committee on Rwandese Refugees in Uganda, Annex: Agreed Minutes of the Second Meeting of the Joint Uganda/Rwanda Ministerial Committee on the Problem of Rwandese Refugees Living in Uganda Held in Kampala from 14th to 17th November 1989," 23 November 1989, "0.10 RWA [C]," UNHCR Archive.
105. Kamara, "Uganda/Rwanda Interministerial Committee," 23 November 1989.
106. Kamara, "Uganda/Rwanda Interministerial Committee," 23 November 1989.
107. "Note pour Dossier: Visite de Monsieur le Ministre des affaires étrangères de la République du Rwanda," 23 November 1989, "0.10 RWA [C]," UNHCR Archives, 1.
108. Kamara, "Uganda/Rwanda Interministerial Committee," 23 November 1989.
109. "Agreed Minutes of the Third Meeting of the Joint Uganda/Rwanda Ministerial Committee on the Problem of Rwandese Refugees Living in Uganda Held in Kigali From 27th to 30th July 1990," 30 July 1990, "100.UGA.RWA [A]," UNHCR Archive.
110. Roger P. Winter, Director US Committee for Refugees, to Jean Pierre de Walincourt, International Council of Voluntary Agencies, 17 September 1990, "100. UGA.RWA [A]," UNHCR Archive.
111. Marjon Kamara, acting representative UNHCR Kampala, to Honourable Minister of Internal Affairs Ibrahim Mukiibi, "Information Campaign for Survey of Rwandese Refugees," 21 September 1990, "0.10 UGA [C]," UNHCR Archive.
112. André Guichaoua, *From War to Genocide: Criminal Politics in Rwanda, 1900–1994,* trans. Don E. Webster (Madison: University of Wisconsin Press, 2015), 24; James K. Gasana, "La Guerre, La Paix et la Démocratie au Rwanda," in *Les crises politiques au Burundi et au Rwanda (1993–1994),* ed. André Guichaoua (Paris: Karthala, 1995), 220.
113. Prunier, *The Rwanda Crisis,* 91.
114. Cullimore to Immediate FCO, "Rwanda/Uganda," 15 October 1990, "JWW 051/1 (Part B), 'Incursion into Rwanda: October 1990,'" FCO; Rusagara, *Resilience of a Nation,* 176.
115. Interview with Caesar Kayizari, 14 October 2018.
116. Paul Whiteway to African Section, Research and Analysis Dept, FCO, "Rwanda: origins of the Civil War," 19 September 1994, "FOI 1024–17_Part_1," FCO; I also interviewed Paul Whiteway on 25 September 2017 during which he provided useful background information on his time in the Great Lakes region.

CHAPTER 5: THE START OF THE STRUGGLE FOR LIBERATION, OCTOBER 1990

1. Cormack to Deskby 031100Z FCO, "Incursion into Rwanda," 3 October 1990, "JWW 051/1 (Part A), 'Incursion into Rwanda: October 1990,'" FCO.

2. Several parts of this chapter are based on material (interviews and documents) that the author collected but which cannot be shared with the public. In this case the footnotes have been marked as "Author's archive."
3. Author's archive.
4. Author's archive.
5. Author's archive; see also Levy, Firestone, Muse, *A Foreseeable Genocide* (Washington, DC: Levy, Firestone, Muse, 2021), 43.
6. Author's archive.
7. Lt. Col. G. B. Molyneux-Carter, "DA Report on Visit to Rwanda border Area—18 October 1990," 22 October 1990, "JWW 051/1 (part C), 'Incursion into Rwanda: October 1990,'" FCO, 2; On Ugandans in the RPA see also Paul Quilès, *Rapport d'information par la mission d'information de la commission de la défense nationale et des forces armées et de la commission des affaires étrangères, sur les opérations militaires menées par la France, d'autres pays et l'ONU au Rwanda entre 1990 et 1994* (Assemblée nationale, Paris, 15 December 1998), Annexes, 185.
8. Interview with Logan Ndahiro, 26 October 2018.
9. Interview with Peter Kalimba, 23 October 2018; Correspondence with Peter Kalimba, 12 November 2018. For a similar story, see Theogene Rudasingwa, *Healing a Nation: A Testimony* (North Charleston, SC: CreateSpace, 2013), 66.
10. Author's archive.
11. Author's archive.
12. Author's archive.
13. Cormack, "Incursion into Rwanda," 3 October 1990.
14. There have been many rumors surrounding Fred Rwigyema's death and some suggest he was murdered by Bunyenyezi and Bayingana, possibly under orders from Paul Kagame. As far as I can tell, there is no truth to this. Not a single interviewee gave credence to these theories.
15. Interview with Caesar Kayizari, 14 October 2018.
16. Cormack to Immediate FCO, "Military Incursion into Rwanda," 4 October 1990, "JWW 051/1 (Part B), 'Incursion into Rwanda: October 1990,'" FCO.
17. Cormack, "Incursion into Rwanda," 3 October 1990.
18. Ambabel Nairobi to Belext Bru, "Incursion armée dissidents Ougandais au Rwanda," 3 October 1990, "18.955–144, Politique intérieure 1990–1992," FPFSA.
19. Major Bogaert, "Rwanda: Incident de frontière—Réservé Exclusivement aux Autorités Belges," 2 October 1990, "18.955–144, Politique intérieure 1990–1992," FPFSA; Ambabel Kigali to Belext Bru, "Sitrep le 041330Z OCT 90," 4 October 1990, "18.955–144, Politique intérieure 1990–1992," FPFSA; Ambabel Kigali to Belext Bru, "Développements incident du 01 oct," 2 October 1990, "18.955–144, Politique intérieure 1990–1992," FPFSA.
20. Interview with Ndore Rurinda, 22 September 2018; this is confirmed by Charles Kayonga and Joseph Karemera in Levy, Firestone, and Muse, *Foreseeable Genocide,* 61.
21. Interview with Peter Kalimba, 23 October 2018.
22. Interview with Caesar Kayizari, 14 October 2018.

23. Cormack to Immediate FCO, "Military Incursion into Rwanda," 5 October 1990, "JWW 051/1 (Part A), 'Incursion into Rwanda: October 1990,'" FCO; Ambabel Kigali to Belext Bru, "Situatie—Rebellen," 4 October 1990, "18.955–144, Politique intérieure 1990–1992," FPFSA.
24. Cormack to Immediate FCO, "Military Incursion into Rwanda," 4 October 1990, "JWW 051/1 (Part A), 'Incursion into Rwanda: October 1990,'" FCO.
25. Author's archive.
26. Charles Mwanguhya Mpagi, "Muntu's Walk from Makarere to the Bush War and Back," *Daily Monitor,* 28 March 2010.
27. Interview with Tito Rutaremara, 9 October 2018.
28. *Africa Confidential,* 12 October 1990, 1; Gérard Prunier, *The Rwanda Crisis: History of a Genocide* (London: Hurst, 1997), 97.
29. Cullimore to Deskby FCO, "Ugandan Military Incursion into Rwanda," 2 October 1990, "JWW 051/1 (Part A), 'Incursion into Rwanda: October 1990,'" FCO.
30. Cullimore to Immediate FCO, "Incursion into Rwanda," 4 October 1990, "JWW 051/1 (Part A), 'Incursion into Rwanda: October 1990,'" FCO; I also had the pleasure of interviewing Charles Cullimore on 15 January 2019 by telephone.
31. Cullimore, "Incursion into Rwanda," 4 October 1990.
32. Prunier, *The Rwanda Crisis,* 98.
33. Cullimore, "Incursion into Rwanda," 4 October 1990.
34. Correspondence with Lt. Col. G. B. Molyneux-Carter, 4 January 2019; correspondence with Molyneux-Carter, 29 May 2017.
35. Lt. Col. G. B. Molyneux-Carter, "DA Report on Visit to Rwanda border Area—18 October 1990," 22 October 1990, FCO.
36. Interview with Caesar Kayizari, 14 October 2018.
37. Correspondence with Gérard Prunier, 22 January 2014.
38. Prunier, *The Rwanda Crisis,* 100–101.
39. The exact timing of Mitterrand's decision is unclear as Prunier (*The Rwanda Crisis,* 100) and Bernard Lugan (*François Mitterrand: l'Armée française et la Rwanda* [Monaco: Editions du Rocher, 2005], 52–53) disagree on it.
40. Interview with Mark Eyskens, 22 January 2019.
41. Johan Swinnen, *Rwanda: Mijn verhaal* (Kalmthout, Belgium: Polis, 2016), 42; Philippe Mahoux and Guy Verhofstadt, *Commission d'enquête parlementaire concernant les événements du Rwanda* (Sénat de Belgique, 6 December 1997), 187–89.
42. Barateau to Ministère des affaires étrangères, "Attaque de Rwanda," 4 October 1990. Quilès, *Rapport d'information,* Annexes, 142.
43. "2e Régiment Etranger de Parachutistes, Journal des Marches et Opérations 1 janvier au 30 juin 1991," GR7U 3440, SHD; Lugan, *François Mitterrand,* 55.
44. "2e REP, JMO 1 juillet au 31 décembre 1990," GR7U 3440, SHD; Lugan, *François Mitterrand,* 56–57.
45. "2e REP, JMO 1 juillet au 31 décembre 1990," GR7U 3440, SHD. "Selon un renseignement de dernière minute en provenance de l'ambassade des Etats-Unis Kigali serait attaquée cette nuit." The Duclert report does not discuss this episode

in detail. However, it seems that Colonel Huchon was also informed of the warning by the US Embassy. The French troops on the ground, which had direct communications to Paris, received the message at 19:15. Colonel Huchon then sent a cable to President Mitterrand's chief of staff Jean Louis Bianco at 19:45, "Des actions ponctuelles de type terroriste sont possibles dans les villes, dès cette nuit, y compris dans la capitale." See Vincent Duclert, *La France, le Rwanda et le génocide des Tutsi (1990–1994)—Rapport remis au Président de la République le 26 mars 2021* (Paris: Armand Colin, 2021), 50–51, 997.

46. "2e REP, JMO 1 juillet au 31 décembre 1990," GR7U 3440, SHD.
47. Cormack to Deskby 051200Z FCO, "Incursion into Rwanda," 5 October 1990, "JWW 051/1 (Part B), 'Incursion into Rwanda: October 1990,'" FCO.
48. Correspondence with Caesar Kayizari, 14 November 2018.
49. Prunier, *The Rwanda Crisis,* 102; James K. Gasana, *Rwanda: Du parti-État à l'État-garnison* (Paris: L'Harmattan, 2002), 66.
50. Lugan, *François Mitterrand,* 59–60.
51. Swinnen, *Rwanda: Mijn verhaal,* 44.
52. In early 2017, the author made a Freedom of Information Act request to the US Department of State regarding the warning sent to the French Embassy. Despite several follow-ups, no reply has been received to date.
53. Cormack to Immediate FCO, "Military Incursion into Rwanda," 5 October 1990, "JWW 051/1 (Part A), 'Incursion into Rwanda: October 1990,'" FCO.
54. *Rapport Duclert,* 91–92; Ministry of Foreign Affairs Brussels to Ambabel Kigali, "Mensenrechten," 8 October 1990, "18.888-I-3, Télégrammes Entrée Kigali 1989–1991," FPFSA.
55. Africa Watch, *Rwanda: Talking Peace and Waging War; Human Rights since the October 1990 Invasion* (Washington, DC: Africa Watch, 27 February 1992).
56. Comité pour le respect des droits de l'Homme et la démocratie au Rwanda (CRDDR), *Rwanda: Rapport de deux missions effectuées par Eric Gillet & André Jadoul, avocats au barreau de Bruxelles au Rwanda du 9 au 17 janvier et du 2 au 5 février 1992* (Brussels: CRDDR, May 1992), 5–7.
57. Prunier, *The Rwanda Crisis,* 99.
58. French Embassy in Paris to International Organizations, "Message à la Nation du Chef de l'Etat le 5 Octobre 1990 à la suite de l'attaque perpétrée contre le Rwanda (1/10/1990)," 8 October 1990, "JWW 014/2, 'Rwanda: Internal Political Situation,'" FCO.
59. Cormack to Immediate FCO, "Incursion into Rwanda," 9 October 1990, "JWW 051/1 (Part A), 'Incursion into Rwanda: October 1990,'" FCO.
60. "Zaire: The Military under Mobutu," "0000267101," CIA Library, accessed 24 June 2019, https://www.cia.gov/library/readingroom/document/0000267101.
61. "Zaire: The Military under Mobutu," 17.
62. Cormack, "Incursion into Rwanda," 9 October 1990; Cormack to Immediate FCO, "Incursion into Rwanda," 10 October 1990, "JWW 051/1 (Part A), 'Incursion into Rwanda: October 1990,'" FCO.

63. Cormack to Immediate FCO, "Incursion into Rwanda," 12 October 1990, "JWW 051/1 (Part A), 'Incursion into Rwanda: October 1990,'" FCO.
64. Col. Galinié and Martres to AD SEGEDEFNAT, "Situation générale le 13 octobre 1990 à 12 heures locales," 13 October 1990, FGT.
65. Cormack to Immediate FCO, "Incursion into Rwanda," 17 October 1990, "JWW 051/1 (Part B), 'Incursion into Rwanda: October 1990,'" FCO.
66. Claude Arnaud to Monsieur le Président de la République, "Entretien avec le Président Habyarimana Jeudi 18 Octobre 1990 à 18h30," 18 October 1990, FGT.
67. "Zaire: A Crumbling Power," *Africa Confidential,* 7 December 1990.
68. Cormack, "Incursion into Rwanda," 17 October 1990.
69. Arnaud, "Entretien avec le Président Habyarimana," 18 October 1990; At Nyagatare, for example, the Forces armées zaïroises supported a FAR counterattack and overran the HQs of the RPA's 6 and 9 Battalions. Author's archive.
70. Anatole Nsengiyumva to —, "N084/G2.2.2.1.4," 7 October 1990, "File 1990/Planning," Linda Melvern Rwanda Genocide Archive.
71. Nsengiyumva, 7 October 1990.
72. Nsengiyumva, 7 October 1990.
73. There is much debate on this point: Did Fred Rwigyema intend to wage a short sharp war or a more protracted guerrilla? The author feels that a short campaign is more logical in view of the military situation, but many prominent RPA veterans, like Sam Kaka, disagree and insist Rwigyema had wanted to carry out a guerrilla during which the RPF would slowly win the hearts and minds of the Rwandan population. Such a plan would have used the NRA Resistance War as a blueprint. According to Kaka, the new high command decided after Rwigyema's death that an immediate attack on Kigali had the best chance of success. Author's archive.
74. Interview with James Kabarebe, 16 October 2018.
75. Quoted in Stephen Kinzer, *A Thousand Hills: Rwanda's Rebirth and the Man Who Dreamed It* (Hoboken, NJ: John Wiley, 2008), 76.
76. Kinzer, 76, 77.
77. Interview with Caesar Kayizari, 14 October 2018; Kinzer, *A Thousand Hills,* 78–79.
78. Cormack to Immediate FCO, "Rwanda: Military Situation," 25 October 1990, "JWW 051/1 (Part B), 'Incursion into Rwanda: October 1990,'" FCO.
79. Cormack, "Rwanda: Military Situation," 25 October 1990.
80. Interview with Caesar Kayizari, 14 October 2018; see also, "Trip Report Kagitumba-Nyagatare-Gabiro by US Embassy in Rwanda," 8 November 1990, "Exhibit Number: DNT 226, Date Admitted: 18-09-2006," ICTR-98–41-T.
81. Correspondence with former RPF member, 27 August 2017.
82. Interview with Ndore Rurinda, 22 September 2018.
83. Cullimore to Immediate FCO, "Incursion into Rwanda," 1 November 1990, "JWW 051/1 (Part C), 'Incursion into Rwanda: October 1990,'" FCO.
84. Cormack to Immediate FCO, "Incursion into Rwanda," 12 October 1990. FCO.

85. O'Niel to Priority FCO, "Incursion into Rwanda," 9 October 1990, "JWW 051/1 (Part A), 'Incursion into Rwanda: October 1990,'" FCO.
86. "Audientienota over het onderhoud van de heer Eerste Minister met de President van Oeganda, Dhr. Museveni, Lambermont, 7 oktober 1990," "18.888-III-1, Onlusten in Rwanda Oktober-November 1990," FPFSA.
87. O'Niel, "Incursion into Rwanda," 9 October 1990; see also Oscar Garschagen, "Martens: Oeganda zat achter invasie Rwanda," *De Volkskrant* (Amsterdam), 16 October 1990.
88. Cormack, "Incursion into Rwanda," 12 October 1990.
89. Cullimore to Immediate FCO, "Incursion into Rwanda," 11 October 1990, "JWW 051/1 (Part A), 'Incursion into Rwanda: October 1990,'" FCO.
90. Cullimore, "Incursion into Rwanda," 11 October 1990.
91. Cullimore to Immediate FCO, "Rwanda/Uganda," 15 October 1990, "JWW 051/1 (Part B), 'Incursion into Rwanda: October 1990,'" FCO.
92. Fergusson to Priority FCO, "Rwanda: French Assessment," 13 October 1990, "JWW 051/1 (Part B), 'Incursion into Rwanda: October 1990,'" FCO.
93. Fergusson, "Rwanda: French Assessment," 13 October 1990.
94. As did much of the French military and diplomatic establishment. See *Rapport Duclert,* 50–51.
95. Martres to French Foreign Ministry, "Analyse de la Situation par la Population d'Origine Tutsi," Quilès, *Rapport d'information,* Annexes, 133. It is worth noting that the Belgian ambassador also saw the specter of genocidal violence. Ambabel Kigali to Belext Bru, "Toestand in Rwanda," 7 October 1990, "18.888-I-3, Télégrammes Entrée Kigali 1989–1991," FPFSA.
96. Interview with Georges Martres, 22 April 2014, Narbonne, France, conducted by Michael Dobbs, https://www.ushmm.org/confront-genocide/speakers-and-events/all-speakers-and-events/rwanda-conference/voices/georges-martres.
97. Interview with Charles Cullimore, 20 May 2009, conducted by Jimmy Jamieson, British Diplomatic Oral History Programme, https://bdohp.chu.cam.ac.uk/transcripts/.
98. McCarthy to Immediate FCO, "Surprise Belgian Initiative on Rwanda," 15 October 1990, "JWW 051/1 (Part B), 'Incursion into Rwanda: October 1990,'" FCO.
99. "België zoekt oplossing voor strijd in Rwanda," *De Telegraaf,* 15 October 1990.
100. Cullimore to Immediate FCO, "Rwanda/Uganda," 16 October 1990, "JWW 051/1 (Part B), 'Incursion into Rwanda: October 1990,'" FCO.
101. Cullimore, "Rwanda/Uganda," 16 October 1990.
102. Cullimore to Deskby FCO, "Rwandan Refugees," 18 October 1990, "JWW 051/1 (Part B), 'Incursion into Rwanda: October 1990,'" FCO.
103. Cullimore, "Rwandan Refugees," 18 October 1990.
104. Arnaud, "Entretien avec le Président Habyarimana," 18 October 1990; Fergusson to Immediate FCO, "Visit to Paris by President Habyarimana 18 October," 22 October 1990, "JWW 051/1 (Part B), 'Incursion into Rwanda: October 1990,'" FCO.

105. Cormack to Immediate FCO, "Rwanda," 22 October 1990, "JWW 051/1 (Part B), 'Incursion into Rwanda: October 1990,'" FCO.
106. Cullimore to Immediate FCO, "Rwanda," 23 October 1990, "JWW 051/1 (Part B), 'Incursion into Rwanda: October 1990,'" FCO.
107. There is no doubt that the RPF communicated its agreement with a ceasefire to Presidents Hassan Mwinyi (Tanzania) and Museveni and to Prime Minister Martens on 21 October 1990. Ambassade van België, Nairobi to Belex Bru, "Déclaration rebelles rwandais," 23 October 1990, "18.888-III-1, Onlusten in Rwanda Oktober-November 1990," FPFSA; UNHCR Nairobi to KEN/RWA/HCR, "Meeting at 09:45P.M. with Belg/Prime Minister Martens and his Minister of Defence Coëme at Ambassador's Residence," 22 October 1990, "010 RWA [D]," UNHCR Archive.
108. Cormack to Immediate FCO, "Incursion into Rwanda," 25 October 1990, "JWW 051/1 (Part B), 'Incursion into Rwanda: October 1990,'" FCO.
109. Cormack to Priority FCO, "Incursion into Rwanda," 26 October 1990, "JWW 051/1 (Part B), 'Incursion into Rwanda: October 1990,'" FCO.
110. Glaze, Addis Ababa, to Routine FCO, "Incursions into Rwanda," 25 October 1990, "JWW 051/1 (Part B), 'Incursion into Rwanda: October 1990,'" FCO.
111. Mahmood Mamdani, *When Victims Become Killers: Colonialism, Nativism, and Genocide in Rwanda* (Princeton, NJ: Princeton University Press, 2002), 183.
112. Lt. Col. G. B. Molyneux-Carter to High Commissioner, Kampala, "DA Report on Visit to Rwanda 16–20 Feb 91," no date but received in registry 5 June 1991, "JWW 014/1 (Part B), 'Rwanda: Internal Political Situation,'" FCO; Correspondence with G. B. Molyneux-Carter, 29 May 2017; Cormack to Immediate FCO, "Rwanda: Military Situation," 25 October 1990, "JWW 051/1 (Part B), 'Incursion into Rwanda: October 1990,'" FCO.
113. Quoted in Prunier, *The Rwanda Crisis,* 119.
114. Quoted in Kinzer, *A Thousand Hills,* 80.
115. Correspondence with former RPF member, 31 August 2017; Kinzer, *A Thousand Hills,* 82.

CHAPTER 6: FORGING THE RPA, NOVEMBER 1990–JANUARY 1991

1. Cullimore to Immediate FCO, "Incursion into Rwanda," 1 November 1990, "JWW 051/1 (Part C), 'Incursion into Rwanda: October 1990,'" FCO.
2. Cullimore to Immediate FCO, "Incursion into Rwanda," 5 November 1990, "JWW 051/1 (Part C), 'Incursion into Rwanda: October 1990,'" FCO.
3. Cormack to Priority FCO, "Rwanda," 9 November 1990, JWW 051/1 (Part C), "Incursion into Rwanda: October 1990," FCO.
4. Gérard Prunier, *The Rwanda Crisis: History of a Genocide* (London: Hurst, 1997), 115; Stephen Kinzer, *A Thousand Hills: Rwanda's Rebirth and the Man Who Dreamed It* (Hoboken, NJ: John Wiley, 2008), 79–88.
5. Cormack to Routine FCO, "Rwanda," 21 November 1990, "JWW 051/1 (Part C), 'Incursion into Rwanda: October 1990,'" FCO; also Lt. Col. G. B.

Molyneux-Carter to High Commissioner, Kampala, "DA Report on Visit to Rwanda 16–20 Feb 91," no date but received in registry 5 June 1991, FCO.

6. Interview with Ndore Rurinda, 22 September 2018.
7. Author's archive.
8. Kinzer, *A Thousand Hills,* 69, 76.
9. Martin van Creveld, *Fighting Power: German and U.S. Army Performance, 1939–1945* (Westport, CT: Greenwood Press, 1982), 3.
10. Creveld, *Fighting Power,* 3; Carl von Clausewitz, *On War* (Herefordshire, UK: Woodworth, 1997), 153–57; the 2022 invasion of Ukraine by Russia has clearly reaffirmed this point.
11. Interview with Caesar Kayizari, 14 October 2018.
12. Interview with Jill Rutaremara, 7 September 2018.
13. Interview with Caesar Kayizari, 14 October 2018.
14. Quoted in Catherine Watson, "War and Waiting," *Africa Report* 37, no. 6 (November 1992): 54.
15. Roméo Dallaire, *Shake Hands with the Devil* (London: Arrow Books, 2004), 67.
16. Fergal Keane, *Season of Blood: A Rwandan Journey* (London: Penguin, 1996), 51.
17. Interview with James Kabarebe, 16 October 2018.
18. M. Anderson, M. Arnsten, and H. Averch, *Insurgent Organization and Operations: A Case Study of the Viet Cong in the Delta, 1964–1966* (Santa Monica, CA: RAND Corporation, August 1967), 9.
19. John C. Donnel, Guy J. Pauker, and Joseph J. Zasloff, *Viet Cong Motivation and Morale in 1964: A Preliminary Report* (Santa Monica, CA: RAND Corporation, March 1965), 21–22.
20. David Kilcullen, *The Accidental Guerrilla: Fighting Small Wars in the Midst of a Big One* (London: Hurst, 2017), 50–51.
21. Kilcullen, 54.
22. Interview with Caesar Kayizari, 14 October 2018.
23. Note that the RPA are familiar of this kind of literature. When I first arrived in Rwanda, I was told by an RPA veteran that I ought to read Liddell Hart if I wanted to understand the Struggle for Liberation.
24. Pascal G. Ngoga, "Guerrilla Insurgency and Conflict Resolution in Africa: A Case Study of Uganda" (PhD diss., Lancaster University, 1997), 230, 241–42.
25. Interview with Caesar Kayizari, 14 October 2018.
26. Interview with Caesar Kayizari, 14 October 2018.
27. Interview with Ndore Rurinda, 22 September 2018.
28. Lt. Col. EJK O'Brien, British High Commission to Lt. Col. JP Cameron, MoD, "Rwanda—Meeting with RPA Commander," 4 September 1992, "FOI 0421–17," FCO.
29. For some instructive quotes, see Hermann Balck, *An Interview, 12 January 1974* (Bennington, VT: Merriam Press, 2006), 59–60; BDM Corporation, Director of Net Assessment, Office of the Secretary of Defence, *Generals Balck and von Mellenthin on Tactics: Implication for NATO Military Doctrine* (Tysons Corner, VA: BDM Corporation, 19 December 1980), 22.

30. Creveld, *Fighting Power,* 73–76. To get familiar and up to date on the latest experience, German troops often received extra training in the field from veterans before being put in the line; Balck, *An Interview,* 38–39.
31. Edward A. Shils and Morris Janowitz, "Cohesion and Disintegration in the Wehrmacht in World War II," *Public Opinion Quarterly* 12, no. 2 (1948): 280–315; Guy L. Siebold, "The Evolution of the Measurement of Cohesion," *Military Psychology* 11, no. 1 (1999): 5–26; Guy L. Siebold, "The Essence of Military Group Cohesion," *Armed Forces & Society* 33, no. 2 (2007): 286–95.
32. Prunier, *The Rwanda Crisis,* 116.
33. Interview, 13 May 2017.
34. Author's archive.
35. Clausewitz, *On War,* 156–57.
36. Author's archive.
37. Interview with Vianney Shumbusho, 18 October 2018; interview with Christine Umutoni, 14 May 2019.
38. Kinzer, *A Thousand Hills,* 82.
39. Correspondence with Ndore Rurinda, 18 March 2019.
40. Kinzer, *A Thousand Hills,* 82–83.
41. Interview with Tito Rutaremara, 9 October 2018.
42. Interview with Christine Umutoni, 14 May 2019.
43. Interview with Christine Umutoni, 14 May 2019; An indication of the RPF's international organization and reach is the number of letters that were addressed to various Belgian and international organizations at the outbreak of the war on 1 October 1990. In the FPFSA (18.888-III-1) I have discovered letters of support for the RPF from the Organizzazione Italo-Rwandese per la pace; the Rwandan community in Washington, DC; L'association des canadiens d'origine rwandaise; Comité pour les droits de l'homme et la démocratie au Rwanda in Geneva; Communauté Rwandaise du Sénégal; the Rwandan Community in Nigeria; and the Commutauté [*sic*] Rwandaise en Allemagne—Comité de soutien.
44. Interview with Christine Umutoni, 14 May 2019.
45. Quoted in Watson, "War and Waiting," 55.
46. Interview with Caesar Kayizari, 14 October 2018.
47. Interview with Peter Kalimba, 23 October 2018; this view was echoed by Logan Ndahiro, interview, 26 October 2018.
48. As it would be for any soldiers, see for example: Field Marshall Lord Carver, "Morale in Battle: The Medical and the Military," *Journal of the Royal Society of Medicine* 82 (February 1989): 68.
49. Interview with Caesar Kayizari, 14 October 2018.
50. Interview with Caesar Kayizari, 14 October 2018.
51. Interview with Peter Kalimba, 23 October 2018.
52. Interview, 13 May 2017.
53. Cormack to Immediate FCO, "Incursion into Rwanda," 1 November 1990, "JWW 051/1 (Part C), 'Incursion into Rwanda: October 1990,'" FCO.
54. Cormack, "Incursion into Rwanda," 1 November 1990.

55. Cormack to Immediate FCO, "Incursion into Rwanda," 2 November 1990, "JWW 051/1 (Part C), 'Incursion into Rwanda: October 1990,'" FCO.
56. Cullimore to Immediate FCO, "Troika Demarche on Rwanda," 7 November 1990, "JWW 051/1 (Part C), 'Incursion into Rwanda: October 1990,'" FCO; Cullimore to Mr Smith, Mr Innes, "Rwanda, and Zaire/Uganda Relations," 8 November 1990, "JWW 051/1 (Part C), 'Incursion into Rwanda: October 1990,'" FCO.
57. Cormack to Priority FCO, "Rwanda," 9 November 1990, "JWW 051/1 (Part C), 'Incursion into Rwanda: October 1990,'" FCO.
58. Cormack to Priority FCO, "Rwanda," 12 November 1990, "JWW 051/1 (Part C), 'Incursion into Rwanda: October 1990,'" FCO.
59. Cormack to Routine FCO, "Rwanda Refugees," 21 November 1990, "JWW 051/1 (Part C), 'Incursion into Rwanda: October 1990,'" FCO.
60. Cullimore to Priority FCO, "Rwanda," 23 November 1990, "JWW 051/1 (Part C), 'Incursion into Rwanda: October 1990,'" FCO.
61. Cullimore, "Rwanda," 23 November 1990.
62. DS Schroeder to Teleletter FCO, "GOB views on Rwanda conflict," 10 December 1990, "JWW 051/1 (Part C), 'Incursion into Rwanda: October 1990,'" FCO.
63. Schroeder, "GOB views on Rwanda conflict," 10 December 1990.
64. Général de Division Varret, Chef de la Mission Militaire de Coopération, to Ministre de la Coopération et du Développement, "Compte rendu de mission au Burundi et au Rwanda," 19 December 1990, FGT.
65. Varret, "Compte rendu de mission," 19 December 1990.
66. Varret, "Compte rendu de mission," 19 December 1990.
67. I discussed the matter with Brigadier General Rwivanga, the RDF spokesman, who believes the ten points are probably a combination of the two. He believes they existed, perhaps in a more abstract form, during the start of the Struggle for Liberation, but were crystallized into a ten-point list after the conflict.
68. Quoted in Kinzer, *A Thousand Hills,* 88.
69. Author's archive.
70. The following section is based on Logan Ndahiro, "Liberation Diary: The Attack on Ruhengeri and Release of Political and Other Prisoners," *New Times,* 27 August 2015; and correspondence with Logan Ndahiro, 19 and 20 March 2019.
71. Logan Ndahiro, "Liberation Diary."
72. Ambabel Kigali to Belext Bru, "Inval uit Oeganda via Noorden van Ruhengeri," 22 January 1991, "18.955–145, Politique intérieure 1990–1992 (10)," FPFSA.
73. Oliver to Immediate FCO, "New RPF Activity in Rwanda," 23 January 1991, "JWW 014/1 (Part A), 'Rwanda: Internal Political Situation,'" FCO.
74. Kinzer, *A Thousand Hills,* 88–89; Paul Quilès, *Rapport d'information par la mission d'information de la commission de la défense nationale et des forces armées et de la commission des affaires étrangères, sur les opérations militaires menées par la France, d'autres pays et l'ONU au Rwanda entre 1990 et 1994* (Assemblée nationale, Paris, 15 December 1998), Annexes, 152; Transcripts of Tuesday, 4 December 2007, Examination-in-chief by Mr. St-Laurent, ICTR-00-56-T, 46.

75. Quilès, *Rapport d'information,* Comptes Rendus 6 Mai–3 Juin 1998, 225–29.
76. Prunier, *The Rwanda Crisis,* 120.
77. Ambabel Kigali to Belext Bru, "Toestand Ruhengeri," 23 January 1991; Ambabel Kigali to Belext Bru, "Evakuatie uit Ruhengeri," 24 January 1991, "18.955–145, Politique intérieure 1990–1992 (10)," FPFSA.
78. Quilès, *Rapport d'information,* 136.
79. Martres to Paris, "Situation au Rwanda," 24 January 1991. Quilès, *Rapport d'information,* Annexes, 153.
80. Lt. Col. EJK O'Brien, British High Commission, to Lt. Col. JP Cameron, MoD, "Rwanda—Meeting with RPA Commander," 4 September 1992, FCO; Bernard Lugan, *François Mitterrand: l'Armée française et la Rwanda* (Monaco: Editions du Rocher, 2005), 78, concurs that, from January 1991 onward, the RPA outclassed the FAR.

CHAPTER 7: THE FAR

1. Lt. Col. G. B. Molyneux-Carter to High Commissioner, Kampala, "DA Report on Visit to Rwanda 16–20 Feb 91," no date but received in registry 5 June 1991, "JWW 014/1 (Part B), Rwanda: Internal Political Situation,'" FCO.
2. Molyneux-Carter, "DA Report on Visit to Rwanda."
3. Defense Intelligence Report, Defense Intelligence Agency, "Rwanda: The Rwandan Patriotic Front's Offensive," 9 May 1994, "The US and the Genocide in Rwanda, 1994," NSA, 3.
4. Interestingly one of the key books on the subject fails to even discuss the Belgian military presence in Rwanda between 1963 and 1990: Patrick Lefèvre and Jean-Noël Lefèvre, *Les militaires belges et le Rwanda 1916–2006* (Brussels: Editions Racine, 2006).
5. "Expert Report requested by the International Criminal Tribunal for Rwanda: Positions of Authority in the Forces Armées Rwandaises (FAR): Power and authority that a civilian could exercise in FAR," 1 August 2006, "Exhibit Number: Unknown, Date Admitted: 27-11-2006," *The Prosecutor v. Protais Zigiranyirazo,* ICTR-2001–73, 51.
6. The US Armed Forces have been grappling with this problem for a while; see, for example, William McCoy, *Senegal and Liberia: Case Studies in US IMET Training and Its Role in Internal Defense and Development,* N-3637-USDP (Santa Monica, CA: RAND, 1994), 26; Stephen Watts, *Identifying and Mitigating Risks in Security Sector Assistance for Africa's Fragile States* (Santa Monica, CA: RAND, 2015); Christopher Paul et al., *What Works Best When Building Capacity in Challenging Contexts?* (Santa Monica, CA: RAND, 2015). For the peacekeeping context specifically, see Marco Jowell, *Peacekeeping in Africa: Politics, Security and the Failure of Foreign Military Assistance* (London: I. B. Tauris, 2018).
7. Correspondence with French officer, 11 September 2016.

8. Philippe Mahoux and Guy Verhofstadt, *Commission d'enquête parlementaire concernant les événements du Rwanda* (Sénat de Belgique, 6 December 1997), 698; See also Colonel Cussac to Armées Paris, "Coopération militaires belge au Rwanda," 20 October 1991, FGT.
9. James K. Gasana, *Rwanda: Du parti-État à l'État-garnison* (Paris: L'Harmattan, 2002), 67.
10. General de Division Varret, Chef de la Mission Militaire de Coopération, to Ministre de la Coopération et du Développement, "Compte rendu de mission au Burundi et au Rwanda," 19 December 1990, FGT.
11. Paul Quilès, *Rapport d'information par la mission d'information de la commission de la défense nationale et des forces armées et de la commission des affaires étrangères, sur les opérations militaires menées par la France, d'autres pays et l'ONU au Rwanda entre 1990 et 1994* (Assemblée nationale, Paris, 15 December 1998), 28.
12. Didier Tauzin, *Rwanda: Je demande justice pour la France et ses soldats* (Paris: Editions Jacob-Duvernet, 2011), 53; Quilès, *Rapport d'information,* 355–56.
13. Colonel Léonidas Rusatira to —, "Note d'appréciation de l'Assistance Militaire française au Rwanda," 17 November 1990, FGT; The same appreciation was also expressed for the French officers who supported the Gendarmerie. See: Lt Col Pontien Hakizimana, G3 EM Gd N to Son Excellence Monsieur le Ministre de la Défense nationale, Kigali, "Prolongation de séjour," 18 November 1990, FGT; see also Ministre des affaires étrangères to Ambassade de France, Kigali, "L'assistance militaire de la France au Rwanda," 23 November 1990, FGT.
14. Quilès, *Rapport d'information,* Annexes, 137–38.
15. "2e régiment étranger de parachutistes, Journal des Marches et Operations 1 janvier an 30 juin 1991," GR7U 3440, SHD.
16. Chollet, DAMI to Colonel Cussac, "Réunion des militaires français en poste au RWANDA," 25 July 1991, FGT.
17. Quilès, *Rapport d'information,* 144–46.
18. "Expert Report requested by the International Criminal Tribunal for Rwanda: Positions of Authority in the Forces Armées Rwandaises (FAR): Power and authority that a civilian could exercise in FAR," 1 August 2006, ICTR-2001-73, 42.
19. "Expert Report," 1 August 2006, 31–32.
20. Defense Intelligence Report, Defense Intelligence Agency, "Rwanda: The Rwandan Patriotic Front's Offensive," 9 May 1994, 3.
21. Ambabel WN to Belext Bru, "VS-Beoordeling van Situatie in Rwanda," 13 February 1991, "18.955–145, Politique intérieure 1990–1992 (10)," FPFSA.
22. Chollet to Galinié, "Compte-rendu du lieutenant-colonel Chollet, chef du Détachement d'assistance militaire et d'instruction au Rwanda [Bilan de l'instruction du bataillon Gitarama]," 22 April 1991, FGT.
23. Chollet, DAMI to Colonel Cussac, "Bilan du 63° bataillon," 12 November 1991, FGT.
24. Chollet, DAMI to Colonel Cussac, "Bilan de l'instruction du 32° bataillon," 22 July 1991, FGT.

25. Chollet, DAMI to Colonel Cussac, "Bilan de l'instruction du bataillon CECODE (41° bataillon) 2° et 3° compagnies," 19 August 1991, FGT.
26. Chollet, "Bilan de l'instruction," 19 August 1991.
27. Chollet to Galinié, "Compte-rendu du lieutenant-colonel Chollet, chef du Détachement d'assistance militaire et d'instruction au Rwanda [Bilan de l'instruction du bataillon Gitarama]," 22 April 1991, FGT.
28. Chollet, DAMI, to Colonel Galinié, "Bilan de l'instruction du 64° bataillon," 2 July 1991, FGT.
29. Chollet, "[Bilan de l'instruction du bataillon Gitarama]," 22 April 1991. Ambassade van België to P/Geo 04, "Intrep CTM van 20 en 21 April 1991," 22 April 1991, "18.955–145, Politique intérieure 1990–1992 (12)," FPFSA.
30. Ambabel Kigali to P/Geo 04, "Intrep van 05 91," 5 March 1991, "18.955–145, Politique intérieure 1990–1992 (11)," FPFSA.
31. Correspondence with French officer, 11 September 2016.
32. Ambabel Kigali to Belext Bru, "Intrep 29 january 1991," 30 January 1991, "18.955–145, Politique intérieure 1990–1992 (10)," FPFSA.
33. Ambabel Kigali to belext Bru, "Situation sur le plan militaire," 8 February 1991, "18.955–145, Politique intérieure 1990–1992," FPFSA; Ambabel Kigali to belext Bru, "Situation sur le plan militaire," 9 February 1991, "18.955–145, Politique intérieure 1990–1992 (10)," FPFSA.
34. Ambabel Kigali, "Situation sur le plan militaire," 8 February 1991; Ambabel Kigali to belext Bru, "Situation sur le plan militaire," 9 February 1991, "18.955–145, Politique intérieure 1990–1992 (10)," FPFSA.
35. Ambabel Kigali to belext Bru, "Situation militaire au Rwanda," 13 February 1991, "18.955–145, Politique intérieure 1990–1992 (10)," FPFSA.
36. Ambabel Kigali to belext Bru, "Situation militaire au Rwanda," 14 February 1991, "18.955–145, Politique intérieure 1990–1992 (10)," FPFSA.
37. Ambabel Kigali to So3—P/Geo 04, "Intrep CTM de ce jour," 14 February 1991, "18.955–145, Politique intérieure 1990–1992 (10)," FPFSA.
38. Ambabel Kigali to P/Geo 04, "Intrep CTM du 15.02.91," 15 February 1991. "18.955–145, Politique intérieure 1990–1992 (10)" FPFSA.
39. Ambabel Kigali to P/Geo 04, "Intrep CTM de ce jour," 18 February 1991, "18.955–145, Politique intérieure 1990–1992 (10)," FPFSA; Ambabel Kigali to P/Geo 04, "Intrep CTM 27/02/91," 28 February 1991, "18.955–145, Politique intérieure 1990–1992 (11)," FPFSA.
40. Ambabel Kigali to P/Geo 04, "Intrep CTM du 26/02/91," 26 February 1991, "18.955–145, Politique intérieure 1990–1992 (11)," FPFSA.
41. Ambabel Kigali to Belext Bru, "Intrep afgesloten op 24 1600 Feb 91," 26 February 1991, "18.955–145, Politique intérieure 1990–1992 (11)," FPFSA.
42. Ambabel Kigali to P/Geo 04, "Intrep van 04 Maart 91," 4 March 1991, "18.955–145, Politique intérieure 1990–1992 (11)," FPFSA; Ambabel Kigali to P/Geo 04, "Intrep van 05 91," 5 March 1991, "18.955–145, Politique intérieure 1990–1992 (11)," FPFSA.

43. Ambabel Kigali to Belext Bru, "Intrep van 7 Maart 1991," 7 March 1991, "18.955–145, Politique intérieure 1990–1992 (11)," FPFSA; Ambabel Kigali to P/Geo 04, "Intrep van 08.03.91," 8 March 1991, "18.955–145, Politique intérieure 1990–1992 (11)," FPFSA; Ambabel Kigali to Belext Bru, "Intrep van 09 en 10 maart 91," 11 March 1991, "18.955–145, Politique intérieure 1990–1992 (11)," FPFSA.
44. Swinnen to P/Geo 04, "Intrep van 07 Mar 91," 7 March 1991, "18.955–145, Politique intérieure 1990–1992 (11)," FPFSA; 80 is the number given to the author by the RPF; the number of 145 comes from the intelligence the FAR passed on to the Belgians.
45. Author's archive.
46. Ambabel Kigali, "Intrep van 09 en 10 maart 91," 11 March 1991.
47. Ambabel Kigali to Belext Bru, "Situation Militaire au Rwanda," 18 February 1991, "18.955–145, Politique intérieure 1990–1992 (10)," FPFSA.
48. Transcripts of Tuesday, 4 December 2007, examination-in-chief by Mr. St-Laurent, ICTR-00-56-T, 46.
49. Kaye Oliver to C Shute Esq, WAD, "Rwanda Internal: Government Reshuffle," 12 February 1991, "JWW 014/1 (Part A), Rwanda: Internal Political Situation,'" FCO.
50. Bruce D. Jones, *Peacemaking in Rwanda: The Dynamics of Failure* (Boulder, CO: Lynne Rienner, 2001), 1.
51. Ambabel D.S.S. Dar Es Salaam [?] to Belext Bru, "Conference de Dar-Es-Salaam," 19 February 1991, "18.955–145, Politique intérieure 1990–1992," FPFSA.
52. Ambabel Kinshasa to Belext Bru, "Rwanda: Rencontre Mobutu-Habyarimana," 26 February 1991, "18.955–145, Politique intérieure 1990–1992 (11)," FPFSA.
53. Details are sketchy. See Cormack to Teleletter FCO, "Rwanda Internal," 4 April 1991, "JWW 014/1 (Part A), Rwanda: Internal Political Situation,'" FCO.
54. Cormack, "Rwanda Internal," 4 April 1991.
55. Transcripts of Tuesday, 4 December 2007, examination-in-chief by Mr. St-Laurent, ICTR-00-56-T, 50.
56. Logan Ndahiro, "From Canopy to Open Savannah: An Incursion into Akagera National Park," *New Times,* 1 February 2016.
57. Ndahiro.
58. Martres to Armées Paris, "Situation Militaire et Renseignements Divers," 2 May 1991, FGT.
59. Martres, "Situation Militaire," 2 May 1991.
60. Ambabel Kigali to Belext Bru, "Mécontentement au sein des FAR," 7 May 1991, "18.955–145, Politique intérieure 1990–1992 (12)," FPFSA.
61. Swinnen to Belext Bru, "Intrep ctm des 03, 04 et 05 mai 1991," 6 May 1991, FGT.
62. Ambabel Kigali to Belext Bru, "Rapport sur les troubles au sein des FAR," 7 May 1991, "18.955–145, Politique intérieure 1990–1992 (12)," FPFSA.
63. Cormack to DHM, "Visit to Rwanda 28 April–1 May," 7 May 1991, "JWW 014/1 (Part B), Rwanda: Internal Political Situation,'" FCO.

64. Ambabel Kigali, "Rapport sur les troubles," 7 May 1991.
65. CTM/B Rwanda to SGR, "Intrep van 06 mei 91," 7 May 1991, "18.955–145, Politique intérieure 1990–1992 (12)," FPFSA; Ambabel Kigali, "Mécontentement au sein des FAR," 7 May 1991.
66. Ndahiro, "From Canopy to Open Savannah."
67. Martres to Armées Paris, "Situation militaire et renseignements divers," 13 May 1991, FGT; Ambabel Kigali to Belext Bru, "Intrep 22 mei 1991," 24 May 1991, "18.955–145, Politique intérieure 1990–1992 (12)," FPFSA.
68. Martres to Armées Paris, "Situation militaire et renseignements divers," 16 May 1991, FGT.
69. Martres to Armées Paris, "Situation militaire et renseignements divers," 17 May 1991, FGT.
70. Ndahiro, "From Canopy to Open Savannah."
71. Swinnen to belext Bru "Intrep du 17 au 20 mai 91," 21 May 1991, FGT.
72. Martres to Armées Paris, "Situation militaire et renseignements divers," 21 May 1991, FGT; Martres to Armées Paris, "Situation tactique le 22 mai 1991 à 16H00' 22 mai 1991," FGT; Swinnen to belext Bru, "Intrep van 22 mei 91," 24 May 1991, FGT.
73. Martres to Armées Paris, "situation militaire et renseignements divers," 29 May 1991, FGT.
74. André Guichaoua, *From War to Genocide: Criminal Politics in Rwanda, 1990–1994,* trans. Don E. Webster (Madison: University of Wisconsin Press, 2015), 72.
75. Transcript of Thursday, 20 October 2005, testimony of Witness LE1. ICTR-98-41-T, 36–37.
76. Gérard Prunier, *The Rwanda Crisis: History of a Genocide* (London: Hurst, 1997), 87. The importance of Mayuya is emphasized by the fact that Camp Kanombe, one of Rwanda's largest military bases, was renamed Camp Colonel Mayuya in his honor. He was in command of the base when he was murdered there. Transcript of Monday, 18 September 2006, testimony of Aloys Ntabakuze, ICTR-98-41-T, 13. Additional information on Mayuya can be found in the transcript of Tuesday, 25 October 2005, testimony of Théoneste Bagosora, ICTR-98-41-T, 49–59.
77. Transcript of Monday, 27 November 2006, testimony of Laurien Uwizeyimana, ICTR-98-41-T, 8.
78. Colonel Anselme Nkilikibona and Déogratias Ndibwani had been arrested around the time of Mayuya's murder. They were released during an amnesty in 1993. Transcript of 31 October 2005, testimony of Théoneste Bagosora, ICTR-98-41-T, 12, 13. There were several commissions into Mayuya's death. The third commission was led by Nkubitu, Nsengiyumva, and Colonel Pontien Hakizimana. See Transcript of Wednesday, 11 October 2006, testimony of Anatole Nsengiyumva, ICTR-98-41-T, 79; see Guichaoua, *From War to Genocide,* 72–73.
79. Anatole Nsengiyumva to —, "N042/G2.2.0," 22 May 1990, "File 1990/Planning," Linda Melvern Rwanda Genocide Archive.
80. Gasana, *Rwanda: Du parti-État,* 66–67.

81. Ambabel Kigali to Belext Bru, "Greve a la prison de Kigali," 7 May 1991, "18.955–145, Politique intérieure 1990–1992 (12)," FPFSA; Ambabel Kigali to Belext Bru, "Situation des droits de l'homme au Rwanda, suite aux evenements d'octobre," 12 April 1991, "18.955–145, Politique intérieure 1990–1992 (12)," FPFSA.
82. Swinnen to belext Bru, "Sitrep 19-20-21/07/91," 22 July 1991, FGT.
83. Gasana, *Rwanda: Du parti-État,* 159.
84. Ambabel Kigali to Belext Bru, "Rwanda—Militaire Processen," 16 July 1991, "18.955–145, Politique intérieure 1990–1992 (12)," FPFSA.
85. Gasana, *Rwanda: Du parti-État,* 159.
86. Major Nyampame to His Excellency the President of the Republic of Rwanda, "Amicale de Byumba," 22 October 1991, "Exhibit Number: P431A, Date Admitted: 9-11-2006 (English Translation)," ICTR-98-41-T.
87. Nyampame, "Amicale de Byumba," 22 October 1991.
88. Nyampame, "Amicale de Byumba," 22 October 1991.
89. Martin van Creveld, *Fighting Power: German and U.S. Army Performance, 1939–1945* (Westport, CT: Greenwood Press, 1982), 3.

CHAPTER 8: MULTIPARTY POLITICS AND THE BATTLE OF AGASENTIMITA, AUGUST 1991–JULY 1992

1. Ambabel Kigali to Belext Bru, "Getuigenis over de politico-militaire toestand in Rwanda," 10 March 1992, "18.955–148, Dossier General Janvier–Mai 1992," FPFSA.
2. Lt. Col. G. B. Molyneux-Carter to High Commissioner, Kampala, "DA Report on Visit to Rwanda 16–20 Feb 91," no date but received in registry 5 June 1991, FCO.
3. "Rapport de la Commission Nationale de Synthèse sur les réformes politiques au Rwanda," March 1991, "Exhibit Number: DB 243, Date Admitted: 1-11-2005," ICTR-98-41-T, 38.
4. "Rapport de la Commission Nationale de Synthèse," March 1991.
5. Ambabel Kigali to Belext Bru, "Grondwetsherziening door pres. Habyarimana ondertekend," 11 June 1991, "18.955–145, Politique intérieure 1990–1992 (12)," FPFSA.
6. Swinnen to Eyskens "Rwandese oppositiepartijen," 28 May 1991, "18.955–145, Politique intérieure 1990–1992 (12)," FPFSA.
7. Gérard Prunier, *The Rwanda Crisis: History of a Genocide* (London: Hurst, 1997), 122–23.
8. "The Three Victors Who Will Lead Rwanda," *New York Times,* 20 July 1994; André Guichaoua, *From War to Genocide: Criminal Politics in Rwanda, 1990–1994,* trans. Don E. Webster (Madison: University of Wisconsin Press, 2015), 81.
9. Dismas Nsengiyaremye, "La transition démocratique au Rwanda (1989–1993)," in *Les crises politiques au Burundi et au Rwanda (1993–1994),* ed. André Guichaoua (Paris: Karthala, 1995), 249–50.

10. Swinnen, "Rwandese oppositiepartijen," 28 May 1991.
11. Swinnen, "Rwandese oppositiepartijen," 28 May 1991.
12. Prunier, *The Rwanda Crisis,* 124–25.
13. Flaten, US Embassy, Kigali, to Secretary of State, Washington DC, "The Military and the Political Process," 11 June 1993, "Rwanda, the failure of the Arusha Peace Accords," NSA.
14. Nsengiyumva to Chef EM AR, "Sûreté intérieure de l'Etat," 2 July 1992, "Exhibit Number: P20(b), Date Admitted: 11-9-2002 (English Translation)," ICTR-98-41-T, 1.
15. Nsengiyumva, "Sûreté intérieure de l'Etat," 2 July 1992, 3.
16. Colonel Cussac to Armées Paris, "Situation militaire et renseignements divers," 13 August 1991, FGT.
17. Colonel Cussac to Armées Paris, "Situation militaire et renseignements divers," 15 August 1991, FGT.
18. Cussac, "Situation militaire," 15 August 1991.
19. Cussac, "Situation militaire," 15 August 1991.
20. Colonel Cussac to Armées Paris, "Situation militaire et renseignements divers," 21 August 1991, FGT.
21. Colonel Cussac to Armées Paris, "Situation militaire et renseignements divers," 31 August 1991, FGT.
22. Colonel Cussac to Armées Paris, "Situation Tactique le 3 septembre 1991 à 12H00 locales," 3 September 1991, FGT; Colonel Cussac to Armées Paris, "Situation militaire et renseignements divers," 5 September 1991, FGT.
23. Colonel Cussac to Armées Paris, "Situation militaire et renseignements divers," 6 September 1991, FGT; Colonel Cussac to Armées Paris, "Situation tactique 7 Septembre 1991 à 12H00 locales," 7 September 1991, FGT.
24. Interview with Caesar Kayizari, 14 October 2018.
25. Interview with Caesar Kayizari, 14 October 2018.
26. Correspondence with French officer, 11 September 2016.
27. Lt. Col. G. B. Molyneux-Carter to High Commissioner, Kampala, "DA Report on Visit to Rwanda 16–20 Feb 91," no date but received in registry 5 June 1991, FCO.
28. Lt. Col. G. B. Molyneux-Carter, "DA Report on Visit to Rwanda border Area—18 October 1990," 22 October 1990, "JWW 051/1 (part C), 'Incursion into Rwanda: October 1990,'" FCO.
29. Kinshasa to—, "Protection Issues Related to Influx Rwandese Refugees in Kivu, Zaire, Status of Deserters from Rwanda Patriotic Front," 15 February 1991, "100. RWA.GEN [A]," UNHCR Archive.
30. Molyneux-Carter, "DA Report on Visit to Rwanda 16–20 Feb 91."
31. Colonel Cussac to Armées Paris, "Renseignements transmis par ambassadeur du Rwanda à Kampala," 5 September 1991, FGT. "Signale que, dans la nuit du 4 au 5 septembre des véhicules ont été observés sur la route Mbarara-Gisoro (40kms nord de Ruhengeri). (ce renseignement est confirmé par les CRAP

des FAR.).” That the CRAP did carry out operations behind enemy lines is confirmed by the commander of the Para-Commando Battalion, Major Aloys Ntabakuze: “The CRAP executed the operational missions (reconnaissance and action in the enemy lines) for the benefit of army HQ or of operational sector on demand or on initiative of the Army HQ.” See “III. The Army and the Para Cdo Bn Background,” “Exhibit Number: DNT235, Date Admitted: 21-9-2006,” ICTR-98-41-T, 42.

32. Colonel Cussac to Armées Paris, “Conversations entre gouvernement rwandais et FPR,” 16 September 1991, FGT; Bruce D. Jones, *Peacemaking in Rwanda: The Dynamics of Failure* (Boulder, CO: Lynne Rienner, 2001), 56.
33. Johan Swinnen, *Rwanda: Mijn verhaal* (Kalmthout, Belgium: Polis, 2016), 141–45.
34. Dijoud to —, “Visite à Paris du major Kagame,” 27 September 1991. Paul Quilès, *Rapport d'information par la mission d'information de la commission de la défense nationale et des forces armées et de la commission des affaires étrangères, sur les opérations militaires menées par la France, d'autres pays et l'ONU au Rwanda entre 1990 et 1994* (Assemblée nationale, Paris, 15 December 1998), Annexes, 206.
35. Quilès.
36. Interview with Ndore Rurinda, 12 October 2018.
37. Author's archive.
38. Interview with James Kabarebe, 16 October 2018.
39. The exact date of these operations is difficult to determine. My interviewees seemed certain they took place toward the very end of 1991, but Abdul Ruzibiza places them a couple of months earlier. While the exact timing of the fighting is not of great importance during this episode, it is something to keep in mind. Abdul Joshua Ruzibiza, *Rwanda: L'histoire secrète* (Paris: Editions du Panama, 2005), 146–51.
40. Author's archive.
41. Personal correspondence between the author and Gérard Prunier, 23 January 2014. It should be noted that this description might not relate to the fighting in Sector Centimeter as such, but rather to that around the Virunga Mountains. The point, however, is that it seems to be a good description of recurring features of the fighting between the FAR and the RPA and confirms many of the stories I was told by RPA veterans.
42. Interview with James Kabarebe, 16 October 2018.
43. Logan Ndahiro, “The Capture of Enemy Territory—The Agasentimita,” *New Times,* 16 May 2016.
44. Colonel B. Cussac, Attaché de Défense près l'Ambassade de France au Rwanda, to Chef d'Etat-Major des Armées, “Rapport de renseignement bimestriel (Septembre-Octobre 1991),” 5 December 1991, FGT.
45. Cullimore to Priority FCO, “Rwandese Patriotic Front (RPF),” 29 January 1992, “FOI: 0421–17,” FCO.
46. Prunier, *The Rwanda Crisis,* 134.

47. Colonel Cussac to Armées Paris, "Désignation d'un premier ministre," 15 October 1991, FGT.
48. In Guichaoua, *Les crises politiques,* 253. Note that Prunier suggests that Nsanzimana did not enjoy support from within the MRND either; Prunier, *The Rwanda Crisis,* 134. For another assessment of Nsanzimana's character and history, see Swinnen, *Rwanda: Mijn verhaal,* 172, 176.
49. Swinnen, *Rwanda: Mijn verhaal,* 179, 184; Swinnen to Eyskens, "Rwanda—open brief van groep intellektuelen aan President Habyarimana," 22 January 1992, "18.955–148, Dossier General Janvier–Mai 1992," FPFSA.
50. Timothy Longman, *Christianity and Genocide in Rwanda* (Cambridge: Cambridge University Press, 2011), 138–39; Swinnen, *Rwanda: Mijn verhaal,* 185–86.
51. James K. Gasana, *Rwanda: Du parti-État à l'État-garnison* (Paris: L'Harmattan, 2002), 103; see also Transcript, 27 November 2002, Examination-in-Chief by Ms. Mulvaney of Witness ZF. ICTR-98-41-T, 23–26.
52. Prunier argues that "as soon as the Nsengiyaremye cabinet was sworn-in, the President asked the new Prime Minister and his Minister of Defence, MRND(D) moderate James Gasana, to prepare a plan for reorganising the Armed Forces top leadership, with the aim of eliminating the most resolute extremists." Prunier, *The Rwanda Crisis,* 167. However, Gasana specifically mentions in his book that this was not the case. Gasana, *Rwanda: du parti-État,* 124.
53. "Détachement NOROIT du 2e RIMa, Journal des Marches et Opérations 05 mars 1992–13 juillet 1992," GR 2000Z 114 455, SHD.
54. "Détachement NOROIT du 2e RIMa."
55. "Détachement NOROIT du 2e RIMa."
56. Gasana, *Rwanda: Du parti-État,* 109.
57. Gasana, 110.
58. US Embassy Kigali to Secretary of State Washington, "Council of Ministers retires top military officers," 11 June 1992, FGT; Transcript of 6 February 2008, Testimony of Witness CBP67, ICTR-00-56-T, 56, 73.
59. US Embassy, "Council of Ministers retires," 11 June 1992. Roméo Dallaire's assessment of Nsabimana was rather less positive: "What I saw was an army chief of staff, who, in my book, did not have the same leadership qualities, charismatic qualities and the calmness in his command that I would have expected from somebody of that rank." Transcript of 21 January 2004, cross-examination by Mr. Constant of Roméo Dallaire, ICTR-98-41-T, 13.
60. US Embassy, "Council of Ministers retires," 11 June 1992.
61. Guichaoua, *From War to Genocide,* 74.
62. Transcript, 21 September 2004, Testimony of Filip Reyntjens, ICTR-98–41-T, 11. "I would not have considered General Nsabimana a member of the *Akazu,* and I think I would have considered him, like others, to be essentially a professional soldier. This would have been the view of the opposition, too, because when he, together with General Ndindiliyimana at the head of the gendarmerie, when he was appointed in replacement of members that were clearly *Akazu,* Colonel

Serubuga for the army and Colonel Rwagafilita for the gendarmerie. That being said, and I must be very hesitant here if only because General Nsabimana is dead, there are a number of sources that suggest that he may have been less the saint that I would have thought he was."

63. Gasana, *Rwanda: Du parti-État,* 123–24.
64. Fergusson to Priority FCO, "Rwanda," 12 June 1992, "FOI 0421–17," FCO.
65. Fergusson, "Rwanda," 12 June 1992.
66. Carl von Clausewitz, *On War* (Hertfordshire, UK: Woodworth, 1997), 27, 28.
67. "Joint Communique Issued at the End of the Negotiations on the Ceasefire between the Rwandese Government and the Rwandese Patriotic Front Arusha 10–12 July 1992," 12 July 1992, FGT.
68. Interview with Ndore Rurinda, 12 October 2018.
69. The following section is based on Logan Ndahiro, "The Capture of Enemy Territory," *New Times,* 16 May 2016; Logan Ndahiro, "Expansion of Territory and the Mukarange Targeted Enemy Shelling," *New Times,* 19 September 2016; and interview with Ndore Rurinda, 12 October 2018.
70. Ndahiro, "Expansion of territory."
71. "Détachement NOROIT du 2e RIMa, JMO 5 mars—13 juillet 1992," GR 2000Z 114 455, SHD.
72. "Détachement NOROIT du 2e RIMa, JMO 5 mars—13 juillet 1992."
73. "Détachement NOROIT du 2e RIMa, JMO 5 mars—13 juillet 1992."
74. "Détachement NOROIT du 2e RIMa, JMO 5 mars—13 juillet 1992."
75. Bernard Lugan, *François Mitterrand: l'Armée française et la Rwanda* (Monaco: Editions du Rocher, 2005), 101–2.
76. "Détachement NOROIT du 2e RIMa, JMO 5 mars—13 juillet 1992."
77. Lugan, *François Mitterrand,* 102.
78. Lugan, 103.
79. "Détachement NOROIT du 2e RIMa, JMO 5 mars—13 juillet 1992."
80. "Détachement NOROIT du 2e RIMa, JMO 5 mars—13 juillet 1992."
81. "Détachement NOROIT du 2e RIMa, JMO 5 mars—13 juillet 1992."
82. "Détachement NOROIT du 2e RIMa, JMO 5 mars—13 juillet 1992."
83. "Détachement NOROIT du 2e RIMa, JMO 5 mars—13 juillet 1992."
84. Ndahiro, "Expansion of Territory."
85. Lugan, *François Mitterrand,* 103.
86. Lugan, 103, quoting General Rosier.

CHAPTER 9: A STRUGGLE FOR PEACE, JULY 1992–MARCH 1993

1. FIDH in collaboration with Africa Watch, *Report of the International Commission of Investigation on Human Rights Violations in Rwanda since October 1, 1990 (January 7–21, 1993)* (Paris: FIDH in collaboration with Africa Watch, March 1993), 11–13; Africa Watch, *Rwanda: Talking Peace and Waging War; Human Rights since the October 1990 Invasion* (Washington, DC: Africa Watch, 27 February 1992).

See Association rwandaise pour la défense des droits de la personne et des libertés publiques (ADL), *Rapport sur les droits de l'homme au Rwanda (Septembre 1991–Septembre 1992)* (Kigali: ADL, December 1992), 109–16, for a list of those who were killed.

2. ADL, *Rapport (Septembre 1991–Septembre 1992),* 101.
3. ADL, 102.
4. FIDH, *Report of International Commission,* 14.
5. Gérard Prunier, *The Rwanda Crisis: History of a Genocide* (London: Hurst, 1997), 99.
6. Vincent Duclert, *La France, le Rwanda et le génocide des Tutsi (1990–1994)—Rapport remis au Président de la République le 26 mars 2021* (Paris: Armand Colin, 2021), 319.
7. Prunier, *The Rwanda Crisis,* 57, 141. Besides Prunier, see Filip Reyntjens, "Rwanda, Genocide and Beyond," *Journal of Refugee Studies* 9, no. 3 (1996): 245; Peter Langford, "The Rwandan Path to Genocide: The Genesis of the Capacity of the Rwandan Post-Colonial State to Organise and Unleash a Project of Extermination," *Civil Wars* 7, no. 1 (2005): 12, 15; and René Lemarchand, "Disconnecting the Threads: Rwanda and the Holocaust Reconsidered," *Journal of Genocide Research* 4, no. 4 (2002): 513. For earlier challenges to the notions of conformity and absolute authority, see Mahmood Mamdani, *When Victims Become Killers: Colonialism, Nativism, and Genocide in Rwanda* (Princeton, NJ: Princeton University Press, 2002), 199–200; and Timothy Longman, "Placing Genocide in Context: Research Priorities for the Rwandan Genocide," *Journal of Genocide Research* 6, no. 1 (2004): 37.
8. Prunier, *The Rwanda Crisis,* 141–42.
9. ADL, *Rapport (Septembre 1991–Septembre 1992),* 117–34.
10. Africa Watch, *Rwanda: Talking Peace and Waging War.*
11. Ambabel Kigali to belext Bru, "Militaire situatie aan 010291," 2 February 1991, "18.955–145, Politique intérieure 1990–1992 (10)," FPFSA.
12. Comité pour le respect des droits de l'Homme et la démocratie au Rwanda (CRDDR), *Rwanda: Rapport de deux missions effectuées par Eric Gillet & André Jadoul, avocats au barreau de Bruxelles au Rwanda du 9 au 17 janvier et du 2 au 5 février 1992* (Brussels: CRDDR, May 1992), 23.
13. FIDH, *Report of International Commission,* 19.
14. Transcript of 11 October 2004, ICTR-99-50-T, 42–44.
15. FIDH, *Report of International Commission,* 19.
16. FIDH, 21–22.
17. Association rwandaise pour la défense des droits de la personne et des libertés publiques (ADL), *Rapport sur les droits de l'homme au Rwanda (Octobre 1992–Octobre 1993)* (Kigali, ADL, December 1993), 165; FIDH, *Report of International Commission,* 29.
18. Swinnen to belext Bru, "Etnische onlusten in de bugesera—mijn bezoek aan nyamata," 7 March 1992, FGT.

19. FIDH, *Report of International Commission,* 27.
20. FIDH, 27.
21. ADL, *Rapport (Septembre 1991–Septembre 1992),* 203.
22. SOURCE, Ambabel Kigali to belext Bru, "Ernstige onlusten in de Bugesera (zuiden van Kigali)," 7 March 1992, "18.955–148, Dossier General Janvier–Mai 1992," FPFSA.
23. Swinnen, Belgian Embassy, Kigali, to belext Bru, "Etnische onlusten in de bugesera—mijn bezoek aan nyamata," 7 March 1992, FGT.
24. Martres, French Embassy, Kigali, to —, "Situation au Rwanda," 9 March 1992. Paul Quilès, *Rapport d'information par la mission d'information de la commission de la défense nationale et des forces armées et de la commission des affaires étrangères, sur les opérations militaires menées par la France, d'autres pays et l'ONU au Rwanda entre 1990 et 1994* (Assemblée nationale, Paris, 15 December 1998), Annexes, 166.
25. Swinnen, Belgian Embassy, Kigali, to belext Bru, "Onlusten bugesera—demarches—mijn onderhoud met pl-voorzitter Mugenzi," 9 March 1992, FGT.
26. Swinnen, Belgian Embassy, Kigali, to belext Bru, "Getuigenis van rwandees officier over politieke toestand," 25 March 1992, FGT. Swinnen spells the name as "Nhizirungu," though the correct spelling seems to be "Nshizirungu."
27. "Détachement NOROIT du 2e RIMa, Journal des Marches et Opérations 05 mars 1992–13 juillet 1992," GR 2000Z 114 455, SHD.
28. Jacques Morel, *La France au cœur du genocide des Tutsi* (Paris: L'Esprit Frappeur, 2016), 82–84. Considering how closely Swinnen kept the French Embassy informed of what was happening in Bugesera, it is peculiar that the *Rapport Duclert* only touches briefly on this episode. *Rapport Duclert,* 152–55.
29. Swinnen, Belgian Embassy, Kigali, to belext Bru, "Etnische onlusten—demarche bij de rwandese overheid," 8 March 1992, FGT.
30. Swinnen, Belgian Embassy, Kigali, to Willy Claes, "Rwanda—Onlusten Bugesera," 27 March 1992, FGT.
31. US Holocaust Museum and The Hague Institute for Global Justice, *International Decision-Making in the Age of Genocide: Rwanda 1990–1994; Annotated Transcript* (The Hague: US Holocaust Museum and The Hague Institute for Global Justice, 1–3 June 2014), 1–10.
32. US Holocaust Museum, 1–26.
33. US Holocaust Museum, 1–17.
34. Flaten, US Embassy, Kigali, to Secretary of State, Washington, DC, "GOR outlines Strategy to Negotiations to End War," 13 May 1992, "Rwanda: The Failure of the Arusha Peace Accords," NSA.
35. Flaten, "GOR outlines Strategy," 13 May 1992.
36. Protocol of Agreement between the Government of the Republic of Rwanda and the Rwandese Patriotic Front on the Rule of Law, Annex III of the Arusha Accords, United Nations Peacemaker.
37. US Holocaust Museum, *International Decision-Making,* 1–17.
38. Prime Minister Dismas Nsengiyaremye to President Habyarimana, "Etat d'exécution et situation de blocage du programme du Gouvernement de transition,"

22 September 1992, "010.RWA[G]," UNHCR Archive. This comment was also a dig at the president, as many in the opposition thought that his powers had not been curtailed sufficiently during the formation of the multiparty government.

39. Nsengiyaremye, "Etat d'exécution," 22 September 1992.
40. Nsengiyaremye, 22 September 1992.
41. Nsengiyaremye, 22 September 1992.
42. US Holocaust Museum, *International Decision-Making,* 1-34, 1-35.
43. Lt-Col EJK O'Brien to Deputy High Commissioner, "Conversation with Brigadier Shaban: Arusha Talks," 16 October 1992, "FOI 0421–17," FCO.
44. O'Brien, "Conversation with Brigadier Shaban," 16 October 1992.
45. Ewing, US Embassy, Dar es Salaam, to Secretary of State, Washington, DC, "Arusha V—Going ahead on nov 23, military integration to top agenda," 20 November 1992, "Rwanda: The Failure of the Arusha Peace Accords," NSA.
46. Leader, US Embassy, Kigali, to Secretary of State, Washington, DC, "Internal Insecurity: An Ongoing Problem," 21 August 1992, NSA.
47. Protocol of Agreement on Power-Sharing within the Framework of a Board-Based Transitional Government between the Government of the Republic of Rwanda and the Rwandese Patriotic Front, Annex IX of the Arusha Accords, United Nations Peacemaker.
48. Protocol of Agreement on Power-Sharing.
49. Johan Swinnen, *Rwanda: Mijn verhaal* (Kalmthout, Belgium: Polis, 2016), 271.
50. US Holocaust Museum, *International Decision-Making,* 1-21-22.
51. Prime Minister Dismas Nsengiyaremye to President Habyarimana, 17 November 1992, "010.RWA[G]," UNHCR Archive.
52. Ewing, US Embassy, Dar es Salaam, to Secretary of State, Washington, DC, "Arusha V—Going ahead on nov 23, military integration to top agenda," 20 November 1992, "Rwanda, the failure of the Arusha Peace Accords," NSA.
53. Prime Minister Dismas Nsengiyaremye to President Habyarimana, 17 November 1992, UNHCR Archive. Note that while this letter has been mentioned by Guichaoua (André Guichaoua, *From War to Genocide: Criminal Politics in Rwanda, 1990–1994,* trans. Don E. Webster [Madison: University of Wisconsin Press, 2015], 77–78), he does not give it the attention and prominence it deserves.
54. Nsengiyaremye, 17 November 1992.
55. Nsengiyaremye, 17 November 1992.
56. Nsengiyaremye, 17 November 1992.
57. Nsengiyaremye, 17 November 1992.
58. Nsengiyaremye, 17 November 1992.
59. Ewing, "Arusha V—Going ahead," 20 November 1992, NSA.
60. Flaten, US Embassy, Kigali, to Secretary of State, Washington, DC, "Integration of the Armies and Demobilisation," 20 November 1992, "Rwanda, the failure of the Arusha Peace Accords," NSA.
61. Hearing held at Quebec 28 and 29 April 2003, Judgement at Ottawa 8 September 2003, *Leon Mugesera et al. v. The Minister of Citizenship and Immigration,* 23–24.

62. US Embassy, Kigali, to Secretary of State, Washington, DC, "Demarches to President and Prime Minister," 14 December 1992, FGT.
63. Ewing, "Arusha V—Going ahead," 20 November 1992.
64. US Holocaust Museum, *International Decision-Making,* 1–26; see also Ambabel Nairobi to Belext Bru, "Arusha—Toestand op maandag 07.12.92," 8 December 1992, "18.955–147, Politique intérieure 1990–1992, Arusha," FPFSA.
65. US Embassy, Kigali, "Demarches to President and Prime Minister," 14 December 1992; and Bagosora to Habyarimana, "Negotiations in Arusha from 22 November 1992 to 9 January 1993," 15 January 1993, "Rwanda, the failure of the Arusha Peace Accords," NSA.
66. Tshitungi, UNHCR Kigali, to UNHCR, "Political Situation Rwanda," 21 January 1993, "010.RWA[G]," UNHCR.
67. Tshitungi, "Political Situation Rwanda," 21 January 1993.
68. AMASASU to His Excellency the President, "Creation of AMASASU," 20 January 1993, "Exhibit Number: P3D1(b), Date Admitted: 78-09-2002," ICTR-98-41-T.
69. AMASASU, "Creation of AMASASU," 20 January 1993.
70. Secretary of State, Washington, DC, to US Embassy, Kigali, "Demarche on President Habyarimana," 27 January 1993, FGT. "The recent episode of ethnically-motivated violence against employees of a USAID-funded CARE project requires an immediate response. Moreover, it seems increasingly obvious that it is symptomatic of a pattern whereby the President is tolerating if not encouraging political violence in order to create a situation where only he can save the country."
71. Prime Minister Dismas Nsengiyaremye to President Habyarimana, "Poursuite des négociations d'Arusha," 24 January 1993, FGT.
72. ADL, *Rapport (Octobre 1992–Octobre 1993),* 160–64.
73. Ambabel Kigali to belext Bru, "Troubles dans le nord-ouest du pays," 27 January 1993, FGT.
74. Cullimore to Deskby FCO, "Unrest in Rwanda," 11 February 1993, "FOI 0676–17," FCO.
75. The N'Sele Ceasefire Agreement between the Government of the Rwandese Republic and the Rwandese Patriotic Front, UN Peacemaker, 14.
76. Philip Roessler and Harry Verhoeven, *Why Comrades Go to War: Liberation Politics and the Outbreak of Africa's Deadliest Conflict* (London: Hurst, 2016), 124.
77. Interview with Caesar Kayizari, 18 October 2018.
78. Interview with Christine Umutoni, 30 May 2019.
79. Correspondence with Christine Umutoni, 23 July 2019.
80. Correspondence with Christine Umutoni, 23 July 2019.
81. There is much documentation of the weapons imported by the FAR; see, for example, Human Rights Watch, *Arming Rwanda: The Arms Trade and Human Rights Abuses in the Rwandan War* (New York: Human Rights Watch, January 1994).
82. Linda Melvern, *A People Betrayed: The Role of the West in Rwanda's Genocide* (London: Zed Books, 2009), 65; Bruce Jones, "The Arusha Peace Process," in *The Path*

of a Genocide: The Rwanda Crisis from Uganda to Zaire, ed. Howard Adelman and Astri Suhrke (New Brunswick, NJ: Transaction Publishers, 1999), 141.

83. Interview with Caesar Kayizari, 18 October 2018.
84. Bernard Lugan, *François Mitterrand: l'Armée française et la Rwanda* (Monaco: Editions du Rocher, 2005), 122.
85. Interview with Caesar Kayizari, 18 October 2018.
86. Author's archive.
87. Interview with Caesar Kayizari, 18 October 2018.
88. Interview with Caesar Kayizari, 18 October 2018.
89. Interview with Caesar Kayizari, 18 October 2018.
90. Or, in military technical lingo, it reduced the RPA's John Boyd's observe-orient-decide-act (OODA) cycle.
91. Bruno Delaye to Président de la République, "Rwanda: Mission à Kigali et Kampala," 15 February 1993, FGT.
92. Delaye, "Rwanda: Mission à Kigali et Kampala," 15 February 1993.
93. Delaye, "Rwanda: Mission à Kigali et Kampala," 15 February 1993.
94. Prunier, *The Rwanda Crisis,* 177.
95. Interview with Caesar Kayizari, 18 October 2018; Stephen Kinzer, *A Thousand Hills: Rwanda's Rebirth and the Man Who Dreamed It* (Hoboken, NJ: John Wiley, 2008), 104–5.
96. Quilès, *Rapport d'information,* 164.
97. Didier Tauzin, *Rwanda: Je demande justice pour la France et ses soldats* (Paris: Editions Jacob-Duvernet, 2011), 67–68.
98. Tauzin, 71.
99. Tauzin, 72.
100. Tauzin, 74; Interview with Caesar Kayizari, 18 October 2018.
101. Tauzin, *Rwanda,* 76.
102. Tauzin, 79.
103. Tauzin, 76.
104. Pierre Joxe to Président François Mitterrand, "Rwanda," 26 February 1993, "The Rwandan Crisis seen Through the Eyes of France," NSA.
105. Interview with Tito Rutaremara, 9 October 2018; Kinzer, *A Thousand Hills,* 106–7.
106. Interview with James Kabarebe, 16 October 2018. I am paraphrasing Kabarebe here, as the interview was not recorded.
107. Interview with Caesar Kayizari, 18 October 2018; Interview with Ndore Rurinda, 5 October 2018.
108. Africa Watch, *Rwanda: Talking Peace and Waging War,* 22–23.
109. FIDH, *Report of International Commission,* 37.
110. Ambabel Kigali to belext Bru, "Intsum 04–07 dec 92," 7 December 1992, "18.955–147, Politique intérieure 1990–1992, Arusha," FPFSA.
111. Prunier, *The Rwanda Crisis,* 175.
112. Note that there is some confusion about the meaning of the abbreviation CLADHO. In ADL, *Rapport (Octobre 1992–Octobre 1993),* the name is given

two explanations. On p. 175 it is rendered as "Comité de liaison des associations rwandaises de défense des droits de l'Homme," while on p. 301 it is the "Collectif des lingues et associations de defence des droits de l'homme au Rwanda."

113. ADL, *Rapport (Octobre 1992–Octobre 1993),* 172; Africa Watch / Human Rights Watch, *Beyond the Rhetoric: Continuing Human Rights Abuses in Rwanda* (Washington, DC: Africa Watch / Human Rights Watch, June 1993).
114. FIDH, *Report of International Commission,* 39.
115. Prunier, *The Rwanda Crisis,* 179–80; James K. Gasana, *Rwanda: Du parti-État à l'État-garnison* (Paris: L'Harmattan, 2002), 188–89.
116. Carl von Clausewitz, *On War,* ed. and trans. Michael Howard and Peter Paret (Princeton, NJ: Princeton University Press, 1976), 87.

CHAPTER 10: "CRY 'HAVOC!'"

1. Gérard Prunier, *The Rwanda Crisis: History of a Genocide* (London: Hurst, 1997), 183, 185–86; André Guichaoua, ed., *Les crises politiques au Burundi et au Rwanda (1993–1994)* (Paris: Karthala, 1995), 629.
2. C. A. Rodriguez to M. N. Bwakira, 1 June 1993, with attached "Note au Président de la République sur le problème de la sécurité," 24 May 1993, signed by Faustin Twagiramungu, Dr. Théoneste Gafaranga, and Justin Mugenzi, "010.RWA[G]," UNHCR.
3. Rodriguez, "Note au Président de la République," 24 May 1993.
4. Rodriguez, "Note au Président de la République," 24 May 1993.
5. Transcript of 28 November 2003, ICTR-98-41-T, 11.
6. Transcript of 28 November 2003, ICTR-98-41-T, 42.
7. Transcript of 1 November 2005, ICTR-99-50-T, 51.
8. Transcript of 26 January 2004, ICTR-99-50-T, 19; Transcript of 20 October 2004, ICTR-99-50-T, 13; Transcripts of 29 January 2004, ICTR-99-50-T, 13–14.
9. "Study of Terrorism in Rwanda since 1990," "Exhibit Number: 3D41, Date Admitted: 19-9-2007," ICTR-99-50-T, 13.
10. FIDH in collaboration with Africa Watch, *Report of the International Commission of Investigation on Human Rights Violations in Rwanda since October 1, 1990 (January 7–21, 1993)* (Paris: FIDH in collaboration with Africa Watch, March 1993), 44.
11. André Sibomana, *Hope for Rwanda* (London: Pluto Press, 1999), 50.
12. Antonia Locatelli was killed on 10 March 1992 and Francois Cardinal on 29 November of the same year. Ambabel Kigali to belext Bru, "Assassinat d'un religieux canadien—menaces contre un religieux belge," 8 December 1992, "18.955–147, Politique intérieure 1990–1992, Arusha," FPFSA.
13. 4 October 2004, ICTR-99-50-T, 40. See also the incident where an MDR politician was beat up by twenty "bandits" in her house: Ambabel Kigali to Belext Bru, "Rwanda—Terrorisme," 9 May 1992, "18.955–148, Dossier General Janvier–Mai 1992," FPFSA. See also Ambabel Kigali to Belext Bru, "Rwanda—Weekoverzicht,"

4–10 May 1992, "18.955-148, Dossier General Janvier–Mai 1992," FPFSA. The MDR was convinced the Interahamwe were behind the many political assassinations; Swinnen to Claes, "Rwanda—MDR standpunt over de onveiligheid van het land," 30 October 1992, "18.955-147, Politique intérieure 1990–1992, Arusha," FPFSA.

14. Guichaoua, *Les crises politiques,* 266; Comité pour le Respect des droits de l'Homme et la démocratie au Rwanda (CRDDR), *Rwanda: Rapport de deux missions effectuées par Eric Gillet & André Jadoul, avocats au barreau de Bruxelles au Rwanda du 9 au 17 janvier et du 2 au 5 février 1992* (Brussels: CRDDR, May 1992), 21–23.
15. Johan Swinnen, *Rwanda: Mijn verhaal* (Kalmthout, Belgium: Polis, 2016), 164–65; CRDDR, *Rwanda: Rapport de deux missions,* 21–22; "Media Situation in Rwanda," 10 January 1992, "Exhibit: DNS7, Date Admitted: 22-11-2002," ICTR-98-41-T, 13.
16. Swinnen, *Rwanda: Mijn verhaal,* 164.
17. Prunier, *The Rwanda Crisis,* 203.
18. "Study of Terrorism in Rwanda since 1990," ICTR-99-50-T.
19. Correspondence with French officer, 1 October 2016.
20. Justus Muhanguzi Kampe, *Eyes of a Journalist* (Kampala: Worlds of Inspiration, 2016), 158–61.
21. Swinnen to Willy Claes, "Rwanda—Onlusten Bugesera," 27 March 1992, FGT; Swinnen, *Rwanda: Mijn verhaal,* 181.
22. Ambabel Kigali to Belext Bru, "Terrorisme en Banditisme in Rwanda," 7 March 1992, "18.955-147, Politique intérieure 1990–1992, Arusha," FPFSA.
23. MAM to Ministère de Coopération et Développement, Paris "Actes de terrorisme perpétrés au Rwanda depuis décembre 1991," 31 May 1992, FGT, 2.
24. From various documents the LOT numbers assigned to the mines were as follows: PRB-M3 Anti-Tank Mines: Lot LAR 1.7 (1960?), Lot LAR 1.9, BMP 1.11; PRB-M409 Anti-Personnel Mine: Lot BMP 1.20; TM-57 Anti-Tank Mine: Lot 55-6-71; MUV-2 Traction Igniter: Lot 156 (Engraved on mine MBY-2, 583-); Other batches, mines/igniter unknown: LOT-RAR-1-9 ATK, CR-6-8702, MYB-25-83-156-69.
25. Colonel P-C Rwagafilita to le Ministre de la Défense Nationale, "Lutte contre le terrorisme," 8 May 1992, FGT.
26. Transcript of Monday, 5 December 2004, witness Pie Betabura, ICTR-99-50-T, 14; Human Rights Watch, *Leave None to Tell the Story: Genocide in Rwanda,* written by Alison Des Forges (New York, March 1999), 90.
27. Correspondence with French officer, 15 September 2016.
28. Correspondence with French officer, 11 September 2016; Swinnen to Eyskens, "Toenemende onveiligheid in Rwanda," 3 March 1992, "18.955-147, Politique intérieure 1990–1992, Arusha," FPFSA.
29. "Détachement NOROIT du 2e RIMa, Journal des Marches et Opérations 05 mars 1992–13 juillet 1992."

30. "Détachement NOROIT du 2e RIMa, Journal des Marches et Opérations 05 mars 1992–13 juillet 1992."
31. "Détachement NOROIT du 2e RIMa, Journal des Marches et Opérations 05 mars 1992–13 juillet 1992."
32. "Détachement NOROIT du 2e RIMa, Journal des Marches et Opérations 05 mars 1992–13 juillet 1992." There are other cases as well; see, for example, Swinnen, *Rwanda: Mijn verhaal,* 161.
33. "Détachement NOROIT du 2e RIMa, JMO 5 mars–13 juillet 1992," GR 2000Z 114 455, SHD.
34. Correspondence with French officer, 6 November 2016.
35. Transcript of Friday, 25 January 2008. ICTR-00-56-T, 21–22.
36. "Détachement NOROIT du 2e RIMa, JMO 5 mars–13 juillet 1992."
37. "Détachement NOROIT du 2e RIMa, JMO 5 mars–13 juillet 1992."
38. CRDDR, *Rwanda: Rapport de deux missions,* 33.
39. FIDH, *Report of International Commission,* 33; a similar story can also be found in Ambabel Kigali to Belext Bru, "Assassinat d'un religieux canadien / menaces contre un religieux belge," 8 December 1992, "18.955–147, Politique intérieure 1990–1992, Arusha," FPFSA.
40. Prunier, *The Rwanda Crisis,* 174.
41. "Study of Terrorism in Rwanda since 1990," ICTR-99-50-T, 5.
42. "S-1062-0004-0004-00001," UNAMIR, 35/152.
43. "First Meeting with the Gendarmerie," 16 November 1993, "S-1062-0008-0002-00001," UNAMIR, 4, 7–8/22; Dallaire would later go on to call Ndindiliyimana "by far the most helpful, candid and open" officer he worked with on the side of the Rwandan government. Roméo Dallaire, *Shake Hands with the Devil* (London: Arrow Books, 2004), 70.
44. "Special Report From: PMT Nyarugenge To: PC Kigali," 20 February 1994, "S-1060-0009-0002-00001," UNAMIR, 33/38.
45. PMT Kicukiro to CPMT Kigali, "Brief Presentation of Kicukiro Territorial's Gendarmerie Company," date unknown, "S-1060-0009-0002-00001," UNAMIR, 18/38.
46. Kicukiro, "Brief Presentation," date unknown.
47. Transcript of Thursday, 17 January 2008, ICTR-00-56-T, 15–16.
48. Tom Franklin, "Confidential Note to the File: Visit to the FPR Displaced Camp, Gishambashayo—Commune of Cyumba and Kivuye," 25 August 1993, "619.8.RWA (B) Special Protection problems Rwanda: Displaced Persons," UNHCR.
49. Randolph Kent, Coordinator LASU, DHA, to Mr. Tshitungi, "Rough draft of Rwanda Appeal," 24 March 1993, "619.8.RWA (A)," UNHCR, 3–4.
50. "ICRC Warns Against Major Catastrophe, Launches Urgent Appeal," 13 April 1993, "619.8.RWA (A)," UNHCR.
51. James Gasana to Prime Minister, "Weekly report on the Country's External Security," 26 September 1992, "Exhibit Number: 1D233(E), Date Admitted: 31-5-2007," ICTR-99-50-T.

52. James K. Gasana, *Rwanda: Du parti-État à l'État-garnison* (Paris: L'Harmattan, 2002), 101.
53. For examples of their violence, see Human Rights Watch, *Leave None,* 46–47, 83; and Gasana, "Weekly report," 26 September 1992.
54. US Holocaust Museum and The Hague Institute for Global Justice, *International Decision-Making in the Age of Genocide: Rwanda 1990–1994; Annotated Transcript* (The Hague: US Holocaust Museum and The Hague Institute for Global Justice, 1–3 June 2014), 1–59.
55. "Study of Terrorism in Rwanda since 1990," ICTR-99-50-T, 9.
56. Ambabel Kigali to Belext Bru, "Synthèse Hebdomadaire (16–29 novembre 1992)," 7 December 1992, "18.955-147, Politique intérieure 1990–1992, Arusha," FPFSA.
57. Ambabel Kigali, "Synthèse Hebdomadaire," 7 December 1992.
58. "Study of Terrorism in Rwanda since 1990," ICTR-99-50-T, 9.
59. Ambabel Kigali, "Synthèse Hebdomadaire," 7 December 1992.
60. Ambabel Kigali to Belext Bru, "Terrorisme en Banditisme in Rwanda," 7 March 1992, "18.955-148, Dossier General Janvier–Mai 1992," FPFSA.
61. FIDH, *Report of International Commission,* 45.
62. "Study of Terrorism in Rwanda since 1990," ICTR-99-50-T, 12.
63. "Study of Terrorism in Rwanda since 1990," ICTR-99-50-T, 12, 14; see also FIDH, *Report of International Commission,* 44.
64. "Study of Terrorism in Rwanda since 1990," ICTR-99-50-T, 9.
65. See, for example, Lt. Col. G. B. Molyneux-Carter to High Commissioner, Kampala, "DA Report on Visit to Rwanda 16–20 Feb 91," no date but received in registry 5 June 1991, "JWW 014/1 (Part B), 'Rwanda: Internal Political Situation,'" FCO.
66. Cussac to —, "Armements des Populations civiles," 22 January 1992, FGT.
67. Colonel P-C Rwagafilita to le Ministre de la Défense Nationale, "Lutte contre le terrorisme," 8 May 1992, FGT.
68. Flaten, US Embassy Kigali, to Secretary of State, "The Military and the Political Process," 11 June 1993, "Rwanda, the failure of the Arusha Peace Accords," NSA. The French noted the same; see Cussac to Armées Paris, "Situation de la Gendarmerie Rwandaise," 20 July 1992, FGT.
69. Dallaire, *Shake Hands,* 166.
70. "Rwanda-The *Interahamwe* Militia," "Date Admitted: 18-2-1997," *Prosecutor v. Akayesu* ICTR-96-4, 4.
71. de Vos, US Embassy, Dar Es Salaam, to Secretary of State, Washington, DC, "Background to Rwanda talks concerning military force size," 26 March 1993, "Rwanda, the failure of the Arusha Peace Accords," NSA.
72. de Vos, "Background to Rwanda talks," 26 March 1993.
73. Secretary of State, Washington, DC, to US Embassy, Dar Es Salaam, "Rwanda Negotiations Weekend Update," 6 April 1993, FGT.
74. Bruce D. Jones, *Peacemaking in Rwanda: The Dynamics of Failure* (Boulder, CO: Lynne Rienner, 2001), 87.

75. Eagleburger, Secretary of State, Washington, DC, to US Embassy, Kigali, "Rwandan Minister of Defense on Integration of Forces," 16 November 1992, "Rwanda, the failure of the Arusha Peace Accords," NSA.
76. Flaten, US Embassy Kigali, to Secretary of State, Washington, DC, "Integration of the Armies and Demobilization," 20 November 1992, "Rwanda, the failure of the Arusha Peace Accords," NSA.
77. Ewing, US Embassy, Dar es Salaam, to Secretary of State, Washington, DC, "Arusha V—Going ahead on nov 23, military integration to top agenda," 20 November 1992, "Rwanda, the failure of the Arusha Peace Accords," NSA.
78. Colonel Bagosora to Rwandan Minister of Foreign Affairs, "Negotiation Strategy," 1 June 1993, "Rwanda, the failure of the Arusha Peace Accords," NSA; Browning, US Embassy Dar es Salaam to Secretary of State, Washington, DC, "Notes from Arusha Peace Talks on Rwanda," 2 June 1993, FGT.
79. Christopher, US Embassy Dar es Salaam, to Secretary of State, Washington, DC, "Rwanda: atmosphere at Arusha talks deteriorates markedly," 4 June 1993, FGT.
80. Christopher, "Rwanda: atmosphere at Arusha talks," 4 June 1993.
81. Christopher, "Rwanda: atmosphere at Arusha talks," 4 June 1993.
82. Christopher, "Rwanda: atmosphere at Arusha talks," 4 June 1993.
83. Browning, US Embassy, Dar es Salaam, to Secretary of State, Washington, DC, "Arusha peace Talks: Tanzanian Presses both sides toward conclusion," 7 June 1993, FGT; Browning, US Embassy, Dar es Salaam, to Secretary of State, Washington, DC, "Arusha Peace Talks: parties conclude protocol on refugee repatriation and reintegration of displaced," 8 June 1993, FGT.
84. de Vos, US Embassy, Dar es Salaam, to Secretary of State, Washington, DC, "Background to Rwanda talks concerning military force size," 26 March 1993, "Rwanda, the failure of the Arusha Peace Accords," NSA.
85. Hurd, FCO to Immediate UKMIS New York, "Rwanda Peace Talks," 29 June 1993, "FOI 0676-17," FCO.
86. Prime Minister Dismas Nsengiyaremye to President Habyarimana, 6 July 1993, "FOI 0676-17," FCO.
87. Gasana, *Rwanda: Du parti-État,* 210. Note that the whole episode surrounding Dismas's ouster is particularly confused in the current scholarship.
88. Gasana, Annexes "Resignation of James Gasana," France Génocide Tutsi Database, accessed 9 January 2025, https://francegenocidetutsi.org/GasanaDemission20juillet1993.pdf.
89. Flaten, US Embassy, Kigali, to Secretary of State, Washington, DC, "The MDR vs. the MDR," 26 July 1993, Department of State FOI.
90. André Guichaoua, *From War to Genocide: Criminal Politics in Rwanda, 1990–1994,* trans. Don E. Webster (Madison: University of Wisconsin Press, 2015), 88–89.
91. Guichaoua, 88–89.
92. Guichaoua, 93; Gasana, *Rwanda: Du parti-État,* 213.
93. Guichaoua, 88.
94. Mahmood Mamdani, *When Victims Become Killers: Colonialism, Nativism, and Genocide in Rwanda* (Princeton, NJ: Princeton University Press, 2002), 210–15.

95. Alan J. Kuperman, "Provoking Genocide: A Revised History of the Rwandan Patriotic Front," *Journal of Genocide Research* 6, no. 1 (2004): 75.
96. Barrie Collins, "The Rwandan War 1990–1994: Interrogating the Dominant Narrative" (PhD diss., SOAS, 2009), 141.
97. Interview with Tito Rutaremara, 9 October 2018.
98. "United Nations Assistance Mission for Rwanda, UNAMIR: Guidelines for Governments Contributing Military Personnel to UNAMIR," 26 October 1993, FGT, 5.
99. Dallaire, *Shake Hands,* 58.
100. Dallaire, 81.
101. US Holocaust Museum, *International Decision-Making,* 1–36.
102. US Holocaust Museum, 1–107.
103. Dallaire, *Shake Hands,* 82.
104. Burundi has its own long and nuanced history, and it would be too simple to explain the strife the country has known since the 1960s as a simple "Hutu" versus "Tutsi" dynamic—as in Rwanda, things are more complicated than that. Not to mention that important regional issues are also at play in Burundi. For more information beyond the rough brushstrokes provided here, see René Lemarchand, *Rwanda and Burundi* (New York: Praeger, 1970); Jean-Pierre Chrétien and Jean-Francois Dupaquier, *Burundi 1972: Au bord des génocides* (Paris: Karthala, 2007).
105. Aidan Russel, "Rebel and Rule in Burundi in 1972," *International Journal of African Historical Studies* 48, no. 1 (2015): 73–97.
106. René Lemarchand, *Forgotten Genocides: Oblivion, Denial, and Memory* (Philadelphia: University of Pennsylvania Press, 2011), 39.
107. Lemarchand, 40.
108. René Lemarchand, *The Dynamics of Violence in Central Africa* (Philadelphia: University of Pennsylvania Press, 2009), 132.
109. The numbers are contested; I take my numbers from Lemarchand, *Forgotten Genocides* (chapter 2), and Lemarchand, *The Dynamics of Violence* (chapter 9).
110. Filip Reyntjens, "The Proof of the Pudding Is in the Eating: The June 1993 Elections in Burundi," *Journal of Modern African Studies* 31, no. 4 (1993): 564.
111. UN Security Council, *International Commission of Inquiry Concerning the Assassination of the President of Burundi: Final Report,* S/1996/682 (23 July 1996) United Nations, 25.
112. UN Security Council, 34–38.
113. UN Security Council, 30–32.
114. UN Security Council, 29.
115. Vincent Duclert, *La France, le Rwanda et le génocide des Tutsi (1990–1994)—Rapport remis au Président de la République le 26 mars 2021* (Paris: Armand Colin, 2021), 300; Quesnot and Delaye to President de la Republique, "Burundi," 25 October 1993, FGT.
116. Catherine Watson wrote in a prescient article that "an army coup would have set the country on fire. Frodebu enjoys rapturous support. If Ndadaye or his team were harmed, every Tutsi family in Burundi would be in danger." Catherine

Watson, "Burundi: Freed from Fear," *Africa Report* 38, no. 5 (1993): 58–61, 60; Filip Reyntjens echoed this warning: "Proof of the Pudding," 578: "Given that Burundi has a history of political assassinations, it is hardly necessary to point out that any serious attempt against Ndadaye's life would result in a massive violence throughout the country. There can be little doubt that, at least in the near future, the Damocles sword of mutinies, attempted coups, or more isolated forms of violence, hangs over Burundi's democratic experience."

117. UN Security Council, *International Commission,* 71.
118. UN Security Council, 71.
119. Tom Bundervoet, "Livestock, Land, and Political Power: The 1993 Killings in Burundi," *Journal of Peace Research* 46, no. 3 (May 2009): 357; Prunier, *The Rwanda Crisis,* 199.
120. Dallaire to Baril, "Arrival of UNAMIR Force Commander," 25 October 1993, FGT.
121. Reyntjens, "Proof of the Pudding," 583; many other experts agree on the importance of this moment. See Prunier, *The Rwanda Crisis,* 199–203 and transcripts of Tuesday 31 May 2005, ICTR-99-50-T, 46.
122. Transcript of 1 December 2005, ICTR-90-55-T, 30–31; see also the testimony of Prosper Higiro Transcript of 26 January 2004, ICTR-99-50-T, 33.
123. Human Rights Watch, *Leave None,* 103.
124. Human Rights Watch, 103; Transcript of 1 June 2005, ICTR-99-50-T, 61.
125. *Rapport Duclert,* 301. "In any case, the Arusha Accords are in serious danger. Hutu-Tutsi tensions in Rwanda will worsen. A speed race is underway between now and the arrival of the peacekeepers in Kigali."
126. Dallaire to Annan UNHQ New York, "UNAMIR Situation Report no. 2," 28 October 1993, FGT.
127. Dallaire to Annan UNHQ New York, "weekly sitrep no. 4," 9 November 1993, FGT.
128. Dallaire, *Shake Hands,* 87.
129. Dallaire to Annan UNHQ New York, "weekly sitrep no. 5," 16 November 1993, FGT.
130. Dallaire to Annan UNHQ New York, "weekly sitrep no. 5," 23 November 1993, FGT.
131. Dallaire, "weekly sitrep no. 5," 23 November 1993.
132. Marlaud to —, "Retrait du Détachement Noroit," 14 December 1993. Paul Quilès, *Rapport d'information par la mission d'information de la commission de la défense nationale et des forces armées et de la commission des affaires étrangères, sur les opérations militaires menées par la France, d'autres pays et l'ONU au Rwanda entre 1990 et 1994* (Assemblée nationale, Paris, 15 December 1998), Annexes, 175.
133. Dallaire, *Shake Hands,* 130.
134. Dallaire, 131.
135. Interview with former RPF member.
136. Dallaire, *Shake Hands,* 138–39.

137. Dallaire, 141.
138. Transcript of 29 January 2004, ICTR-99-50-T, 52; Transcript of 10 June 2004, ICTR-99-50-T, 24–25.
139. Dallaire, *Shake Hands,* 166.
140. Dallaire, 178.
141. Dallaire, 186–87.
142. Dallaire, 187.
143. Dallaire, 188.
144. Transcript of 27 January 2004, ICTR-99-50-T, 4.
145. Dallaire, *Shake Hands,* 189.
146. Dallaire, 210–12; Rawson, US Embassy Kigali, to Secretary of State, Washington, DC, "DAS Bushnell meets Habyarimana and RPF," 25 March 1994, FGT; US Embassy, Kigali, to Secretary of State, Washington, DC, "CDR Issue proves Intractable," 28 March 1994, FGT.
147. Timothy Longman, *Memory and Justice in Post-Genocide Rwanda* (Cambridge: Cambridge University Press, 2017), 19.

CHAPTER 11: THE CAMPAIGN AGAINST GENOCIDE, APRIL–JULY 1994

1. Roméo Dallaire, *Shake Hands with the Devil* (London: Arrow Books, 2004), 222–26.
2. Jean-Louis Bruguière, *Délivrance de mandats d'arrêt internationaux,* Tribunal de Grande Instance de Paris—Cabinet de Jean-Louis Bruguière, Premier Vice-Président, Parquet: 97.295.2303/0 Cabinet: 1341, 17 November 2006; Republic of Rwanda, independent committee of experts charged with investigation into the crash on 06/04/1994 of Falcon 50 Aeroplane, registration number 9XR-NN, *Report of the Investigation into the Causes and Circumstances of and Responsibility for the Attack of 06/04/1994 against the Falcon 50 Rwandan Presidential Aeroplane, Registration Number 9XR-NN,* Kigali, 20 April 2009; Filip Reyntjens, "A Fake Enquiry on a Major Event: Analysis of the Mutsinzi Report on the 6th April 1994 Attack on the Rwandan President's Aeroplane," Institute of Development Policy and Management Working Paper, University of Antwerp (July 2010); Marc Trévidic and Nathalie Poux, *Rapport d'expertise: Destruction en vol du Falcon 50 Kigali (Rwanda),* Cour d'Appel de Paris Tribunal de Grande Instance de Paris (5 January 2012).
3. Gérard Prunier, *The Rwanda Crisis: History of a Genocide* (London: Hurst, 1997), 213–15.
4. Prunier, 217–18.
5. Trévidic and Poux, *Rapport d'expertise,* 239.
6. Transcript of 27 November 2003, Examination-in-Chief by Ms. Mulvaney of Annonciate Kavaruganda, ICTR-98-41-T, 18. The story of the Kavaruganda family that follows is based on ICTR transcripts. In this particular case there were confusing approximations and tense discrepancies in the court translation from

the original French to English. As such, the translations have been improved, especially for readability.

7. ICTR-98-41-T, 19.
8. ICTR-98-41-T, 20; Dallaire, *Shake Hands,* 224.
9. ICTR-98-41-T, 21.
10. ICTR-98-41-T, 22.
11. ICTR-98-41-T, 32.
12. ICTR-98-41-T, 32.
13. ICTR-98-41-T, 24.
14. ICTR-98-41-T, 27.
15. ICTR-98-41-T, 32.
16. ICTR-98-41-T, 33–35.
17. Dallaire, *Shake Hands,* 232.
18. Human Rights Watch, *Leave None to Tell the Story: Genocide in Rwanda,* written by Alison Des Forges (New York, March 1999), 156.
19. This section is based on discussion with the staff of the Campaign Against Genocide Museum in the CND during October 2017; and "Compte rendu du colonel Cussac et lieutenant-colonel Maurin, Paris, 19 avril 1994," Annexes 8.2, Paul Quilès, *Rapport d'information par la mission d'information de la commission de la défense nationale et des forces armées et de la commission des affaires étrangères, sur les opérations militaires menées par la France, d'autres pays et l'ONU au Rwanda entre 1990 et 1994* (Assemblée nationale, Paris, 15 December 1998), 350.
20. Johan Swinnen, *Rwanda: Mijn verhaal* (Kalmthout, Belgium: Polis, 2016), 528–34; Alan J. Kuperman, "Provoking Genocide: A Revised History of the Rwandan Patriotic Front," *Journal of Genocide Research* 6, no. 1 (2004): 79.
21. This gives a theoretical strength of 8,000–16,000. I see the 16,000 number as the absolute maximum theoretically possible. US intelligence estimated the RPA had about 15,000 combat troops. Defense Intelligence Report, Defense Intelligence Agency, "Rwanda: The Rwandan Patriotic Front's Offensive," 9 May 1994, "The US and the Genocide in Rwanda, 1994," NSA.
22. "Rwanda: The Rwandan Patriotic Front's Offensive," 9 May 1994; André Guichaoua, ed., *Les crises politiques au Burundi et au Rwanda (1993–1994): Analyses, faits et documents* (Paris: Karthala, 1995), 767–68. Guichaoua's estimate is slightly different: FAR 35,000 (including gendarmes) in 1994. For the RPF in 1994 he quotes "over 25,000," which seems unlikely, especially as the estimate is based on a comment by vice president of the RPF Patrick Mazimhaka made during the Campaign Against Genocide—no organization would give away its true strength in the middle of a crucial campaign. The estimate he gives for April 1993 of 12,000 seems much more realistic.
23. Henry Kwami Anyidoho, *Guns over Kigali* (Accra: Woeli Publishing Services, 1997), 36.
24. Correspondence with former RPF member, 27 August 2017.
25. Edwin Musoni, "How RPA Deployed 600 Soldiers in the Heart of Kigali against All Odds," *New Times,* 3 July 2014.

26. Musoni.
27. Logan Ndahiro, "The Rpa's Quest to Stop Genocide and Subsequent Liberation of Rwanda," *New Times,* 5 July 2017.
28. Ndahiro.
29. Philippe Mahoux and Guy Verhofstadt, *Commission d'enquête parlementaire concernant les événements du Rwanda* (Sénat de Belgique, 6 December 1997), 516–18.
30. Quilès, *Rapport d'information,* 270–72.
31. Swinnen, *Rwanda: Mijn verhaal,* 535–46.
32. Mahoux and Verhofstadt, *Commission d'enquête,* 518–21.
33. Anyidoho, *Guns over Kigali,* 32.
34. Ndahiro, "Rpa's Quest to Stop Genocide."
35. Interview with James Kabarebe, 16 October 2018.
36. Interview with Caesar Kayizari, 23 October 2018.
37. Interview with Caesar Kayizari, 23 October 2018.
38. "Rwanda: The Rwandan Patriotic Front's Offensive," 9 May 1994, "The US and the Genocide in Rwanda, 1994," NSA.
39. Human Rights Watch, *Leave None,* 157–58.
40. Jason Stearns, *Dancing in the Glory of Monsters* (New York: Public Affairs, 2012), 19.
41. Stearns, 20.
42. Ndahiro, "Rpa's Quest to Stop Genocide."
43. Transcript of 20 January 2004, Examination-in-Chief of Brent Beardsley by Mr. White, ICTR-98-41-T, 9–14.
44. Interview with Caesar Kayizari, 23 October 2018.
45. Interview with James Kabarebe, 16 October 2018.
46. Dallaire, *Shake Hands,* 421.
47. Colonel Mustafizur Rahman, "Investigation Report of the Nyamirambo Killings," 17 June 1994, FGT.
48. UNAMIR Sitrep Dallaire to Annan UN, "Daily sitrep," 5 June 1994, FGT.
49. UNAMIR Sitrep Dallaire to Annan UN, "Daily sitrep," 10 June 1994, FGT.
50. UNAMIR Sitrep Dallaire to Annan UN, "Daily sitrep," 13 June 1994, FGT.
51. UNAMIR Sitrep Dallaire to Annan UN, "Daily sitrep," 22 June 1994, FGT; UNAMIR to Annan UN, "Weekly Sitrep," 28 June 1994, FGT.
52. Interview with Caesar Kayizari, 23 October 2018.
53. The best available accounts of Opération Turquoise, which I do not propose to cover in detail here, are to be found in Prunier, *The Rwanda Crisis,* and Daniela Kroslak, *The Role of France in the Rwandan Genocide* (London: Hurst, 2007).
54. Prunier, *The Rwanda Crisis,* 281.
55. Dallaire, *Shake Hands,* 342.
56. Prunier, *The Rwanda Crisis,* 289.
57. Prunier, 289–90.
58. Linda Melvern, *A People Betrayed: The Role of the West in Rwanda's Genocide* (London: Zed Books, 2009), 237; Prunier, *The Rwanda Crisis,* 289, 293; Dallaire, *Shake Hands,* 449; Kroslak, *The Role of France,* 228–31.

59. UNHCR to Palais des Nations, "Summary of UNHCR Presentation Before Commission of Experts, 10 October 1994: Prospect for Early Repatriation of Rwandan Refugees Currently in Burundi, Tanzania and Zaire," 11 October 1994. Also known as the Gersony Report, 12.
60. A good example is the case of Abdul Ruzibiza. Claudine Vidal, "Les contradictions d'un lieutenant rwandais: Abdul Ruzibiza, témoin, acteur, faux-témoin," in *L'Afrique des Grands Lacs, annuaire 2008–2009,* ed. S. Marysse, F. Reyntjens, and S. Vandeginste (Paris: L'Harmattan, 2009), 43–55.
61. Robert Kaplan, *The Good American: The Epic Life of Bob Gersony, The U.S. Government's Greatest Humanitarian* (New York: Random House, 2021).
62. Kaplan, 274–85, 275.
63. Gersony Report.
64. Kaplan, *The Good American,* 276.
65. Kaplan, 276.
66. Kaplan, 280.
67. Gersony Report.
68. Gersony Report.
69. Human Rights Watch, *Leave None,* 555; The numbers mentioned by Gersony vary slightly. See also Kaplan, *The Good American,* 263–301, 283, where mention is made of "a minimum of 30,000"; Prunier puts the total killed by RPA troops at somewhere between 10,000 and 100,000. *The Rwanda Crisis,* 360.
70. Gersony Report.
71. Kaplan, *The Good American,* 284.
72. Kaplan, 294.
73. Kaplan, 285.
74. Human Rights Watch, *Leave None,* 543.
75. Human Rights Watch, 548.
76. Human Rights Watch, 558.
77. Human Rights Watch, 550.
78. Human Rights Watch, 558; see also André Sibomana, *Hope for Rwanda* (London: Pluto Press, 1999), 143.
79. Quoted in Philip Roessler and Harry Verhoeven, *Why Comrades Go to War: Liberation Politics and the Outbreak of Africa's Deadliest Conflict* (London: Hurst, 2016), 131–32.
80. Interview with Caesar Kayizari, 23 October 2018; see also Prunier, *The Rwanda Crisis,* 301.
81. Due to its still controversial nature, the sources of several quotes in this section are withheld.
82. Roessler and Verhoeven, *Why Comrades Go to War,* 131.
83. Interview with a high-ranking official in the Rwandan Ministry of Defense.
84. Human Rights Watch, *Leave None,* 557.
85. Dallaire, *Shake Hands,* 466.

CONCLUSION

1. Mahmood Mamdani, *When Victims Become Killers: Colonialism, Nativism, and Genocide in Rwanda* (Princeton, NJ: Princeton University Press, 2002), xiv.
2. Alan J. Kuperman, "Provoking Genocide: A Revised History of the Rwandan Patriotic Front," *Journal of Genocide Research* 6, no. 1 (2004): 82.
3. Kuperman, 82.
4. Kuperman seems to generally believe that giving dictators what they want is a way to avoid violence. In 2022 he wrote on Ukraine that "Putin's pre-war request of Zelensky is largely forgotten but was relatively modest—to implement an agreement that Ukraine had signed in 2015 to guarantee political autonomy to two enclaves that Russian forces had helped establish. . . . Zelensky might have averted war by agreeing to implement that deal signed by his predecessor. But he refused. . . . Putin responded on Feb. 21 by recognizing the two enclaves as independent countries and deploying troops there for 'peacekeeping.' Further aggression still might have been averted if Zelensky had renounced his desire for NATO weapons and membership, as Moscow demanded, but instead he amplified such calls, so Russian forces invaded Ukraine proper on Feb. 24, aiming to overthrow its government." "Why Military Aid to Ukraine Is Backfiring," *New York Daily News,* 25 March 2022.
5. Judi Rever, *In Praise of Blood* (Toronto: Random House Canada, 2018), 61.
6. International Criminal Tribunal for Rwanda, Lejmi Alo to Hassan Jallow, 1 October 2003.
7. Rever's sourcing is often unclear. The section in which she suggests that RPF technicians killed Tutsi, quoted above (Rever, *In Praise of Blood,* 61), has no footnote. However, throughout the paragraph before she mentions the "SIU Summary." The Summary notes that "during the war, the 'technicians' appeared at the side of the Interhamwe [*sic*] on barriers. . . . Their role was to take part in the killings and to incite the interhamwe [*sic*] to do more massacres." It notes pages 052, 053, and 065 of the main investigation as proof on this assertion. However, in the documents Rever released to the public, pages 49–66 are missing; DocumentCloud, accessed 17 March 2024, https://www.documentcloud.org/app?q=user%3Abenedict-moran-23693%20project%3Arwanda-47032%20.
8. Kuperman, "Provoking Genocide," 78.
9. Helen Epstein, *Another Fine Mess: America, Uganda and the War on Terror* (New York: Columbia Global Reports, 2017), 112–13; Epstein's source is Roméo Dallaire, *Shake Hands with the Devil* (London: Arrow Books, 2004). In the paragraph she cites, Dallaire is indeed unclear, although he does mention on page 292 that the RPA arrived north of Kigali. However, Prunier is quite clear that the RPF arrived in Kigali on 11 April 1994. Gérard Prunier, *The Rwanda Crisis: History of a Genocide* (London: Hurst, 1997), 268. Des Forges also notes the RPA arrived on 11 April; see Human Rights Watch, *Leave None to Tell the Story: Genocide in Rwanda,* written by Alison Des Forges (New York, March 1999), 538.

10. Susan Thomson, *Rwanda: From Genocide to Precarious Peace* (New Haven, CT: Yale University Press, 2018), 23–24.
11. Dallaire, *Shake Hands,* 421.
12. Dallaire, 24.
13. Human Rights Watch, *Leave None,* 535. The similarity between Thomson's and Des Forges's wording makes me suspect Thomson is well aware of this passage.
14. Rever, *In Praise of Blood,* 232.
15. Philip Verwimp, "Testing the Double-Genocide Thesis for Central and Southern Rwanda," *Journal of Conflict Resolution* 47, no. 4 (2003): 423–42, 441; see also Scott Straus, "The Limits of a Genocide Lens: Violence against Rwandans in the 1990s," *Journal of Genocide Research* 21, no. 4 (2019): 5.
16. Robert Kaplan, *The Good American: The Epic Life of Bob Gersony, the U.S. Government's Greatest Humanitarian* (New York: Random House, 2021), 284. "I have always made the distinction between the mass murder of tens of thousands of people and the genocide of hundreds of thousands."
17. Rever, *In Praise of Blood,* introduction.
18. Straus, "Limits of a Genocide Lens," 13.
19. Susan Thomson, *Whispering Truth to Power: Everyday Resistance to Reconciliation in Postgenocide Rwanda* (Madison: University of Wisconsin Press, 2013), xiii.

Bibliography

ARCHIVAL AND DIGITAL COLLECTIONS

Archives of the (Belgian) Federal Public Service of Foreign Affairs. Brussels. (FPFSA)
18.888-I-1 Télégrammes 'Sortie' Kigali 1983–1984, 18.888-I-1 Télégrammes 'Sortie' Kigali 1985–1986, 18.888-I-3 Télégrammes 'Entrée' Kigali 1974–1988, 18.888-I-3 Télégrammes 'Entrée' Kigali 1989–1991, 18.888-II Constitution Rwanda, 18.888-II MRND-RPF 1988–1989, 18.888-III-1 Onlusten in Rwanda 1972–1973, 18.888-III-1 Onlusten in Rwanda Décembre 1990–Mars 1991, 18.888-III-1 Onlusten in Rwanda Oktober-November 1990, 18.955–144 (Politique intérieure 1990–1992), 18.955–145 (Politique intérieure 1990–1992), 18.955–146 (Politique intérieure 1990–1992), 18.955–147 (Arusha—Politique intérieure 1990–1992), 18.955–148 (Terrorisme et banditisme—incidents ethniques de Bugesera), 18.955–149 (Conference de la Table Ronde—Arusha—Troubles Ethniques)

British Diplomatic Oral History Programme. https://bdohp.chu.cam.ac.uk/.

CIA Library. https://www.cia.gov/library/readingroom/.

Food and Agricultural Organisation of the United Nations. http://www.fao.org/faostat/. (FAO)

France Génocide Tutsi. http://francegenocidetutsi.org/. (FGT)

Government of the United Kingdom. FOI release: Rwanda 1992 to 1993. https://www.gov.uk/government/publications/foi-release-rwanda-1992-to-1993. (FCO)

International Criminal Tribunal for Rwanda. The Hague.
The Prosecutor of the Tribunal v. Augustin Ndindiliyimana, François-Xavier Nzuwonemeye, Innocent Sagahutu, Augustin Bizimungu, ICTR-00-56-T.
The Prosecutor of the Tribunal v. Casimir Bizimungu, Justin Mugenzi, Jérôme-Clément Bicamumpaka, ICTR-99-50-T.
The Prosecutor of the Tribunal v. Theoneste Bagosora, Gratien Kabaligi, Aloys Ntabakuze, Anatole Nsengiyumva, ICTR-98-41-T.
The Prosecutor v. Protais Zigiranyirazo. ICTR-01-73-T.

The Linda Melvern Rwanda Genocide Archive. The Hugh Owens Library, University of Wales, Cardiff.
File 1990/Planning

National Archive of Rwanda. Kigali.
MIN 237, MIN 238, PRES 68, PRES 80

National Archives of the Netherlands. The Hague. (NL-NA)
Archiefbloknr: Z162 Inv.nr.: 1, 2, 3, 4, 20, 23, 24, 25
National Archives of the United Kingdom. Kew, England. (NAUK)
FCO 25/262, FO 371/177017, FO 371/177022, FO 371/181948
National Security Archive. https://nsarchive.gwu.edu/. (NSA)
Office of the UN High Commissioner on Refugees Archive. Geneva. (UNHCR)
321.HUMRIGHTS
001.HC.UGA, 001.UGA, 010.UGA Vol. 1, 010.UGA Vol. 2, 010.UGA Vol. 3, 013.UGA, 022.UGA, 025.UGA, 027.UGA, 100.RWA.UGA, 100.UGA.RWA, 110.3.UGA, 110.4.UGA, 110.5.UGA, 118.UGA, 120.UGA, 130.UGA, 205.1.UGA, 254.UGA, 321.UGA, 321.UNDP.UGA, 400.UGA, 400.ICRC.UGA, 410.LRCS.UGA, 410.MSF.UGA, 410.OXFAM.GBR.UGA, 507.UGA, 521.UGA, 513.UGA, 531.UGA, 542.UGA, 600.UGA, 607.UGA, 610.RWA.UGA, 610.UGA.RWA, 620.UGA, 641.UGA, 656.UGA, 812.UGA, 813.UGA, 854.UGA
001.HC.RWA, 001.RWA, 010.RWA, 013.RWA, 023.RWA, 100.BEL.RWA, 100.GEN.RWA, 100.RWA.GEN, 101.RWA, 118.RWA, 120.RWA, 130.RWA, 254.RADIO.RWA, 301.RWA, 321.UNDP.RWA, 321.WFP.RWA, 322.FAO.RWA, 350.RWA, 400.RWA, 410.ICRC.RWA, 410.LRCS.RWA, 520.1.RWA, 521.RWA, 522.RWA, 523.RWA.BEL, 523.RWA.FRA, 600.RWA, 610.GEN.RWA, 619.8.RWA, 631.RWA, 641.RWA, 801.RWA, 813.RWA, 816.RWA, 841.RWA
Service Historique de la Défense. Paris. (SHD)
GR 6Q 50, GR 2000Z 114 455, GR7U 3440
United Nations Archive. https://archives.un.org/. (UN Archive; UNAMIR)
United Nations International Residual Mechanism for Criminal Tribunals. Judicial Records and Archives Database. https://unictr.irmct.org/en/documents.
United Nations Peacemaker. https://peacemaker.un.org.
US Department of State, FOI. https://foia.state.gov/.
US Holocaust Memorial Museum. https://www.ushmm.org/.
US National Archives and Records Administration. (US-NA; USNARA)
Access to Archival Databases. https://aad.archives.gov/aad/series-description.jsp?s=4073.
Central Foreign Policy Files, created, 7/1/1973–12/31/1979, documenting the period ca. 1973—12/31/1979. Series from Record Group 59: General Records of the Department of State. Access to Archival Databases (ADD)
World Bank. Rwanda Reports. https://documents.worldbank.org/en/publication/documents-reports.

BOOKS AND ARTICLES

Adelman, Howard, and Astri Suhrke, eds. *The Path of a Genocide: The Rwanda Crisis from Uganda to Zaire.* New Brunswick, NJ: Transaction Publishers, 1999.

Amselle, Jean-Loup, and Elikia M'Bokolo, eds. *Au coeur de l'ethnie.* Paris: La Decouverte, 2005.

Anderson, David. *Histories of the Hanged: Britain's Dirty War in Kenya and the End of Empire.* London: Phoenix, 2006.

André, Catherine, and Jean-Philippe Platteau. "Land Relations under Unbearable Stress: Rwanda Caught in the Malthusian Trap." *Journal of Economic Behaviour and Organisation* 34, no. 1 (1998): 1–47.

Angstrom, Jan, and Isabelle Duyvesteyn, eds. *Rethinking the Nature of War.* London: Routledge, 2005.

Anyidoho, Henry Kwami. *Guns over Kigali.* Accra: Woeli Publishing Services, 1997.

Balck, Hermann. *An Interview, 12 January 1974.* Bennington, VT: Merriam Press, 2006.

Biddle, Tami Davis, and Robert M. Citino. "The Role of Military History in the Contemporary Academy." *Army History* (Summer 2015): 24–30.

Black, Jeremy. *Rethinking Military History.* London: Routledge, 2004.

Botte, Roger. "Rwanda and Burundi, 1889–1930: Chronology of a Slow Assassination, Part 2." *International Journal of African Historical Studies* 18, no. 2 (1985): 289–314.

Bourgeois, R. *Banyarwanda et Barundi, tome 1 Ethnographie.* Brussels: ARSOM, 1957.

———. *Témoignages: Tome 1—Volume 2, Fonctionnaire territorial (1931–1961).* Brussels: MRAC, 1987.

Braeckman, Colette. *Rwanda, histoire d'un génocide.* Paris: Editions Fayard, 1994.

Branch, Daniel. *Defeating Mau Mau, Creating Kenya: Counterinsurgency, Civil War and Decolonisation.* Cambridge: Cambridge University Press, 2009.

Bundervoet, Tom. "Livestock, Land, and Political Power: The 1993 Killings in Burundi." *Journal of Peace Research* 46, no. 3 (May 2009): 357–76.

Carney, James J. "From Democratization to Ethnic Revolution: Catholic Politics in Rwanda, 1950–1962." PhD diss., Catholic University of America, 2011.

———. *Rwanda before the Genocide: Catholic Politics and Ethnic Discourse in the Late Colonial Era.* Oxford: Oxford University Press, 2014.

Carver, Field Marshall Lord. "Morale in Battle: The Medical and the Military." *Journal of the Royal Society of Medicine* 82 (February 1989): 67–71.

Chemouni, Benjamin, and Assumpta Mugiraneza. "Ideology and Interests in the Rwandan Patriotic Front: Singing the Struggle in Pre-Genocide Rwanda." *African Affairs* (2019): 1–26.

Chrétien, Jean-Pierre. *The Great Lakes of Africa: Two Thousand Years of History.* Translated by Scott Straus. New York: Zone Books, 2006.

Chrétien, Jean-Pierre, and Jean-Francois Dupaquier. *Burundi 1972: Au bord des genocides.* Paris: Karthala, 2007.

Chrétien, Jean-Pierre, and Marcel Kabanda. *Rwanda: Racisme et génocide.* Berlin: Alpha, 2016.

Clapham, Christopher. *Africa and the International System: The Politics of State Survival.* Cambridge: Cambridge University Press, 1996.

———, ed. *African Guerrillas.* Oxford: James Currey, 1998.

———. "Rwanda: The Perils of Peacemaking." *Journal of Peace Research* 35, no. 2 (March 1998): 193–210.

Clausewitz, Carl von. *On War.* Edited and Translated by Michael Howard and Peter Paret. Princeton, NJ: Princeton University Press, 1976.

———. *On War.* Hertfordshire, UK: Woodworth, 1997.

Collins, Barrie. *Rwanda 1994: The Myth of the Akazu Genocide Conspiracy and Its Consequences.* London: Palgrave Macmillan, 2014.

———. "The Rwandan War 1990–1994: Interrogating the Dominant Narrative." PhD diss., SOAS, 2009.

Creveld, Martin van. *Fighting Power: German and U.S. Army Performance, 1939–1945.* Westport, CT: Greenwood Press, 1982.

———. "Thoughts on Military History." *Journal of Contemporary History* 18, no. 4 (October 1983): 549–66.

———. *The Transformation of War.* London: The Free Press, 1991.

Dallaire, Roméo. *Shake Hands with the Devil.* London: Arrow Books, 2004.

Decker, Alicia C. *In Idi Amin's Shadow: Women, Gender, and Militarism in Uganda.* Athens: Ohio University Press, 2014.

Des Forges, Alison L. *Defeat Is the Only Bad News: Rwanda under Musinga, 1896–1931.* Madison: University of Wisconsin Press, 2011.

Desmedt, Christiane. "Poteries anciennes décorées à la roulette dans la Région des Grands Lacs." *African Archaeological Review* 9 (1991): 161–96.

Desrosiers, Marie-Eve. *Trajectories of Authoritarianism in Rwanda: Elusive Control before the Genocide.* Cambridge: Cambridge University Press, 2023.

d'Hertefelt, M., A. A. Trouwborst, and J. H. Scherer. *Les anciens royaumes de la zone interlacustre méridionale Rwanda, Burundi, Buha.* Tervuren, Belgium: MRAC, 1962.

Dorsey, Leathern. "The Rwandan Colonial Economy, 1916–1941." PhD diss., Michigan State University, 1983.

Douek, Daniel. *Insurgency and Counterinsurgency in South Africa.* London: Hurst, 2020.

Epstein, Helen. *Another Fine Mess: America, Uganda, and the War on Terror.* New York: Columbia Global Reports, 2017.

Evrard, Camille, Muriel Gomez-Perez, Martin Mourre, Florent Piton, Nathaniel Powell, and Romain Tiquet. "Dossier: Au-delà du rapport Duclert; Décentrer l'histoire du génocide des Tutsi du Rwanda." Special issue, *Revue d'histoire contemporaine de l'Afrique* (November 2021).

Fontanellaz, Adrien, and Tom Cooper. *The Rwandan Patriotic Front: 1990–1994.* Solihull, UK: Helion, 2015.

Gasana, James K. *Rwanda: Du parti-état à l'état-garnison.* Paris: L'Harmattan, 2002.

George, Edward. *The Cuban Intervention in Angola, 1965–1991.* London: Frank Cass, 2005.

Gourevitch, Philip. *We Wish to Inform You That Tomorrow We Will Be Killed with Our Families.* New York: Picador, 2000.

Guichaoua, André. *From War to Genocide: Criminal Politics in Rwanda, 1990–1994.* Translated by Don E. Webster. Madison: University of Wisconsin Press, 2015.

———, ed. *Les crises politiques au Burundi et au Rwanda (1993–1994): Analyses, faits et documents.* Paris: Karthala, 1995.

Hartmann, B., and J. K. Boyce. *A Quiet Violence: View from a Bangladesh Village.* Dhaka: The University Press, 1988.

Hatzfeld, Jean. *A Time for Machetes: The Rwandan Genocide; Let the Killers Speak.* Translated by Linda Coverdale. London: Serpent's Tail, 2008.

Heldring, Leander. "The Origins of Violence in Rwanda." *Review of Economic Studies* 88, no. 2 (March 2021): 730–63.

Hiernaux, J. *Analyse de la variation des caractères physiques humains en une région de l'Afrique centrale: Ruanda-Urundi et Kivu.* Tervuren, Belgium: Musée Royal du Congo Belge, 1956.

Horowitz, Donald L. *The Deadly Ethnic Riot.* Los Angeles: University of California Press, 2002.

Jones, Bruce D. *Peacemaking in Rwanda: The Dynamics of Failure.* Boulder, CO: Lynne Rienner, 2001.

Jowell, Marco. "Cohesion through Socialization: Liberation, Tradition and Modernity in the Forging of the Rwanda Defence Force (RDF)." *Journal of Eastern African Studies* 8, no. 2 (2014): 278–93.

———. *Peacekeeping in Africa: Politics, Security and the Failure of Foreign Military Assistance.* London: I. B. Tauris, 2018.

Kagame, Alexis. *Un abrégé de l'ethno-histoire du Rwanda I & II.* Butare, Rwanda: Éditions universitaires du Rwanda, 1972, 1975.

Kamola, Isaac A. "The Global Coffee Economy and the Production of Genocide in Rwanda." *Third World Quarterly* 28, no. 3 (2007): 571–92.

Kampe, Justus Muhanguzi. *Eyes of a Journalist.* Kampala: Worlds of Inspiration, 2016.

Kaplan, Robert D. *The Good American: The Epic Life of Bob Gersony, The U.S. Government's Greatest Humanitarian.* New York: Random House, 2021.

Keane, Fergal. *Season of Blood: A Rwandan Journey.* London: Penguin, 1996.

Kegel, John Burton. "Post-Genocide Rwanda." *Africa: Rivista semestrale di studi e ricerche* 1, no. 1 (2019): 123–28.

Kennes, Erik, and Miles Larmer. *The Katangese Gendarmes and War in Central Africa.* Bloomington: Indiana University Press, 2016.

Kilcullen, David. *The Accidental Guerrilla: Fighting Small Wars in the Midst of a Big One.* London: Hurst, 2017.

Kinzer, Stephen. *A Thousand Hills: Rwanda's Rebirth and the Man Who Dreamed It.* Hoboken, NJ: John Wiley, 2008.

Kroslak, Daniela. *The Role of France in the Rwandan Genocide.* London: Hurst, 2007.

Kuperman, Alan J. "Provoking Genocide: A Revised History of the Rwandan Patriotic Front." *Journal of Genocide Research* 6, no. 1 (2004): 61–84.

Langford, Peter. "The Rwandan Path to Genocide: The Genesis of the Capacity of the Rwandan Post-Colonial State to Organise and Unleash a Project of Extermination." *Civil Wars* 7, no. 1 (2005): 1–27.

Larsen, Josefine Kühnel. "Peace by Peace: The Construction of National-Military Identity in Post-Genocide Rwanda." PhD diss., University of Copenhagen, 2014.

Lefèvre, Patrick, and Jean-Noël Lefèvre. *Les militaires belges et le Rwanda 1916–2006.* Brussels: Editions Racine, 2006.

Lemarchand, René. "Controversy within the Cataclysm: Review of *Rwanda: L'histoire secrète* by Abdul Ruzibiza." *African Studies Review* 50, no. 1 (April 2007): 140–44.

———. "Disconnecting the Threads: Rwanda and the Holocaust Reconsidered." *Journal of Genocide Research* 4, no. 4 (2002): 499–518.

———. *The Dynamics of Violence in Central Africa.* Philadelphia: University of Pennsylvania Press, 2009.

———. *Forgotten Genocides: Oblivion, Denial, and Memory.* Philadelphia: University of Pennsylvania Press, 2011.

———. *Rwanda and Burundi.* New York: Praeger, 1970.

———. "Rwanda: The Rationality of Genocide." *Issue: A Journal of Opinion* 23, no. 2 (1995): 8–11.

———. *The World Bank in Rwanda: The Case of the Office de valorisation agricole et pastorale du Mutara (OVAPAM).* Bloomington: Indiana University Press, 1982.

Logiest, Guy. *Mission au Rwanda: Un blanc dans la bagarre Tutsi-Hutu.* Brussels: Didier Hautier, 1988.

Longman, Timothy. *Christianity and Genocide in Rwanda.* Cambridge: Cambridge University Press, 2011.

———. *Memory and Justice in Post-Genocide Rwanda.* Cambridge: Cambridge University Press, 2017.

———. "Placing Genocide in Context: Research Priorities for the Rwandan Genocide." *Journal of Genocide Research* 6, no. 1 (2004): 29–45.

Lucier, Richard L. *The International Political Economy of Coffee: From Juan Valdez to Yank's Diner.* New York: Praeger, 1988.

Lugan, Bernard. "Causes et effets de la famine 'Rumanura' au Rwanda, 1916–18." *Canadian Journal of African Studies* 10, no. 2 (1976): 347–56.

———. *François Mitterrand: l'Armée française et le Rwanda.* Monaco: Editions du Rocher, 2005.

Mamdani, Mahmood. *When Victims Become Killers: Colonialism, Nativism, and Genocide in Rwanda.* Princeton, NJ: Princeton University Press, 2002.

Maquet, Jacques. *The Premise of Inequality in Ruanda.* Oxford: Oxford University Press, 1961.

Maquet, Jacques, and Marcel d'Hertefelt. *Elections en société féodale: Une étude sur l'introduction du vote populaire au Ruanda-Urundi.* Brussels: Académie royale des Sciences coloniales, 1959.

McDoom, Omar Shahabudin. *The Path to Genocide in Rwanda: Security, Opportunity, and Authority in an Ethnocratic State.* Cambridge: Cambridge University Press, 2021.

Melvern, Linda. *Conspiracy to Murder: The Rwandan Genocide.* London: Verso, 2006.

———. *A People Betrayed: The Role of the West in Rwanda's Genocide.* London: Zed Books, 2009.

Morel, Jacques. *La France au cœur du genocide des Tutsi.* Paris: L'Esprit Frappeur, 2016.

Moyar, Mark. "The Current State of Military History." *Historical Journal* 50, no. 1 (March 2007): 225–40.

Mushemeza, Elijah Dicken. "Politics and the Refugee Experience: The Case of the Banyarwanda Refugees in Uganda (1959–1994)." PhD diss., Makerere University, 2002.

Newbury, Catherine. "The Cohesion of Oppression: A Century of Clientship in Kinyaga, Rwanda." PhD diss., University of Wisconsin–Madison, 1975.

———. *The Cohesion of Oppression: Clientship and Ethnicity in Rwanda, 1860–1960.* New York: Columbia University Press, 1988.

Newbury, Catherine, and David Newbury. "Bringing the Peasants Back In: Agrarian Themes in the Construction and Corrosion of Statist Historiography in Rwanda." *American Historical Review* 105, no. 3 (June 2000): 832–77.

Newbury, David. *Kings and Clans: Ijwi Island and the Lake Kivu Rift, 1780–1840.* Madison: University of Wisconsin Press, 1991.

———. *The Lands beyond the Mists: Essays on identity and Authority in Precolonial Congo and Rwanda.* Athens: Ohio University Press, 2009.

———. "Precolonial Burundi and Rwanda: Local Loyalties, Regional Royalties." *International Journal of African Historical Studies* 34, no. 2 (2001): 255–314.

Ngoga, Pascal G. "Guerrilla Insurgency and Conflict Resolution in Africa: A Case Study of Uganda." PhD diss., Lancaster University, 1997.

Olson, Jennifer Maria. "Farmer Responses to Land Degradation in Gikongoro." PhD diss., Michigan State University, 1994.

Parker, Geoffrey, ed. *The Cambridge History of Warfare.* Cambridge: Cambridge University Press, 2009.

Paul, Christopher, Jennifer D. P. Moroney, Beth Grill, Colin P. Clarke, Lisa Saum-Manning, Heather Peterson, and Brian Gordon. *What Works Best When Building Capacity in Challenging Contexts?* Santa Monica, CA: RAND, 2015.

Percival, Val, and Thomas Homer-Dixon. "Environmental Scarcity and Violent Conflict: The Case of Rwanda." *Journal of Environment & Development* 5, no. 3 (September 1996): 270–91.

Pottier, Johan P. "Taking Stock: Food Marketing Reform in Rwanda, 1982–89." *African Affairs* 92, no. 36 (January 1993): 5–30.

Prunier, Gérard. *The Rwanda Crisis: History of a Genocide.* London: Hurst, 1997.

Reed, Cyrus. "Exile, Reform and the Rise of the Rwandan Patriotic Front." *Journal of Modern African Studies* 34, no. 3 (September 1996): 479–501.

Reid, Richard J. "Past and Presentism: The 'Precolonial' and the Foreshortening of African History." *Journal of African History* 52, no. 2 (2011): 135–55.

———. *Warfare in African History.* Cambridge: Cambridge University Press, 2012.

———. *War in Pre-Colonial Eastern Africa.* London: James Currey, 2007.

Rever, Judi. *In Praise of Blood.* Toronto: Random House Canada, 2018.

Reyntjens, Filip. "A Fake Enquiry on a Major Event: Analysis of the Mutsinzi Report on the 6th April 1994 Attack on the Rwandan President's Aeroplane." Institute of Development Policy and Management Working Paper, University of Antwerp, July 2010.

———. *Political Governance in Post-Genocide Rwanda.* Cambridge: Cambridge University Press, 2013.

———. *Pouvoir et droit au Rwanda: Droit public et evolution politique, 1916–1973.* Tervuren, Belgium: MRAC, 1985.

———. "The Proof of the Pudding Is in the Eating: The June 1993 Elections in Burundi." *Journal of Modern African Studies* 31, no. 4 (1993): 563–83.

———. "Rwanda, Genocide and Beyond." *Journal of Refugee Studies* 9, no. 3 (1996): 240–51.

———. "'*Rwanda: L'histoire secrète* by Abdul Ruzibiza': Review of *Rwanda: L'histoire secrète* by Abdul Ruzibiza." *Africa Today* 54, no. 3 (2008): 141–44.

Roessler, Philip. *Ethnic Politics and State Power in Africa: The Logic of the Coup–Civil War Trap.* Cambridge: Cambridge University Press, 2016.

Roessler, Philip, and Harry Verhoeven. *Why Comrades Go to War: Liberation Politics and the Outbreak of Africa's Deadliest Conflict.* London: Hurst, 2016.

Rudasingwa, Theogene. *Healing a Nation: A Testimony.* North Charleston, SC: CreateSpace, 2013.

Rusagara, Frank K. *Resilience of a Nation: A History of the Military in Rwanda.* Kigali: Fountain Publishers, 2009.

Russell, Aidan. "Rebel and Rule in Burundi in 1972." *International Journal of African Historical Studies* 48, no. 1 (2015): 73–97.

Ruzibiza, Abdul Joshua. *Rwanda: L'histoire secrète.* Paris: Editions du Panama, 2005.

Schoenbrun, David L. "Cattle Herds and Banana Gardens: The Historical Geography of the Western Great Lakes Region, ca AD 800–1500." *African Archaeological Review* 11 (1993): 39–72.

Shils, Edward A., and Morris Janowitz. "Cohesion and Disintegration in the Wehrmacht in World War II." *Public Opinion Quarterly* 12, no. 2 (1948): 280–315.

Sibomana, André. *Hope for Rwanda.* London: Pluto Press, 1999.

Siebold, Guy L. "The Essence of Military Group Cohesion." *Armed Forces & Society* 33, no. 2 (2007): 286–95.

———. "The Evolution of the Measurement of Cohesion." *Military Psychology* 11, no. 1 (1999): 5–26.

Sierra, Raul Sanchez de la. "On the Origins of the State: Stationary Bandits and Taxation in Eastern Congo." *Journal of Political Economy* 128, no. 11 (2020): 32–74.

Singiza, Dantès. "La famine Ruzagayura (Rwanda, 1943–1944): Causes, conséquences et réactions des autorités." PhD diss., Université de Liège & Musée royal de l'Afrique centrale, Tervuren, 2011.

Speke, John Hanning. *Journal of the Discovery of the Source of the Nile.* London: William Blackwood and Sons, 1863.

Stapleton, Timothy. "The Importance of Operational Accounts in African Military History." *Journal of African Military History* 5, no. 2 (2021): 73–76.

Stearns, Jason. *Dancing in the Glory of Monsters.* New York: Public Affairs, 2012.

Storey, Andy. "Structural Adjustment, State Power and Genocide: The World Bank and Rwanda." *Review of African Political Economy* 28, no. 89 (2001): 365–85.

Straus, Scott. "The Limits of a Genocide Lens: Violence against Rwandans in the 1990s." *Journal of Genocide Research* 21, no. 4 (2019): 1–21.

———. *The Order of Genocide: Race, Power, and War in Rwanda.* Ithaca, NY: Cornell University Press, 2006.

Swinnen, Johan. *Rwanda: Mijn verhaal.* Kalmthout, Belgium: Polis, 2016.

Tauzin, Didier. *Rwanda: je demande justice pour la France et ses soldats.* Paris: Editions Jacob-Duvernet, 2011.

Thomas, C. G., and R. Doron. "Out of Africa: The Challenges, Evolution, and Opportunities of African Military History." *Journal of African Military History* 1, no. 1 (2017): 3–23.

Thomson, Susan. *Rwanda: From Genocide to Precarious Peace.* New Haven, CT: Yale University Press, 2018.

———. *Whispering Truth to Power: Everyday Resistance to Reconciliation in Postgenocide Rwanda.* Madison: University of Wisconsin Press, 2013.

Tsuruta, Aya. "'It Is Difficult to Understand Rwanda History': Contested History of Ethnicity and Dynamics of Conflicts in Rwanda during Revolution and Independence." PhD diss., University of Edinburgh, 2013.

Uvin, Peter. *Aiding Violence: The Development Enterprise in Rwanda.* West Hartford, CT: Kumarian Press, 1998.

———. *Development, Aid and Conflict: Reflections from the Case of Rwanda.* Helsinki: United Nations University, 1996.

———. "Reading the Rwandan Genocide." *International Studies Review* 3, no. 3 (2001): 75–99.

Uwizeyimana, Laurien. *Octobre et novembre 1990: Le Front patriotique rwandais à l'assaut du Mutara.* Ruhengeri: Éditions universitaires du Rwanda, September 1992.

Vansina, Jan. *Antecedents to Modern Rwanda: The Nyiginya Kingdom.* Madison: University of Wisconsin Press, 2004.

———. *L'évolution du royaume Rwanda des origines à 1900.* Brussels: Belgian Royal Colonial Institute, 1962.

———. *Living with Africa.* Madison: University of Wisconsin Press, 1994.

———. *Oral Tradition as History.* Madison: University of Wisconsin Press, 1985.

Verpoorten, Marijke. "Leave None to Claim the Land: A Malthusian Catastrophe in Rwanda?" *Journal of Peace Research* 49 (July 2012): 547–63.

Verwimp, Philip. "Agricultural Policy, Crop Failure and the 'Ruriganiza' Famine (1989) in Southern Rwanda: A Prelude to Genocide?" Centre for Economic Studies Discussion Paper Series, Katholieke Universiteit Leuven, June 2002.

———. "Development Ideology, the Peasantry and Genocide: Rwanda represented in Habyarimana's speeches." Yale Genocide Studies Program: Working Paper GS13, 1999.

———. *Peasants in Power: The Political Economy of Development and Genocide in Rwanda.* New York: Springer, 2013.

———. "Testing the Double-Genocide Thesis for Central and Southern Rwanda." *Journal of Conflict Resolution* 47, no. 4 (2003): 423–42.

Vidal, Claudine. "Le Rwanda des anthropologues ou le fétichisme de la vache." *Cahiers d'études africaines* 9, no. 3 (1969): 384–401.

———. "Les contradictions d'un lieutenant rwandais: Abdul Ruzibiza, témoin, acteur, faux-témoin." In *L'Afrique des Grands Lacs, annuaire 2008–2009,* edited by S. Marysse, F. Reyntjens, and S. Vandeginste, 43–55. Paris: L'Harmattan, 2009.

Wallis, Andrew. *Silent Accomplice: The Untold Story of France's Role in the Rwandan Genocide.* London: I. B. Tauris, 2014.

———. *Stepp'd in Blood.* Winchester, UK: Zero Books, 2019.

Watson, Catherine. "Burundi: Freed from Fear." *Africa Report* 38, no. 5 (1993): 58–61.
———. "War and Waiting." *Africa Report* 37, no. 6 (November 1992): 51–55.
Watts, Stephen. *Identifying and Mitigating Risks in Security Sector Assistance for Africa's Fragile States.* Santa Monica, CA: RAND, 2015.

REPORTS AND PARLIAMENTARY INQUIRIES

Africa Watch. *Rwanda: Talking Peace and Waging War; Human Rights since the October 1990 Invasion.* Washington, DC: Africa Watch, 27 February 1992.
Africa Watch / Human Rights Watch. *Beyond the Rhetoric: Continuing Human Rights Abuses in Rwanda.* Washington, DC: Africa Watch / Human Rights Watch, June 1993.
Anderson, M., M. Arnsten, and H. Averch. *Insurgent Organization and Operations: A Case Study of the Viet Cong in the Delta, 1964–1966.* Santa Monica, CA: RAND Corporation, August 1967.
Association rwandaise pour la défense des droits de la personne et des libertés publiques (ADL). *Rapport sur les droits de l'homme au Rwanda (Septembre 1991–Septembre 1992).* Kigali: ADL, December 1992.
———. *Rapport sur les droits de l'homme au Rwanda (Octobre 1992–Octobre 1993).* Kigali: ADL, December 1993.
BDM Corporation, Director of Net Assessment, Office of the Secretary of Defense. *Generals Balck and von Mellenthin on Tactics: Implication for NATO Military Doctrine.* Tysons Corner, VA: BDM Corporation 19 December 1980.
Bruguière, Jean-Louis. *Délivrance de dandats d'arrêt internationaux.* Tribunal de Grande Instance de Paris—Cabinet de Jean-Louis Bruguière, Premier Vice-Président. Parquet: 97.295.2303/0 Cabinet: 1341, 17 November 2006.
Comité pour le respect des droits de l'Homme et la démocratie au Rwanda (CRDDR). *Rwanda: Rapport de deux missions effectuées par Eric Gillet & André Jadoul, avocats au barreau de Bruxelles au Rwanda du 9 au 17 Janvier et du 2 au 5 Février 1992.* Brussels: CRDDR, May 1992.
Donnel, John C., Guy J. Pauker, and Joseph J. Zasloff. *Viet Cong Motivation and Morale in 1964: A Preliminary Report.* Santa Monica, CA: RAND Corporation, March 1965.
Duclert, Vincent. *La France, le Rwanda et le génocide des Tutsi (1990–1994)—Rapport remis au Président de la République le 26 mars 2021.* Paris: Armand Colin, 2021.
FIDH in collaboration with Africa Watch. *Commission Internationale d'Enquête (7–21 Janvier 1993): Violations massives et systématiques des droits de l'homme depuis le 1er octobre 1990.* Paris: FIDH in collaboration with Africa Watch, 8 March 1993.
———. *Report of the International Commission of Investigation on Human Rights Violations in Rwanda since October 1, 1990 (January 7–21, 1993).* Paris: FIDH in collaboration with Africa Watch, March 1993.
Gersony, Robert. "Summary of UNHCR Presentation before Commission of Experts, 10 October 1994: Prospect for Early Repatriation of Rwandan Refugees Currently in Burundi, Tanzania and Zaire." 11 October 1994. [unpublished]

Gouvernement Belge. *Rapport présenté par le gouvernement belge au Conseil de la société des nations de l'administration du Ruanda-Urundi pendant l'année 1924.* Geneva: Société des nations, 1925.

———. *Rapport soumis par le gouvernement belge à l'Assemblée Générale des Nations Unies au sujet de l'administration du Ruanda-Urundi pendant l'année 1949.* Brussels: Etablissements Généraux d'Imprimerie, 1950.

———. *Rapport soumis par le gouvernement belge à l'Assemblée Générale des Nations Unies au sujet de l'administration du Ruanda-Urundi pendant l'année 1955.* Brussels: Imprimerie Fr. van Muysewinkel, 1956.

High Commissioner for Refugees. *1964 Programme—New Projects: Projects for the Settlement of Approximately 20,000 Refugees from Rwanda.* New York: United Nations, 10 April 1964.

———. *Proposal for Assistance to Refugees from Rwanda in the Kivu Province of the Congo.* New York: United Nations, 13 April 1964.

———. *Report on the Situation of Refugees from Rwanda.* New York: United Nations, 1963.

Human Rights Watch. *Arming Rwanda: The Arms Trade and Human Rights Abuses in the Rwandan War.* New York: Human Rights Watch, January 1994.

———. *Leave None to Tell the Story: Genocide in Rwanda.* Written by Alison Des Forges. New York: Human Rights Watch, March 1999.

International Coffee Organisation. *The International Coffee Organisation 1963–2013: 50 Years Serving the World Coffee Community.* International Coffee Organisation, 2013.

Kamer der Volksvertegenwoordigers. *Parlementaire Handelingen: Vergadering van dinsdag 17 november 1959.* Brussels: Belgisch Staatsblad, 17 November 1959.

Levy, Firestone, Muze. *A Foreseeable Genocide.* Washington, DC: 2021.

Mahoux, Philippe and Guy Verhofstadt. *Commission d'enquête parlementaire concernant les événements du Rwanda.* Sénat de Belgique, 6 December 1997.

McCoy, William. *Senegal and Liberia: Case Studies in US IMET Training and Its Role in Internal Defense and Development.* Santa Monica, CA: RAND Corporation, 1994.

M. le Ministre des Colonies. *Rapport sur l'administration belge du Ruanda-Urundi pendant l'année 1930.* Brussels: Etablissement Emile Bruylant, 1931.

———. *Rapport sur l'administration belge du Ruanda-Urundi pendant l'année 1936.* Brussels: Etablissement Emile Bruylant, 1937.

———. *Rapport sur l'administration belge du Ruanda-Urundi pendant l'année 1953.* Brussels: Etablissements Généraux d'Imprimerie, 1954.

———. *Rapport sur l'administration belge du Ruanda-Urundi pendant l'année 1954.* Brussels: Imprimerie Fr. van Muysewinkel, 1955.

Nordic Africa Institute. *The International Response to Conflict and Genocide: Lessons from the Rwanda Experience, Historical Perspective; Some Explanatory Factors.* Written by Tor Sellström and Lennart Wohlgemut. Uppsala, Sweden: Nordic Africa Institute, 1996.

Peigneux, MM. Fr., G. Malengreau, and S. Frédéricq. *Rapport de la Commission d'Enquete au Ruanda.* Brussels, 1960.

Quilès, Paul. *Rapport d'information par la mission d'information de la commission de la défense nationale et des forces armées et de la commission des affaires étrangères, sur les opérations militaires menées par la France, d'autres pays et l'ONU au Rwanda entre 1990 et 1994.* Paris: Assemblée nationale, 15 December 1998.

Refugee Policy Group. *Older Refugee Settlements in Africa—Final Report.* Written by Lance Clark and Barry Stein. Washington, DC: Refugee Policy Group, November 1985.

Republic of Rwanda, independent committee of experts charged with investigation into the crash on 06/04/1994 of Falcon 50 Aeroplane, registration number 9XR-NN. *Report of the Investigation into the Causes and Circumstances of and Responsibility for the Attack of 06/04/1994 against the Falcon 50 Rwandan Presidential Aeroplane, Registration Number 9XR-NN.* Kigali: Republic of Rwanda, 20 April 2009.

Rijckmans, Pierre. *Rapport du groupe de travail pour l'etude du problème politique au Congo Belge.* Brussels: Chambre des Représentants, 20 January 1959.

Services d'information du ministère des affaires étrangères du Rwanda. *Toute la vérité sur le terrorisme 'Inyenzi' au Rwanda: Une mise au point du ministère des affaires étrangères du Rwanda.* Kigali: Services d'information du ministère des affaires étrangères du Rwanda, 1964.

Trévidic, Marc, and Nathalie Poux. *Rapport d'expertise: Destruction en vol du Falcon 50 Kigali (Rwanda).* Cour d'Appel de Paris Tribunal de Grande Instance de Paris, 5 January 2012.

Trusteeship Council. *United Nations Visiting Mission to Trust Territories in East Africa, 1948: Report on Ruanda-Urundi.* New York: United Nations, 1948.

———. *United Nations Visiting Mission to Trust Territories in East Africa, 1957: Report on Ruanda-Urundi.* New York: United Nations, 1958.

———. *Visiting Mission to Trust Territories in East Africa, 1960: Report on Ruanda-Urundi.* New York: United Nations, 1960.

UN Security Council. *International Commission of Inquiry Concerning the Assassination of the President of Burundi: Final Report.* S/1996/682. United Nations, 23 July 1996.

US Committee for Refugees. *Exile from Rwanda: Background to an Invasion.* Written by Catherine Watson. Arlington, VA: US Committee for Refugees, February 1991.

———. *Human Rights in Uganda: The Reasons for Refugees.* Arlington, VA: US Committee for Refugees, 1985.

———. *Refugees in Uganda and Rwanda: The Banyarwandan Tragedy.* Written by Roger Winter. Arlington, VA: US Committee for Refugees, 1983.

US Department of State. *Uganda, 4 Annual Human Rights Report Submitted to Congress.* Washington, DC: US Department of State, 1980.

———. *Uganda, 6 Annual Human Rights Report Submitted to Congress.* Washington, DC: US Department of State, 1981.

US Holocaust Museum and The Hague Institute for Global Justice. *International Decision-Making in the Age of Genocide: Rwanda 1990–1994; Annotated Transcript.* The Hague: US Holocaust Museum and The Hague Institute for Global Justice, 1–3 June 2014.

Winter, Roger. "Human Rights in Uganda: The Past, Present and Future." In *Three Papers Presented before the Commission of Inquiry into Violations of Human Rights.* Kampala, 15–16 February 1990.

World Bank. *Mutara Agricultural and Livestock Development Project—Phase II, Staff Appraisal Report.* Washington, DC: World Bank, 1979.

———. *Recent Economic Development and Prospects of Rwanda.* Vol. I, *The Main Report.* Written by Attila Sönmez. Washington, DC: World Bank, 1974.

NEWSPAPERS

Africa Confidential (London)
Centre de recherche et d'information socio-politiques—CRISP
Chicago Daily Tribune
Daily Express
Daily Mail (London)
Daily Monitor
De Standaard
De Telegraaf (Amsterdam)
De Volkskrant (Amsterdam)
The Economist
Financial Times (London)
Friese Koerier (Heereveen, Netherlands)
The Guardian
Le Courrier d'Afrique (Léopoldville, Belgian Congo)
Le Monde (Paris)
Le Soir (Brussels)
New Times
New Vision
New York Times
Sunday Times (London)
The Times (London)

Index

Page numbers in italics indicate illustrations.